HELEN BARRETT MONTGOMERY

HELEN BARRETT MONTGOMERY

The Global Mission of Domestic Feminism

KENDAL P. MOBLEY

BAYLOR UNIVERSITY PRESS

Cover Design: Pamela Poll
Cover Image: Helen Barrett Montgomery, portrait, 1920-1930? Used by permission of the Rochester Public Library Local History Division. Image number rpf02291.

Library of Congress Cataloging-in-Publication Data

Mobley, Kendal P., 1962-
 Helen Barrett Montgomery : the global mission of domestic feminism / Kendal P. Mobley.
   p. cm.
 Includes bibliographical references and index.
 ISBN 978-1-60258-187-6 (pbk. : alk. paper)
 1. Montgomery, Helen Barrett, 1861-1934. 2. Women in missionary work. 3. Feminism--History. 4. Feminism--Religious aspects--Christianity. 5. Women missionaries--Biography. I. Title.

BV2610.M58 2009
286'.1092--dc22
 [B]
                            2008029391

To my father

George Judson Mobley

in loving memory

Contents

Acknowledgments   ix

1   Helen Barrett Montgomery: The Interpretive Challenge   1

2   "The Fatherhood of God and the Victorian Family": The Childhood and Early Education of Helen Barrett   11

3   Evangelicalism, Progressivism, and Domesticity: Helen Barrett's Wellesley   25

4   The "New Woman" at Work, Home, and in Public: Helen Barrett Montgomery's Return to Rochester   47

5   Montgomery's "New Woman" and the Limitless Scope of Woman as Citizen   71

6   Susan B. Anthony and Helen Barrett Montgomery: An Intergenerational Feminist Partnership   101

7   The Rochester Women's Educational and Industrial Union: Montgomery's Platform for Municipal Housekeeping   129

8   Helen Barrett Montgomery, Walter Rauschenbusch, and the Battle for Progressive Public Education   155

9   The Hackett House Episode and the Birth of Social Centers   183

10 "A Great Theme": Domestic Feminism and the Gospel
of the Women's Jubilee   201

11 After the Jubilee: Women's Colleges and "World Friendship"   225

12 A "Middle-of-the-Road Baptist": Creedalism and
the Defense of Baptist Liberty, 1921–1922   245

13 Conclusion   259

Notes   265

Bibliography   303

Index of Personal Names   323

Index of Subjects   327

ACKNOWLEDGMENTS

I am indebted to many people who helped me bring this book to completion. The ones who are mentioned below must stand as representatives of that "exceeding great army" of family, friends, colleagues, and teachers whose generosity and collaboration improved the quality of my work and made the whole endeavor much more enjoyable.

This book began as a dissertation at the Boston University School of Theology. To Dana L. Robert, my first reader, I owe a tremendous debt of gratitude. She introduced me to Helen Barrett Montgomery in a doctoral seminar in 1997 and encouraged me to write Montgomery's story. Working as her research assistant contributed to the support of my family and to my growth as a scholar. As I developed my thesis, I benefited constantly from her expert guidance and criticism.

Finding a second reader for my dissertation was not easy, but Providence was kind in the end. Nancy T. Ammerman was still new to the School of Theology in 2004, but certainly not to the scholarly study of the Baptist movement. She kindly agreed to lend her considerable expertise, and I am indeed grateful. Her incisive questions helped me to understand how much more remains to be learned about Montgomery.

I also wish to thank Christopher H. Evans and Liah Greenfeld, who generously offered trenchant criticism on portions of the text, and Wendy J. Deichmann Edwards, who edited my first publication on Montgomery.

I am grateful for the assistance of Caroline Christian and Dawn Piscitello of the Boston University School of Theology Library, Jean Nielson Berry of the Margaret Clapp Library at Wellesley College, Thomas Haverly and Evanna DiSalvo of the Ambrose Swasey Library at Colgate Rochester Crozer Divinity School, Lara Little and Cindy Newport of the G. A. Pfeiffer Library at Pfeiffer University, the Local History Department of the Central Library of Rochester and Monroe County, and the Rare Books, Special Collections and Preservation Department of the Rush Rhees Library of the University of Rochester.

I made several profitable visits to the American Baptist–Samuel Colgate Library of the American Baptist Historical Society (ABHS) in Rochester, N.Y. Former director H. W. Walker Pipkin; his assistant, Nancy Blostein; and former director Stuart W. Campbell earned my deep appreciation. The ABHS collection has been relocated to Mercer University in Atlanta, Georgia, and I have changed my citations to reflect its new home.

At the offices of the Rochester Board of Education, Kimberly Rohring, executive assistant to the board, kindly provided access to documents, photocopies, an empty office, and a computer. Jack Handy, Jane Grant, and Peter J. B. Carman assisted me in the archives of Lake Avenue Baptist Church in Rochester. I have never met my fellow Montgomery scholars, Conda Delite Hitch Abbott and Julie Fewster, but both of them were kind enough to share information with me through e-mails and telephone calls.

My wife, Rhonda Brady-Mobley, prayed for me, encouraged me, and facilitated my work in countless ways. Our children, Rachel and George, have been remarkably patient. I am eternally grateful for my mother, Bettie Mobley, who is deeply invested, spiritually and materially, in this endeavor.

Cheryl and John Gagliardi, Sandy and Bob Harbick, Kelly and Paul Hughett, Joy Reis, and Gus Rocha were the members of my CARE Group at Bay Community Church, Swansea, Massachusetts. They purchased the laptop computer that I used to record my research and write the dissertation. For that excellent and serviceable gift, as well as for much prayer and encouragement, I owe them a debt of gratitude. Gus Rocha went the extra mile when he patiently and carefully proofread the entire final draft of my dissertation. Serving the people of Bay Community Baptist Church as their interim pastor was a tremendous privilege and blessing. I must also thank

Mike Lewis, my good friend and former pastor, who proofread early drafts of the first few chapters of my dissertation.

The members of Enon Baptist Church in Salisbury, North Carolina, where I currently serve as pastor, are unfailingly gracious and supportive to my family and me. Kathy Vestal, one of our deacons, did me the tremendous service of reading and rereading my drafts for the manuscript. Her suggestions were always helpful.

Sharyn Dowd's research and encouragement have been invaluable. She is the reason I submitted my dissertation to Baylor University Press. It has been a pleasure to work with Diane E. Smith and Carey C. Newman of Baylor University Press. Their patient professionalism and guidance made this experience very positive for me.

With so much help and support, one ought to be able to produce a flawless book. I fear that I have fallen short of that mark and wish to acknowledge that any flaws that my readers discover are my responsibility alone.

One

Helen Barrett Montgomery
The Interpretive Challenge

On 24 July 1923, Helen Barrett Montgomery stood before the Third Baptist World Congress in Stockholm, Sweden, where two thousand delegates from thirty-five countries had gathered, and told the assembled delegates:

> Jesus Christ is the great Emancipator of woman. He alone among the founders of the great religions of the world looked upon men and women with level eyes, seeing not their differences but their oneness, their humanity. He alone put no barriers before women in his religious teaching, but promulgated one law, equally binding upon men and women; opened one gate to which men and women were admitted upon equal terms. . . .
>
> In the mind of the Founder of Christianity there is no area of religious privilege fenced off for the exclusive use of men. In this attitude Jesus Christ stands absolutely alone among religious teachers.[1]

As radically feminist as her words must have sounded in 1923, they led to a conclusion that today would be welcomed by many fundamentalists. Montgomery applauded the new avenues of education, organization, and service that were opening to women, but she ended her address with a call that sounded quite traditional. She said,

> The *home* is calling as never before, for women to adopt and to glorify as a vocation the one absolutely essential profession. God is calling for *mothers*!

1

. . . The profession of motherhood, being the highest in the world, is also the most difficult. . . . To the brave soldiers of the kingdom who, turning their backs on fame and glory, shall find in a humble home their sphere of service, God himself shall stoop with a fadeless garland to place it on the brow of a mother![2]

To many modern ears, there is a jarring discord between Montgomery's feminist and domestic values. She was a social reformer and the first woman elected to the school board in Rochester, N.Y. She was licensed to preach by Lake Avenue Baptist Church. She was the first woman elected president of the Northern Baptist Convention, and she is still the only Baptist woman to publish an original English translation of the New Testament. She was all of these and more, and yet she was also a Victorian wife and mother who would not accept speaking engagements that took her away from home until she had her husband's permission. Apparent contradictions such as these are the heart of the interpretive challenge surrounding her legacy.

Montgomery was one of the most influential leaders in the history of the ecumenical woman's missionary movement in America. Her greatest contribution to the movement was the 1910 mission study book *Western Women in Eastern Lands*, which she wrote to commemorate fifty years of women's foreign missionary work. The book sold 100,000 copies and launched the great Golden Jubilee tour of 1910–1911—the largest mission celebration in the history of the United States. *Western Women in Eastern Lands* epitomizes "Woman's Work for Woman," the first missiology developed by the ecumenical woman's missionary movement. In the fifth chapter, "The New Woman of the Orient," Montgomery offered an interpretation of the first half-century of American women's missionary effort. She interpreted the ecumenical woman's missionary movement as the leading edge of a "worldwide woman's movement," and she claimed to find "evidences that age-long habits of subserviency are loosening, that women are shaking off the lion's paw of cruel custom and are daring to stand on their feet, 'an exceeding great army.'"[3] The global women's movement, Montgomery asserted, was not limited by "race or country." The impulse for women's freedom in America, Europe, and the Orient had "a common source" in "certain principles which Christ enunciated . . . (1) the supreme worth of the individual, (2) his direct responsibility to God, (3) the obligation of unselfish service laid on all irrespective of sex, (4) human brotherhood, (5) divine fatherhood."[4]

In the following paragraph, Montgomery offered perhaps the clearest statement of what Lucy W. Peabody called Montgomery's "great theme"[5]—the emancipation of women through the gospel of Jesus Christ.

> The Gospel is the most tremendous engine of democracy ever forged. It is destined to break into pieces all castes, privileges, and oppressions. Perhaps the last caste to be destroyed will be that of sex. It is not surprising that, while the main problem of democracy is still undemonstrated, the corollary of women's rights should remain to be grappled with. The surprising thing is that, not only in countries where there is most light and freedom is the impulse felt, but also in the most backward and despotic, so far as women are concerned. This can be accounted for only on the ground that there is a wider adumbration of the spirit of Christ than we dream. He being lifted up, even as he said, is drawing the whole world unto his perfect charity, justice, friendliness, democracy, to that redeemed humanity in which there shall be no male or female, bond nor free, but only free men and free women, whose lives, like His, are given them not to be ministered to, but to minister.[6]

Many thousands of women responded with an enormous outpouring of enthusiasm in the great Women's Missionary Jubilee of 1910–1911. But Montgomery's theme is not remarkable simply because it inspired such a powerful response. It is remarkable primarily because of its character. This theme, despite its religious language, is profoundly mundane. Montgomery did not write about heaven or a world to come; she focused instead on the power of Christianity to transform the material, social, and political conditions of life for women in the present world, which is precisely why her message thrilled thousands of American women. Montgomery claimed that the global women's movement, which was in turn part of a larger democratic impulse, was not only legitimated by the gospel, but was in fact the core meaning of the gospel for human civilization. How Montgomery's "great theme" developed is the interpretive challenge of this book.

Key Terms

Several terms that will be central to the argument of the book require definition. The expression "ecumenical woman's missionary movement" refers to the emergence and development of an organizational infrastructure to promote growth and cooperation among the independent women's mission boards across denominational lines, so that women could serve as missionaries in ministries explicitly designed to meet the needs of women and children in the mission field. This movement promoted an explicitly feminist missionary agenda. In the United States, leaders of the movement advocated for women to be appointed as full-fledged missionaries and created organizations and publications to educate women for support of missionary endeavors. In the educational materials produced by the movement, gender was a specific category of analysis.[7] In mission fields around the world, the movement funded evangelistic outreach programs, schools, medical services, and social services for women.

Until World War I, the underlying missiology of the movement was "Woman's Work for Woman": American women would emancipate their sisters around the world through the holistic proclamation and application of the gospel of Jesus Christ. Jesus was, as Montgomery wrote in the 25 August 1923 issue of the *The Baptist*, "the Great Emancipator of woman" who "alone among the founders of the great religions of the world looked upon men and women with level eyes, seeing not their differences, but their oneness, their humanity. He alone put no barriers before women in his religious teaching, but promulgated one law, equally binding upon men and women; opened one gate to which men and women were admitted upon equal terms."[8] While other religions oppressed women, Christianity liberated them, and in the liberation of women the kingdom of God was advanced.[9]

While it is impossible to set exact boundary dates for the ecumenical woman's missionary movement, several events are helpful in understanding its emergence, apex, decline, and demise. In 1888 the creation of the World's Missionary Committee of Christian Women signified the birth of the movement. In 1900 the women's foreign missionary boards created the Central Committee on the United Study of Foreign Missions—perhaps the movement's most characteristic and successful institution. The event that was most indicative of the movement at its apex, in terms of grassroots participation and influence on American culture, was the still unmatched Jubilee of 1910–1911. The Jubilee was a transcontinental series of woman's missionary celebrations that marked the fiftieth anniversary of the founding of the Woman's Union Missionary Society.

Following World War I, as the mission theory of "Woman's Work for Woman" evolved into a theory of "World Friendship," reflecting a host of theological and cultural changes in America and on the mission field, the movement fell into sharp decline. By the Second World War, the organizational resources of the women's movement had been absorbed by the various denominational structures.[10]

In this book, the term *feminism* refers specifically to late nineteenth- and early twentieth-century feminism. In that context, the term is used to indicate individuals or groups who responded to "woman's sphere" by promoting the autonomy of women. Feminism is really a term of convenience. As Nancy F. Cott has noted, the term is largely an anachronism in the nineteenth century, and it did not come into common usage before 1920. Still, the elements that define feminism were present in the nineteenth century in what is commonly called the "woman movement."[11]

The white middle-class feminist movement of the nineteenth century had to contend with certain key ideas that were deeply imbedded in the social structure, codified in the legal and political system, affirmed by the science of the day, and given a mantle of religious legitimacy by the dominant theologies of both Protestantism and Roman Catholicism. These ideas, which developed in response to social changes in the late colonial and early republican periods, were crystallized into a Victorian-era social institution that Barbara Welter called "the Cult of True Womanhood,"[12] otherwise known to scholars as "domesticity" or "woman's sphere." Domesticity was a social edifice that overshadowed every other aspect of a woman's existence in the Victorian Era.

As Aileen Kraditor has shown, the nineteenth-century debate over feminism was essentially a debate over how family structure related to social order. According to the conventional wisdom, "The home was the bulwark against social disorder, and woman was the creator of the home."[13] In the home, mothers taught children to behave properly when they were in the world. Paradoxically, the home was a retreat from the public world, but its function was to equip its members (especially the males) to regulate their own behavior in the world. Far from being a challenge to the world, the home depended upon the world for its meaning, and in return supported the world by providing social agents with a moral code for self-regulation that was appropriate for their increasingly specialized and individualized roles in society.

The ideology of domesticity was predicated on a central dualism between woman's sphere of home and family, where piety, virtue, and affection were esteemed and cultivated, and the man's sphere of business, politics, and labor, where shrewd dealing, selfish ambition, and cutthroat competition were more common. Woman's sphere was relational. The duties of women were other-directed. A woman's love was to be "disinterested"—that is, not selfishly motivated. She was to put the needs and concerns of others above her own.

In the language of the day, the home was "woman's sphere." While a middle-class white man might more or less freely choose a field of endeavor based on talent and opportunity, the role and work of a woman was regarded as determined by her "nature"—that is, her sex. According to the conventions of domesticity, God endowed women with natural capacities and virtues that suited them for the care and nurture of home and hearth—the very foundations of civilization—while men were suited for the striving and competition of public life. The goal of a woman's life was to marry well and establish a happy home where she could bring her moral influence to bear for the good of her husband, her children, and her community. In "the Cult of True Womanhood," the cardinal feminine virtues were piety, purity, submissiveness, and domesticity, and a woman without them was a failure, no matter what else she achieved. By the virtue of their influence, women—working subtly from the moral citadel of the home—would civilize the world.

The idea that mothers were responsible for the moral and spiritual education of children represented a shift from the eighteenth-century view of the patriarchal family, in which, while the mother was responsible for the physical care of the children, the father was responsible for their spiritual, moral, and intellectual growth. This shift in responsibility was due to the fact that fathers were more and more absent from the family because of their employment, and it reflected the impact of the moderate Calvinism of the Second Great Awakening and the influence of Lockean educational psychology.[14]

Helen Barrett Montgomery was a "New Woman" of the Progressive Era. She approached social problems with a consciousness influenced as deeply by progressivism as by feminism. Historians use the term *progressivism* to describe the many interconnected reform movements that developed between 1890 and 1920, as well as the style of thought that characterized the reformers who led the movements. The term became popular because some reformers used it to define themselves as enlightened, forward-looking, and optimistic leaders. It has remained useful because it helps to describe a generation at the turn of the twentieth century "who made the first comprehensive efforts to grapple with the ills of modern urban-industrial society."[15]

Progressives inherited from their predecessors the belief that America, as a Christian and democratic nation, was destined to lead the world into a new age of prosperity, social harmony, and peace, and many of them were motivated by a desire to speed the arrival of the millennium. Consequently, many were eager to baptize any means or theory that seemed modern and progressive—including theories and means that tended to undercut traditional evangelical piety and biblical interpretation, such as Darwinian evolution and modern biblical criticism. As the supernatural elements of millennial thought receded, what remained was a faith in divinely directed progress—a manifest destiny for the United States in which engineers were viewed as coagents with God.[16] By the end of the nineteenth century, the vision of the coming kingdom of God remained, but it was a project, not a miracle.

At the beginning of the Progressive Era, many Americans believed that Western civilization, and especially American culture, was involved in a process of evolutionary development toward greater and greater social perfection. To that extent, progressives were indistinguishable from conservatives. What set the progressives apart was their belief that society could ameliorate social evils. Conservatives tended to prefer the so-called Social Darwinism of English social philosopher Herbert Spencer. Conservative intellectuals found Spencer attractive because his theory seemed to validate their belief in America's manifest destiny, individual self-determination, and laissez faire capitalism supported by a strictly limited federal government. Rather than believing that social progress ought to be left to destiny or providence, progressives believed that people could either promote or retard the progressive development of history. They developed a critique of Social Darwinism that has become known as Reform Darwinism.[17]

The progressive movement developed in the context of the Victorian Era and shared the Victorian moral perspective. In fact, the progressive movement was, to a great extent, a response to the moral crisis of Victorian culture caused by the unprecedented growth of urban-industrial society in the post-Civil War era. The mainstream of progressivism was conservative in spirit. In the face of an increasingly complex society, the progressives tried to "hold a reluctant society to its basic values" by infusing public life with the moral code of the Victorian home and family.[18] They were engaged in a struggle to maintain a middle-class Protestant cultural hegemony against a multiplicity of social and economic forces.

The Purpose of This Book

The complex roots and significance of Helen Barrett Montgomery's contributions have been largely overlooked. Some know her as a social and educational reformer in late nineteenth-century Rochester, New York. Others know her as one of the first women to produce an original translation of the New Testament, as one of the most influential figures of the ecumenical woman's missionary movement of the early twentieth century, or as a leading Baptist of her day and the first woman to be elected to the presidency of a major American Protestant denomination. But no one has attempted a comprehensive analysis of her thought that reveals the underlying framework that connected her religious and secular work.

This book shows how Montgomery emerged as an intellectual of the American ecumenical woman's missionary movement and how the missionary apologetic she developed combined her Baptist piety with political and social views shaped by feminism and progressivism. Montgomery was a second-generation "domestic feminist," whose views provided a link between what has been labeled the "liberal feminism" of predecessors such as Elizabeth Cady Stanton and Susan B. Anthony and the "evangelical feminism" of women such as Frances Willard. She was a "New Woman" who wanted to maintain the values and virtues of "True Womanhood" as she widened the sphere of woman's activity and influence—a sphere that Montgomery eventually extended to encompass the entire world.

Montgomery was also a progressive in her social, theological, and political views. Thirty-six years of public life and leadership, 1893 to 1929, placed her squarely in the Progressive Era. Often blending the liberal feminist and evangelical maternalist perspectives, she worked for progressive reforms as a leader of the Women's Educational and Industrial Union of Rochester, and as an elected member of the city's school board, which was itself a product of municipal political reform. Progressivism shaped her optimism about the future, her evangelical determination to combat what she considered to be social evil, her eagerness to harness the latest learning for redemptive purposes, and her confidence in the democratic ideal. In her view, Christianity, science, and democracy were inextricably linked, and they were forging a new age of salvation, enlightenment, and freedom for the world—the kingdom of God.

Montgomery was convinced that Christianity was inherently superior to all other world religions because of the freedom and enlightenment it engendered in civilization. In her mind, the American foreign missionary movement combined spiritual and material ends. Given sufficient time and effort, she was certain that the truth of the gospel, combined with the growing power of scientific achievement to cure the world's greatest ills, and the inevitable triumph of democracy over tyranny, would emancipate humanity and bring in the kingdom of God. But this vision would not be accomplished without great human effort, and she believed Christian women were assigned a special role in the scheme of redemption—they were called by God to work for the emancipation of their sisters everywhere.

The synthesis of religion, science, and democracy into a theory of progressive cultural development, what Jean B. Quandt called "the secularization of postmillennialism," also marked Montgomery as a progressive. Postmillennialism was a widely held view of eschatology among nineteenth-century American Protestants, characterized by a belief that the spiritual rule of Christ over the world (rather than his physical presence) would become manifest in the gradual perfection of society through inspired human agency, culminating in the realization of the kingdom of God on earth. It was, at least in the minds of many evangelicals at the end of the nineteenth century, compatible with evolutionary science and political notions of manifest destiny. The social gospel in particular emphasized an increasingly secularized version of postmillennialism. But the influence of postmillennialism went far beyond institutional Protestantism and is evident in the thought of many progressive intellectuals and reformers, such as Herbert Croly, Richard Ely, Albion Small, and even the pragmatist John Dewey.[19]

For many scholars, Montgomery's theological progressivism and the fact that she was a contemporary of Walter Rauschenbusch in Rochester beg the question of a connection between her theological views and the social gospel. While it is a valid question, it is strange that Montgomery's earlier and apparently more intimate relationship with suffragist Susan B. Anthony has not raised similar questions. All of those whom historians usually consider to be the leading figures of the Social Gospel movement were men, and Janet

Forsythe Fishburn once characterized the movement as "a theology written by men for men."[20] Recent scholarship is moving in the direction of including women as shapers of the social gospel.[21] Nevertheless, it is more helpful and more appropriate to view Montgomery's theology as a contribution to the ecumenical woman's missionary movement, which was a separate but related development—a theology written by women for women. At least in Montgomery's case, her theology was influenced by political progressivism, domestic feminism, and the historical experience of women on the foreign mission field. These influences were prior to, and more important than, the impact of the social gospel—if by the social gospel one means primarily the thought of Walter Rauschenbusch. That is not to say that Rauschenbusch's influence was unimportant. But it does not deserve the interpretive privilege it has sometimes been given. This book examines Montgomery's relationship with suffragist Susan B. Anthony in chapter 6 and her connections with Rauschenbusch in chapter 8.

Two

"The Fatherhood of God and the Victorian Family"
The Childhood and Early Education of Helen Barrett

Helen Barrett's childhood experience was crucial to her mature development as a domestic feminist and a progressive. This chapter shows how her family, religious training, and early education helped to shape her worldview consistent with the intellectual and moral presuppositions of evangelical piety in the Victorian Era.

A key feature of young Helen's moral worldview, which she learned by precept and by example, was the conviction that the home was the basic moral and spiritual unit of society and the cornerstone of civilization. She learned that womanly virtue and the tender influence of a pious mother—a True Woman—were essential in maintaining and safeguarding the moral and spiritual atmosphere of the home.

At her grandfather's knee, Helen learned to believe in the integration and continuity of scientific knowledge with evangelical Christianity. From her parents, especially from her father, she gained an early appreciation for education. Like most educated young women of her era, she was taught that those who were educated had an obligation to make themselves "useful" in some way—to use their learning for the benefit of others and for the advancement of Christianity.

Helen's family and religious experience inculcated in her a warmhearted personal piety. Evangelical Christian faith was seamlessly integrated with the rest of her cultural experience. She did not experience "conversion" in the traditional evangelical sense. While conversion was a theoretical possibility that she understood and affirmed, her assimilation into the Christian faith lacked the moral crisis that evangelicals have traditionally ascribed to the conversion process. Nevertheless, her Christian faith was activist, evangelical, and missionary in spirit from the very beginning.

Family Influences

Helen Barrett was born to Amos Judson Barrett and Emily B. Barrows Barrett on 31 July 1861, in Kingsville, Ohio, the home of her grandparents on the Barrett side. Her grandparents on both sides of the family were descendants of New England Puritans. On the Barrett side, her grandparents practiced family prayer, conducted spelling drills, and taught their children and grandchildren the Bible. They frowned upon hair-curling, gum-chewing, pantalettes, and parties.[1] The Barretts had helped to settle Ohio's Western Reserve, and in a memorial written at the death of her father, the adult Montgomery reflected on the values that shaped their lives. "Whenever a cluster of rude log cabins broke the solitude of the forest, there might also be found the plain church, with its small steeple faithfully pointing upward, and the village school, with its ever open door. Full of privations and difficulties, yet withal eager, questioning, aspiring, self-restrained was life in these new communities, amid whose influences and under whose training were reared some of the noblest sons and daughters of the Republic."[2]

From her parents and grandparents, Helen learned to value simplicity, piety, intellectual curiosity, self-sufficiency, self-discipline, and patriotism. These values were part of the legacy she received from her Yankee roots, and they were glorified in the Victorian culture of her youth. Her father's generation lived in settlements that were essentially New England villages removed westward; and in the romanticized memories of progressives, the New England village was a place where face-to-face relationships prevailed and Christian faith, republican duty, and human sympathy characterized social intercourse.

In her memorial to her father, the adult Helen Barrett Montgomery portrayed the rustic life of the Yankee settlers as one of refined simplicity and ideal domesticity. Her father's boyhood cabin offered few material comforts or conveniences, and just to survive required much labor.

Yet that home which he remembered was a beautiful home; full of the light of love and grace of courtesy, and glorified by a womanly presence that softened every bare outline with nameless charm, and made the log house a very Bethany. How he loved to tell of the long winter evenings when the great open fire-place, filled with glowing logs, flooded the room with light; when mother sat at her spinning-wheel, and father, book in hand, gave out to his eager boys the hardest words in Webster's Spelling Book, or gathered them about him to hear brave stories of the Revolution in which his father fought, or to listen reverently to the Book ever central in that home.[3]

True Womanhood softened the harsh wilderness existence of the settlers of the Western Reserve, according to Montgomery, and made a home where, under the firm, intelligent discipline of a Christian father, the learning, piety, and patriotism of Victorian civilization could flourish. If this brief reminiscence is an accurate indication, Montgomery's grandfather apparently took the central role in the moral education of his children. Her grandmother's role was to lend "charm" to the bare existence, and, apparently, to contribute to household production in the age of homespun. Montgomery's father was born in 1832, so his reminiscences can probably be dated to the late 1830s and early 1840s. This is precisely the era when the ideology of domesticity was taking definite shape. The separation of the domestic sphere of the True Woman from the public sphere of man was still under way, and the delegation of moral education in the home from the father to the mother was incomplete.[4]

Helen's grandfather Barrows, of South Trenton, was an amateur scientist who for many years made weather reports to the Smithsonian Institute based on observations from his own barometer. She once wrote that her grandfather (probably Barrows) was "expelled from the Baptist Church because he insisted on studying Geology," and his fellow church members felt it was a threat to the authority of the Genesis account of creation.[5] Her grandmother Barrows taught her to work—to cook, bake, sew, and knit; to do farm chores; and to manage a household. In the Barrows farmhouse, young Helen gained her first exposure to classics of piety such as Foxe's *Book of Martyrs* and Bunyan's *Pilgrim's Progress*.[6]

In "Coming of Age in America," Barbara Welter offered several generalizations that bear directly on the early life of Helen Barrett Montgomery.

The most important virtues for the nineteenth-century girl, said Welter, were obedience and self-control, and the father was "the god-on-earth who must not be disobeyed . . . subject to the prior claims of the heavenly father."[7] Welter went on to describe the general family pattern that emerged in the lives of woman suffragists:

> The girl is usually the firstborn, often without any male children in the family, or at least not for several years. The father assumes direction of his daughter's education and character, while the mother is relegated to the role of invalid or nurse-housekeeper for younger children. The girl and her father develop an extraordinarily close relationship, as a part of which she feels that she must compensate him for the son she is sure he wished her to be. In later life these women, who achieved much more than most of their contemporaries, look back on their father with some ambivalence, and see their mother's role as that of a silent martyr. They both blame and credit their fathers with their own desire for achievement, which, in nineteenth century values, was not a desirable quality in a woman. Many of these women choose weak husbands, whose careers they eclipse, and they themselves are preoccupied, in their reforms or their writings, with finding a suitable definition of woman's nature and role.[8]

While Welter's generalizations do not match perfectly with Montgomery's career, the correspondence is very close indeed. Montgomery did not look upon her father with ambivalence. Every word she ever wrote about him for a public audience was filled with admiration and respect, and her private communications to him and about him were warm and affectionate. But he did take a dominant role in her education, while her mother's role—especially in her early life—was clearly secondary. In her childhood and young adulthood, at least until her marriage, Helen wanted nothing so much as to make her father proud.

Helen's mother, Emily B. Barrows, was the preceptress of the Nunda Institute, where she met Amos Judson Barrett, the principal, and they were married.[9] Helen recorded little about her mother, other than that she loved her, and that she was "obeyed because she belonged."[10] In her letters home from college and just after college, however, it is evident that her relationship with her mother grew as she matured. In 1881 she wrote to her mother on her mother's birthday: "As I remember the past, and think of the care, the trouble, and the heartache I have caused you, always taking, and you always giving so freely, so patiently, I realize the depth and beauty of a life and love that has surrounded me so completely that sometimes I have not felt its presence."[11] After her graduation, while teaching in Philadelphia, Helen wrote to her parents that she had "noticed the character" of her mother and had come to love her "not merely because she was Mama but because Mama was lovely." For many years, she wrote, "this conception of my mother as a person" had been growing, and every year she found it "sweeter and better and dearer."[12] Implied in that statement was that for many years she had not considered her mother as a person—at least not with the same regard that she accorded to her father. According to Helen's description, her mother was the epitome of the True Woman—self-sacrificial, subordinate, pious, pure, and domestic. Helen loved her mother, and as she matured she grew to appreciate and respect her mother; but Helen never wanted to emulate her mother. That honor went to her father.

Clearly Amos Judson Barrett was the most powerful influence upon Helen's early life. She wrote: "To this child God always looked like her father, and obedience to her father became the basis of submission to the will of God. There was reverence, there was fear, the right kind of fear, a dread of doing what was wrong in my father's sight."[13]

Judson Barrett entered the University of Rochester in Rochester, New York, in 1851 as a sophomore. He taught school at Little Falls while he finished his degree, and then for six years he was principal of Nunda Academy in Livingstone County. In 1860 he married Emily B. Barrows of Trenton, New York. After Helen came another daughter, Anne Louise, who died in Denver, Colorado, on 14 June 1906,[14] and a son, Storrs Barrows, who eventually became an astronomer at the University of Chicago[15] and the Yerkes Observatory in Wisconsin.[16]

Judson Barrett became the principal of an academy at Lowville, New York, in 1868, when Helen was seven years old. In 1868 the South (except for Tennessee) remained under military Reconstruction, although eight of the eleven states of the Confederacy were readmitted to representation in Congress. Ulysses S. Grant, the greatest hero of the Republic, was elected president with campaign slogans like "Scratch a Democrat and You Will Find a Rebel," "The Party that Saved the Union Must Rule It," and "Vote As You Shot."[17] Helen was introduced to the passions of post-Civil War

nationalism when several of her new playmates asked if her father was a
Republican. Mistaking the party of Lincoln for the "publicans" that she had
learned were sinners in the New Testament, she "denied the allegation with
some heat."[18] Word soon got around, and the townspeople required Judson
Barrett to clarify his political views.

In the early 1870s Judson Barrett gave up the academy and returned to
Rochester as principal of the Collegiate Institute, a preparatory school for the
university. He felt called to ministry, however, so he gave up his position as a
principal, retained a professorship in Latin and Greek, and entered Rochester
Theological Seminary. He graduated in 1876 and became pastor of Lake
Avenue Baptist Church in Rochester, where he continued in ministry until
his death. In 1888, he took a year's leave of absence from the pulpit because
of vision problems, and he traveled extensively in the South and West. In
1889, he died on his way to Sunday evening services, after having preached in
the morning and at a funeral in the afternoon.[19] Soon after his death, Helen
Montgomery wrote a privately published memorial volume commemorating
his life.

Evangelical Zeal, Christian Nurture, and Progressive Piety

Helen demonstrated a capacity for evangelical zeal very early in her life.
Her grandfather Barrett's neighbors were Spiritualists. Young Helen
watched "Mrs. Jones waving her apron aloft and driving 'sperrits' [spirits]
from the door," and she debated theology with Mr. Jones as he milked his
cow.[20] Modern Spiritualism began with the "mysterious rappings" heard in
the home of John D. Fox, a blacksmith, in Hydesville, a small village near
Rochester in 1848. Fox's wife and three daughters alleged that the noises
were communications from invisible beings in the spirit world. The Fox family soon moved into Rochester, whence their notoriety spread rapidly. Baptist
luminary Augustus H. Strong was an eyewitness to the phenomenon when
he was a teenager, but he regarded it as "a farce."[21] Many other noteworthy
persons took a more favorable view. Several members of the famous Beecher
family became Spiritualists, as did Abby Ann Judson, daughter of the famous
Baptist missionary Adoniram Judson. Between 1848 and the turn of the century, thousands became convinced that they could speak to the dead through
mediums, and thousands of others seriously investigated the phenomena.
Spiritualism provided a radical, individualistic, nonconformist alternative

to orthodox Protestantism, and many radical political activists, especially women suffragists, were active in the movement. Women, who were assumed to be naturally more spiritual and emotional than men, held important positions of leadership and authority in Spiritualism from the beginning, although the movement was never organized and institutionalized to the extent that orthodox Protestant denominations were.[22]

Helen was unable to convert her grandfather's neighbors, but her failure left her undaunted. As a self-proclaimed theological conservative,[23] she remained a committed opponent of Spiritualism throughout her life. Many years later, during a postwar resurgence of Spiritualism, the adult Montgomery continued her polemical engagement with Spiritualism.[24] But Montgomery's evangelical zeal was by no means limited to combating Spiritualism. Throughout her life she maintained a commitment to personal evangelism, even though her own conversion was a product of spiritual nurture rather than confrontational evangelism.

Helen's father was called to the pastorate of Lake Avenue Baptist Church upon his graduation from the Rochester Theological Seminary in 1876. The Reverend Barrett baptized Helen into church membership that winter. Helen was deeply moved by the experience of being baptized by her father, but it was an experience forever marred with regret. When Helen presented herself as a candidate for baptism, she, like all the other candidates, had to appear before the deacons for examination "as to their Christian experience." One elderly deacon, apparently still attached to older ideas about conversion, asked her, "My young sister, did you feel the burden of sin roll away?" Years later, reflecting on the experience, Montgomery expressed exasperation that anyone should expect a conversion experience from "a child of fifteen growing up in a Christian home!" Not knowing what else to do, Helen told the deacon that she had indeed felt the burden roll away, and she felt the sting of guilt. "I had told a lie in order to get into the church. It filled me with bitterness at the very moment when a gracious father was welcoming me into the household of faith."[25]

Membership in the Lake Avenue Baptist Church taught Helen the meaning of Christian duty in an age of Protestant activism. From the beginning of its history, the Lake Avenue congregation was missionary in spirit. The first missionary society was established in the church soon after the church was constituted. The members of the society divided the entire city into districts and assigned each member a district for house-to-house visitation. During its mission phase, from 1865 to 1871, four students from Rochester Theological Seminary served as part-time pastors. Two of these men went on to become foreign missionaries, and four women from the congregation became foreign missionaries between 1877 and 1885.[26]

For young Nellie Barrett, church membership was anything but restful. In addition to attending the morning worship service, she taught a Sunday School class at the Lake Avenue church on Sunday mornings, and on Sunday afternoons, she walked two miles to the Lyell Avenue Mission Sunday school, where she taught a class of "under-privileged" boys. Sunday also included the young people's meeting and evening worship.[27]

At the age of fifteen, Helen demonstrated a capacity for theological reflection and eloquence beyond her years. In reflecting on a sermon she heard, she wrote:

> The preacher showed how God's immutability must be, to correspond to his other attributes, how He knew no such thing as succession or progression, that no such thing as time was of God, how He filled all duration as well as space. The thought that the longest age—in fact the world and all its affairs—shrink into a mere point in the awfulness of his immensity, is grand. My *mind* loves to view this Being and revels in following a little way these incomprehensibly great thoughts, but my *heart* loves better to think of Him as the sorrowing Man of Nazareth, or the gentle Father who is not too far off or too great to be sorry or glad with me, and to lead me by His side. Now is the time for daisies and they look so pretty on their tall stems. From gazing so steadily at the sun, I love to fancy, they have come to bear on their tiny faces a feeble likeness of His glory, and thus it is with us.[28]

With this brief passage, which touches upon God's transcendence and immanence, the Incarnation, natural revelation, and human beings as bearers of the image of God, Helen revealed her inclination to serious theological reflection juxtaposed with warm, heartfelt piety. She was intellectually attracted to the distant, transcendent, impassive, Calvinist God that the preacher described; she was emotionally drawn to the more accessible, warm, and tender figure of Jesus and his loving heavenly Father, who came near, who cared about her personally, and who was affected by her joys and sufferings. Helen's theology was consistent with the "dulcet and sentimental" spirit of middle-class Protestantism of the late Victorian Era.[29]

Early Education

Helen received much of her basic education at home—primarily from her father, but from other family members as well. Her Aunt Susie taught her to play the piano. At the age of nine, she joined the rhetoric class at the academy in Lowville, where her father was the principal, so at an early age, she learned to stand upon a stage before an audience and speak. At some point, probably just after her father took over the Collegiate Institute, she enrolled at the Livingston Park Seminary.[30]

Established by Cathro Mason Curtis in 1858, Livingston Park Seminary was one of the ubiquitous female schools that emerged in the latter half of the nineteenth century to prepare young ladies for the responsibilities of school teaching and True Womanhood. Before the 1780s, New England girls usually learned at home or from private tutors. From 1780 onward, many boys' academies accepted girls as well, segregating them in different rooms or parts of rooms, allowing them fewer hours of instruction or instructing them only during the summer. Around the turn of the nineteenth century, female academies began to appear across New England. These offered basic education, as well as ornamental "accomplishments" such as painting, embroidery, music, and languages, which appealed to wealthy families. Between 1810 and 1830, however, both of these approaches gave way to more pragmatic female academies aimed at preparing women for their socially essential roles in the domestic sphere. If a woman was to be a stimulating companion to her husband and a competent and efficient manager of the household, and if she was to bring up her children in Christian piety and instill them with the morals and virtues necessary for republican citizenship, she needed an education particularly suited to those ends.[31] By the 1830s women were perceived as particularly felicitous candidates for the teaching profession, first of all because they were "naturally" suited to the task of instructing and influencing children with positive moral influence and because they could be employed for much lower salaries than men could. Furthermore, teachers were needed to Christianize and civilize on the western frontier, and many families came to believe that education was a key to improved opportunities and self-support for unmarried daughters.[32] A wave of female seminaries and schools for the training of women teachers emerged in the second quarter of the nineteenth century, notable among them Mary Lyon's Mount Holyoke Female Seminary, chartered in 1836, from which so many pioneer woman missionaries emerged.[33] As the female seminaries (outside of New England they were sometimes called academies or colleges) grew and developed, their curricula included more and more of the liberal arts studies covered at men's colleges.[34]

While it can be argued that women's education did function according to the essentially domestic rationale behind it, there were unintended consequences as well. Following the trend of the Cult of True Womanhood in general, those who structured women's education disregarded economic status and treated women as a class unto themselves. Economic fortunes were precarious in nineteenth-century America, and a woman who employed a domestic servant in one year might have to become a domestic servant the next year. Since all women were assumed to have the same domestic duties and maternal calling, all women were assumed to need the same preparation. Consequently, women's education fostered a kind of feminist consciousness. Furthermore, a few educated women began to look beyond the limitations placed on learning by the ideology of woman's sphere. They sought professions in science, medicine, law, and theology, and their boldness questioned implicitly the sexual determinism at the very foundation of domesticity.[35]

The motto of the Livingston Park Alumnae Association was: "Loyalty—Purity—Sincerity."[36] Curtis' students memorialized her for "the power and influence in the formation of character which so distinguished [her] as an educator."[37] Nevertheless, Curtis' intellectual achievements were substantial for a woman of her era. Like so many heads of female seminaries, she was a generalist by necessity. She was apparently "proficient" in Greek, Latin, German, French, and Italian; she taught Shakespeare, mathematics, fine art, and music. One admirer testified that he had never known a finer "expounder of Bible History."[38] Students studied trigonometry and botany, and they recalled reading Wayland's *Moral Science*, Paley's *Natural Theology*, and Butler's *Analogy of Religion*.[39] These books represented the intellectual cornerstones of post-revolutionary America. They used Scottish Common Sense philosophy (imported through Princeton) and Baconian inductive empiricism to weave a seamless garment of certainty. According to the perspective of Common Sense, anyone could discover that science, the Bible, Christian theology, Victorian morality, republican political institutions, capitalism, and ordinary common sense offered profound and comprehensive mutual confirmation. The key was careful observation, classification of facts, and avoidance of speculation. Even more significantly, they proved the existence of God, who created the universe and invested it with a moral nature and a spiritual destiny.[40] The fact that those books were used at Livingston Park Seminary suggests that Curtis was attempting to make the education she offered as near as possible in quality to that offered to men in the colleges. Even so, the emergence of the new American universities in the latter half of the nineteenth century, and with them a positivist approach that made religious belief irrelevant to the scientific enterprise, led to the rapid disappearance of those books from the curricula of leading colleges and left the female seminaries like Livingston Park lagging behind.

Curtis set an example for her students of lifetime learning. She traveled in Europe, and she was active in the early women's clubs in Rochester—especially the Fortnightly Ignorance Club, which was the second women's club in the state of New York.[41] Founded by Sarah Adamson Dolley, the second woman in America to receive a medical degree,[42] the Ignorance Club was an attempt on the part of some of the leading women of Rochester to educate themselves. At each meeting, women would pass the "Ignorance Book," in which they could write a question about a topic they wanted to discuss. Then they would choose a question from the list and someone to investigate it. At a subsequent meeting, the report would be presented and discussed. The Ignorance Club was an early example in Rochester of the emphasis on womanly self-improvement that characterized the domestic feminism of the woman's club movement.[43]

Curtis' students said that she sowed "seeds of truth and purity" in them during their days at Livingston Park Seminary.[44] Judging from the poetry she wrote for the Ignorance Club, she also sowed seeds of feminist consciousness and maternalist activism:

Let Her Act
O woman grand and glorious;
Let the dawning light appear,
Put forth your power of saving,
Nor stand in servile fear.
Behold the weak are calling,

To shield from sin and death;
Stand up, defend the falling,
From sin's consuming breath.

No longer sip the nectar,
With childish pleasure smile,
And shun the real labors
That save from evils vile.
'Tis sweet to hear of roses,
Of man's protecting care,
Of vines so soft and tender,
And beauties of the fair.

But 'tis sweeter far, and nobler,
In life's broad field to fight,
For purity and goodness,
For home, for God, for right.
Then forward to the rescue,
Break the hateful shackles off,
Free woman from dishonor,
From disrespect and scoff.

The breath of God will quicken,
Make glad the fainting heart
And fill with higher impulse
The earnest woman's part.
Teach man to love and cherish,
With impulses divine,
And hand in hand together,
The higher aims combine.

With righteousness the cap-stone,
This earth our Savior trod,
Will bloom with joy and gladness,
With glory to our God.
And woman, pure and noble,

In honor shall be seen,
Foremost in life's great warfare—
The woman, mother, queen.[45]

Curtis' vision of True Womanhood was missionary and militant. In her view, it was up to women to civilize the world. Another poem written for the Ignorance Club, "Two Theories on the Origin of Man,"[46] is too long to reproduce, but it is characterized by the same theme of maternal mission and activism. Curtis juxtaposed the biblical and evolutionary accounts of human origins. She thought woman was blamed unjustly for the fall of humanity in the biblical account. Nevertheless, with characteristic compassion, patience, submission, and practicality, woman sewed fig leaves together to provide clothing for herself and her husband, and thus made the first contribution to civilization. In the evolutionary account, Curtis thought it was the moral sense that set human beings apart from the animal world and made civilization possible. Since, according to the ideology of True Womanhood, woman was the guardian of morality and religion, it fell to her to guide and defend the progress of civilization. In Curtis' view, no matter which theory of origins one chose to believe, the result was the same: woman was responsible for civilization.

Under Curtis' leadership, the Livingston Park Seminary carefully inculcated a spirit of patriotism in its students. Older alumnae recounted how Curtis was responsible for the first flag-raising in Rochester at the outbreak of the Civil War. Curtis insisted that the seminary must have a flag "proclaiming our loyalty to the Union." They found, however, that there were no flags available for purchase in the city. So Curtis decided that her students could make a flag. When the flag was ready, Curtis invited Dr. Anderson, president of the University of Rochester, and several other local dignitaries to the flag-raising ceremony. Because it was considered unwomanly for the female students to cheer in public when the flag was raised, Dr. Anderson brought along several young men from the university, who gave a rousing cheer as the flag went up. The Livingston Park women sang "America" and "The Star-Spangled Banner," while the newly mustered Fifteenth Regiment lined the street and offered a salute.[47]

For most of the nineteenth century, an education at a place like Livingston Park was the most a young woman could hope to achieve, but the founding of Vassar College in 1861 marked the beginning of a new era in women's education in America. For the first time, there was an educational institution for women that proposed to provide a curriculum that was equal in substance and quality to that of the best colleges for men. Wellesley College, another pioneer college for women, was established in 1875—and unlike Vassar, Wellesley had an all-woman faculty.

Helen set her heart on attending college at Wellesley, and in 1880 her father agreed. She had read the required Latin before the age of fifteen, but her background in mathematics was lacking. She left Livingston Park Seminary in the spring of 1880 so that her father could give her personal instruction. Her mother's contribution to the enterprise was material rather than intellectual. She helped Helen with the formidable task of preparing a suitable wardrobe.[48] Helen entered Wellesley in the fall of 1880 at the age of nineteen.

Three

Evangelicalism, Progressivism, and Domesticity
Helen Barrett's Wellesley

Helen Barrett's experience at Wellesley was crucial in shaping the rest of her life. By attending Wellesley, she entered into the tiny elite of college-educated women in the United States, many of whom provided leadership for the burgeoning movements among women in religion, politics, and social reform in the late nineteenth and early twentieth centuries. Wellesley provided Helen with several examples of strong, well-educated Christian women who were capable of combining the conventions of middle-class domesticity with a missionary passion for social change. These examples empowered her to embrace fearlessly her own strengths and challenged her to reflect seriously upon her own calling, as a Christian and a woman. Furthermore, she was confronted by a diversity of religious, social, and political thought that sometimes challenged her convictions and sometimes confirmed them. In her correspondence to her family during her college years, it is possible to glimpse the emergence of Helen as an activist and an intellectual, and the roots of several of her most profound and important ideas can be identified.

Higher Education for American Women

By the middle of the nineteenth century, young women had begun to clamor for admission to colleges and universities. In the Midwest, beginning with Oberlin College, a few private colleges and some of the new land-grant universities admitted women to special programs. The first female colleges were established in the Northeast just after the Civil War. Despite loud objections from those who, like Harvard's Edward Clarke, believed the stress of higher education would be ruinous to the health and reproductive capacity of young women,[1] these schools self-consciously aimed at providing the same quality of liberal education as men's colleges. They did not openly challenge the conventions of True Womanhood, but their very existence signaled a cultural change.

By the turn of the century, several schools were already experimenting with authentic coeducation, and men and women were admitted and educated under the same standards. Even though True Womanhood was still the dominant cultural social institution for women, its presuppositions about women's inferior intellectual capacity, physical delicacy, and emotional fragility were profoundly challenged by the overwhelming success of women in higher education. Social surveys of female students and alumnae tended to find that they were generally in good physical and mental health, but that they did have lower marriage and childbirth rates than other women.[2]

So many women entered colleges, and they competed so successfully with men, that a backlash against coeducation developed among those who feared what Rosenberg called "the feminization of academe." In many schools, coeducational programs were segregated once again, and a quota was established to limit the number of women admitted.[3] In some cases, the restrictive measures remained in place for several decades. But the implications of women's higher education for the emerging feminist movement were already apparent. If competition in higher education was any indication, women were intellectually and emotionally equal to men. "Woman's sphere" persisted, but the support it drew from the conventional wisdom of women's intellectual inferiority was shattered.

Wellesley: True Womanhood and Academic Excellence

Founded in 1875 by Henry Fowle Durant, Wellesley was a nondenominational Christian college for women that enforced not only academic rigor, but what was considered a womanly domesticity as well. Durant was a Harvard classmate of Dr. Edward Clarke, who was adamantly opposed to the higher education of women for alleged health reasons. Durant believed differently and set out to prove his point. He believed that women were morally superior to men and that their subordinate cultural status was socially constructed rather than biologically determined. He believed higher education would demonstrate women's fitness for public life and prepare them for the work of social reform.[4]

Wellesley in the 1880s was in the business of molding women of "blameless character and fine scholarship and Christian womanliness."[5] Although Durant wanted Wellesley to be the female equivalent to Harvard academically, his plan for molding Christian womanliness and character was based on the female seminary model of Mount Holyoke, where he was a trustee. To fulfill his academic goal, Durant spared no expense equipping the science labs and stocking the library. He designed a curriculum that was broad and progressive, and he took the bold step of hiring an all-female faculty with the best academic qualifications he could find—so long as they were evangelical Christians. To fulfill his moral goal, he incorporated into the facilities and regulations of the college all of the features that he believed would build strong women of Christian character: evangelical Christianity, careful moral supervision, regular exercise, practical dress, a healthy environment, and a proper diet.[6]

Durant emphasized the family atmosphere of Wellesley. Following the Mount Holyoke model, he informed prospective students and their families that all students would "aid to some extent in the domestic work of the family." In Durant's view, it was a measure that served several practical purposes. It would help all the young women to "understand and take part in systematic housekeeping," it would keep the cost of tuition and board low for "young women of moderate means," and the discipline would unite the students "all in one family as helpers in the common good." In fact, Durant declared that domestic work was "invaluable in its influence upon the moral nature and its preparation for social life."[7] Durant believed that Wellesley could provide "the elevating and refining influences of a happy Christian home" that would "make the life of the students refined and noble."[8]

Durant was very sensitive to the charge that women's health would be destroyed by the strain of higher education. In his view, the charge was unjust. "The truth is," he wrote, "hard study, properly directed and regulated, promotes physical health." He believed "unjust prejudice" disregarded the real causes of women's maladies and laid the blame on women's higher education. He believed that when the results of the Wellesley experience became clear, "this calumny, that woman's mind and woman's body are too frail to bear the pursuit of knowledge, will perish with other forgotten prejudices."[9]

To validate his beliefs and meet the concerns of the critics of women's higher education, Durant took great care to guard the health of his students. He boasted that the location of the college was ideal and that the heating systems of the buildings had been constructed so that circulating air was moisturized to "the established health point" and maintained an "equable summer atmosphere." Gas lights were supplemented with special oil lamps for reading, and "the College Home" was equipped with hot and cold water from an Artesian well, bathing rooms, an elevator, and "an abundance of light, sunshine, and fresh air."[10]

Health was also a part of the curriculum. A woman physician and a nurse were on hand to tend to students' medical needs and teach "the laws of Hygiene" and "proper habits of attention and care." Durant purchased fourteen boats so that the women could exercise by rowing on the lake, and he noted that the lake was also suitable for skating in the winter.[11] Students were told to air their bedding for one hour each day and to avoid reading in improper light. They were to bathe regularly, to monitor the temperature and air quality in their rooms, and to maintain a wardrobe that was "neat, very simple, and adapted to the season." Over the years, the college experimented with various styles of gymnastics training.[12]

The tension between the college ideal of academic excellence and the female seminary ideal of Christian womanliness provoked no end of conflict in the early years of Wellesley. Faculty and students chaffed at religious requirements, lifestyle regulations, and administrative policies they found demeaning and restrictive. Durant and Ada Howard, whom Durant brought from Mount Holyoke to be Wellesley's first president, found many of the first students ill-prepared and somewhat unladylike and some of the faculty insubordinate. In addition to the academic requirements, Helen complained that Wellesley's regulations mandated that students "*must* exercise one *hour every* day in the open air . . . and . . . work one hour, and attend chapel twice, and Bible class once, and silent time twice, and spend one hour in elegant leisure at dinner."[13] Students' chores included seeding raisins, peeling apples, sorting beans, filling lamps, washing dishes, and dusting.

In accordance with the seminary tradition, the social lives of the young Wellesley women were closely monitored. Only those students whose parents had given written permission were allowed to leave the campus or receive visitors. Helen wrote home during her freshman year asking her father to send a permission card stating that she could "go to Boston or anywhere I want to go at any time" and also "permitting me to see anyone that calls at any time, whether male or female."[14]

Some of the students were quite unhappy with the lifestyle restrictions, especially the heavy evangelical climate that Durant insisted upon. One student wrote that his "fanaticism" drove her away from Christianity.[15] Although Helen loved Wellesley and looked back fondly on her college days throughout her life, she was not wholly uncritical of the school. She told her parents it was "by no means a paradise. In many ways they are fussy, and in some narrow, but I like it very much." Nevertheless she did not want others to come on her recommendation, for she thought she would "feel the responsibility of them all the time."[16] Her minor criticisms notwithstanding, Helen's years at Wellesley provided her with a wealth of experiences that challenged her intellectually, deepened her faith and piety, stirred her passion for the gospel and her sense of missionary calling, and broadened her view of the world.

Religion and Bible Study at Wellesley

In addition to Mr. Durant, who preached in the chapel on the first Sunday of every year on the text, "God is love,"[17] students heard regularly from guest preachers, including famous liberal clergymen such as Lyman Abbott and Phillips Brooks. Even on a campus that was so obviously evangelical in orientation, the higher education of women apparently made many clergymen nervous. According to faculty member Sarah Frances Whiting, they would often preach "what we used to call a woman-sermon—to tell us what we might and might not do. Finally President Freeman requested that some other subject be selected."[18] The presumption on the part of such clergymen, as guests on campus, to lecture the all-female Wellesley community on domestic propriety, must have stirred and exacerbated the deep vein of hostility toward male power, which feminist scholars have discovered simmering just below the surface of True Womanhood. That hostility was a consequence of the vulnerability of women under the ideology of separate spheres as well as a powerful motivation in nineteenth-century women's efforts for moral and political reform.[19] The resentment of male domination fostered feminist consciousness at Wellesley—a consciousness that Durant feared, despite his advocacy of women's social potential, but which flourished under the leadership of Alice Freeman.[20]

Other notable guests, such as Matthew Arnold and Oliver Wendell Holmes, anthropologist Frank Hamilton Cushing, and English critic Edwin Paxton Hood, visited the campus occasionally. As an upperclassman, Helen was often given the duty of escorting guests on campus tours, and she had the additional privilege of sitting at the faculty table during meals and participating in discussions with visiting dignitaries. Freeman herself took charge of Matthew Arnold's visit, but he proved uncontrollable. Rather than submit to the formalities of meeting the faculty or following the planned tour, the distinguished English poet and literary critic "plunged through the door exclaiming, 'Ah! Really! How beautiful, how like a fairyland!'" After several attempts to return to the planned itinerary, Freeman was finally reduced to following him around and answering his questions "with due meekness." When he observed Helen's Greek class, he was incredulous. She wrote, "He looked on our work as if it were the antic of some strange animal and said, ''Pon honor, they write with the accents, now really!'" Then, with a chauvinistic dig, he asked Freeman, "'Doesn't all this affect their chaunces [chances]?'"[21]

Among the visitors Lyman Abbott in particular seemed to have a profound influence on Helen's thinking, especially in regard to Christian apologetics and religious pluralism. At Wellesley, she first encountered in a significant way the jarring effects of religious pluralism. In her junior year, she wrote to her parents about Abbott's approach to comparative theological education. "If Dr. Abbott were president of a theological seminary he would, when Unitarianism was under consideration, have the principles of Unitarianism presented by the best thinker in the denomination, and with Catholicism the same. His boys should know fully what they had to meet, and their stand should be taken through *intelligent* conviction. I think he is right, don't you?"[22]

Despite her confidence in intelligent conviction, whenever she was shaken or confused in her own beliefs she would write to her father for advice. On one occasion, she wrote him because she needed "some references to arguments for the personality of the devil" in order to answer those in her Bible class who were "unsound on that point."[23] A more fundamental threat to her religious worldview was enjoined by the conflict between her "stiff little Baptist"[24] view of closed communion and the more ecumenical views of other students and faculty. On at least two different occasions, she wrote to her parents because she was troubled by having to isolate herself from her classmates over this "matter of principle." During her freshman year, she wrote: "Oh, you don't know what it seems to *feel* that you are an *out* set, that you are regarded as narrow, bigoted, etc. Then my own heart turned traitor, and it was only by persistently using my reason and remembering that it was a matter of principle and not sentiment that I could make it seem right to go off by myself instead of staying with the others."[25]

During her junior year, her discomfort was intensified. On one particular communion Sunday, she was prevented from traveling to Natick to observe communion with the Baptist church there, as was her usual custom, because of a diphtheria epidemic. Dr. Lyman Abbott, in his communion sermon at Wellesley, explained that communion at Wellesley was "less a church than a family ordinance—in fact, as Christ gave it," and he invited "those who loved the name of Christ—whether having openly professed it or not" to participate. Then he asked those who would not, for the sake of conscience, share in the observance to stay while the others participated. Helen wanted to remain, but when the other Baptist women left the room, she went with them. Once again she wrote to her father for counsel:

> I am sadly shaken and confused, I fear. Generally, in the world, I can hold firmly to the principle. But here, all seems changed—for four years we all work together, with no thought of sect except at the communion table, when I am shut out from all other Christians. You cannot understand how it seems. I never should have unless I had been here. Now, Papa, don't think I am getting adrift—I think my moorings are fast, but I am a bit shaken up in my mind. You would settle me in no time, I presume.[26]

Helen's home church maintained closed communion until 1891, but Montgomery followed her own more ecumenical instincts as time went on, discovering that she could enjoy the fellowship of Christ with the whole church without "getting adrift." In fact, her entire career as an apologist for the women's ecumenical mission movement was based on the idea that for the sake of the gospel, women could "work together, with no thought of sect." In this comment, one finds the first hint of what would become the vision of her "great democracy"—the idea that it is possible for the Christian community to find unity, not organically but practically, by relegating its doctrinal disagreements to the background and by working toward a shared, this-worldly realization of the kingdom of God. Nevertheless, she always maintained her Baptist identity. Several years later, at Northfield (presumably during a summer school for mission study), she remarked, "Well, if it ever happens that we unite in one church, I'll go around with a button under the lapel of my coat which will read, 'I'm a Baptist.'"[27]

Wellesley introduced Helen to several other ideas that were important to her throughout her life and career. One of the most significant was the academic study of the Bible, introduced at Wellesley by Alice Freeman in 1881 when Helen was a sophomore. While some students objected that it detracted from "the sacredness of the Bible to study it just like a common book," Helen replied "all right, the more we know about it the better."[28]

The program of academic Bible study was intended to be "a serious study of the Bible in light of the scholarly research of the best Biblical scholars of the day."[29] In addition to daily chapel services attended by all students and faculty and Sunday worship led by ministers of various denominations, students pursued a systematic study of the Scriptures through a course for credit during all four years of the degree program.

During Helen's era there was no special faculty for the Bible classes. Faculty chosen from other subjects taught the biblical courses and supervised the Sunday evening section meetings. Students attended the required Bible classes for about two hours per week. The weekday class meetings "involved study, recitations and examinations," while the Sunday evening section meetings "were really little meetings for prayer and exhortation, held in a student's room, led by students, though their teacher met with them." The four-year plan of study included: the Bible (Topics from the Gospels) and Ethics for freshmen; the History of the Jewish Church (which was probably a study of 1 and 2 Samuel, 1 and 2 Kings, and 1 and 2 Chronicles) for sophomores; the Life of Christ for juniors; and the Apostolic Age and Epistles for seniors. According to Kendrick, "It was rather from the historical approach than from the literary approach that the Wellesley teaching proceeded."[30]

The views of Scripture taught at Wellesley were "by no means modern critical views."[31] Many of the foundational concepts, such as the documentary hypothesis of the Hexateuch, the priority of the Markan Gospel, the composite nature of the prophetic writings, the existence of Q—things that are today considered the taken-for-granted results of source, form, and redaction criticism—had not yet been fully developed in Europe, had not made their way across the Atlantic, or were widely repudiated among English-speaking scholars. In fact, Kendrick claimed it would have been impossible in 1880–1884 for undergraduates in United States to study the Bible critically from a modern point of view. Instead,

> it may be said that there were three things which the student of the first ten years usually carried away with her: (1) some rather detailed knowledge of the contents of the books of the Bible as they stand; (2) an impression that there is revealed in this literature a unique religious message for the world, in the language of Miss Morgan, the Professor of Philosophy, a "scheme of salvation;" (3) an attitude of mind which we called "liberal," a confidence that the old beliefs are not necessarily better than the new, that scholars will find out more and more concerning the truth within the Scripture and outside it, and that the results of criticism are to be welcomed.[32]

That evangelical focus on the "scheme of salvation" combined with a liberal confidence in the value of biblical scholarship became foundational for Helen's lifetime of serious biblical study and mission advocacy.

Helen's Role Models

Not surprisingly, Helen eschewed "strong-mindedness" as an unenviable trait in a woman. In her letters she reassured her family that she had not become strong-minded, nor were the women she admired.[33] Nevertheless, she admired women who believed and acted as if they were equal to men—women such as "Miss Colman,"[34] who sought to attend postgraduate lectures at Harvard University on political science. Charles William Eliot rebuffed her with a curt reply written on a postcard: "Women are not admitted to Harvard College."[35]

Several other members of the faculty were important influences on Helen. Other than Alice Freeman herself, the one she mentioned most frequently was Sarah Frances Whiting, one of the original faculty members, who spent forty years on the faculty at Wellesley, principally in the physics department. Whiting was a favorite of Durant, who went to great lengths to support her scholarship and to establish experimental science at Wellesley. Consequently, physics became one of the outstanding areas of the curriculum.[36]

Helen learned astronomy from Whiting in the classroom and social reform outside the classroom. Her earliest expression of openness to a missionary vocation came during her freshman year, after a Sunday walk with Whiting and two other students. Whiting read "Summers in Huckleberry Cut," by Jane Grey, a story from a periodical called the *Christian Union*, edited at that time by Henry Ward Beecher and Lyman Abbott. The story told of two women, "'neither strong-minded' nor 'reformers'" involved in "temperance work among the lowly."[37] As Helen reflected on her feelings about the story the professor read, she wrote to her family: "We listened to a cry from out of the dark, a moan, a struggle, a wild wretched tumult with calls for help, and a tender, pitiful, sisterly, womanly answer, 'We will.' Deep down in my heart there was born a purpose that said, 'Yes, Lord, when Thou dost call me.'"[38] Apparently, despite her openness, Helen never believed that she received a missionary call—at least not a call to become a career missionary. Nevertheless, she was true to her commitment and gave a lifetime of service to the cause of missions, both home and foreign, as a teacher, organizer, fund-raiser, and intellectual for missionary causes.

Helen must have been one of Whiting's favorite students because later that year she wrote home that she had received a "lovely Christmas present" from Whiting. It was "a little Parian marble bust of Shakespeare that she bought at Stratford-on-Avon this summer." (Helen was in the Shakespeare Club at Wellesley.) She told her parents, "I have written her a real nice *careful* letter today."[39] Patricia Ann Palmieri characterized the emphasis on faculty relationships with students outside the classroom at Wellesley as "learning through friendship and informality."[40] Perhaps that is an understatement. The relationships were at times almost sisterly. But however the relationships are best characterized, they were profoundly effective in shaping the minds and hearts of the students and preparing them for futures as members of the progressive, socially active "new womanhood."[41]

Perhaps Helen's favorite role model from Wellesley was Alice Freeman herself. Helen wrote often of Freeman, and always with admiration and affection. She commented that chapel under Freeman's leadership was "a spiritual education, and I never thought of it as compulsory, though it was."[42] After Freeman's appointment to the presidency, Helen wrote a very positive endorsement of Freeman's swift policy changes:

> We have had quite a revolution in a small way this past week. . . . Miss Freeman is progressive and is jogging things out of the ruts. She does do

magnificently as President. She reminds me of Papa so much in her way of handling the girls. She can be severe, but in her chapel talks she never uses sarcasm and never comes at us with the meat ax, but she makes the girls feel just as she wants them to feel, and if she but suggests anything most of the girls are eager to do just as she wishes. After one of her lectures we go out feeling that we are "moral agents" and not naughty children who have been scolded.[43]

Helen's comments were a perceptive summary of Freeman's genius for leadership. Freeman was young and brilliant. Her youth made her seem almost sisterly to the students, and her approach to historical scholarship seemed to her students exciting and innovative.[44] But her most important asset in making people "feel just as she wants them to feel" was her detailed attention to personal relationships; her ability to communicate confidence, sympathy and support, and her skillful use of a student's desire not to disappoint her.[45] Freeman kept detailed records about all the women in each freshman class and studied these each night so that she could build personal relationships with students. In her 1903 tribute to Alice Freeman Palmer, Helen Barrett Montgomery said that Freeman "entered by a genius of sympathy, into our lives. She knew our problems, understood our aspirations better than we did ourselves and in our gratitude we determined to achieve great things for the college and for her."[46] Freeman made the students feel empowered, but they also felt responsible to fulfill her moral vision. It is interesting to note that young Helen compared Freeman's ability to exercise moral leadership to her father's—the one person in the world whom Helen most wanted to please.

During Helen's junior year she began sitting with Freeman at the faculty table, and she wrote home with glowing reports of the table talk. She and Freeman discussed the possibility of Helen opening a preparatory school for Wellesley in Rochester. She left Wellesley with a personal recommendation letter from Freeman in hand.[47]

Helen the Student: Ambition and True Womanhood

Wellesley offered two curricular options—classical and scientific. Helen took the classical course and studied Greek—a decision that would lead one day to her publication of an original translation of the Greek New Testament

(1924). Yet she originally resisted the idea of taking an introductory class in Greek during her freshman year. She complained to her father: "They are all perfectly Greek crazy here" and implored him to "remain firm in your wish that I should not take it up." In the end, she gave in and took the class "merely for politic reasons. Miss Howard is so crazy over Greek and it will be for my advantage with her to comply with her wishes. Mr. Durant . . . has eyes for none but the Greek scholars." A short time later, she reported that she had "got on swimmingly in Greek" and had "done their work of four weeks in one." By January 1881 she had changed her mind about Greek completely: "I think the Greek verb is beautiful, not a letter or a sound but it means something, not an accent but comes from some reason."[48]

Helen's letters home from Wellesley revealed her persistent and growing ambition to excel in some way, as well as her efforts to maintain an attitude of humility and keep her ambitions in check. In her freshman year, she frankly admitted her desire to "be a phenomenon in some direction." She believed her father would be disappointed if she did not "shine," and she feared she would not. She regarded her "thinking and arguing powers" as her most systematically developed assets, and hoped they would carry her through. She felt that her limited experience of formal education in a preparatory school was a disadvantage in competing with her peers, and she questioned whether her "ambition to be thought smart and to lead the class" was a good one. Yet she found it difficult to settle for an average standing when she longed to take the first place. Nevertheless, she tried to lower her family's expectations for her, telling them, "I can never be more than one of the average." She claimed she did not mind being average and would not change it if she could. "I feel content if I can only conquer myself as to be able to do some good to others."[49] Her protestations of humility notwithstanding, Helen soon found several areas in which to excel.

Aside from her academic success, Helen became an influential force in her class and among the students of Wellesley. This was due in part to her skill as a debater. "I may be wrong," she wrote to her family, "but I do love argument. I feel just in my element. I sniff the battle from afar."[50] While Helen did enjoy the study of argumentation in her classes on logic and rhetoric, much of her success as a leader among the students at Wellesley was due to her political skills, which she often used to control events from behind the scenes. In one class election, she boasted, "There were five in the committee and of these I nominated three—not I personally—I was very quiet." In another case, she worked to have "two girls who represent sets whose noses are a little of the broken order" appointed for honors, to "conciliate all factions."[51] Nevertheless, she was not always successful. When she failed in her bid to be elected class president during her junior year, she tried to accept defeat graciously; but it was not easy. She wrote to her family: "I find that one of the hardest things for me to do is not to be glad and proud when I am honored, and depressed when I feel I am overlooked."[52]

In keeping with her middle-class Victorian upbringing, Helen's social views were antiaristocratic. She often expressed a preference for simplicity of dress and manners, and she tended to regard all persons as social equals. Her egalitarian views, learned from her Yankee ancestors, seem to have matured during her experience at Wellesley, where the administration made efforts to mitigate social distinctions among the students.[53] Helen liked the domestic work at Wellesley because it "made for a unified democracy," she said. During her freshman year, her chores included washing the lunch dishes and dusting. During her sophomore year, she worked seeding raisins, sorting beans, and paring fruit. She filled lamps for one term, and her sister Anne, who also attended Wellesley, did domestic chores for President Freeman.[54]

The Wellesley College rules went so far as to proscribe food that was not supplied by the college. Durant set out the "Wellesley diet" when he established the college to staunch "the pernicious habit of eating confectionary and sweetmeats at irregular hours."[55] Students were *pledged in honor* neither to buy nor receive in any manner whatsoever any confectionary or eatables of any kind not provided for them by the College," nor any wines or liquors for medicinal use; and parental interference in these rules was not tolerated.[56] When Helen's father, apparently unaware of the restrictions on food, sent her some apples, she had to give them to a professor because she might have been expelled if she had eaten them herself.[57] The restrictions on food did not apply to students who remained at school during holidays. Helen stayed at Wellesley over the Christmas vacation of her freshman year. She wrote to her parents that she was "under no laws whatever" and "could eat candy every hour of the day." Nevertheless, she asked her parents not to send bon-bons because of the expense. She said she could "enjoy the thought of them just as much as if I had them and have none of the protests of an indignant stomach to endure."[58]

There were also restrictions on the type of physical exercise in which Wellesley women could participate. According to a Wellesley dean, "Fiercely competitive athletics," while dangerous for men, helped to "develop manly strength." But while they were even more physically dangerous for women, "the qualities they tend to develop are not womanly."[59] Wellesley women went on brisk walks, rowed, skated, or did gymnastics. Durant even provided them with a tennis set, "but had some difficulty in persuading many of the students to take such very violent exercise."[60]

For health reasons, as well as to build a sense of community, Durant wanted students' clothing to be simple, short enough to permit ease of walking, not too heavy, and not too expensive.[61] The restrictions did not extend to uniformity in dress, since Helen reported, "I am dressed just as well as there is any necessity for, and look a good deal better than many of the other girls, even those who have more extensive wardrobes." She went on to note that her clothes were not "conspicuous in any way, whether for elegance or plainness."[62]

The college administration made efforts to prevent economic disparities among the students from intruding into community life on campus. According to Helen, the class organizations were informed that "if they grew to be extravagant, so that the poorest girl would not feel able to be in the class organization, why, this would be shut down."[63] Nevertheless, Helen was aware of economic disparities. Some students, she believed, spent too liberally on shopping trips to Boston, room decorations, sending laundry out to be done, and other nonessentials. One student in particular, Helen reported, had spent $125 on such items, and her mother was "well satisfied—she knows these little expenses will come in," while Helen herself had spent only $15 including her subscriptions to the missionary society and the concert fund.[64]

Characteristic of her frugality, Helen gave a great deal of thought to how to make the best use of her wardrobe. Despite faculty efforts to discourage preoccupation with fashion, clothing was an important issue among students.[65] During her freshman year, she wrote to her parents of her plan: "I am saving my silk. Have worn it but once. Sundays, wear my bunting. Mornings, wear my gray calico with red trimmings. Afternoons, my gingham. Shall finish this month with calico as school dress, next month shall wear gingham and then shall put on my blue."[66] Later that same year, she told her parents that they need not go to the expense of providing her with a gymnastic suit. "I find that by removing my dress waist and corset (ssh!) and wearing my blue flannel sack with my blue dress skirt I get along splendidly."[67] During her senior year, she asked that her grandmother knit her some new stockings; her old ones were so worn that they would not stay darned.[68]

Helen contemplated women's fashions for yet another reason—feminist concerns regarding women's health. The faculty at Wellesley shared Durant's progressive views on the relationship between clothing and women's health. Helen's elocution teacher, Dr. Mary Walker, made Helen "an entire convert to the non-corset theory." "I shan't violate my physiological conscience any longer," she wrote, condemning the "false taste" that compelled women to have their clothes fit "like sausage skins." According to Helen, many of the students and teachers had already eschewed corsets, as she would if she had the time to modify her clothing. "Next summer I am going to have every-thing made *right*," she declared. "I can't bear the idea of living in a box any longer." Women, she thought, would be "a great deal happier and stronger" if they valued health more than a narrow waist.[69]

Women's clothing was politicized in the last third of the nineteenth century. One's position on the corset said something about one's view of women. For example, suffragist and free-love advocate Tennie C. Claflin also objected to the standards of women's dress: "A woman rigged with the entire paraphernalia of fashion is only a fit subject for a show. . . . Practically, the present styles of dress for women of business, so far as convenience is con-cerned, are simply absurd, not to say ridiculous, while from the health point of view they are suicidal."[70]

By her junior year, Helen had obtained a gymnastic suit, and she found wearing it quite energizing: "so light and free and unconfined!" She thought women could accomplish a great deal more if they would adopt such clothing on a regular basis. "We lift tons every year just in carrying about our clothes," she wrote, asserting that women would have much more energy if only they "had the freedom to breathe and move as they wanted to."[71]

Yet for all her protestations of liberation, Helen was still complaining about women's apparel in 1886 or 1887, long after her graduation from Wellesley: "I wonder if ever women will go back to some artistic loose easy costume. I fear that we shall burden ourselves with heavy skirts and pinch ourselves into corsets to the end of the chapter."[72]

While Helen found the fashion in women's apparel objectionable from a feminist perspective, she did not offer a similar critique of women's domesticity. On the contrary, like many nineteenth-century feminists, she thought domesticity was an essential aspect of the sort of womanliness to which she aspired. During her freshman year, she stayed at Wellesley for Christmas. It was her first Christmas away from home, and she regretted missing the holiday preparations. "How I would like to step into that kitchen," she wrote, "and send Grandma and Mama and Anne all flying to the sitting room and then just evolve the most marvelous Christmas dinner. How I would revel in pies and cakes and delectable puddings. I am just aching for a chance to putter over a cook stove."[73] Indeed, the Wellesley of Helen's era encouraged the domestic ideal. Students were expected to cultivate refined manners and tastes, to "hang pictures, decorate with flowers, and attend concerts."[74] In a letter to her family, Helen fretted about having attended a performance of Haydn's oratorio, "The Creation," on Easter Sunday in Boston, finally deciding it was "appropriate for Sunday" though she wished it could have been "given freely and not as a money-making enterprise."[75]

Feminism at Wellesley: Symmetrical Womanhood

Roberta Wein perceived a growing divide over the proper end of women's education in the last quarter of the nineteenth century. One tradition, epitomized in Wein's view, by Bryn Mawr under M. Carey Thomas, the first dean and second president, promoted an ideology of women's professional development beyond the domestic sphere. The other, represented by Wellesley under Alice Freeman, the second president, promoted an ideology of women's professional development within the domestic sphere. While Bryn Mawr women were prepared for independent professional careers, particularly in academia, and were discouraged from entering into "suffocating marriages," Wellesley women received quite a different message and goal. Alice Freeman regarded motherhood as "the most sacred work of women, and the dearest to them, of every class." She believed college education could make women better wives and mothers. Furthermore, she regarded women as the only leisure class in society, and she believed college education would prepare women to use their leisure time to enlarge the domestic sphere by improving public schools and managing benevolent and philanthropic enterprises.[76]

Palmieri, on the other hand, by focusing on the work of the much more radical Vida Scudder, found the Wellesley faculty committed to "Symmetrical Womanhood" as early as 1887. The so-called symmetrical woman did not need a man to be complete. She was healthy, emotionally well balanced, educated, and able to be happy without marriage. But whether married or not, her goal was to be a useful citizen and activist in the life of her community.[77] The symmetrical woman maintained the moral purity of True Womanhood, but she augmented it with education, so she brought an intelligent, well-informed social and ethical insight to the problems afflicting late nineteenth-century civilization. According to Scudder, the "disintegration of older cultures [has] precipitated society into a chaos before which men are helpless," and at the crucial moment "this throng of educated women has been released into the larger life."[78] The main focus of the symmetrical woman as citizen and activist would be to apply her educated virtue to the study and melioration of social problems.

In Helen Barrett Montgomery's case, at least, both impulses were merged. She believed that women had a major role to play in public life, but she also valued the domestic ideal and made determined attempts to realize it in her own life. In a tribute Montgomery wrote for Alice Freeman Palmer in the *Wellesley Magazine* in 1903, Montgomery described Palmer as the ideal woman who "made real to us the possibility of a rounded and symmetrical womanhood. To add to one's attainment in scholarship, culture; to culture, social tact; to conjoin high enthusiasm with a sense of proportion; it was this that we believed should belong to the ideal of every college woman."[79] Alice Freeman Palmer, who later gave up her career for married life, was, in Montgomery's view, the ideal symmetrical woman.

At the same time, Montgomery believed that her duty could not be circumscribed by any particular definition of the private sphere. For her, the sphere of woman was ever-expanding, and it included any problem or issue that affected the lives of women anywhere. Montgomery's subsequent life and career can be viewed as a complex interweaving of the two impulses of domesticity and citizenship—of True Womanhood and Symmetrical Womanhood. In the combination of the two, as subsequent chapters show, Montgomery tried to construct a satisfying balance that she called the "New Woman."

Progressive Reform at Wellesley: Maternalism and Missions

Another significant idea that Helen encountered was temperance. As a sophomore, she attended a Prohibition lecture at Tremont Temple in Boston by a Mrs. Foster of Iowa, a lawyer. She was greatly impressed. "I don't know but I am a convert to prohibition myself—at least her kind of prohibition." As a senior, she herself "gave a temperance talk" (perhaps her first) to "the Saturday Night Club for the working girls of South Natick."[80] She became a lifelong and committed advocate of temperance (and ultimately of Prohibition).[81] The visit to the Saturday Night Club of Natick was indicative of another cause she embraced in college that became a lifelong endeavor—the social uplift of women.

Wellesley provided students like Helen with plenty of opportunities for practical experience in reform work. One incident in particular, which Helen related to her family in a letter, which her father then sent to a local newspaper for publication, is especially noteworthy. It reveals many unconscious assumptions on young Helen's part. The article, "Thanksgiving at Wellesley," recounts her first Thanksgiving at Wellesley, when she joined several other students in visiting the women's prison in South Farmington, Massachusetts. As gifts for the four hundred inmates, the girls made bunches of flowers with hand-written Bible verses tied to them with ribbon. Once at the prison the Wellesley students performed a program of songs, readings, and recitations. In keeping with Victorian religious assumptions about the fatherhood of God and the brotherhood of man, Helen was convinced that the prisoners were her "sorrowful, sinful sisters, all children of our common father." Still she had the sensation of "a weird dream" as she "looked over the hard dull faces—hopeless, depraved, pitiful, with only here and there a face of ordinary intelligence." She was impressed in the cleanliness and orderliness of the institution, although she was saddened at the thought of the fifty or so babies being cared for in the prison nursery. During the program Helen was happy to see some of the women's "hard faces soften, to see them smile or laugh." But she was saddened to see "how little sensibility there was to their emotions."[82] To Helen, "they seemed as uncontrollable and impulsive as children—the mere slaves of their impulses." In her comments about the inmates, Helen reflected a Victorian assumption about civilization and savagery. According to the Victorian way of thinking, civilization was a way of life based on reasoned self-control of animal instincts and impulses, reflection on the accumulated experience of the past, and the anticipated consequences of future actions. Savages lived immoral lives because they were incapable of using, or had not learned how to use, reason, reflection, and impulse control.[83] In depicting the women as dull and incapable of self-control, Helen was suggesting that they had become uncivilized.

The savagery of the inmates stood in sharp contrast to the ideal Christian civility of their matrons, according to Helen. The prison was unusual, she thought, because it was run entirely by women—"lovely, refined christian [*sic*] ladies" who cared enough about the inmates to "work over them, study them, pray for them and with them, and when they are ready to go out into the world again, get them a place and keep watch over them." Here indeed were True Women, using their time, wealth, intelligence, and moral influence to restore "fallen sisters" to a semblance of womanliness.

Before returning to Wellesley, the students were invited to the house of the president of the institution, where they were "served to a very dainty lunch, being waited upon by some of the most trusty of the prisoners." Here, in an atmosphere of middle-class gentility, Helen found confirmation that the regimen of the prison was redeeming fallen women to Christian civility. Two of the prisoners, whom she found very "ladylike," were in prison for arson, but the prison matron assured her that "both seem to be changed women and when released will lead respectable and useful lives."[84] In Helen's mind, sin and crime were associated in these women with a lack of intelligence and an immature, undisciplined impulsiveness. But Christian benevolence and maternal discipline could overcome the hardness and impulsiveness of their hearts and make them respectable and useful—even "ladylike."

Wellesley's atmosphere of benevolence and social reform confronted Helen with several possible options for living out a vocation of Christian service. In her sophomore year she wrote to her family: "When I hear about the South, it seems to me I must go there; when of the Indians, I don't see how I can stay away from them. And now the Mormons, they need teachers so much." And in the same letter she wrote that she was considering a career in medicine. "Seriously I think that if educated women would become physicians, they might do a great deal of good."[85] Many of the options she considered would probably have meant following the example of her teachers and many others who were regarded as role models, who pursued the separatist strategy of Victorian women's culture. While they lauded and defended the ideal of the Victorian family, motherhood, and the home, many of these women spent their entire adult lives in separate female communities. Those gender-segregated enclaves "served as crucibles for the creation of attitudes, values, and practices" that the female reformers attempted to use to effect change on society at large.[86]

In the end, Helen chose a different path. She did not, like so many of her teachers and other educated women, follow the path of sexual separatism as a strategy for her personal feminist and social reform activities. After a brief career as a teacher, she chose to marry and have a family. Nevertheless, she found ways to use her education for citizenship, for social activism, Christian mission, and the uplift of women. In fact she used and adapted many aspects of her Wellesley experience to serve women who would never have an opportunity to go to college.

Politics at Wellesley: Nationalism, Feminism, and Suffrage

One of the more unusual incidents Helen reported in her letters from Wellesley revealed the unconscious nationalism (or perhaps conscious feminism) of the students. It was November 1880, Helen's first semester and a presidential election year. The ill-fated James A. Garfield, the Republican candidate, won an electoral college victory over Winfield S. Hancock, the Democratic nominee, although Garfield received less than 50 percent of the popular vote in a three-way race where emotions over the Civil War and Reconstruction still ran hot. Of course, none of the students or teachers at Wellesley, being women, could vote in the election; but that did not prevent them from becoming partisans. Helen reported that three professors went to Boston and brought back Garfield badges for their students and that there was "not a girl in the building but wears a badge of some sort." Many students had decorated their doors, transoms, and hallways with patriotic colors and political themes. Helen and four or five others were touring the halls and admiring the displays when they came upon a student, a southerner, putting up pictures of Hancock. A loud political disagreement ensued, and the Hancock booster's display was torn down. Another Democrat found it necessary to guard her display by pouring chalk dust through the transom upon the heads of those who dared to approach her door.[87]

Why would these women become so emotionally involved in an election when they could not even vote? At least in part, it was a pro-suffrage symbolic ritual. Although Wellesley College did not take an official position regarding suffrage in the nineteenth century, several of the faculty declared themselves personally as suffragists. Katherine Coman, one of Helen's favorite teachers, declared that teaching political economy was intended to prepare women for the franchise.[88] As feminists, the faculty and students were declaring themselves as citizens, as members of the nation—despite their alienation from the franchise—and as members of the collective solidarity known as "Americans." Participation in the election of a president—even the mock participation that the women of Wellesley contrived for themselves—reaffirmed their identification as Americans. Indeed, they celebrated the ideals of the nation, even though they were in many ways denied its benefits, because they believed so strongly that the ideals belonged to them just as much as they belonged to anyone. In her senior year, Helen wrote: "We are now taking up the civil service reform in England as contrasted with our system, or lack of system. It seemed to me that I must get right up and do something to help this country. What are the gentlemen of the United States thinking of that they are not more interested in politics? Don't they know that indifference is the disgrace and death of republican institutions?"[89] These few lines make clear that Helen regarded the American system as "our" system, and perceiving it to be in dysfunction, she expressed a desire to participate in its rescue. She regarded apathy and nonparticipation as dereliction of duty—and if the "gentlemen of the United States" defaulted on the duties of citizenship, she stood ready to fill the gap.

Evidently faculty and students at other women's colleges held mock elections as well. Lynn D. Gordon claimed these activities, as well as others, such as college-sponsored athletics, student government, and debate, were intended to train women "to think and act like men" in the protected environment of single-sex institutions. Separatism offered an unexpected "creative function" when it allowed college women to practice new skills and gain confidence in new areas of knowledge before having to exercise them in competition with men.[90]

When Helen received her diploma in 1884, she was a rarity. In 1880 only 1.9 percent of American women, eighteen to twenty-one years of age, attended college. In 1890 that figure was only 2.2 percent.[91] American society still waited to see what the results of the bold experiment of higher education for women would be. Helen also felt the need to measure up to the expectations of her parents, who made a major financial sacrifice in paying the $250 per year for tuition and board that Wellesley College required. It was time for her to "be a phenomenon in some direction."[92]

Four

The "New Woman" at Work, Home, and in Public
Helen Barrett Montgomery's Return to Rochester

When Helen Barrett left Wellesley, it appeared that she was about to follow a trajectory that was becoming increasingly familiar among the first two generations of college-educated women in America. Many women of this new elite class remained single and entered a profession. For a while, it seemed Helen would enter the teaching profession and pursue an academic career. Her decision to marry William A. Montgomery changed her professional trajectory. Helen Barrett Montgomery chose to integrate her marriage, family, and career goals at a time when such integration was almost unheard of and most difficult to achieve. She became a "New Woman" of the Progressive Era. She maintained middle-class Victorian values and virtues, but she used her college education and her professional skills to engage in causes and enter roles that transcended the traditional boundaries of the "woman's sphere."

For most of the nineteenth century, women were banned from the most influential and lucrative professions, such as medicine, law, or ordained ministry. The one profession that did admit women, that of school teaching, was open to them in large part because it came to be viewed as an extension of the domestic sphere and in part because women entered the occupation before it was regarded as a profession.[1]

As more and more women gained basic education and therefore literacy, a new genre of popular women's literature developed and opened a new professional avenue for educated women. Popular women's literature grew rapidly from 1820 to 1850, as women's magazines multiplied and domestic novels proliferated.[2] While this literature ostensibly legitimated traditional roles for women in society, it provided a means for women to expand the limits of domesticity to include intellectual and professional labor, and it provided a vehicle for women to speak with their own voices on the nature and meaning of domesticity.

Even among the resolute pioneers who challenged the boundaries of "woman's sphere," Victorian constructions of gender retained tremendous force in shaping their perceptions of themselves and their world. Elizabeth Blackwell, the first woman to graduate from an American medical school, who had to fight for the right to attend classes with men and view dissections, decided not to march in the Commencement procession when she graduated in 1849, fearing it would be "unladylike."[3] Nevertheless, she gained a medical degree, and after great struggle she opened a hospital in New York City eight years later, staffed entirely by women, where she pioneered in the training of nurses. Dr. Anna Howard Shaw, a physician and a Methodist minister, entered the Boston University School of Theology in 1875, where she endured poverty and hunger in order to complete a theological degree. Myra Bradwell appealed all the way to the U.S. Supreme Court, albeit unsuccessfully, for the right to practice law in the state of Illinois in 1873.[4] In each case, whether successful or not, these women's efforts, and others like them, tested and ultimately expanded the theoretical boundaries of woman's sphere, inscribing an ever-widening circle that encompassed more and more of the public world within its limits.

Teaching was a well-established profession for single women by 1884—and more than two-thirds of female college graduates from the first two generations taught at some point in their lives—but college-educated women also helped to shape new professions. Social work and journalism, for example, were two fields where female college graduates became prominent.[5]

Fewer than 50 percent of female college graduates married soon after college. At the same time, the culture of domesticity was still very strong, and a large number of college-educated women gave up the possibility of an independent career in order to marry and raise families. Over 90 percent of female college graduates did marry at some point in their lives, although they married later and had fewer children than other women, thus giving rise to the fear that the higher education of women would lead to "race suicide."[6]

Even college women who married found ways to be involved in activities outside their homes, as members of cultural or civic clubs, or volunteers in religious or benevolent enterprises.[7] Describing herself and her peers, Madeleine Wallin, a female graduate student at the University of Chicago in 1894, wrote that college-educated women "are just as much in earnest about their aims and career as they are about marriage. . . . They don't know which they want, and they are trying the first one that comes until they can decide. They don't make an ironclad resolution about either one."[8] These early graduates felt they had options, but the options were apparently mutually exclusive. Once they made "an ironclad resolution" to follow one route, they believed they had closed off the other possibility.

While Helen Barrett was typical of the college women of her era in many ways, she was unusual in that she found a way to have a family and a career. She had parents who supported her ambitions and released her from what Jane Addams called the "family claim."[9] But far more important was her choice of a spouse. William A. Montgomery entered his relationship with Helen Barrett with the understanding that he would not stand in the way of her career. His willingness, not only to permit, but to support her achievements was a key factor in her successful merger of professionalism and domesticity.

William Montgomery's attitude was somewhat unconventional. In the 1890s, many people still regarded the "notoriety" of women with alarm. Helen Barrett Montgomery pressed the limits of social convention by becoming a female preacher and public lecturer, and she did it in the name of "womanhood." But the womanhood she represented was not the True Womanhood of the mid-nineteenth century, it was a progressive New Womanhood that was still under construction in the late 1800s.

Helen Barrett Montgomery's Rochester

The village of Rochesterville, as it was known to its earliest permanent settlers in 1812, was conceived as a milling and market town on the northward-flowing Genesee River in western New York, but the completion of the Erie Canal in 1825 transformed the village into the nation's first boomtown. From a population of 332 in 1815, the city swelled to more than 9,000 by 1830 and more than 20,000 by 1840.[10] Rochester became known as the "Flour City" in the late 1830s because of the high quality and huge quantities of flour produced by the city's grist mills, but ascendancy in that industry was brief. As western competitors such as St. Louis and Minneapolis overshadowed Rochester in the production of flour in the 1850s, Rochester emerged as a leader in several other industries, such as clothing, shoes, and horticulture. Indeed, the "Flour City" of the 1830s and 1840s became the "Flower City" in the latter half of the nineteenth century. Meanwhile the population exceeded 36,000 in 1850 and 63,000 in 1870.[11]

Rochester grew into a city of 134,000 by 1890, and even though the city was originally settled mostly by westward-moving New Englanders, most Rochesterians of the 1890s were immigrants (40,000) or the children of immigrants (54,000). A decade later, the city had 160,000 residents with 41,000 immigrants and 48,000 children of immigrants, and in 1910, the population was 218,000, with 59,000 immigrants and 57,000 children of immigrants.[12]

To support such rapid population growth, Rochester became a leader in several industries as well as a center of technological innovation. German immigrants John Jacob Bausch and Henry Lomb began an optics business in 1853 with an investment of $60. Bausch and Lomb was the leading optical manufacturer in the United States by the 1880s and became a major industry in Rochester, employing twelve hundred workers in 1903.[13]

George Eastman developed the world's first commercially successful flexible photographic film in 1884, and in 1888, the first successful film camera designed for amateur use. By 1900, when Eastman introduced the one-dollar Brownie camera, his company was the world's largest manufacturer of photographic materials. Eastman Kodak became a global empire and a major leader among Rochester's industries, and Eastman himself became a leading philanthropist and civic booster in Rochester.[14]

Chainless bicycles, the voting machine, a dial-system telephone, George B. Selden's internal combustion engine—all originated in Rochester. Foundries and machine shops, such as Yawman & Erbe, grew and multiplied, despite many consolidations and buyouts. In 1908 the Chamber of Commerce adopted the slogan, "Rochester Made Means Quality," an expression of their faith that the city could, through the pursuit of excellence, create and sustain a competitive advantage over other cities with superior resources. Several industries that were dominant in earlier decades remained profitable, including some horticulture firms, clothing and shoe manufacturers, and furniture manufacturers. The men's clothing industry continued to be the largest source of jobs, and half the buttons made in America came from Rochester in 1910. The number of locally owned corporations in Rochester grew so large that a local stock exchange, Wortham & Company, began listing the stock of twenty-five Rochester companies in 1901, and the company traded 128,680 shares of stock in 1906.[15]

Much of the creativity and labor for these industries came from the immigrant communities in Rochester. Among the earliest were the Irish, who first arrived in 1817 and whose numbers increased with the construction and opening of the Erie Canal. By 1855, a quarter of Rochester's residents were either Irish-born or their children, and their numbers stirred anti-Catholic and nativist resentments.[16] In the 1870s and 1880s, new waves of immigrants from other countries flowed into Rochester. The Irish began to assimilate, even though they maintained a vital interest in the economic and political questions affecting Ireland. By the 1880s, immigration from Ireland was declining, and members of the second and subsequent generations worked in factories, skilled trades, and civil service. Many representatives of the Irish community assumed positions in Rochester's leadership, such as Bernard J. McQuaid, the first Roman Catholic bishop of Rochester, carriage manufacturer James E. Cunningham, liquor distiller Walter B. Duffy, *Post Express* editor Joseph O'Connor, Mayor Michael Curran, and Congressman James O'Grady.[17]

The first German immigrant to Rochester, Jacob Hau, arrived only two years after the original settlement, but Germans did not arrive in significant numbers until the 1830s. By 1855 German immigrants were one-seventh of the population of Rochester, and their children accounted for another seventh.[18] Like the Irish, Germans were targets of nativism and (in the case of the Roman Catholics among them) anti-Catholicism. They also maintained close political and cultural ties to the old country, but because Germany was politically and religiously divided, such ties sometimes inhibited the unity of Rochester's German community. German immigrants were predominant in numerous industries, including breweries, optics, horticulture, shoes, and clothing, as well as in trades, such as carpentry and masonry. They sustained a healthy German-language press and exerted significant leadership in religious and cultural pursuits. By 1890 the number of German immigrants in Rochester trebled, but their numbers declined after the turn of the century.[19]

While German-born immigrants such as George Ellwanger and John Jacob Bausch were leaders of industry, many of the second generation, such as Isaac Adler and Walter Rauschenbusch, were leaders in intellectual, social, and political life.

Compared to the Irish and Germans, the Italians were relative latecomers to the Rochester scene, but when they came, they came in force. Only 516 appeared in the 1890 census, but there were more than 10,000 by 1910.[20] Most Italian immigrants were single young men who arrived in labor gangs under the authority of a *padrone*. Initially, they lived in work camps or moved into the poorest sections of the city, but as they achieved permanent residency, many swiftly moved into factory work or small commercial enterprises of their own. For example, Salvatore M. Vella, the first Italian to graduate from the Rochester Free Academy, established a weekly newspaper, *Corrier di Rodete*, in 1905. Although a few married local women, most sought wives from Italy. The community was plagued by outbursts of violence, at least some of which was instigated by the Black Hand, which had followed the community from the Old World. Nevertheless, they were eager to embrace American political and social institutions, and nearly 2,000 Italians achieved full citizenship in Rochester by 1915.[21]

Several other ethnic and immigrant communities—most rather small in comparison to the Irish, German, and Italian communities—found their way to Rochester. Among them were African Americans, Russians, Poles, Belgians, Dutch, French and French Canadians, Swiss, and Swedes. By 1910, Rochester was home to a Jewish community of 10,000 persons, comprising mostly Germans, Russians, and Poles, which supported eleven synagogues, two schools, and a home for the elderly.[22] Each ethnic and immigrant community typically established its own religious institutions as soon as the community was large enough to support them. Each celebrated its own holidays and established its own social, cultural, political, and benevolent societies.

In addition to its commerce and industry, Rochester also possessed a strong tradition of religious faith and social reform activism. The revival meetings of Charles Finney in 1830–1831 left Rochester in a spirit of "self-conscious restraint," according to the city's greatest historian.[23] By the 1850s there were fifty Protestant and Catholic churches in the city (one church for every 720 people in the city); a strong temperance movement; an orphan asylum; many vigorous Sunday schools; regional Bible, tract, and mission societies; and other charities. Secular reform movements included antislavery and suffrage. Spiritualism emerged in the Rochester area in the 1840s, joining the Millerites, the Mormons, the Shakers, and numerous other religious movements that scorched the "burned-over district" in the mid-nineteenth century.[24]

By the early 1890s the number of churches had doubled to one hundred, but with one church to every 1,300 residents, they had not kept up with the growth of the population. There were sixteen Roman Catholic parishes, most with parish schools, and a Roman Catholic seminary. Although the Presbyterians outnumbered the Baptists, the Baptists supported a university and a seminary in Rochester. The Episcopalians, Lutherans, and Methodists, along with several smaller Protestant groups, were prospering. Membership in the Young Men's Christian Association (YMCA) reached 1,236 in 1893, and the Woman's Christian Temperance Union (WCTU) was active and robust in the city.[25]

Like many cities at the turn of the century, Rochester was still adjusting to several major transitions of the last half-century: the largely unregulated transition from small, home-based manufacturing to large industries of mass production; rapid urban growth and expansion, requiring expanded public works and city services; and growing religious and ethnic pluralism, with its attendant social and political tensions. Rochester attempted to meet these challenges with a combination of expanded, more efficient, and more open city government, private and faith-based charity and reform, and the creation of new city services. As in the past, Rochester's citizens approached the city's challenges with a spirit of civic duty and pride. Yet in the 1890s, a new group of citizens stepped from the sidelines to the front lines of the municipal cause. The women of Rochester's middle and upper classes emerged from their kitchens and parlors with militant and maternal passion, ready to do battle with ignorance, poverty, and corruption, and Helen Barrett Montgomery would become their most gifted and effective leader.

Helen Barrett, the Schoolteacher

After graduating from Wellesley, Helen spent a year teaching high school at the Rochester Free Academy in Rochester, New York,[26] and two more years as co-principal of the Wellesley Preparatory School in Philadelphia, Pennsylvania. Her letters to her family reveal further evidence of her middle-class Victorian values: her distaste for ostentation, her love of frugality and simplicity, and her tendency toward social leveling. During her walks in Fairmount Park, she observed families of different economic classes as they toured in carriages. She contrasted the "trim little box-buggies containing happy young men and pretty young ladies" with the "elegant carriages with horses glittering with silver" and "coachmen and footmen resplendent in livery." The latter "seemed absurd," she thought. The people in the more lavish carriages appeared to her "bored and unhappy," while she found it "pleasant to see the modest little one-horse rigs containing father and mother and a chick or two stowed away up front, all having such a good time." Likewise, she found attractive the "fine old family rigs" with a "substantial team of horses" and "the keen prosperous proprietor driving them instead of sitting behind a betogged mummy of a coachman." She saw it as a contest of "comfort versus display, and I said, give me comfort every time."[27]

Helen's intellectual abilities did not go unnoticed. She contemplated returning to Wellesley as a member of the faculty. Meanwhile two women's colleges were considering her as a candidate for their presidencies. She was discovering her powers as a public speaker, and her parents encouraged her professional ambitions. But Helen's plans for her future were complicated when she fell in love with William A. Montgomery, a businessman from Rochester and a faithful member of Lake Avenue Baptist Church.[28]

William A. Montgomery and Christian Chivalry

William Montgomery was a widower,[29] and he was seven years her senior. He had little formal education, and Helen's parents doubted the marriage would succeed. Apparently Helen had arrived at the point where "an ironclad resolution" was demanded. She had a choice between the traditional domestic expectations for women in late-nineteenth-century America and the personal and professional development her education and abilities had made possible. To follow her role models on the Wellesley faculty, she had to remain single and pursue a professional career. A career meant rejecting—or at least deferring—the domestic roles of wife and mother that her faith and culture recognized as most important for women—roles, in fact, that Alice Freeman had lifted up as the very reasons for which women ought to become educated.[30] Yet, if she married and started a family, she risked the possibility that she would never be able to realize fully her potential as an individual—she might never "shine in some direction," to the disappointment of her father.[31]

William Montgomery was a child of the Victorian Era. The Victorian moral imagination conceptualized the individual (especially the male individual) as moral agent and shaper of personal destiny. Consequently the Victorian moral code demanded rigorous effort on the part of the individual. As shaper of his own destiny, the man had a duty to self-improvement. At the same time, in light of one's Christian duties to family and society and the temptations that abounded in the world, the Victorian man must be capable of self-sacrifice as well as self-discipline and self-restraint.

All of the virtues of the individual were inculcated in the context of the family, which was, according to the Victorian moral code, the source of civilization. Men, as husbands and fathers, and women, as wives and mothers, had different natures and roles, but they were complementary. According to the Cult of True Womanhood, women's moral authority was anchored in the home and in the crucial role of mother. Virtuous motherhood was the key to the development of virtuous citizenship in children and to the Christianization of American culture.

For men, the Victorian moral code prescribed a set of values that contained the potential for profound inner tension. The limited scope of the liberal state allowed very wide latitude to the individual, so the self-made Victorian man had to be strong and self-assertive in order to achieve success in the world. At the same time, he needed self-discipline and self-restraint because the deferral of gratification and conservation of resources often offered greater possibilities for economic success. Furthermore, the Victorian moral code assigned positive duties to a man in respect to his neighbors. The Victorian imagined society as a commonwealth of peers, where everyone's individual interests were equally represented in the "public interest." Consequently, in self-discipline and self-restraint, the ideal Victorian man was required to make political and economic decisions based on the public interest rather than his private interests. Furthermore, he was required to exercise chivalry—that is, honorable self-restraint in the behavior of the stronger toward the weaker and of men toward women in particular. Victorians believed virtuous manhood would yield "conspicuous evidence of success" in prosperity for the individual and the community, and that it contributed to social harmony.[32] Consequently, individual virtue was believed to be the key to civic virtue, and the Victorian moral code became institutionalized in Protestantism and American nationalism.

The Victorian moral code was advocated in the family, church, school, and public opinion. Despite its ubiquity, for most people, it proved to be too difficult a moral standard for political and economic life, and they adopted a double standard of morality that differentiated between the private and public spheres. Robert Wiebe noted that the "segmented morality" of the late nineteenth century called for different standards of behavior in different settings: "A gracious warmth in the living room, decent manners in the street, pious thoughts on Sunday, a formal honesty in dealing with acquaintances, and animal cunning before the rest of the world all passed at the bar of justice."[33] Progressives came to believe that one sphere or the other would eventually prevail. Either the private sphere of home and family—the engine of civilization—would infuse its values into the public sphere and bring about a reformation of social institutions, or the conflict, corruption, and rapacity of the public sphere would desecrate the sanctuary of the home. For the sake of civilization, they were determined to protect and extend the values of the home.

William Montgomery was born in Rochester, New York, on April 26, 1854.[34] His father, Abel S. Montgomery, had been a successful businessman before the Civil War, but when the war started, he recruited a company of men, trained them, and led them off to battle. He returned from the war with his health broken, and he was never able to rebuild his business.[35] William quit school at the age of fourteen and went to work for four dollars per week. He gave two dollars per week to his mother for room and board. As long as he lived with his parents, he paid his mother half his weekly wages, and yet he was able to save a thousand dollars by the time he was twenty-one. At the time of his marriage to Helen, he was "a junior member of the Woodbury Engine Company,"[36] and he became secretary and treasurer before the business was sold to a Pennsylvania firm in 1891.[37] Deacon D. A. Woodbury, the company's owner, was a charter member of the Lake Avenue Baptist Church.[38]

After leaving the Woodbury Engine Company, Montgomery went into business with W. G. Ricker making agricultural implements, until a fire destroyed the factory in 1893 and left him without employment or income. Subsequently, he went into business with C. E. Meade in shoe manufacturing. In 1897 Montgomery entered a shoe manufacturing partnership with Edmund Venor under the name Venor & Montgomery.[39]

In 1910 Venor & Montgomery was dissolved, and Montgomery founded the North East Electric Company.[40] That company pioneered the mass production of electric automobile starters and was ultimately purchased by General Motors. It became the Rochester Products Division of General Motors.[41] Soon after selling the North East Electric Company, he established the Electromatic Typewriter Company,[42] which was purchased by IBM in 1933, three years after Montgomery's death.[43] Though cautious in business, he believed in entrepreneurialism. By the end of his life, his business ventures and cautious stewardship had made him a wealthy man.

Montgomery joined the Lake Avenue Baptist Church in about 1873, where he rented a pew and paid his share of the church's expenses.[44] A faithful churchman, he took over Helen's class of five boys at the Lake Avenue Baptist Church Sunday school when she went off to college, and this became the subject of their earliest correspondence.[45] Over a span of forty-three years, he developed the group into one of Rochester's leading men's Sunday school classes.

Barbara Welter, in her description of what she called the "family pattern" of nineteenth century suffragists, said that the women often married "weak husbands, whose careers they eclipse[d]," while they were "preoccupied, in their reforms or their writings, with finding a suitable definition of woman's nature and role."[46] While Helen Barrett Montgomery certainly eclipsed William Montgomery in terms of intellectual achievement and fame, it would be a mistake to understand his quiet support for his wife's career as weakness or failure. In fact he wielded significant personal influence in the Rochester community, and by the end of his life, his economic achievements were substantial. In the Lake Avenue church he was a trustee, deacon, church clerk, teacher of a large men's Sunday school class, and chairman of three different pastor search committees. He served on the board of trustees of the Colgate-Rochester Divinity School from 1922 until his death, where he was a substantial contributor and served on several important committees.[47] Eight months before his death, he was elected president of that board, but he never had the opportunity to preside at a meeting. He was a member and officer of the Rochester chapter of Walter Rauschenbusch's Brotherhood of the Kingdom.[48] In addition to the Colgate-Rochester Divinity School, he was a contributor to the University of Rochester, the Rochester Mechanics Institute, Wellesley College, and Keuka College. Those who knew him well believed that he was a man of great spiritual strength and virtue, despite his unassuming manner.

Rather than weakness or failure, William Montgomery's relationship to power is better characterized as one of chivalrous self-restraint and sacrifice. He exemplified the chivalry of the Victorian "Christian gentleman" described by Janet Fishburn in *The Fatherhood of God and the Victorian Family*:

> The Christian gentleman as "knight-errant" was potentially a man of spiritual and material success. The spirit of chivalry was the self-sacrificing motive of the knight-errant fighting the forces of evil out of his love for woman, God, and country. He could easily appear to be successful from a worldly point of view. But he was distinguished from the "Victorian gentleman" of the male-achiever ethos primarily by his motivation, which was not self-serving, although his vocation did demand aggression. The knight-errant was motivated by love, not by a desire for economic gratification and personal power held at the expense of others. The aggression of the knight-errant was moral because it was not economically or sexually motivated.[49]

William Montgomery's willingness to lead a life of duty and self-sacrifice was frequently noted by his contemporaries. Albert W. Beaven said that William Montgomery was "a fine example of the workability of Christianity, operating in the life of a man and making him an instrument for the Kingdom of God."[50] According to all accounts, his life was marked by a sense of devotion to duty, Christian stewardship, and generosity. One manifestation of that devotion was his lifelong commitment to simplicity and frugality, a commitment that Helen Barrett Montgomery respected and shared.

As Helen prepared for married life with William, she tried to see how much less than the two-hundred-dollar budget William had given her she could spend on furnishing their rooms. She wrote to her family, "Whatever we get out of this big self-restraint and economy we are going to give to God as a thank-offering." While she did not regard herself as "fanatical or foolish" in this regard, she found frugality spiritually satisfying.[51] Indeed, she and William were of one mind on this question, and it was one of the things she most admired about him. After his death she wrote: "I don't think he wanted money for its own sake, but he loved to see what splendid uses men could make of it."[52]

William Montgomery began the practice of tithing—contributing one-tenth of his personal income to the church—when Judson Barrett was pastor of the Lake Avenue Church. At one point in his marriage to Helen, after he had invested his life savings in developing the electric automobile starter, he had no income. The Montgomerys were forced to sell their house and most of their furniture (including Helen's beloved piano), and they moved into a duplex where Helen had to get along without servants. Despite such measures, Montgomery refused to cut his contribution to the Lake Avenue Church, even when the pastor asked him to, saying, "I may have to do it, but it will be the last thing I cut, not the first." He never cut his contribution; instead, he increased it as soon as he could, and by the end of his life he was giving far beyond one-tenth.[53]

Apparently he did not care much for material possessions. His wife once asked him how he had supported his parents when he was young. He replied: "My tastes were very simple, I bought good clothes and took care of them, I had no bad habits, and I had the habit of persistent, regular saving."[54] Although he owned a company that manufactured parts for automobiles, he never owned a car until the last year of his life, when his doctors insisted for health reasons that he must have transportation.[55]

Although William Montgomery was never one to seek the spotlight, he did feel a duty to publicly profess his Christian faith. His sense of religious duty led him to the Christian Endeavor Society, which he joined as a young man. Although he was "painfully shy, and the dread of speaking of his religious life in public was a positive torture to him," he would "pull himself to his feet with his hands on the chair in front of him while he gave his testimony." Once he had professed his faith publicly, he felt he had to do his best to live up to his words.[56]

At the time of their engagement, William Montgomery did not want to deter Helen from her dreams and goals. When he proposed marriage, he offered to lengthen their engagement five years so that Helen would have time to pursue her career. Helen decided no delay was necessary. In William's attitude toward her talent and ambition, she found the tension between domesticity and professionalism adequately resolved. William, she discovered, would help her and sympathize with her "in every high aspiration and unselfish purpose." She wrote, "I am growing more and more anxious that my life may be given without reserve to God's service." After he visited her in Philadelphia before their marriage, she wrote to her family, "he knelt down with me and we consecrated our lives to God's work in the world, promising to make this work our first thought and asking for His strength to keep us unspotted from the world."[57] With William, Helen believed it would be possible for her to enjoy the blessings of domesticity without sacrificing her ambition to serve God in the wider world. They were married on 6 September 1887, in her parents' home at 182 Fulton Avenue, Rochester, where her father performed the ceremony.

William Montgomery's willingness to sacrifice his own desires for the sake of Helen's sense of calling continued throughout their marriage. When, in 1910, the national committee that was responsible for organizing the Women's Jubilee tour asked her to lead the group of speakers, Helen first had to ask her husband if he would give his permission for her to go. She soon responded to the committee: "W. says if our missionaries can do what they have to do, he has no right to withhold me if I can help."[58] Ever the chivalrous, Christian gentleman, he was, by all accounts, notable for the restraint with which he utilized power and authority. William Montgomery died 10 July 1930.

The New Woman: Making a Living and Becoming a Mother

After her marriage to William Montgomery, Helen gave up her position in the Wellesley Preparatory School, and the couple settled in Rochester. Helen put her education to work in respectable Victorian fashion. She became a private tutor for young women preparing for college, from which in 1894 she earned approximately five dollars per week. About the same time, she collected five dollars apiece from the women (or most of them) who attended her series of Monday lectures, and her mother expected that she would earn at least one thousand dollars from the fees.[59] It was perhaps a little less ladylike than private tutoring, especially when the women started bringing their husbands to hear the lectures, but her mother was very proud of her. She also earned seventy-five dollars for a series of six lectures on "Grecian History," which she gave to a boys' school. Several churches in Rochester sought her out for lecture courses. The money was sorely needed, for William Montgomery was unemployed because of the fire that destroyed his factory, and Helen supported the family from her income plus the board Helen's mother paid to live with them. Her mother wrote: "Nellie can keep the boat afloat for a time, and I am glad.[60]

In 1895 Helen and William Montgomery adopted a five-year-old daughter named Edith.[61] Like many female college graduates of her generation, Helen Montgomery had postponed motherhood. The Montgomerys had been married about eight years when they finally decided to become parents. Helen was about thirty-four years old, and William was about forty-one. In 1887, just after her wedding, Helen mused about motherhood: "If I ever have children, I wonder if they will grow beyond and away from me? I'd want to be the one they'd soonest be with. Does every mother have the sword pierce her heart of being no longer necessary to her children?"[62] Motherhood was an important part of Montgomery's life. Like most American women of her age, she believed that a woman's children were her first responsibility and her greatest legacy. In 1922, she was quoted in the *Literary Digest*: "Perhaps not all women should marry. I am quite sure that those who plan to shift the burden of responsibility for the care of their children onto others should not marry. It is a harder thing to build a good child than to paint a picture or write a book or carve a statue. It requires absolute devotion of self; but the task is worthwhile. A group of beautiful, good, and clever children is the best work that a woman can contribute to her own generation."[63] Although she never bore children of her own, and Edith was her only child, Montgomery viewed motherhood as a sacred duty. She often asserted that the responsibilities of home and family were more important than any other duties a woman could bear, and she claimed that she would rather give up her outside activities than neglect her home life.[64] Edith often traveled with Helen and even accompanied her on a world tour after she graduated from Wellesley in 1913.

Montgomery loved children and she delighted in amusing them. In 1905 she planned a Christmas party for Edith and her five cousins. Montgomery decorated her yard with a fishpond for the occasion. One niece received a small toy "with a mirror on the outside and carved wooden goose on the inside." It was inscribed in German: "Here is the smallest and largest goose in the world." Edith got a little swan with a poem by Montgomery:

When this swan you look upon
darling light daughter
think of all the things
your mother says that you hadn't ought'er.[65]

Montgomery's Leadership in the Monroe Baptist Association

When Helen returned to Rochester as Mrs. Montgomery, she became involved once again in the life of Lake Avenue Baptist Church and the Monroe Baptist Association. In fact, it was at the 1887 meeting of the Monroe Baptist Association, at Penfield, New York, where Montgomery first met Lucy (Mrs. N. M.) Waterbury, who would later become Lucy Waterbury Peabody—her partner in so many endeavors on behalf of the ecumenical woman's missionary movement. According to the Monroe Baptist Association minutes for 1887, Montgomery and Waterbury, the missionary widow returned from India, "spoke in the interest of Foreign Missions" for fifteen minutes each.[66] Caroline Atwater Mason, who would become the author of two books for the ecumenical woman's missionary movement, also joined them on the platform that day.

At the annual meeting of the Women's Home Mission Union of 1888, the proceedings of which are recorded in the minutes of the Monroe Baptist Association meeting of 1888, Montgomery was elected to the executive committee of the Women's Home Mission Union. In an open discussion at that meeting, she advocated combining the Home and Foreign Mission societies of the local church and having separate committees to carry on "the Lord's work" in each area. Later on, she "urged the necessity of a suitable building" for the Baptist Missionary Training School in Chicago, where women went to be trained for service as Baptist missionaries. Montgomery tried to motivate the ladies of the Monroe Association to contribute to the cause.[67] In June, at the annual meeting of the Women's Foreign Missionary Society, also reported in the minutes of the association's annual meeting, she was elected second vice president.

Montgomery and Waterbury mounted the platform of the Monroe Baptist Association together a second time in 1888. According to the minutes for the meeting, Montgomery offered a ten-minute address on "Our Work among the Mormons," while Waterbury used her ten minutes to address the enigmatic topic "Shadows." Later in the meeting, Montgomery led a discussion of a presentation by Rev. William Elgin, D.D., on the "Actual and Possible Power of the Sunday School." Montgomery also reported briefly on the work of the Women's Home Mission Union, where she, along with another speaker "fired [the women's] hearts anew to press forward in the woman's work for women."[68]

In 1889 Montgomery was elected president of the Monroe Association's Women's Home Mission Union. She was also elected to a second term as second vice president of the Women's Foreign Missionary Society. Nevertheless, she did not get to address the entire association meeting at Pittsford that year. According to the minutes, "Our good brothers at the Association found so many important subjects demanding discussion . . . that they felt unable to yield any of the time to the sisters, to be used in talking about missions," so the women held their meeting in the Methodist church.[69] Montgomery continued as president of the Women's Home Mission Union until 1897. She concluded her presidency that year with a paean to the greatness of America, "so full of fields and opportunities for work." After the singing of "My Country 'tis of Thee," the meeting of the society was adjourned.[70]

Montgomery as Licensed Preacher

Montgomery's father died suddenly on a Sunday afternoon, 20 September 1889. According to an account given by Wilhermina C. Livingstone, Montgomery preached at Lake Avenue on the Sunday following his death,[71] but that account is probably incorrect. An article in the *Democrat and Chronicle* entitled "Tributes to a Brother" reported that Rev. Dr. T. Harwood Pattison preached at Lake Avenue "both morning and evening" on the Sunday after Barrett's death.[72] Livingstone, apparently following the account of Alice A. Chester as reported by Albert W. Beaven, went on to assert that Helen Montgomery filled the Lake Avenue pulpit on many subsequent occasions, before and during the pastorate of Clarence A. Barbour.[73] While not completely false, that account needs some qualification.

After Rev. Barrett's death, the congregation called T. Harwood Pattison, a professor of homiletics at Rochester Theological Seminary, to be interim pastor. Apparently, he served until the congregation called Clarence A. Barbour in 1891.[74] Consequently, there would have been few opportunities for Montgomery to preach during those years.

Helen Montgomery was licensed to preach by the Lake Avenue congregation. In the Baptist tradition, there is a distinction between licensing and ordination. A license to preach is an endorsement, given by the church that issues the license, of one's doctrinal soundness and preaching ability. It is like a letter of reference from one's home church that is traditionally recognized by other Baptist churches. Unlike ordination, a license to preach is not recognition of pastoral gifts, calling, or skills, nor is it necessarily indicative of an intention to seek ordination or pursue pastoral ministry; rather, it is indicative of an intention to stand before the public and preach the gospel. The Lake Avenue Church would not have licensed Montgomery to preach until the congregation had heard her preach and was satisfied as to her sound doctrine and ability. Thus it is important to establish when the church licensed her. That would give some indication as to when she had in fact preached at Lake Avenue.

A collection of material apparently gathered by her brother, Storrs Barrett, contains a quotation from an article that appeared in the *Northwestern Christian Advocate* on 26 July 1922, which reported the date of her license as 1892. One other early source, the obituary for Montgomery that appeared in the *Times-Union* on 19 October 1934, also reported that date as 1892.[75] Other references to 1892 in secondary sources apparently come from those reports. Despite those early testimonials, there is good reason to doubt that Montgomery was licensed in 1892.

First of all, according to the minutes of the Monroe Baptist Association, Lake Avenue did not report Montgomery as a licensed preacher until 1898. William A. Montgomery was the church secretary for Lake Avenue during the years in question, so it is unlikely that the omission of her name was an oversight. In the Lake Avenue Baptist Church archives there is a manuscript copy of the 1896 "church letter"—the form that church secretaries completed to report church statistics to the association. Apparently William Montgomery himself completed the form. It does not list Helen Montgomery's name under licentiates.

Montgomery preached from the Lake Avenue pulpit on at least two Sundays in 1898. According to reports in the *Democrat and Chronicle*, she preached on 8 August and 15 August. Apparently she spoke morning and evening on both Sundays in the absence of the pastor, Clarence A. Barbour. It is possible that Montgomery preached on other Sundays, both before and after August 1898 and that the local press missed or failed to report the event. But unless convincing evidence to the contrary is discovered in the future, it appears likely that the reports of the *Northwestern Christian Advocate* and the *Times-Union*, that Montgomery was licensed in 1892, were incorrect. It is more likely that Montgomery's August 1898 sermons were the basis on which the Lake Avenue congregation voted to license her as a preacher of the gospel, and the church reported the action to the Monroe Baptist Association the same year.

Lake Avenue Baptist Church maintains in its archives a collection of its weekly church calendars dating back to 1872. The calendars provide the order of services for morning and evening worship of a particular Sunday, as well as other news and events for the subsequent week. The collection is incomplete from 1872 to September 1905. After that, the collection is apparently complete for the duration of Montgomery's life except for the weeks of 28 June through 30 August 1908, when no calendars were printed. An examination of the collection through 1930 revealed several "addresses" given by Montgomery over the years, but they can hardly be characterized as frequent. It is worth noting that the calendars never referred to her presentations as "sermons." Like other laypersons who spoke at Lake Avenue, she gave "addresses."

According to the calendars in the collection, Montgomery spoke seventeen times before 1930, when she retired from public life due to illness. She gave an address for Children's Day, 14 June 1908; on "Reminiscences of Mr. and Mrs. Bawden" (missionaries supported by Lake Avenue), 19 December 1909; on "Prayer," 28 January 1912; on "What Baptists are Doing in Asia," 24 May 1914; an untitled address, 3 January 1915. She was one of four people who gave memorial addresses, 21 March 1915; she gave an untitled address at the evening service, 20 June 1915; another untitled address at the evening service, 7 October 1915. She spoke on "The Girl in War Time" at the evening service, 16 September 1917; on "Our First Church," 29 November 1917, when she was one of several speakers at a service in celebration of laying the cornerstone for a new meetinghouse. She gave an untitled address, 26 May 1918. She and Albert W. Beaven shared the platform on 16 May 1920 as Lake Avenue celebrated the completion of their New World Movement campaign with a "Victory Service." She gave a vespers meditation, 20 November 1921; an "Illustrated Address" on the topic, "Around the World Under the Christian Flag," at the evening service, 23 July 1922; an "Illustrated Address" on "John Huss, a Great Reformer and Martyr," 25 November 1923. She was one of five who gave memorial addresses after the death of Rev. S. W. Beaven, father of Albert W. Beaven and assistant pastor at Lake Avenue, 8 March 1925. Her final address to Lake Avenue was on "Mothers of Men," 12 May 1929.

There were other speakers who were men, both lay and ordained, who appeared more frequently over the years, such as Clinton Howard, Rev. Paul

Moore Strayer, Conrad H. Moehlman, and others. Some of these men preached on several consecutive Sundays during the summer vacations of Barbour or Beaven. Perhaps Montgomery was not called upon because she was unavailable during the summer. She was a frequent lecturer at the summer mission schools for women at Northfield, Massachusetts; Winona Lake, Indiana; and Chautauqua, New York. Nevertheless, it is safe to say that Montgomery was the most frequent female speaker in the Lake Avenue pulpit during her lifetime.

It is important to remember that after the death of her father, Montgomery organized the Barrett Memorial Sunday School Class for women at Lake Avenue Baptist Church. This grew until it enrolled two hundred and fifty women, and it became an important base of power for Montgomery in the church and in the city. For forty-four years, Montgomery taught the class whenever she was in town. Her lessons covered a wide range of topics, from the Bible to social issues to politics, and the weekly meetings gave her a regular and influential platform for her views. Even though the class grew quite large, it was Montgomery's custom to greet each of her "girls" by name and welcome visitors or new members. According to Alice A. Chester, many of the members were teachers and principals in the public schools, and Montgomery was to all of the women "a revelation of the possibilities of Christian womanhood."[76] Her niece recalled how she exhorted her class: "She would say, 'Come on, now sing! If you haven't got a good voice make your mouth go!' At other times she would say, 'Oh, you gals, you sit behind your faces,' meaning you let your mind wool gather. She thought that happened frequently when she spoke to American women but I don't think so."[77] Albert W. Beaven, who was Montgomery's pastor, and Wilhermina C. Livingstone, who was a member of the class, regarded Montgomery's class as one of the most influential in the city of Rochester, and they believed its influence was global.[78]

Forays into Broader Public Life

In addition to her local lectures, local Baptist leadership, and preaching and teaching at Lake Avenue Baptist Church, Montgomery gained a wider reputation as a speaker and writer. In 1893 the woman suffragists of New York were engaged in an effort to add a suffrage amendment to the New York State Constitution, which was to be revised in a constitutional convention in

1894. Mrs. Jean Brooks Greenleaf, president of the New York State Woman's Suffrage Association, directed the statewide campaign from Rochester. Mary S. Anthony, Susan B. Anthony's sister, organized the Rochester women's clubs in a petition drive in favor of the amendment, and she was so successful that the number of signatures on the petitions in Rochester exceeded the number of registered voters by 25 percent. No other city had such a successful petition drive, and Rochester became known as a suffrage "hotbed."[79]

Montgomery participated in the effort to gain the suffrage amendment. In April 1894 her mother wrote, "Nellie is invited to speak again in New York. This time before a group of forty women in the parlors of Margaret Olivia Slocum Sage. Bishop Huntington and another gentleman speaking against, and Nellie and Mrs. Jacobi for, woman suffrage. Do not think of her as a woman suffragist. She gives what seems to her the true reasons and some of the wealthiest women in New York are working in these parlor meetings to influence the coming constitutional convention. She has been asked to contribute a paper on the question to *Harper's Bazaar*."[80]

Margaret Sage was the wife of Russell Sage, a wealthy New York financier. Russell Sage made his fortune in groceries, banking, stock speculation, and, with Jay Gould, in railroads and the Western Union Telegraph Company. He was a congressman and a benefactor of Cornell University.[81] After Russell Sage's death in 1906, Margaret Sage used her husband's fortune to fund a wide variety of educational and benevolent causes—especially those related to women's causes. In Troy, New York, where her husband had started his business career, she gave endowments to Emma Willard College and Rensselaer Polytechnic Institute and established Russell Sage College for women. She bought Marsh Island in the Gulf of Mexico as a bird sanctuary for the state of Louisiana, and in 1907, she established the Russell Sage Foundation in New York City for "the improvement of social and living conditions in the United States." In its early years, the foundation initiated research for progressive causes such as social welfare, urban planning, public health, low-income housing, education, and labor reform. Today the foundation is dedicated to improving social policy by refining the methods, data, and theoretical foundations of social science.[82] Mrs. Sage was also a benefactor of the Woman's Missionary Jubilee of 1910.

In an example of issue-oriented Progressive coalition building, the suffragists enlisted the support of the labor unions and farmers' granges. New

York suffrage leader Carrie Chapman Catt, who came to suffrage leadership through the temperance movement, gave over forty speeches and organized political equality clubs in support of the campaign. She also encouraged "parlor meetings" to enlist the support of New York's wealthiest and most prominent women.[83]

Apparently Mrs. Sage's parlor meeting was one of those organized by Catt, and Montgomery was a pro-suffrage speaker. Montgomery's ally in the debate on the suffrage side was Dr. Mary Putnam Jacobi. In 1876 Jacobi's essay, "The Question of Rest for Women During Menstruation," won Harvard's Boylston Prize and helped turn the tide against those who claimed that higher education was ruinous for women's health, such as Dr. Edward Clarke of Harvard.[84] She was one of the organizers of the New York Consumers' League in 1890.[85] In 1894, when she and Montgomery appeared together in Mrs. Sage's parlor, Jacobi wrote "'Common Sense' Applied to Woman Suffrage." In the pamphlet, she utilized data related to the vast changes in women's work and the large number of women industrial workers to argue against the idea that women workers could be adequately represented and protected by the political and economic rights of a husband or father. Women workers acted as independent economic agents, she argued, and they needed the sort of independent legal protection that could only be enforced by independent political rights.[86]

The debate in Mrs. Sage's home is a fine example of how the values implicit in Victorian gender construction were utilized in the transformation of the woman's sphere, and of Montgomery's contribution to that transformation. Parlor meetings were private affairs attended by invitation only. Respectable, wealthy women, whose modesty and fear of public notoriety might have prevented them from attending a public suffrage meeting, could attend a parlor meeting without embarrassment. But the subject of the meeting—suffrage—was the primary objective in a protracted effort to dismantle the dividing wall that separated the private woman's sphere from public life and made their scruples necessary.

According to Mrs. Barrett's account, Bishop Frederic Dan Huntington defended the antisuffrage position in Mrs. Sage's parlor meeting. Huntington was the first bishop of the Episcopal Diocese of Central New York. Scion of an old Puritan family from Boston, his father was a Congregational clergyman, but his mother had become a Unitarian. Huntington graduated from the Harvard Divinity School and was ordained a Unitarian clergyman. In 1855, he accepted a call to become the preacher at the College Chapel and the Plummer Professor of Christian Morals at Harvard. In 1859, after a long spiritual struggle, he made a profession of faith in the Episcopal Church. He left Harvard in 1860 to enter the Episcopal ministry, and in 1869, he was consecrated the first bishop of the Diocese of Central New York. He was interested in the social implications of Christianity throughout his career, and according to one source, he favored woman's suffrage.[87] If so, it is curious that he defended the antisuffrage position in his debate with Montgomery and Jacobi in 1894.

Elizabeth Cady Stanton mentioned Dr. Mary Putnam Jacobi and Margaret Sage among the chief advocates of the suffrage amendment in the New York campaign of 1894. The constitutional convention's Committee on Suffrage never even submitted a report to the convention, despite the fact that, in Stanton's words, "half a million of our most intelligent and respectable citizens had signed the petition requesting them to do so."[88] Actually 600,000 people signed the suffragists' petition, with an additional 211,000 signatures from the labor union petitions as well as 50,000 signatures from the grange petitions.[89] Nevertheless, antisuffrage political maneuvering assured that the suffrage amendment failed overwhelmingly.

Mrs. Barrett, despite her obvious pride in Montgomery's achievement, wanted to defend her daughter against the negative stereotype associated with woman suffragists. She was emphatic that her daughter was not a suffragist. She believed that Montgomery merely expressed her honest convictions— "what seems to her the true reasons." Her daughter was no partisan, just a reasoned critic of the status quo. As the next chapter will show, Montgomery's own arguments reflect the same hesitancy to embrace the appellation of "suffragist." In fact, the label was immaterial to the effect of her public actions. In the very activities she chose—preaching, public lecturing, and serving in public office—she expanded the role for women in society.

After her marriage, Montgomery was forced to resolve—to her own satisfaction, at least—the tension between the expectations of the woman's sphere and the expectations placed on her as a "college woman." Montgomery's abilities drew her steadily into increasingly public and controversial roles. In the Lake Avenue Baptist Church, she emerged from traditional women's venues, such as her Sunday school classroom and the women's missionary meetings, with such obvious leadership and oratorical ability that the church gave her a license to preach—a most unusual step for a Baptist church in the late nineteenth century. As a public lecturer, she became one of the most popular speakers in the city among both men and women, and the leaders of the suffrage cause recruited her.

Nevertheless, it is clear that Montgomery generally affirmed middle-class Victorian assumptions regarding the different but complementary roles of men and women in society. From the titles and content of her addresses, it is obvious that she saw herself as a defender of virtuous womanhood. In fact, as the next chapter shows, she frequently defended her departures from traditional gender roles as necessary to the protection of the domestic ideals of motherhood and family. As a progressive New Woman, Montgomery believed that her ventures into public life did not undercut the dignity and moral influence of women in society. On the contrary, she believed her activism would make it possible to extend the ideals of domesticity into the public sphere. By translating "womanly" virtues into the public sphere, she hoped to universalize them.

Five

Montgomery's "New Woman" and the Limitless Scope of Woman as Citizen

Helen Barrett Montgomery was a college graduate and, by 1893, a club-woman. At Wellesley she learned to augment the traditional feminine virtues of moral purity, piety, and duty to home and family with duty to the community, a commitment to education and professionalism, and a passion for social reform. In Rochester she soon found an outlet for those values in the "domestic feminism" of several of Rochester's women's clubs.

Women's Political Strategies and the Varieties of Feminism

In Victorian society, women's power originated in the private sphere, and it was indirect power—the power of moral influence. The political philosophy originally developed by the women of the antebellum reform movement was maternal. That is, their model for political power was that moral influence of women, and mothers in particular, and their model for proper social relationships was the well-ordered Victorian home and family. Consistent with the Victorian social ethic and their experience in the antebellum reform movement, they believed in the protection of women and children, of the family, and in the duty of the strong to protect the weak. To the extent that they sought equal political rights for women, they did so in the belief that rights were necessary in order for women to perform their social duties and fulfill their obligations to the community. They did not believe that equality necessarily meant sameness. According to Elizabeth Battelle Clark: "Although

71

women demanded equality, they also predicated their entry into the political world on a moral sensibility which most saw as uniquely feminine, and which served as the basis for their political agenda and theory of rights."[1]

Antebellum female reformers were able to use the moral authority of women as an effective political strategy as long as the communities in which they worked were small and the franchise was limited to the men to whom the women were somehow connected. But as communities grew, or their goals for reform transcended the local community, or political networks became more complex and the franchise was extended to men beyond the moral influence of the women, their moral authority became less effective as a political strategy. The institutions of electoral politics, at once public and anonymous, were largely beyond the reach of the informal and relational sources of women's power in the domestic sphere, and antithetical to them. Women became conscious of the danger that the widening gap between public and private morals and the separation of political power from women's moral influence presented to them and their families. Increasingly they came to resent the division of spheres and to desire their eradication.[2]

To meet the challenge, the intellectual elite of the nascent suffrage movement developed a theoretical justification for the political emancipation of women based on individualistic-civic nationalism, which they linked to the core traditions and symbols of American democracy—the American Revolution and the Declaration of Independence. The suffragists cause was the political recognition of "the individual autonomy of woman in all her relations."[3]

The suffragists' justification for the emancipation of women was an extension of the natural rights theory used by the founders of the American republic. They wanted women to be recognized as competent individuals in civil society, whose autonomy and rights were protected by the state. But the suffragists wanted more than a mere recognition of equal political rights. They wanted an extension of liberal democratic political theory into the domestic sphere. They wanted the protective power of the state expanded into the domestic (that is, private) sphere of woman, so that a woman's ownership of her own person and her right to privacy were established and protected by law. These issues were never contemplated by the free white men who created the American republic because their rights to personal self-ownership and privacy were never in doubt. The suffragists wanted to reform liberal democratic political theory in a way that would eradicate the gender-based separation of spheres.[4]

Suffrage leaders matched their rhetoric to their intended audiences. When they engaged male audiences of legislators or voters, they utilized the language of individualistic-civic nationalism. When they spoke with their largely female constituency, they used the religious and moral vocabulary of maternalism.[5] The majority of female reformers, working from a maternalist political philosophy, believed social justice would be achieved through moral influence. They wanted to arouse public sentiment in the interest of social control. They were less interested in majority rule than in community consensus achieved through the voluntary assent of each individual conscience to the will of God. For them the reform of public sentiment, rather than the coercive power of law, represented actual progress toward the perfection of social institutions.[6] But the intellectual elite who shaped the suffrage movement pursued a political strategy based on the direct power of a limited state to protect the autonomous individual.

In the pluralism of antebellum female reform, the emphasis on individual civil liberties coexisted with the emphasis on the moral obligations of maternalism. After the Civil War, they developed organizationally and ideologically into three different types of feminism, which historians have labeled "liberal feminism," "evangelical feminism," and "domestic feminism."

Liberal Feminism

After the Civil War, when suffragists resumed their efforts, the uneasy alliance of maternalism and liberal feminism—that is, feminism based on the extension of liberal democratic theory—was sundered. While many proponents of reform viewed suffrage as one need among many, advocates of women's rights were convinced of the need to focus exclusively on obtaining suffrage. Initially they envisioned a millennial era of democratic reform that would include both political liberty and economic opportunity. A coalition of women, blacks, and the working classes, they believed, would strive in unity to secure the promises of democracy for all.[7] The coalition was soon disrupted, however, when the Republican Party refused to support suffrage along with the extension of the franchise to black men. Reformers found themselves forced to choose sides, and even the suffrage leadership was divided over the issue.

A new suffrage movement emerged from the rubble of their disillusionment in the form of two national organizations. Disappointed and divided by the fact that women were excluded from the Fourteenth and Fifteenth Amendments' redefinition of American democracy and feeling betrayed by the Republicans and abolitionists, Elizabeth Cady Stanton and Susan B. Anthony organized the National Woman Suffrage Association (NWSA) in May 1869—for women only. In November, Lucy Stone and her husband Henry Blackwell, along with Julia Ward Howe, author of the "Battle Hymn of the Republic," who supported the Fourteenth and Fifteenth Amendments and the Republican Party, organized the American Woman Suffrage Association, which included men. These two organizations became the main channels through which suffragist leaders renewed their efforts to expand liberal democracy to include women's rights, and they had a major influence on the emerging feminist consciousness. While the NWSA focused on a state-by-state effort to win suffrage, the AWSA worked toward an amendment to the federal constitution. But both organizations were committed to the extension of liberal democracy to include women as competent individuals in civil society, and the two groups merged into a single organization, the National American Woman Suffrage Association, in 1890. Although liberal feminists made pragmatic alliances with their evangelical sisters from time to time, they remained convinced that the maternalist justification of "home protection" was simply inadequate as a basis for the emancipation of women and protection of their individual rights in civil society.

Evangelical Feminism

As the suffragists who followed the liberal feminist strategy organized separately following the Civil War, the remaining forces of the female reform movement continued to utilize the indirect political power of women's moral influence and maintained their emphasis on maternalism as the basic motivation for reform. These reformers maintained much closer relations with evangelical Protestants than the liberal feminists did (even though they, too, sometimes advocated suffrage), and they often expressed their motivations in missionary terms. These evangelical feminists continued the tradition of religiously motivated moral reform inherited from the antebellum reformers, who were in turn inspired by the Second Great Awakening. The organizations they created were Protestant in character, but they avoided sectarian identifications and focused on the implications of evangelical religion for social reform. The massive Woman's Christian Temperance Union (WCTU) was the largest and most influential organization created by evangelical feminists. Led to its zenith by Frances Willard, the bulk of the WCTU's strength was in the Midwest.

According to Clark, one key difference between the liberal feminists and evangelical feminists was religious in nature. The absent God of the liberals required "individual growth and autonomy," while the ever-present God of the evangelicals "stressed kinship and care."[8] The evangelical feminists wanted to reform the political world created by men with a political world that would at once be more Christian and more democratic. In contrast to the naked power struggle and corruption of backroom deals, vote buying, and gerrymandering, evangelical feminists envisioned an open democracy perfected through "voluntary obedience." According to Hannah Whitall Smith, "Voluntary obedience is a deed which is performed after the right state of feeling towards the object has been induced."[9] The evangelical feminists believed they could induce "the right state of feeling" through moral influence. They imputed to motherhood a moral privilege that sometimes amounted to condescension and coercion.

Unlike the liberal feminists who emphasized women's political impotence in civil society, WCTU president and evangelical feminist Frances Willard rejected the analogy that compared the condition of women with slavery and called for women's emancipation. For Willard, maternalism constituted a powerful and practical political force, and the analogy to slavery had "associations and . . . history . . . not to our advantage."[10] In the view of evangelical feminists, one was not just an autonomous, anonymous *individual* pursuing self-interest in civil society. One was a *person* with duties and obligations, pursuing the public interest through a web of relationships. Those relationships linked the person, the home, the community, the state, and God.

Domestic Feminism

A third variety of feminism, and the most significant for understanding Helen Barrett Montgomery, developed as a sort of middle way between liberal and evangelical feminism. Contemporary historians sometimes refer to it as "domestic feminism." Although the roots of the movement reach back to the beginning of the nineteenth century, the period of its most rapid proliferation followed 1868, the era of the women's club movement. Both Jane Cunningham Croly, founder of Sorosis in New York City (1868), and Caroline Severance, founder of the New England Woman's Club in Boston (1868), might be considered exemplars of domestic feminism. The differences between them give some indication of the diversity encompassed by the term. Both were married women and mothers, but Croly was a career-oriented journalist whose primary interest was women's self-improvement and culture study. Severance was primarily a liberal reformer whose associations and interests embraced a panoply of nineteenth-century reform movements from temperance to Transcendentalism. Those twin foci—self-improvement and reform—characterize the movement, along with its inclusiveness and diversity. The women's clubs of the domestic feminist movement were nonsectarian in many respects. They usually made room for Christians and non-Christians, for liberals and evangelicals, for suffragists and antisuffragists. The distinguishing characteristic of the movement, however, was its affirmation and utilization of the ideology of domesticity. Domestic feminists embraced the cultural conventions of True Womanhood and used them as a justification for expanding women's social and political roles.[11] For the most part, domestic feminist organizations remained officially neutral on the suffrage question and claimed a unique and practical political role for women in so-called municipal housekeeping.

Montgomery as a Domestic Feminist

Montgomery was chosen as the first president of the Rochester Women's Educational Industrial Union (WEIU) in 1893,[12] and she used that position as a platform to articulate a broad intellectual, political, and social agenda for domestic feminism. The goal of the WEIU was to provide social, educational, and protective services for women—especially poor and working women. The WEIU was the first woman's club in Rochester to move beyond culture study and self-improvement into municipal housekeeping. The mission of the WEIU attracted the attention and support of many of the most prominent women in Rochester. Montgomery's lectures to the WEIU quickly became very popular and earned her a reputation as an intellectual leader of the women in the city.[13]

Karen Blair identified the crucial role of the Women's Educational and Industrial Unions in the reorientation of the woman's club movement from culture study to municipal housekeeping.[14] Montgomery's role was key in the case of the Rochester WEIU. Her WEIU lectures reflected that transformation from culture study to municipal housekeeping, but they also transcended it. Montgomery's vision for women's public role was theoretically unlimited. Montgomery utilized the Victorian stereotype that assigned special virtues, unique maternal skills, and particular character traits to women as a justification for women's unrestricted political involvement based on the special qualifications of their gender. Nevertheless, while she claimed a special role for women as women in municipal housekeeping, she believed women must think and act as citizens as well as women and mothers. Through her lectures, she challenged the women of the WEIU to move beyond the logic of municipal housekeeping and to think about national and international political questions.

Montgomery in Rochester's Women's Clubs

According to the notes of an interview with Mary T. L. Gannett,[15] Montgomery was a charter member of the Wednesday Morning Club (1890), a women's literary club.[16] According to one historian, it was "the smallest, the youngest, and undoubtedly the best of the women's literary societies" in Rochester and its members were "chosen for ability to contribute something of real worth to the discussions."[17] At the beginning, the members of the Wednesday Morning Club focused strictly on literary interests. They met every third Wednesday morning for hourlong readings and discussions that continued over lunch. They considered authors such as Blake, Browning, Tolstoy, George Eliot, Emerson, Longfellow, and many others. Soon however, the reform-minded members of the club, including Mary T. L. Gannett, Mrs. Max Landsberg, Mrs. Joseph T. Alling, and Mrs. Henry Danforth (all future members of the WEIU) desired a broader field of discussion. The club began to hear papers with titles such as "Modern Municipal Reforms," "The Mission of the Liberal Thinker," "Women's Task Masters," and "Women's Legal Rights in Various States." The Wednesday Morning Club was still in existence in 1986.[18] Some papers presented to the Wednesday Morning Club were thought so valuable they were read to the Ignorance Club or the Woman's Ethical Club, where some Wednesday Morning ladies were also members.[19]

In 1897 Montgomery joined the College Women's Club. Although the club was not limited to literary interests, it included a study group that met at the Reynolds Library and pursued year-long discussions of topics such as Russian literature or the history of the Netherlands. The College Women's Club was absorbed into the American Association of University Women in 1917.[20]

Montgomery was also a charter member of the critically important Woman's Ethical Club (1889).[21]Founded by Mary T. L. Gannett, the wife of Unitarian minister William Gannett, the Woman's Ethical Club was the first to unite women from the various churches of Rochester. The club did not directly endorse the suffrage cause, but it educated women on various social questions and often enlisted their support for benevolent causes, and it became one of the most popular clubs in Rochester. By encouraging women to become municipal housekeepers, the Woman's Ethical Club made practical feminists of many women without having to take an official stand on suffrage. By the mid-1890s, the meetings of the Woman's Ethical Club attracted three hundred to a thousand women.[22]

It is very likely that, despite her early reticence to adopt the "suffragist" label, Montgomery eventually became a member of the Political Equality Club (before 1891 it was the Woman's Political Club). Miss Mary S. Anthony and Mrs. Ellen Sully Fray established the club in 1886. It was patterned after a similar organization with which Mrs. Fray was connected in Toledo, Ohio.[23] The purpose of the club was "to secure for women the unrestricted exercise of all rights of citizenship, and equal constitutional rights with men, and equal protection of the law." The Political Equality Club affiliated with the National Woman Suffrage Association in 1890, and it became the Woman Suffrage Party of Monroe County in 1916.[24] In addition to suffrage activism, the Political Equality Club was a key force behind several important reform movements in Rochester in which Montgomery participated, such as Montgomery's election to the school board, the effort to bring coeducation to the University of Rochester, and the woman's campaign against vice, which Montgomery led in 1905. Montgomery spoke at several Political Equality Club events, and the newspapers assumed she was a part of the club, as did city historian Blake McKelvey. The *Herald* noted that it was "the suffragists" who called her Helen Barrett Montgomery, rather than Mrs. W. A. Montgomery.[25]

Montgomery's Concept of the "New Woman"

Montgomery had very clear ideas about the role of what she called the "New Woman" in American society—ideas that were quite consistent with the domestic feminism of the woman's club movement. Montgomery's New Woman was warm and tenderhearted toward her family, but she organized her family life in a way that was rational and scientific. Patriotism, piety, and moral purity motivated her, but she based her actions on factual information and practical good sense, not sentiment. The New Woman wanted to do everything in a "womanly" way, but as the Woman's Christian Temperance Union said, she wanted to "Do Everything." Home and family came first for the New Woman, and she always submitted to her duty; but everything in the world touched the home and family, so her duty was as wide as the world. While maintaining formal allegiance to the gender distinctions of Victorian culture, Montgomery's definition of the New Woman expanded the woman's sphere until it encompassed all of life.

Montgomery and "Equal Suffrage"

Harper's Bazaar published Montgomery's article on "Equal Suffrage," which Emily Barrett mentioned in 1894. In the article, Montgomery exhibited some of her mother's reticence to assume the mantle of suffragist. She was swift to point out that support for suffrage did not require one to become "a man-hater nor an advocate of bloomers." She wanted her readers to picture suffrage advocates as "sensible, patriotic women, saying to the husbands and fathers and brothers whom they trust and love, 'May we not help you in the struggle for good government and happy homes. [*sic*] We do not wish any longer to be a privileged class in the State, let us share in the political as we already do in the social and religious life of the nation.'"[26]

Montgomery did not want her readers to think suffrage was a passing fad or the whim of a few "discontented women"; it was "a wave on the surface of a mighty current that is altering the face of the earth. We call this current democracy." She claimed that the history of the nineteenth century was the history of the spread of democracy around the world and argued that "each extension of the franchise has tended directly to the purity of the government." Nevertheless, according to Montgomery, in the progress of democracy as "the expression of the universal will," the political condition of woman remained "an anachronism." Women could hold and bequeath property, choose their own professions, work, pay taxes, and exercise a variety of rights, but they could not vote to elect legislators who levied the taxes and protected their rights. In most states, women had no right to their own children in the case of divorce. Women teachers, educated, moral, and organized, had much less influence with government than "the most ignorant trades-union." Trades dominated by women were "wretchedly paid" in comparison with those dominated by men. All of these circumstances could be remedied with women's suffrage because "the political condition largely determines the economic condition."[27]

Montgomery asserted that women were well suited to join in deliberations on certain important matters of public policy precisely *because* they were women. Women were endowed with high moral character, which she believed was demonstrated in the fact that women made up only fifteen percent of the prison population while they accounted for three-fourths of the membership of the Protestant churches. They were especially concerned about questions of "education, public morality, and the reform of old abuses," while "municipal questions, too, are only an extended housekeeping." Women would "stand for the interests of little children" and "oppose the influences hostile to the home." Finally Montgomery reasoned that one of the best arguments in favor of women's suffrage is an examination of its enemies—especially the liquor interests.[28]

In a few brief paragraphs, Montgomery touched upon many of the cardinal arguments of the suffrage movement. The failure to extend suffrage to women was inconsistent with justice and the political principles of the nation.[29] Aileen Kraditor called this the "core of the suffrage argument" that never disappeared, even though by the 1890s, with the pressures of immigration, industrialization, and colonization affecting American society, many people no longer took the equality of all men for granted.[30]

In the 1890s some suffragists believed it was to their own advantage to utilize, as an argument of expediency, the idea that educated white women were more entitled to the franchise than some men.[31] Montgomery did not make that argument explicitly, but she did suggest that without suffrage, educated white women were at a political disadvantage to their intellectual inferiors.[32] Like other suffragists, she argued that women suffered economic discrimination because they lacked the vote.[33] Finally she employed the maternalist argument that suffrage would benefit the state because it would empower women to fulfill the mandate of their gender to defend the home, combat vice, and exert a positive moral influence on social and political relations.[34]

Kraditor attributed the origin of the idea that government was house-keeping on a broad scale to Frances Willard, who in 1898 wrote to Susan B. Anthony, "Men have made a dead failure of municipal government, just about as they would of housekeeping, and government is only housekeeping on the broadest scale."[35] But Montgomery used essentially the same thought four years earlier: "Municipal questions, too, are only an extended house-keeping, and the peculiar training of women has admirably fitted them to cope with the perplexing details of city administration."[36] Whether it was original to Montgomery or Willard or someone else, the effect of the idea was to extend the woman's sphere into the public realm and to blur the line between the responsibilities of men and women for the public good. Kraditor attributed this response to the increasing government regulation and control of traditional women's functions, such as the production of food and cloth-ing, and education. As women's functions became politicized, women them-selves became politicized.[37]

Montgomery's Maternalist Politics

Montgomery's ideas about equality transcended the public political realm. She asserted that wives ought to be equal partners, not dependents, in mar-riage and family relations. Speaking on "The Money Value of the Home Service of the Wife and Mother," she pointed out that the money value of the wife could be estimated as the amount needed to replace the services she rendered to the family. In most cases, according to Montgomery, that meant the employment of "a servant, a housekeeper, a governess, a chaper-one." Regarding wives as dependents rather than partners degraded "true marriage," she believed.[38]

Women were as interested as men in political issues, according to Montgomery. She asserted that "one of the most prominent New York dai-lies" had recently done some market research to find out which part of the paper women read first, and they found that "a very large majority" turned to the political news first. Montgomery thought this would come as a shock to most men, "who expect us to look first in the 'Woman's Page,' and to take no interest in the big world around us."[39] She addressed the 1899 meeting of the New York State Federation of Women's Clubs on "Political Study for Mothers and Teachers," and she asserted that the best municipal government could not be achieved until mothers and teachers were "united in political duties."[40] Montgomery did all she could to help women think and act as informed citizens. The press reported on twenty public lectures given by Montgomery under the sponsorship of the Women's Educational and Industrial Union (WEIU) between 1895 and 1899. Of the twenty, nine were devoted to global political affairs, four were concerned with national political questions, four addressed municipal issues, one stated Montgomery's views on "the New Woman," and two addressed more than one political issue from different levels of government.

In her lecture on the New Woman, Montgomery provided a historical argument for the development of the new opportunities open to the women of her day and outlined her views on how women ought to make the best advantage of those opportunities. The lecture reflected the middle-class status of Montgomery and her audience. According to Montgomery, two conditions separated women of the late nineteenth century from women of earlier periods. She believed the women of her day had more leisure time and more talent than women had ever had before. Furthermore, she believed that the increase in women's leisure time was achieved by making men busier. Still, she believed there was more to the emergence of the New Woman than the industrial reorganization of means of production. She believed the New Woman came of age in the midst of national conflict. "When woman received her baptism in the civil war, man also received his, and the change dates back to the war."[41]

Montgomery's characterization of women's leisure betrayed an ignorance of the realities of factory life. "The spinning, weaving, sewing, the making of the lights burnt that were fifty years ago performed by the women, are now all done outside."[42] Those tasks, she said, were "taken out of the hands of women and organized as great industries, so that women who do not feel the pressure of poverty, or the burden of family, or the need of self-support, have leisure hours every day that their grandmothers had to give to the superintendence of household matters."[43] In fact, contrary to Montgomery's claim, many women still did the same work they had always done. The difference was that they did it for low wages in the mechanical and highly structured environment of the factory instead of at home. Furthermore, when they left the factory, they went home to do domestic chores. But Montgomery's listeners were middle-class Victorian ladies. Most of them had probably never seen the inside of a factory.

According to Montgomery, women's leisure was purchased at the expense of men's increased labor. She claimed that "in the tremendous stress of business competition, the husbands and fathers of women in comfortable circumstances are far more busy than were their grandfathers." So, while the businessman trying to support his family was busier than ever before, the "well-to-do woman" could count on unprecedented hours of leisure time "without neglecting her home."[44]

Montgomery feared that "this accession to leisure would be a curse to women with empty heads and idle hands," but it did not need to be so. Educational opportunities for women were increasing, as were opportunities for service. "The time is past when women are content to play with dolls, or devote themselves to their little calling list, and the association of a few social friends; but their ideas and desires are daily broadening, and they are looking about for greater variety of work." In her view, a woman of "well developed intellect" must "take a woman's part in this glorious life." They must "realize that work is their birthright and not idleness."[45] According to Montgomery, the New Woman had a moral responsibility to make her leisure productive for the common good.

Montgomery was an active churchwoman, and she knew very well that women had long been meeting together in denominational organizations and societies related to the local church. But the time had come, she said, for women to "bury their creeds and meet together for mutual study and advantage."[46] Judging from Montgomery's own record of involvement with Christian organizations, it is doubtful that she meant to secularize the New Woman by this comment. Probably she intended to open the way for a broad and inclusive ecumenism in women's cooperative activities—an ecumenism that was inclusive enough even for Jewish women, such as Mrs. Max Landsberg, whose husband was the rabbi of Berith Kodesh. Mrs. Landsberg was one of the original members of the board of Rochester's WEIU, and Montgomery was president.[47] Mary T. Gannett, wife of the Unitarian pastor and social gospel leader, Rev. William C. Gannett, was another guiding light of the WEIU who influenced Montgomery. Mary Gannett founded the

Woman's Ethical Club on the same broad cooperative principle.[48] The New Woman, despite her piety, was not necessarily a Christian.

Montgomery believed the New Woman did not need "political suffrage" to "exert a beneficial influence." In fact, Montgomery thought that demonstrating the usefulness of women to the community might contribute to the suffrage cause. "Perhaps the surest way to command recognition is to occupy the present time in study and activity. We have no lack of opinions; the only trouble is they are ill founded, and not fully matured by careful study."[49]

Montgomery and Educated Motherhood

The modern woman ought to engage in three subjects of study in particular: child culture, household economics, and civic life. A new mother herself by adoption, Montgomery believed it was a mistake to think that understanding of child culture would develop naturally "with the mother love." Even though it was "our specialty, our God-given right of dominion,"[50] motherhood ought to be pursued as a science, particularly by the modern woman, who had overlooked the subject, in Montgomery's opinion. "When there are more children well born and well bred, we will need fewer reformatories," she told her audience, and she lauded Rochester's kindergarten program as an example of what she meant by "scientific child culture."[51]

Montgomery believed household economics, studied and applied scientifically, might relieve household drudgery. Women who hated managing a home because they could not do it well might be empowered by a scientific approach. For example, she pointed out that nutrition could be studied scientifically in relation to the development of the body, disease prevention, the problem of intemperance, and limited economic resources.

Those two subjects, child culture and home economics, place Montgomery in the Progressive Era tradition of "educated motherhood." The post-revolutionary ideal of "Republican motherhood" taught women that it was their job to inculcate in their children the virtues necessary for citizenship, and the Victorian ideal of True Womanhood taught them that women's moral natures made them especially suited to the task. According to the ideology of educated motherhood, woman's natural gifts and inclination toward motherhood were not enough. Women must make motherhood a field of practical, scientific study that included the topics of child psychology, physical development, health, nutrition, sanitation, and education. The realm of responsibility encompassed by motherhood expanded from the home into the kindergartens, schools, markets, factories, streets, and community at large. Wherever children and families lived and moved, educated motherhood had an interest and a duty.

Educated motherhood inspired women to pursue an impressive range of maternal reforms in the Progressive Era, including free kindergartens, child labor legislation, compulsory education legislation, and municipal clinics for pregnant women and children. According to Sheila Rothman, "To an unprecedented degree, it became the charge of the mother and the state to pursue the best interests of the child."[52] Educated motherhood became a major rationalization and motivation for women's higher education, careers in social service, and advocacy of equal suffrage.

Montgomery offered a practical suggestion for maternal reform. At Hull House in Chicago, she said, one of the "original founders" gathered a collection of pictures for a lending library, where for five cents poor people could rent a picture for two weeks and then exchange it for another. In this way, she thought, the poor enjoyed the "great advantage" of viewing beautiful and inspiring pictures.[53]

Likewise, a group of women could purchase a "home library" of eighteen books and two periodicals that were "of special interest to children." This library, kept in a "rough case," could be delivered to "some poor home in the most wretched quarter of the city." The child who lived there would take a turn as "the librarian." That child would be responsible for issuing books to a group of about ten children, with whom "some noted woman" would meet weekly in the librarian's home. There she would read with the children and discuss the books until the group exhausted the supply. Then it would be traded for the library of another group. In this way, Montgomery asserted, the children of the poor gained "the reading habit." It kept girls "off the street, and the boys from the saloons," and it planted "the seeds of intellectual culture."[54]

Montgomery believed the modern woman ought to be involved in the civic life of the city. Women could do a great deal, she thought, without waiting for full political rights. Like child culture and household economics, civic life yielded itself to a scientific approach. "There are all the elements of sociology right in our little city," she said. The WEIU ought to study Rochester's life, streets, educational system, parks, government, social services, and charities. The modern woman could do a great deal of good for the city by asking questions related to politics and referenda, or by studying art, architecture and aesthetics, and applying this knowledge to the development of the city and its buildings.[55]

A Theoretically Limitless Woman's Sphere

The basic strategy at work in Montgomery's maternalist approach was to redefine the woman's sphere to include more and more of public life. This strategy allowed women the protection of respectability and conservatism while actually undercutting the status quo and empowering women for public political action. Montgomery found disagreement among her constituency of women on the question of suffrage, so she decided to work pragmatically on the issues where there was agreement. To the women of the WEIU she wrote: "The whole belongs to us—every one. Whether we believe in the desirability of women expressing their convictions at the polls or not, and there is a very decided difference of opinion in our membership on that question, there can be no doubt as to the propriety and duty of each true woman doing her part in the betterment of the city here and now."[56] She encouraged her women to assert their "city patriotism," and to begin where they were, with the problems that presented themselves at the women's doorsteps.

> Whatever our views or lack of views on the subject of women's participating in national politics, what rational creature can deny their ability and duty to take a hand in city affairs? The management of a city is simply bigger housekeeping, involving questions upon which the women of a city are quite as intelligent and far more interested than are men. Clean streets, pure food supplies, efficient schools, protection of the young, these are our subjects, this is our preserve. What right have we to stand one side in placid bovine stupidity while they are being settled?[57]

Montgomery viewed her own work of educating the women of WEIU as a contribution to broader democracy. "Time spent in study, discussion, dissemination of information, is not wasted if it is slowly training a body of public-spirited women who realize that they have duties to the whole body politic."[58] Through her lectures, which covered a broad array of topics, from home economics to municipal reform to international politics, Montgomery was trying to equip women intellectually for the challenges, responsibilities, and duties of citizenship. Feminist scholar Aileen Kraditor found that late nineteenth-century suffragists sometimes acknowledged that, while women were theoretically equal to men in terms of their humanity, they were at a practical disadvantage because of their subjection; but they needed only remedial education to become equal in fact.[59] From this point of view, Montgomery's educational work for the WEIU can be seen as remedial political education for women.

Woman's Influence in American Democracy

Even though Montgomery was willing to help women engage the public sphere at whatever level they felt comfortable, she believed women's voices needed to be heard in national and international affairs. She believed women's voices were needed to counterbalance the perspectives and prejudices of men. For example, in 1896 during the prelude to the Spanish-American War, she told the women of the WEIU that the voices of women in national affairs would help to bring about "a more pacific tone" and that "the flippancy of some people in treating of war" was "disgusting." Why, she asked, "should we regard in a nation as glorious that which we despise in an individual?" She declared that "we [presumably women] are horrified" at the thought of the "billions of treasure wrung from the people" and the "millions of lives sacrificed to sate the ambitions of statesmen." She urged her audience to "read and think about it, that we may act intelligently, and not hastily like a lot of schoolboys."[60]

Montgomery gave a great deal of her time and energy to ensure that the women of Rochester would be able to think and act intelligently on major national and international issues. For example, one lecture in 1895 was dedicated exclusively to explaining in detail the committee structure of the U.S. Congress and how that structure influenced the legislative process, and another in 1897 covered the electoral college, the powers of the president, and the powers and duties of cabinet officials.[61] The journalist who reported the meeting for the *Democrat and Chronicle* believed that the large attendance was evidence of "the interest which women are taking in politics," as if it were a novelty.[62] Montgomery cherished the openness of American politics although she recognized it was a rarity in her world. She once told the WEIU women: "Our political life . . . is very little understood by foreign nations. In their eyes our habit of criticizing public men is an evidence of weakness rather than as we look at it, merely an expression of our approval or disapproval of public acts."[63]

Montgomery believed women had a duty to be politically informed, and she told her audience that "the time was coming when an American woman not interested in politics would be as rare as a French woman who does not care for art." She insisted that America's political institutions were a "gift" to the "stock of ideas" that had "enriched the world." She reminded her audience that "the American people will be expressing their will" through the upcoming session of Congress and their acts would "make our history." She thought it was "a wholesome thing" for elected officials to know that "the voice of the people can rise up and put them all out." Montgomery warned her audience not to be distracted by the pageantry of the Congress and not to put too much stock in the public speeches. Most of the real business of the Congress went on behind closed doors in the committee process, she asserted. She encouraged women to pay attention to the issues and to how their representatives actually voted, and to inform their representatives of their opinions on important issues. Women "need not wait for the suffrage to use their influence in directing affairs," she said.[64]

Women's historians and historians of the Progressive movement have noted the significance of the maternalist political influence for the expansion of government regulation and intervention in the Progressive Era.[65] At the municipal level, through the expanded social welfare role of the educational system, and at the state and federal levels, through protective labor legislation and ultimately the creation of the public welfare agencies such as the Children's Bureau, maternalist political thinkers usually favored an expanding role for government in the lives of individuals and families. Montgomery was no exception.

In 1897 Montgomery gave a lecture before the WEIU in which she advocated nationalization of telegraph lines. Her lecture sparked a local controversy and prodded the editors of the *Herald* to brand her a "socialistic propagandist."[66] In her reply to their critique, Montgomery sketched her views on the relation of individual interests and public interests, and on the difference between political rights and economic interests. She described herself as "a most conservative believer in the right of private property, the value of individual enterprise, the sacredness of the home, the justice and stability of American institutions, and the supreme loveliness and power of the gospel of

Christ." In her view, the nationalization of the postal telegraph was constitutional under Article One, Section Eight of the Constitution of the United
States, which granted to Congress the right to create the federal postal service. She claimed that "rights are sacred, be they the right of many or few,
rich or poor. Interests are not sacred." Consequently she believed that "the
private interests of the few ought not be allowed to interfere" with a policy
that would "be for the benefit of the whole nation." She believed that nation-
alizing the postal telegraph would broaden the service to areas of the country
where the monopolists of the Western Union had found it unprofitable to go,
and it would reduce the price so that telegraph service would become more
affordable to persons of modest means. With the telegraph, like the postal
service, government would provide an essential and legitimate service to the
people of the nation.[67]

A nationalized postal telegraph was just one example of how Montgomery
believed government ought to serve the people. She commended Birmingham,
England, as "almost a perfect city" because of the many municipal services and
reforms it undertook. These included a reduction in the hours of the work-
day from ten to eight with no reduction in wages, "public swimming baths"
and libraries, redevelopment in the tenement district, which Montgomery
credited with a reduction in the death rate from 53 percent to 21 percent over
a decade, and "compulsory thrift among the working classes" and the establishment of a public pension system for city workers.[68] Glasgow, Scotland,
also drew her praise for its many progressive municipal reforms. Among the
most impressive to Montgomery were the many varieties of sanitary inspec-
tors, including women who went house to house "in aid of household cleanliness" and who did "untold good in their systematic visitation among the very
poor: their official position giving weight to their suggestions."[69]

Another area in which Montgomery advocated government regulation
was the liquor traffic. At this point in her career, she was not an advocate of
Prohibition because she did not believe it was a practical solution, and she
was not sure that "the wise and discriminating class" should be completely
prohibited from drinking alcohol. Nevertheless, she did want to see the sales
of intoxicants controlled by the municipal government because she believed a
carefully administered government program would prevent abuse and remove
the profit motive from the liquor trade. Perhaps the best modern comparison
with what Montgomery had in mind is a contemporary state-run lottery.

Under Montgomery's scheme, a city government would grant a franchise to a company to run a number of carefully regulated establishments where patrons could purchase liquor by the drink. Investors in the company would get a return of 6 percent. The remainder of the profits would be invested in a special fund for major municipal expenditures over and above the normal operations funded by taxes. Montgomery believed the regulations placed on the sale of liquor combined with the elimination of the profit motive would help to eliminate drunkenness as well as help to purify municipal politics. In her view, "the immense profits and large fortunes to be made" blinded people to the real consequences of the liquor trade and encouraged government corruption.[70]

Montgomery understood that the plan was controversial. Some people objected that "the taxpayer becomes debauched when it is seen what can be brought from the profits. The thought that charities are supported and public places of amusements and recreation are furnished" was demoralizing to the public, according to some. Nevertheless, Montgomery felt this measure was justified because she believed that the use of liquor was responsible in great measure for "idiocy, blindness, epilepsy and crime." These were problems that affected the interests of the entire community, and Montgomery believed they demanded the response of government.[71]

Educating Women in International Affairs

In addition to domestic political issues, Montgomery often lectured on international political affairs. She examined the political and social institutions of numerous countries and addressed American political interests in relation to those countries. In a lecture on Venezuela, for example, she traced the history of European colonial intervention in the region, the Venezuelan struggle for independence, the Monroe Doctrine, and how it related to President Grover Cleveland's intervention in the border dispute that was ongoing in 1895 between Venezuela and Great Britain.[72]

Montgomery supported the efforts of people everywhere to secure for themselves the rights and freedoms enjoyed by American citizens. In 1896 she spoke very sympathetically about Cuba's efforts to win independence from Spain, and she was critical of the failure of Ulysses S. Grant's administration to aid Cuba in its initial bid for independence in the Ten Years' War (1868–1878). Spain, according to Montgomery, had made the mistake of clinging to a feudal past rather than embracing the liberal influences of the French Revolution represented by the unimplemented constitution of 1812. Spain was "blinded" by "superstitions and traditions" and thus refused to "accord to Cubans the same laws and liberties as those enjoyed by the Spaniards." The Cubans made "a gallant struggle" in this war, but the United States, eager to annex Cuba for itself, failed to recognize the Cubans' right to belligerency. Thus, after losing 45,000 people, "Cuban liberties were again manacled." Spain continued its oppressive policies, and in 1895 the Cubans, "influenced by the same principles which caused our forefathers to throw off the yoke of England," rebelled again, "preferring the evils of war to submission to Spanish tyranny." According to Montgomery, "the whole Cuban people are clamoring and struggling for freedom with an energy born of despair."[73]

It is apparent from her comments on Spain that Montgomery was influenced by the so-called Black Legend, and especially by one version of it, which Richard L. Kagan called "Prescott's Paradigm."[74] Proponents of the Black Legend alleged that Spain developed a peculiar, exceptional, and immutable national character in contrast to the rest of Europe. Alleged character traits included fanatical Catholicism, cruel authoritarianism, rapacious greed, cultural decadence, political corruption, pervasive indolence and unenlightened bigotry.[75] Many of the features of the Black Legend derived from the criticisms of Bartolomé de Las Casas, who objected to the cruelty and greed that he witnessed in Spain's colonial territories in America. Las Casas, a Dominican priest from Seville, Spain, was a missionary to the New World from 1502 to 1547. His most famous work, *The Devastation of the Indies: A Brief Account,*[76] was controversial when it was first published in 1552, and the controversy has hardly abated in the subsequent centuries. Sixteenth-century Protestants in England and the Netherlands capitalized on Las Casas to excoriate all things Spanish. In the seventeenth and eighteenth centuries, the Black Legend was augmented by assertions of Spanish cultural declension and malaise.[77]

That William H. Prescott (1796–1859), the first American historian to specialize in Spanish history, was influenced by the Black Legend is understandable given the influence of that theory in the United States in the nineteenth century. What made Prescott's work significant was the value of his comparative methodology as nationalistic propaganda. He was the first American historian to approach the history of Spain as the antithesis of the history of the United States. For Prescott, Spain was antimodern. In matters of religion, Spain was fanatically Catholic and intolerant. Royal absolutism and corruption paralyzed Spanish political institutions. The unproductive wealth that flowed from the Spanish empire made Spain indolent and disinclined to invest in industry. This combination of defects stunted Spain's economic growth and inhibited her national competitiveness. In contrast, Prescott believed the United States was characterized by broad religious tolerance and republican political institutions that unleashed the creative economic spirit required for a successful nation.[78]

While there is no direct evidence that Montgomery had read Prescott, or perhaps one of his disciples, such as John Lathrop Motley or Henry Charles Lea, her interpretation of Spanish history was so remarkably close to his that the conclusion is almost unavoidable. In any case, most nineteenth-century Baptists would have accepted Prescott's Paradigm as validation of their own anti-Catholic theological and political views. Even twenty-four years later, Montgomery's views of the Roman Catholic Church remained harshly critical.[79]

Montgomery believed Spain was "peculiar in development" among the states of Europe because she maintained "a medieval conservatism in protecting her hierarchy and priesthood" and failed to enlighten and educate the mass of the people. According to Montgomery, the "atrocious cruelty of the Spaniard" was a consequence of Spain's high rate of illiteracy (then 70 percent, according to Montgomery) combined with "excessive religious superstition and bigotry" and "a general inertia of priesthood and people bound in religious subservience."[80] In Montgomery's view Spain lacked all of the qualities that made great and progressive nations: enlightenment, freedom, and equality.

Nevertheless, at the conclusion of the Spanish-American War, Montgomery did not advocate immediate autonomy for any of the former Spanish colonies. The United States annexed Hawaii by an act of congress and by treaty with Spain took control of the Philippines, Guam, Cuba, and Puerto Rico. Montgomery's discussion of the Spanish-American War covered all of the major issues that were debated in the national press by the leading Protestant clergymen of the day.[81] Sydney Ahlstrom said the Protestant churches in America were able in a very short time "to convert the war into a crusade and to rationalize imperialism as a missionary obligation."[82]

Montgomery believed, on the basis of reports commissioned by President McKinley, that the Spanish colonies were incapable of self-rule according to democratic principles. Therefore, it was incumbent upon the United States to exercise a benevolent authority over them until they could be made ready to rule themselves. "We went into the war with the promise to free a people who had been oppressed for hundreds of years. Our sympathies were all with the poor Cubans who had fought to free themselves from the yoke of a powerful tyrant." But post-war examination had made Americans "better informed" on the conditions prevailing in Cuba, and "a change in the sentiment of the people" had occurred. "We find the Cubans to be an illiterate people utterly incapable of self-government. . . . The government of which they boasted never existed except on paper; they have no government and never had." She believed that the Cubans "need to be helped for many years to come. They need to be taught to govern themselves." It would be up to the United States to "develop the best in them, and to keep the worst influence below the surface."[83] The United States, in Montgomery's view, would not be so much an imperial power as the moral guardian of the Cubans as they grew into the responsibilities of liberty.

Christopher A. Vaughan studied responses to the Spanish-American War in the secular and religious press, and he found a prevailing spirit of paternalism, tinged with racism, that regarded native peoples as children in need of benevolent guidance from the United States.[84] Richard Hofstadter found that Social Darwinism contributed to an already substantial myth of Anglo Saxon superiority, and many, such as Theodore Roosevelt, who favored America's expansion into imperialism used both Social Darwinism and the Anglo-Saxon myth to buttress their arguments. Others, not necessarily motivated by economic imperialism, saw the global political landscape as a contest of the survival of the fittest between the races, and they believed that the white races must conquer the dark races or be overwhelmed. Anti-imperialists ignored the Anglo Saxon myth and theories or racial destiny. Instead they appealed to America's republican traditions of individual and civil liberty, and they claimed that imperialism was un-American under any circumstances. They argued from a Darwinian perspective that war made a race unfit because it eliminated the youngest and strongest members of the race.[85]

Montgomery's lectures, as reported in the newspapers, show no evidence that she used arguments based on racial superiority or Social Darwinism. She was more interested in the extension of democracy. Clearly she believed the peoples of the former Spanish colonies were capable of developing and maintaining democratic political institutions, but she believed they had never had the opportunity. America's duty, she believed, was to provide protection until nascent democracy could take root and flourish.

If Cuba required American guardianship, the situation in the Philippines was even worse, according to Montgomery. The question of the disposition of the Philippines was much more troubling to many Americans than that of Cuba. The Philippines fell to America almost by default after the destruction of the Spanish fleet in Manila Bay by Commodore Dewey on 1 May 1898—almost two months before the engagement of American and Spanish forces in Cuba. After the brief war and Spain's capitulation, some in the United States suggested returning the Philippines to Spanish control, or selling them to England, because they believed that the United States could not manage such a far-flung empire and that the practice of holding colonial territories was a threat to America's most sacred political principles and institutions. For example, Presbyterian clergyman Henry Van Dyke wanted to know: "Are we still loyal to the principles of our forefathers . . . or are we now ready to sell the American birthright for a mess of pottage in the Philippines?"[86] David Starr Jordan, president of Stanford University, called the conquest of the Philippines "un-American; it is contrary to our traditions; it is delicious; it is intoxicating."[87] Montgomery disagreed with such sentiments. She asserted that to return the Philippines to Spanish control would be "a turning back the progress of civilization." Nevertheless, she hoped that the United States would "be generous rather than just in dealing with a weaker nation [Spain]" so that the United States would gain credit in the eyes of the world.[88]

As the situation in the Philippines turned ugly and the Filipino freedom fighters turned their guns against the American forces, Montgomery was hard pressed to explain why American occupation remained necessary. Following the report of the Schurman Commission,[89] she came to believe that the Filipinos had never really aimed at political independence anyway, but had taken up arms against Spain to win the expulsion of the Catholic friars who dominated the colony and to expand their civil liberties and political rights. She assured her audience that in the original conflict with Filipino rebels the United States had been attacked first, and that the Filipino rebels had intended to "loot and plunder" Manila until the Americans stopped them. American presence was necessary to maintain peace and good order, and the American authorities were doing everything in their power to establish self-government in the municipalities as a means of training the people for eventual national self-government.[90]

Montgomery believed the United States had a responsibility to the Filipinos as well as the Cubans to govern them benevolently until they could govern themselves. In her view, nothing less than the national character of the United States was at stake in the exercise of global leadership. If great wealth and resources had placed the United States in a position of global power, Montgomery believed only careful use of that power according to the principles of liberty and justice would yield the moral authority necessary for leadership among the nations. She was joined in her sentiments by several prominent American clergymen, including Washington Gladden and eventually Lyman Abbott, who, after some wavering, called the new policy an "imperialism of liberty."[91] Walter Rauschenbusch believed God had "made clear his will for us by the irrepressible force of events" and suggested that God was calling the nation from a youth of national isolation into an adulthood of global leadership. He declared: "As a nation we must walk by faith and not by sight" into a "trackless future."[92]

While Montgomery supported the idea that the United States should maintain control of Cuba and the Philippines, she thought that the nation must "repudiate the old medieval idea of colonization." She believed that Spain's practice represented the old model—using colonies "as plunder to enrich their nobles and aristocracy," and it was this practice that led Spain to ruin. She commended to her audience instead the British model, which she felt was more in keeping with the political principles of the United States. Great Britain, Montgomery claimed, was "the exponent of a new colonial idea, which is to develop her people to the highest civilization and greatest usefulness; not to enrich the mother country, but to develop her colonies for the benefit of the whole world."[93] The power of empire ought to be moral and benevolent, in Montgomery's view. The United States must not exploit the colonies, but serve as a political guardian and cultural mentor of colonized peoples until they were ready to rule themselves according to democratic principles.[94]

In the Philippines, for example, Montgomery lauded efforts to educate Filipinos in democracy by setting up municipal governments according to democratic principles and training natives for the duties of public office. While the early results of this effort were promising, in her view, the Filipinos were still "utterly incapable" of self-government. Nevertheless, she believed in the power of education to remedy the situation and "declared that what is needed more than an army of occupation is an army of good Yankee schoolma'ams."[95] She asked her audience to "have faith in the magnificent citizenship of the American people, who have proved their ability and honesty to deal with perplexing problems."[96]

While Montgomery believed that American democracy was progressive, she did not necessarily believe it was the only progressive democracy on the planet. In fact she said that the Australian Commonwealth, which had been constituted in 1900, was "a compromise between the constitution of the United States and of Canada, and in some respects, it is more democratic than either." Montgomery's lecture on the Australian Commonwealth showed that she shared the well-documented progressive affinity for direct democracy.[97] She believed Australia was "the most radical democracy in expressing the will of the people that we have in the English-speaking world" because it preserved so much authority for the state-level governments and because it was so responsive to direct majority rule. "The will of the majority of the people can be carried into effect in six months after election, while ours is far more difficult and requires four or five years for a change of policy."[98]

The benevolent influence of American nationalism was demonstrated, Montgomery thought, in the slow but steady progress she saw in the empire of China, which she credited in large part to American influence. Montgomery cited the reorganization of the University of China along American lines, a new public school system similar to that in the United States, the granting of franchises for the construction of railroads, as well as other more subtle reforms in the government bureaucracy, as results of American influence. She told her audience that "they should be proud of the part Americans have taken in this change in China."[99] Montgomery's attitude toward China, expressed in the year prior to the Boxer Rebellion, while laced with paternalism, was much more positive than the views Robert McClellan found reflected in missionary sources written about the same time.[100]

Montgomery often expressed concern about America's competitiveness and supremacy among the nations. While she was not an advocate of war, she was pleased that the Spanish-American War had "settled our position as the leading nation of this continent." In fact, she believed that the war had established the United States as a leading world power, and she quoted from a German editorial which, according to Montgomery, suggested that "in thinking of the great resources and wealth of this country, it cannot be compared with any other nation, but it must be compared with the whole world."[101]

The construction of the Panama Canal would be a symbol of the progress of the American nation, according to Montgomery. She quoted a Native American chief who characterized the difference between his people and the whites, saying, "We walk in the paths our fathers trod, while the white men build roads for their children." She thought this symbolized beautifully the difference in general between civilized and primitive peoples. She said, "The highways and waterways of the world have been a true expression of the advance of civilization since the beginning of history. They are the keys which unlock the nations and open them to the outside world." She believed that "the Pacific is the coming sea of the world and seven great nations are struggling for possession of its ports and wrestling for commercial supremacy." She believed the canal would give the United States a competitive advantage over England in relation to trade with Japan and China because it would bring the port of New York closer than Liverpool to the Eastern powers.[102]

Montgomery: A Second-Generation Domestic Feminist

The broad political content of Montgomery's lectures begs the question: was there more to domestic feminism than municipal housekeeping? Apparently there was. Montgomery was trying to educate women for citizenship—not just citizenship in a woman's sphere, but full citizenship albeit exercised in a womanly way. Although Montgomery's tone was generally more conservative than that of Susan B. Anthony and the leaders of the first generation of suffragists, many of her feminist arguments could have come from Anthony herself, and they were certainly characteristic of the more conservative younger generation of late nineteenth-century feminist leaders who were her contemporaries. As the suffrage cause became more respectable and mainstream, and as the women's movement made advances in other areas of society, women who were not radicals in other respects began to join the ranks, and the movement in the last decade of the nineteenth century became more conservative.[103] Montgomery advocated suffrage as one of many causes she supported. Nevertheless, like all good orators, she matched her rhetoric to her audience. When it served her purpose, she was willing to put suffrage aside and focus on other more attainable goals. Still, in substance her ideas were consistent with the broad range of feminist thought in her day.

Like late nineteenth-century domestic feminist thought generally, Montgomery's arguments move in more than one direction at the same time. She insisted on women's equality with men as human beings and as citizens, yet she argued for including women in public life because of the alleged unique contribution only women could make. Nancy F. Cott called this the "Janus face" of nineteenth-century feminism.[104] Montgomery was not "radical" if radical means insistence on suffrage as the test of loyalty to the woman's cause. She did believe in suffrage and said so; and like many of her contemporaries in the women's club movement, she was just as practically involved in political questions as the women of her generation who were more well known as suffragists. Montgomery's feminism was merely expressed in other directions than suffrage. She wanted to educate women for the day when they would have the vote—a day that she believed would inevitably arrive because she believed that democracy was "a mighty current that is altering the face of the earth."[105] She wanted to prepare them to use the vote intelligently.

One might wonder why she did not become more politically active on the suffrage question. Some have suggested a decision on her part to give more emphasis to religious work,[106] but there is no evidence to support that claim in the early years of her career. In fact, while she never stopped teaching her women's Bible class and speaking to religious audiences on various occasions, it is evident that most of her energy was given to the WEIU and its causes.

What about the theory that evangelical feminists were constrained in part by the conservatism of evangelical religious belief? In her examination of the process by which women came to feminist consciousness in nineteenth-century Rochester, Nancy L. Hewett claimed that "Yankee evangelicals" tended to choose forms of association and activism that did not challenge the economic organization, race relations, social stratification, or gender hierarchy of the community, while "agrarian Quakers" tended to question the justice and morality of the status quo.[107] Nancy F. Cott concluded that evangelical religion in the nineteenth century tended both to elevate women—to place them on a pedestal and give them sole responsibility for the woman's sphere—and to subjugate them to men at the same time, for the sake of social stability. Nevertheless, women had to "escape from the containment of conventional evangelical Protestantism" in order to become full-fledged suffragists.[108] Shirley S. Garrett implied a distinction between "church" and "radical" feminism without defining it precisely.[109] Carolyn Haynes concluded that Christian feminists had to choose between fighting pragmatically against the social evils that affected women without attacking institutional Protestantism, or attacking Protestantism and being ineffective when it came to practical reform.[110]

There is no evidence to suggest that Montgomery felt compelled by her evangelical religious convictions to limit her personal activities. On the contrary, by all accounts she felt empowered by her education, her family background, her husband, and her religious community to follow her own sense of vocation. To that extent Montgomery's experience seems to validate Hewett's thesis. Nevertheless, the most convincing answer lies in the direction of Karen Blair's thesis. Montgomery was one of many in the women's club movement whom Blair described as "feminists under the skin, developing a significant and popular strategy for autonomy, however much they may have maintained their ideological cover."[111] Although Montgomery remained quite prominent in her local church and denominational organizations, she chose the WEIU as her main vehicle for municipal reform. That decision reflected her liberty to act beyond the boundaries of church and home, as well as her astute judgment. The WEIU offered a broader base of support and influence in the political life of Rochester than sectarian organizations would have allowed.

Montgomery advocated suffrage, but at the same time she asserted that women did not need suffrage to be effective as agents of change. That she was correct was to a great extent due to the work of her more radical predecessors. Montgomery enjoyed the respectability that she gained by upholding the Victorian ideals of virtuous womanhood, and like many women of her generation, she saw no reason to sacrifice it. The domestic feminists of the second generation stood on the shoulders of their older sisters, whose willingness to suffer indignities because of their strong-mindedness gained much ground for all women. The older generation's determined efforts at reform in the causes of abolition, temperance, education, and suffrage, among others, made the way much easier for the next generation. Their organizations, public speeches, petitions, and leadership created a precedent upon which the next generation built. Even the negative reactions they aroused created a foil against which the next generation could contrast themselves in a more positive light.

Like many of her contemporaries, Montgomery wanted the vote, but empowered by all the resources she already commanded, she found many other causes that seemed to her more pressing. As a well-educated, white, middle-class woman related to a family and church that enjoyed broad respect, her decision to refrain from suffrage agitation was made out of a sense of empowerment rather than apathy or impotence. She attempted to broaden women's sphere of influence and to prepare women for unprecedented roles in community service. But instead of abandoning the ideals and virtues associated with womanliness and motherhood, she utilized them strategically. She led the women of Rochester to access the moral authority associated with domesticity as a source of public political empowerment through municipal housekeeping.

Six

SUSAN B. ANTHONY AND HELEN BARRETT MONTGOMERY
An Intergenerational Feminist Partnership

The name of Susan B. Anthony is synonymous with the struggle for women's suffrage in America, and the identification is well deserved. She worked tirelessly throughout her life for a number of reform causes, but above all else she earned a place in American history as one of the foremost advocates of women's rights in her generation. The name of Helen Barrett Montgomery is much lesser known today, especially in feminist circles. Among those who do remember her, she is identified not with suffrage or women's rights, but with the cause of missions and especially with the ecumenical woman's missionary movement. Montgomery, too, was active in many reform causes, but her greatest passion was the cause of women's missions, to which she devoted the greater portion of her adult life. One of the most important questions addressed in this book is the relationship between the causes of Anthony and Montgomery—between women's rights and women's missions.

Despite their differences, in the eyes of many people Anthony and Montgomery were the two leading women of Rochester for more than a decade before Anthony's death in 1906. While Anthony lived, no woman in Rochester could equal her notoriety; and by the end of her life, "Our Susan," as the newspapers called her, had no peers for the respect and affection of the people of Rochester. After Anthony's death, it was apparent to many people that her mantle as Rochester's leading woman had passed to Helen Barrett Montgomery.

Conventional thinking about women's history would rarely associate two women whose lives seem to have had such different trajectories. Anthony was a Quaker who became a Unitarian; Montgomery, a middle-of-the-road Baptist. Anthony was a suffragist activist; Montgomery regarded the suffrage label with ambivalence. Nevertheless, for more than a decade, Susan B. Anthony and Helen Barrett Montgomery worked side by side as leaders of the women's movement in Rochester. Even as they worked together and supported the same causes, the strategies they used and the rhetoric they employed reflected their different generations and priorities, but Anthony and Montgomery were able to forge an effective partnership because their aims were fundamentally the same. They both wanted to empower women for political engagement as women and as citizens, and they wanted to improve opportunities for women in education.

Susan B. Anthony: Suffrage Radical

Susan B. Anthony[1] was born in 1820. Her father, Daniel Anthony, was a Hicksite Quaker of some prominence in the area of Troy, New York, but financial reversals forced him to relocate to the Rochester area in 1845. Susan, a successful schoolteacher, turned down a proposal of marriage from a wealthy Quaker elder and farmer from Vermont to accompany her father to Rochester. Soon after the relocation, Susan B. Anthony received an offer to teach in the female department of the Canajoharie Academy, so she left Rochester. During her four years away from Rochester, she began her lifelong interest in the temperance cause, and in 1849 she gave her first public address to two hundred Daughters of Temperance at Canajoharie.

Anthony returned to Rochester for personal reasons to find that her family had attended the Woman's Rights Convention in Rochester in 1848, an adjourned session of the Seneca Falls convention. Anthony became interested in the antislavery cause, and she and her family joined the Unitarian church because the Rochester Friends were opposed to abolitionist activism. Her final conversion to the woman's rights cause came when she was prevented from speaking from the floor at a New York state convention of the Sons and Daughters of Temperance in 1852. In the antebellum period and during the Civil War she was an upstate New York agent of the American Anti-Slavery Society, in which she worked with Henry and Elizabeth Cady Stanton, Frederick Douglass, and William Lloyd Garrison, among others; and she was a lifelong activist for temperance and women's rights. She withdrew from the Daughters of Temperance and helped to organize the Woman's State Temperance Society in New York in 1852, in which she was joined by Elizabeth Cady Stanton, Amelia Bloomer, and Antoinette Brown, all of whom became forces in the movement for women's rights. In that convention, Anthony advocated the adoption in New York of the "Maine Law," a strong, statewide Prohibition measure recently adopted in Maine. She regarded that speech as her "first declaration for woman suffrage."[2] She attended her first Woman's Rights Convention in Syracuse, New York, the same year, along with suffrage leaders Lucy Stone, Lucretia Mott, and Ernestine Rose.

The women's rights cause led Anthony into a number of reform movements. She worked for better wages for women laborers, for legal protection for the property rights of married women, for women's rights to their children in divorce, for legal protection of children's rights, for the end of the sexual double standard; and for numerous "social purity" causes.

The feminists ceased agitation for women's rights during the Civil War, but when President Lincoln issued the Emancipation Proclamation in 1863, Anthony and Stanton organized the Woman's National Loyal League. The league was the women's vehicle to lobby for full emancipation of all slaves in the Union, not just those of Rebel masters, as the Emancipation Proclamation said. When Congress passed the Thirteenth Amendment, the league ceased operations. Following the Civil War, the debate among the suffragists over the Fourteenth and Fifteenth Amendments resulted in schism, and Anthony and Stanton withdrew from the American Equal Rights Association and organized the radical National Woman Suffrage Association in 1869. Lucy Stone and Henry Blackwell organized its reformist counterpart, the American Woman Suffrage Association, the same year. The organizations merged in 1890 to become the National American Woman Suffrage Association. Susan B. Anthony remained a driving force behind suffrage radicalism until her death in 1906.

Anthony and Montgomery: Clubwomen and Feminists

Founding the Rochester WEIU

Judging from the available evidence, Anthony and Montgomery became acquainted through the women's clubs of Rochester. Montgomery made such a strong impression on the first-generation feminist leaders of Rochester that they turned to her to lead a key new organization. Dr. Sarah R. Adamson Dolley, one of the nation's first female medical doctors and a founder of Rochester's Ignorance Club (1881); the influential Mrs. Mary T. L. Gannett, founder of the Woman's Ethical Club; Susan B. Anthony; and her sister Mary, who founded Rochester's Political Equality Club (1885), joined forces in 1893 to establish the Women's Educational and Industrial Union (WEIU). They called upon Montgomery to become the organization's first president. Montgomery's presidency of the WEIU (1893–1911) was her gateway to broad influence in the social and political affairs of Rochester at the turn of the century.

The WEIU was founded in Rochester on 26 April 1893. Mrs. Harriet Brown Dow, the first recording secretary, who served during Montgomery's entire presidency, called its formation "a strange miscarriage of purpose."[3] About two weeks earlier, on 10 April, Dr. Dolley invited representatives of several Rochester women's clubs to a meeting for the purpose of establishing a Woman's Alliance—a federation of local women's clubs. But a few days before the meeting, an indigent woman who was a stranger in the city collapsed on the street, and the police, having no other place to accommodate her, locked her in the jail overnight until she could be identified. Newspaper reports of the event prompted Susan B. Anthony and Mary Gannett to propose a different sort of organization to the women who gathered at Dolley's invitation at the Chamber of Commerce. Anthony invited Mrs. George W. Townsend, president of the Buffalo Woman's Educational and Industrial Union, to attend the gathering. When Dolley called the meeting to order, Gannett was elected to chair the meeting, and she called on Townsend to address the group.[4]

Townsend described the Buffalo WEIU as an organization modeled after an earlier one in Boston, which provided social, educational, and protective services for women—especially poor and working women. After her address, Dolley moved that the chair appoint a committee to create a plan of organization for a Woman's (later Women's) Educational and Industrial Union. Anthony seconded, and the motion carried.[5]

The WEIUs were instrumental in redirecting the domestic feminism of the women's literary clubs from their cultural focus to the political and social reform emphasis of municipal housekeeping.[6] Mrs. Townsend's Buffalo WEIU disbanded in 1916, apparently because its members believed the organization was no longer needed. The Rochester Union maintained a vibrant existence well into the 1940s.[7]

Mrs. Jean Brooks Greenleaf, a prominent suffragist in New York state whose husband was Rochester's Democratic congressman,[8] was the chairperson who reported on behalf of the organizing committee at the meeting on 26 April.[9] The organizing committee had drafted a constitution and nominated a slate of officers. According to the constitution, which was adopted without amendment, the purpose of the WEIU was exactly the same as that of the original Boston Union:[10] "to increase fellowship among women, in order to promote the best practical methods for securing their educational, industrial and social advancement." The original committees, modeled after the Buffalo organization, were Finance, Legal Protection, Industries and Employment, Philanthropy, Education, and Social Affairs. The membership fee, like Boston and Buffalo,[11] was one dollar per year with a lifetime membership available for fifty dollars. At the conclusion of the 26 April meeting, membership stood at 130.

Among the members of the board were some of the most prominent women in Rochester, such as Matilda G. Morell Bausch, spouse of the eldest son of John Jacob Bausch, cofounder of Bausch & Lomb. Edward Bausch became a prominent optical technician and businessman in his own right. Edwine Blake Danforth's husband was a well-known judge and politician. Marion E. Keeler Kimball was the wife of a noted businessman, art collector, and horticulturist. Miriam Landsberg was married to the liberal rabbi of Berith Kodesh, a prominent German Jewish synagogue. Finally, there was Margaret Durbin Harper Sibley, an antisuffragist whose husband was an influential banker and a benefactor of the University of Rochester.[12] The women at the helm of the WEIU were not radicals. They were ladies. They believed in God and country and home and family. It would have been impossible for Anthony to unite them around the cause of suffrage, but with Anthony's support and under Montgomery's leadership, they could and did build one of the most influential Progressive Era organizations in the city of Rochester.

President of the New York State Federation of Women's Clubs

Montgomery's influence soon extended beyond Rochester. In November 1896, the New York State Federation of Women's Clubs, meeting in Buffalo, elected Montgomery as its president. Jane Cunningham Croly, the founder of Sorosis, a woman's literary club in New York City, founded the General Federation of Women's Clubs in 1890 to link women's clubs across the nation in cooperation, coordination, and communication. The General Federation of Women's Clubs promoted an agenda of domestic feminism that included women's self-improvement and municipal housekeeping—reforms aimed at protecting women and children and improving the quality of urban life. The state-level federations were organized after the General Federation and followed the same agenda. The New York State Federation of Women's Clubs was organized in 1895, a year before Montgomery became president. By 1897 there were two hundred women's clubs in the New York State Federation, representing about 25,000 women, and there were about a hundred and fifty clubs in the state still outside the federation.[13] Montgomery commended the broad reform agenda of the "Woman's Federation" to the WEIU in her lecture on the "New Woman" in 1896, several months before her election as president of the state federation.[14]

According to newspaper reports in the *Herald* and the *Union and Advertiser,* Montgomery was swept into office on the strength of "electioneering" by the Rochester delegation and an address she gave to the meeting on "Comparative Study of Literature"—perhaps an indication that culture study remained an important item along with reform on the agenda of the women's club movement. That Montgomery's paper on comparative literature could excite enthusiasm was confirmation that self-improvement and culture were still very important to the New York State Federation in 1896.

The *Herald* and the *Union and Advertiser* both exulted that a Rochester lady had been "honored." The editors of the *Herald* claimed that she was "one of the ablest and most accomplished ladies in the country, and it is fit that her talents and her work in behalf of women should be thus recognized. Should her health be spared her, we bespeak for her a distinction not second to that of any lady in the United States."[15] Blair found that the federation movement pushed the women's clubs beyond culture and self-improvement toward an agenda of maternalist municipal reform, but that self-improvement never completely disappeared.[16]

Unfortunately Montgomery was able to serve only six months as president of the federation due to a sudden illness that required removing a kidney. But even during her brief presidency, Montgomery pushed the federation toward reform work. The resolutions adopted by the federation in appreciation for her service noted that she laid "plans for practical work which the federated women of New York State may do for the benefit of their generation."[17]

What precisely the illness was is unclear, but it was perhaps what Rose Lattimore Alling described when she reported that Montgomery's family "had to inform her that she had some alarming symptoms" and convinced her to see a doctor, who took X-rays. Alling did not state what the X-rays revealed, but the doctor said: "Why, Mrs. Montgomery, you must have suffered great pain for a long time." According to Alling, Montgomery seemed "puzzled and mildly amused," and said, "No—no, I don't remember any." She underwent surgery, and when Alling visited her afterward, she said, "Hello, Rose! Well, that's over. Joke, wasn't it?"[18] Apparently during her convalescence from this illness, she became a member of the College Woman's Club (founded 1897, later the College Women's Club and the Rochester Branch of the American Association of University Women).[19]

Sharing the Platform with Susan B. Anthony

Just a week after her election to the presidency of the New York State Federation of Women's Clubs, Helen Barrett Montgomery spoke on the platform at a reception in honor of Susan B. Anthony. During the banquet, Montgomery sat with Anthony at the head table, which was sponsored by the Rochester Political Equality Club. Among the many other notable feminists at the head table were Mary S. Anthony, Rev. Dr. Anna Howard Shaw, and Mrs. Mariana W. Chapman, president of the State Suffrage Association. The event came at the conclusion of the state suffrage convention, which met in Rochester that year.

Perhaps the most controversial aspect of the reception was the accidental substitution of "ornate" sherbet (that is, sherbet with liqueur) for the plain sherbet that the committee on arrangements had ordered. Many of the women, club founder Mary S. Anthony included, were offended. Many suffrage women came to the cause as the Anthony sisters did—through the temperance movement. According to the *Herald,* Mary S. Anthony said that the "compound" they were served "placed many of us in an attitude of compromise, if not entire surrender to all temperance principles." Once she learned that the committee was not responsible for the mistake, it appeared "somewhat less vexatious though very regrettable."[20]

Montgomery's so-called toast to the temperance-minded crowd, reported briefly in the *Union and Advertiser,* was entitled, "Woman Suffrage in the Home." Her remarks before this significant gathering of peers, although quite brief, offered clear insight into her views on suffrage and the woman's sphere. She asserted that "the wooly indifference of the mass of American women" to the cause of suffrage was the worst enemy of the cause, rather than the resistance of men. She believed that the misperception of most women "that those who are fighting for political equality are strong minded universally" was the chief impediment to be overcome. Against this misconception, she asserted: "Our conventions are made up of home women, and this movement is a woman's movement. One effect of the movement will be to bring the state into the home, and then again the home into the state." Montgomery's feminism was based upon the assumption, shared by many people of her day, that men and women were endowed with different but complementary physical, intellectual, and emotional capabilities. While she agreed that a woman's first duty was to her home and family, she believed that it was a mistake to segregate the woman's sphere completely from the public world. "We need the influence and assistance [of the home] in our state affairs," she asserted.[21]

In 1898 Montgomery once again shared the platform with Susan B. Anthony at the dedication of a new building for the Young Women's Christian Association (YWCA) in Rochester. The YWCA movement began in Boston in 1866 and soon spread nationwide. According to Sheila Rothman, its goal was to protect and promote "virtuous womanhood" among country girls moving to the city—an evangelical response to the effects of industrialism and urbanization on young women who worked away from home.[22] The YWCA attempted to provide a wholesome, evangelical, homelike atmosphere where young single women could find fellowship, recreation, self-cultivation, culture, and support. Young single women could rent rooms; hear lectures on a variety of religious, cultural, and reform topics; take classes to improve job skills; get help with job placement; or find an older woman eager to become a friend and mentor in the ways of womanly virtue. The leaders of the YWCA encouraged young women to take jobs as domestic servants in the homes of respectable middle-class families because it was regarded as more digni-fied work than factory labor, and they tried to organize women's clubs to provide the young women with refined entertainment and opportunities for self-improvement.[23] The YWCA promoted the institutions of domestic feminism among its constituency.

According to the report in the *Democrat and Chronicle,* Anthony used the occasion of the YWCA building dedication to give a rousing suffrage address. In her view the essential problem for women was an absence of political power. "Women have not a single power to make the laws that govern these conditions to prevent these miseries among humanity," she said. But like Montgomery and the domestic feminists, she believed that women would purify politics. If women could vote, she said, they would "give us a clean, honest administration." In her view, the strategy of the YWCA was palliative but not remedial. The women of the YWCA were "busy repairing damages instead of going to the bottom and changing the social conditions that make the damages. . . . I would not have you do less than you are doing towards repairing the damages, but I would have you set about changing the conditions that produce these damages." Turning to the assembled clergy who shared the platform with her, she insisted that they ought to support women's suffrage because women were their best allies. Women's suffrage would shift the balance of power in their favor and give them a political advantage over the "saloon men" who helped create the social conditions that institutions like the YWCA sought to mitigate. She did not mind being called "strong minded," she declared, if by her activities she could "make conditions better and easier for women."[24]

In contrast to Anthony's demand for women's political power through the ballot, Montgomery emphasized the more traditional domestic view that women's power rested in their moral influence. "We have been taught to think that men of wealth, the bankers, and the millionaires of the earth, the great statesmen and the politicians are the people who have the greatest influence in the world, but it is a mistake; the young girls are the great but unconscious power in the world." The contrast with Anthony's words could not have been more striking. She remarked that the YWCA and the WEIU were "sister societies" involved in practical reforms. Then, addressing her middle-class audience, she said that it was difficult for women who lived "sheltered lives" to recognize the need for the YWCA. For them it required "consecrated imagination" to understand the danger to the young woman in the city. The YWCA offered a safe, homelike refuge for "thousands of girls who work on the miserable pittances, who have to live in dark, dingy boarding houses in a cheerless seven-by-nine room, many of them almost friendless and alone, and at last there is always the jewel of their womanhood to be cast down."[25] While Montgomery did not disagree with Anthony's analysis, she believed women did have a great wealth of unrealized power— the power of moral influence. Montgomery's comments suggested that the work of the YWCA was important to her not only because it was an example of the moral influence of her middle-class peers, but also because it offered working-class women protection from the corrupting powers of the male-dominated industrial world that would otherwise rob them of their moral purity and destroy the power of their moral influence. Equally important, in Montgomery's view, the YWCA, like the WEIU, was a means of awakening the "unconscious power" of working women and stimulating the "consecrated imagination" of middle-class women, so that both could be applied to the practical needs of the world.

Partners in the Struggle for Coeducation at the University of Rochester

A week after Anthony and Montgomery spoke from the YWCA platform, the trustees of the University of Rochester voted to accept women as students "upon the same terms and under the same conditions as men" if the women of the city could raise the substantial sum of $100,000 for the university.[26] Although a few women had been admitted as special students or allowed to audit classes in the past, they had never been admitted as regular students. Large numbers of women enrolled in the ten-week extension courses offered by the university and were eager for more.[27] The extension movement began in England in the 1870s, but in America it became part of the Progressive agenda to democratize education. Classes were intended for "all classes of men and women" and were designed to give them "systematic university instruction" that would not interfere with their regular employment.[28]

While it was obviously impossible to get the full benefit of a university education in the extension program, it was possible for people to pursue self-improvement through "a broader outlook over the world of literature, science and art." The courses were believed to "stimulate genuine habits of study and research, and thus give assurance of permanent benefit."[29] In addition to the normal lectures, reading lists, and exams, the extension program recommended learning strategies that were familiar to women who were a part of the women's club movement. Students might form Student's Clubs that met between lectures or even after the course was ended, to "continue the study with the advice of the lecturer." If students lived in rural areas that had no library, they were encouraged to ask the state library to supply them with a traveling library for a small fee.[30] Montgomery herself presented a series of university extension lectures in 1895 on "Life in Old Florence."[31]

The women's organizations of the city wanted more than extension education. They had lobbied the trustees for the admission of women since 1890. At that time they were informed that the university was in financial need, and they asked how much money would be required to permit the admission of women.[32] An unrelated attempt on the part of the trustees to raise a $100,000 endowment failed, so the trustees, many of whom supported coeducation anyway, turned to the women in 1898.[33] Susan B. Anthony recognized the facts of the situation and called the decision to accept women students "a war measure . . . a financial necessity now that forces the trustees to take some step to raise money." Characteristic of her aggressive approach, Anthony immediately pressed for even more than the trustees had offered. She thought there should be women on the board of trustees and the faculty. "We would have joint educators as well as joint education," she said. Nevertheless, she and the other leaders of the WEIU immediately started planning to raise the money and prepare the women students for their entrance examinations.[34]

Montgomery was out of town on the day the decision on coeducation was made and announced by the trustees, but she arrived at home on the day of the alumni dinner, and she and other WEIU leaders decided to attend the event. After the other speeches concluded, Montgomery was invited to the platform. She became the first woman ever to address the alumni at the University of Rochester. According to the *Democrat and Chronicle,* she was received in a "hearty manner" with a "lusty college yell" from the assembled alumni as she was escorted to the platform by the interim president of the college, Dr. Samuel A. Lattimore.[35]

The women lost no time in organizing their campaign for the money. The WEIU hosted a meeting at the Watson House (WEIU headquarters) of the officers of all the women's clubs of the city who were interested in the project on 18 June 1898. The women appointed an executive committee of five to lead the effort, including Susan B. Anthony and Montgomery. At least twenty-five women's clubs had representation at the meeting. Several women expressed bitterness that the trustees of the university had put a price on the admission of women. In reply, Rose Lattimore Alling, whose husband was a trustee, explained that the trustees were genuinely in favor of coeducation, but the money was badly needed to build new laboratory facilities and relieve overcrowding. Anthony asserted that "the moneyed people of the city" did not support the university because they regarded it as too narrowly sectarian. The university was begun by Baptists, and in 1898 the by-laws still required the president of the university to be a Baptist. Anthony, a Quaker of broadly democratic sentiments, objected to that rule in particular.[36]

Montgomery, a Baptist, responded to Anthony's concern in a way that both agreed and disagreed: "It ought to be the University of Rochester, not the university of any sect or organization. Jews and Gentiles, Catholics and Protestants have gone through that college, and I don't believe there has ever been a feeling that it belonged to one more than another."[37]

Several of the women were concerned that female students would only be allowed into the university through the back door. Anthony thought that the conditions of the women's entrance ought to be made clear by the trustees. She was already "sounding everyone she knew who had money" and "everyone has said that he would not give a dollar unless it is guaranteed that there is to be no annex and no conditions by which the girls shall not enter on absolutely equal terms with the boys."[38] The University of Rochester came late to coeducation, and by the late 1890s there was a backlash against women in many other schools where women had been admitted. Most colleges and universities considered the education of men their real business and their first priority. The entrance of women was at first a distraction, and later, as women became successful scholars, a threat to male students, educators, and administrators. For example, at the University of Chicago, coeducational from its founding in 1892, women students accounted for 52 percent of the student body and 56 percent of Phi Beta Kappa awards by 1902. That same year, President William Rainey Harper, expressing concerns for the health and welfare of women students, instituted separate classes for women in the freshman and sophomore years. Many other colleges made similar arrangements in the first decade of the twentieth century.[39]

The women finally decided to call a mass meeting to "arouse a strong university sentiment throughout the length and breadth of the city." Montgomery thought the women of the city had an opportunity to promote the university and help it to "unify the whole city intellectually." Anthony asked, "What will have more effect in making happy homes in this country than to educate the women?"[40] In characterizing their appeal to the community in those terms, they pursued two goals simultaneously. They worked for the advancement of women and enlarged opportunities for women's self-improvement, and they worked for the public good of Rochester—for happier homes and a more enlightened community. They wanted to expand the woman's sphere into higher education and at the same time improve the quality of life for their neighbors. It was the agenda of domestic feminism.

At the mass meeting on 23 June the women did not ask for pledges, but did ask for those in attendance to write down the names of everyone they knew who might be interested in contributing to the fund. The women announced their plan to divide the city into districts and assign visitors, "who, if necessary, will make a house to house canvass."[41] Apparently the women initially planned to attack the $100,000 fund in the way women had used petition drives to pursue moral reforms for years—with face-to-face appeals and womanly moral influence. At a subsequent meeting, the executive committee decided to delay its actual fund-raising effort until the fall, but to plan carefully in advance so the work could be done quickly. They planned to pursue large donations first and then go door to door if necessary. They also decided to approach the university trustees and ask if some women might be admitted before the whole amount was raised as a means of interesting people in the project.[42] The trustees were not swayed by the women's appeal.

Apparently the fund-raising work did not go well. The first deadline in 1899 came and went, and the women had not even come close to raising the money. The alumni of the university were "more or less opposed to co-education" even though the faculty favored it.[43] The university trustees, who had been more successful than the women at fund-raising, were able to break ground on a new gymnasium in 1899, which relieved the crowding in Anderson Hall.[44] That, combined with the public sentiment in favor of admitting the women,[45] persuaded the trustees to extend the deadline another year.

Elected to the School Board

Meanwhile, in November 1899, Susan B. Anthony and all of the city's leading women's organizations supported Montgomery's bid to become the first
woman ever elected to the school board in Rochester. This campaign was
another example of an issue-oriented ad hoc Progressive coalition. Rochester's
Good Government movement joined with the women's organizations in
support of Montgomery's candidacy. Without their combined efforts, it is
unlikely that Montgomery could have been elected.

The Good Government Movement in Rochester

In Rochester, as in so many other places, the Progressive Era began with
municipal reforms supported by a coalition of male civic leaders, progressive Protestant clergy, and clubwomen. Under the pressure of a nationwide
depression that affected Rochester from 1893 through 1897, several leading
citizens applied new scrutiny to the performance of city government, and in
the process they discovered waste, incompetence, and outright corruption.
One citizen in particular, Joseph T. Alling, decided to put his energy into an
effort to reform city government. Alling, a successful businessman and dedicated churchman, was a trustee of the University of Rochester, the founder
and leader of the largest men's Bible class in the city, and the president of the
Young Men's Christian Association. He attended in the summer of 1895 in
Cleveland, Ohio, the second National Conference for Good Government,
with three others from the city. Upon their return, a number of other prominent citizens joined them in organizing the bipartisan Good Government
movement in Rochester.[46]

The Good Government movement was a response among municipal
reformers, most of whom represented the older, native-born middle and
upper classes, to the swift growth of cities in the late nineteenth century.
Across the nation, the older urban elite struggled for power with political
bosses, who courted the throngs of immigrants that crowded into tenement
districts. City governments were inadequate to meet the needs of sprawl-
ing urban populations, and they were structured in such a way as to thwart
efforts at coordination. Particular city services were decentralized, disorga-
nized, and largely dominated by ward politics. Political machines and bosses
created corrupt networks that catered to favored business interests and held
power through a spoils system. Middle-class reformers deplored these condi-

tions as wasteful, inefficient, and barbaric. Immigrant laborers, on the other hand, sometimes preferred corrupt ward politics, in which they had some political influence, to reform regimes in which they had little or none.[47]

As early as the 1870s in New York City and in various other cities, citizens formed organizations to oppose government mismanagement and defeat those politicians whom they considered responsible for corruption. They pursued their goals through the classical early Progressive strategies of "investigation, agitation, publication, and the massing of moral forces."[48] The two most important of these groups for the history of the Good Government Movement were the City Club of New York (founded 1892) and the Municipal League of Philadelphia (founded 1891). These two organizations worked together in 1893 to call for a National Conference for Good City Government. The invitation stated that the purpose of the conference was to inquire into the best way to meet "the rapidly growing demand for honest and intelligent government in American cities." Organizers promised that participants would learn how to create public interest in "raising the popular standards of political morality" and facilitate "that feeling of brotherhood and co-operation and that unity of actions and methods, which will multiply their strength and enthusiasm. . . ." Twenty-nine organizations sent delegates to the first conference, and a committee was appointed to organize a National Municipal League, which took place in 1894.[49]

The Cleveland conference, which Alling attended in 1895, was focused on smaller cities like Rochester. The movement was growing. One hundred and eighty municipal reform associations affiliated with the league. Alling went home to Rochester and started a Good Government Club there. Reverend Clarence A. Barbour, the pastor of Lake Avenue Baptist Church, where Montgomery was a member, was Alling's vice president. Alling and his cohorts organized Good Government clubs in every ward of the city and collected seven thousand signatures. While most of the leaders of the new movement were Republicans, the local Democratic Party was the first to endorse their agenda, and the Good Government forces were able to secure the election of their candidate, Democrat George E. Warner, as mayor. Warner was committed to a strict policy of economizing, and he vetoed many appropriations that came to him from the city council.[50]

As the depression waned and prosperity returned to Rochester, Alling and his Good Government forces moved away from strict fiscal economy to support other causes, such as school reform, expanding city services, and beautification. Warner, in his second term, was still committed to fiscal economy, and so he and the Good Government forces parted ways. Although remaining bipartisan, the Good Government movement increasingly aligned itself with Republican leadership. School reform became a central issue. The schools were grossly overcrowded, and many teachers and principals were untrained for the positions they held. Many school buildings were obsolete, unsanitary, or in disrepair, and books and educational materials were often in short supply. Good Government leaders pressed for passage of the Dow Law. Named for Dr. Frank F. Dow, a reform-minded member of the school board whose wife was secretary of the WEIU, the Dow Law provided for a smaller board whose members were elected by the city at-large rather than by wards. The reformers believed a smaller board was the only way to remove cronyism and corruption from the administration of the schools. The measure attracted wide bipartisan support and was passed, so that in 1899 the first members of the new school board were to be elected.[51]

Many of the Good Government leaders' wives were involved with the WEIU or some other club connected with the Local Council of Women. Joseph T. Alling's wife, for example, was a leader in the WEIU and the Woman's Ethical Club. Other Good Government leaders, such as Rev. Clarence A. Barbour, Montgomery's pastor at Lake Avenue Baptist Church, were progressive clergymen who regularly supported their female members' efforts at maternalist municipal reforms. Consequently, Montgomery's candidacy for the school board was regarded as a welcome reform by the Good Government forces, the progressive clergymen, and the clubwomen.

Montgomery as the Women's Candidate

The Ignorance Club had been interested in having a woman on the school board since 1881, but to no avail.[52] In 1891 an organization called the Citizen's Educational Association recommended, among other reforms, the appointment of a woman to the school board. The organization included several professors from the University of Rochester, and it was connected with the Good Government movement, but its impact was hindered by its "fitful existence."[53]

In her 1897 president's address to the WEIU, Montgomery took note of a campaign on the part of a women's club in Philadelphia, the Civic Club, to secure the election of women to the school board of the Seventh Ward of that city. The women were nominated by the Municipal League, one of the founding organizations of the Good Government movement. The Philadelphia women were defeated, but Montgomery said they changed more than 20 percent of the vote. Montgomery carefully explained the strategy used by the Civic Club in a door-to-door canvass of the ward. They tried to verify voter registration lists and eliminate fraudulent entries, to persuade "the woman of the house to influence the men to vote for the woman candidates," to distribute and explain sample ballots, and to collect information and suggestions related to the schools. The women also organized public meetings and parlor meetings, and they supervised polling places on election day. Montgomery emphasized that the Philadelphia women knew from the beginning that they could not win. Their effort was "meant simply to insert the edge of the wedge," she said. She encouraged the WEIU ladies to learn the lessons of the Philadelphia effort because it was a womanly effort. "Forethought, system, care in details, discipline, organization, energy and patience—all these, which we are used to think belong exclusively to our sex—appear clearly and unmistakably in these modest pages." She believed the idea of having a woman on the school board was "perfectly practical and sane."[54] Montgomery and the WEIU worked closely with the Good Government forces to support the Dow Law in 1898.[55]

The passage of the Dow Law created a new opportunity. In January 1899, after the passage of the Dow Law, Susan B. Anthony invited representatives of seventy-three women's organizations to form a Local Council of Women. Forty-seven groups representing more than four thousand women responded to the invitation, and thirty-four groups sent delegates to the organizational meeting.[56] Although initially the local Council of Women declined to name a candidate or call for the election of a woman, they eventually did both, and they made Montgomery their candidate.[57] The women hoped to have both parties nominate Montgomery because they believed that would ensure her election, but the Democrats failed to nominate her. Nevertheless, she stumped as a nonpartisan representative of Rochester's women, who just happened to be nominated by the Republicans. She spoke at Republican ward rallies and at meetings with groups of teachers and mothers.[58] At least one Protestant minister, Dr. Henry H. Stebbins of the Central Church, advocated her election from the pulpit,[59] and the local press was supportive as well.[60]

If Montgomery enjoyed broad support, she was not without critics. In his sermon in support of her candidacy on 30 October, Dr. Stebbins outlined many of the objections raised against her. The objections were plausible because each one was based on a kernel of fact. Consequently, Montgomery was forced to spend a great deal of her time at ward rallies refuting the criticisms. For example, Stebbins said that some people believed her candidacy was "an entering wedge in favor of woman suffrage." In fact, Montgomery had become closely identified with Susan B. Anthony through the work of the WEIU and the coeducational committee. Press reports frequently observed that Montgomery was the most prominent woman in the city, second only to Anthony. Furthermore, Anthony worked as hard as she could in support of Montgomery's candidacy, obviously because she believed it would further the suffrage cause. The Political Equality Club met at Anthony's home on 19 October 1899 to "map out an informal plan of campaign to assist Mrs. Montgomery." The newspaper report noted that the parlors of Anthony's home were decorated with yellow bunting, "the color of the woman suffragists." There is no indication that Montgomery was present, but the association of her name with suffrage was clear.[61] Twelve days later, the Local Council of Women invited Rev. Anna Howard Shaw to Rochester to speak on behalf of the cause of electing a woman to the school board, and Montgomery's behalf.[62] More importantly, Montgomery herself was on the record as in favor of women's suffrage.[63]

Of course Anthony pressed the women's clubs to make Montgomery's candidacy a suffrage issue. The Local Council of Women met at Watson House on the same day as the Political Equality Club meeting. Anthony was there, and she moved that the council thank the Democratic Party delegates who voted for Montgomery at their city convention and the Republican Party for placing her on their ticket. She thought it was appropriate because "it was the first time that a woman had been recognized in this city for a political office." According to press reports, the council voted Anthony's motion down "emphatically" because "that endorsement of it would make a suffrage issue of Mrs. Montgomery's nomination, which issue was not intended or desired." Finally a compromise resolution was passed thanking both parties for nominating several school board candidates, including Montgomery, from the list of candidates that the council had recommended.[64]

Montgomery arrived later, to the applause of the women of the council, and presented a statement that the council adopted as its official platform in regard to her candidacy for the school board. Montgomery wanted to make clear that a woman on the school board was not a novel idea. It had been done elsewhere, and she said that having women on the school board had proven wise in other cities where it had been tried. The remainder of Montgomery's speech epitomized the ideology of domestic feminism. She took the maternal values of True Womanhood and transformed them into reasons that women should become insurgents in the public sphere. She argued that women had a "special fitness" for the work that the school board demanded, a "gift of administration." Furthermore, in her view, caring for the "health, instruction, comfort, culture, and well being of children" was the "province of women." Domesticity and motherhood, she claimed, made women especially fitted for school administration. "Their home life, their intimate association with children, their sympathy with the child's needs and desires" made women particularly suited to the work of the school board. "The mother's point of view is too wise and comprehensive to be unrepresented on the school board," she said.[65]

The moral benefits of womanly influence in the political realm were not lost on Montgomery. The candidacy of a woman would be apolitical and would "help to take the schools out of politics," Montgomery claimed. Women were motivated by maternal rather than political values. A woman on the school board would not seek to "build up political power" because "her constituency will be the school children." A woman would not represent a political party; she would represent "the home." A woman candidate, she claimed, would not be chosen on a political basis; rather, she would be selected on the basis of her "education, general intelligence and special fitness." Consequently, her presence in the contest would raise the standard for all candidates and encourage the voters "to think of the good of the children and not the party" when they made nominations.[66]

Many of Montgomery's comments revealed her middle-class cultural assumptions. A woman on the board would promote economy because women know how to be thrifty, she said. Also women, because of their role as homemakers, have more time to devote to public service than men. As "bread winners," men were forced to devote themselves almost totally to "private business" and had little time to develop the "thorough understanding of the needs of the schools" that was necessary for a school commissioner. Montgomery insisted that there were many educated women who had "large gifts of leisure" to devote to "the general welfare."[67]

Montgomery on the Political Platform

On the campaign trail, even as she delivered speeches from the platform at ward meetings, Montgomery adamantly denied political motives and claimed the legitimacy of domestic benevolence. "I am set to represent the mothers and homes of Rochester. We ask not that women be dragged into politics, but that the schools be lifted out of politics." Her decision to run for a seat on the school board grew out of "a sense of public duty," but it was a duty befitting her gender. "I do not represent women who wish to do the work of men. I wish to do a woman's work in a woman's way."[68]

Late Victorian culture assumed that family was the basic model for society and that the relationships and values of the family, which were based on complementarian gender assumptions, ought to be extended into social relationships. Montgomery drew on those assumptions in her campaign speeches. She believed that fathers and mothers both needed representation on the board, and she asserted that women had a distinctive contribution to make to the administration of the schools. "There is a feminine point of view too valuable to be ignored," she said.[69] She pointed out that families needed mothers as well as fathers to care for them. Often, she observed, mothers looked after details for which fathers had no time or energy. "Why should it be thought a disadvantage for our school system to have the services of a mother and housekeeper?"[70] Furthermore, Montgomery assumed that the differences between men and women complicated communication between the sexes. She believed a woman on the school board would introduce "the mother's tact and sympathy and housewifely experience" to the board's relations with the six hundred women teachers it employed. "They would be brought into closer contact with the aims of the school board by the presence of one of their own sex," she claimed. Likewise, thousands of homes would be "bound by strong ties of interest to the public schools if a woman represented the mothers of the city," she claimed.[71]

Montgomery heard from those who felt a woman's place was in the home, but she refused to allow them to take the high ground of domesticity from her. "I am told that I ought to stay home and wash the dishes," she said, and she agreed that it was "a pretty good objection." In fact, she agreed "perfectly in spirit with those who raised it. The home is first." She admitted that she would be "an untrue woman" if she neglected her responsibility to her family for the sake of any public office. "A wife and mother has and can have no call to any duty that will excuse her for neglecting her home. If the circumstances of that home require that she should wash dishes and sweep floors, and bake bread, and make clothes, any true woman will be glad to do her full share, and will glory in the work done for love's sake." Montgomery affirmed her competency in the domestic sphere: "I can do it, and do it well; for my mother taught all these accomplishments to her daughters."[72] Montgomery turned this argument around on her detractors. She told one audience that she had not "heard that any of the seven gentlemen nominated . . . mean to give up their business if they are elected school commissioners" and she would not give up hers. "They will attend to their work in the office, or factory, or store, or shop, and I will attend to mine in my home."[73] Montgomery believed the responsibilities of men and women were complementary and parallel, not dependent and hierarchical.

In the late nineteenth century, domestic servants were a sign of middle-class respectability, and many middle-class women no longer did the bulk of their own housework. Montgomery believed she had several good reasons for pursuing work outside the home while she hired others to do her domestic work. First of all, it benefited the city's economy. "If all of the women of Rochester were to wash their own dishes and make their own clothes it would mean that thousands of women would have no way to earn their daily bread," she claimed. "It might be cheaper to some individuals, but it would cost the city a great deal." Second, it was a practical benefit to the community. Would anyone tell the trained nurses of the city, "as they perform their beautiful work, that their place is washing dishes?" Or, she asked, do people find fault with women who "care for the unfortunate, or visit the destitute, or relieve suffering, or administer great philanthropies" because they are engaged in public service? Of course, they did not. In fact, Montgomery concluded, those women "whose hands are not fully occupied with household cares" had a positive duty to give "some of their leisure to the general welfare."[74] In her view, the community was a legitimate extension of the domestic sphere.

In fact, duty demanded "an enlarged conception of motherhood"—one large enough to encompass a broad range of municipal reforms. Montgomery believed a "great industrial revolution" had occurred over the previous one hundred years, which had taken much of the drudgery of providing food, clothing, and other daily essentials "out of the house into the factory." This made possible "a higher type of motherhood than the world has ever known." Montgomery believed nineteenth-century industrial civilization gave women (or at least middle-class women like herself) the time to "minister with wise and loving hands to the life that is more than meat, and the body that is more than raiment." Conversely, as women were relieved of the burden of drudgery, "the men of the nation have been put under new burdens of responsibility, and had to meet ever enlarging demands on time and strength." Montgomery disdained the idea that educated women would waste their leisure on "whist clubs and afternoon teas, shopping and matinees." She believed the new circumstances demanded a new definition of the woman's sphere, and women owed "a duty to the commonwealth" in return for the "privilege and influence" they enjoyed. "The enlarging opportunities of our time demand an enlarged conception of motherhood and all that it may mean to the community. We would not destroy the old conceptions of woman's work. We would transform it with new meaning and blessedness."[75]

Against those who might suggest that women serving in public roles would erode the sanctity of motherhood, Montgomery believed that placing a woman in a position of public responsibility on the school board would be good for the institution of motherhood. Montgomery believed it would provide mothers with "a renewed sense of the dignity and privileges of true motherhood" and be a step in the direction of the "higher type of motherhood" that Montgomery desired for Rochester. She envisioned an educated and informed motherhood. "Not more love but more intelligence, not more devotion but better understanding is the great need of us mothers."[76] Montgomery believed in the dignity of motherhood, and she was convinced that giving women the opportunity to leave the isolation of the home and apply their motherly values and skills in the broader sphere of the community would strengthen, elevate, and refine the institution.

Finally, Montgomery made the question a matter of simple fairness. "Is it too much to ask that she who bears and watches and rears the child shall have some part in the direction of that child's education?"[77] It was an obvious point, provided that one agreed with Montgomery's arguments that the material changes in the circumstances of women entailed a new social status, in which women were morally obligated to an enlarged domesticity—to become public citizens and contributing members of the commonwealth.

With these responses, Montgomery deftly engaged the conventional wisdom of her age that placed the woman's sphere in the private world of the home and family. Montgomery asserted that women had a positive *public* duty in those areas where governmental functions touched on questions of home and family. They would enter into that duty, even in the political realm, in an apolitical, feminine way, and their entrance into the public realm would introduce a force of moral transcendence, which tended to raise governmental concerns (in this case, the school question) "out of politics."

Montgomery's critics did not stop with suffrage or the woman's sphere. A group commonly known as the "book ring" (essentially the American Book Company, which supplied textbooks for Rochester's schools, and those connected with city government who had an interest in maintaining the status quo of that relationship, such as Republican Party boss George Aldridge) opposed Montgomery's election. They attributed to Montgomery the comment that if she were elected all public school teachers would be replaced by college graduates within five years.[78] Montgomery flatly denied making the statement. In her denial, she made her egalitarianism clear. "I am against all favoritism and class distinctions and pulls. I would have teachers appointed for merit only. The door ought to be wide open to the daughter of the poorest man for any position for which she can show herself qualified to fill, college training or no college training, influence or no influence."[79]

Others objected that she was liable to act out of narrowly sectarian motives. Montgomery's faith commitment was so well known in the city that it became an issue in the election. Her deepening involvement in social reform and city politics did not force her to curtail her religious activities. When the Monroe Baptist Association met at the Second Baptist Church in Rochester on 5 October 1899, the press reported that Montgomery addressed the meeting on foreign missionary work.[80] Her views on the Spanish-American War were well-known. Some Roman Catholic voters feared that she might harbor bias against Roman Catholic teachers.

Despite her personal views, Montgomery disavowed any such motives. "I hate sectarianism," she told one audience. "I believe that church and state should be entirely separate; that conscience should be absolutely free; that public schools, supported by taxation of all the people, should be free from any tinge of sectarianism. I stand for justice to all religious beliefs, and to those who hold no religious belief."[81] She believed religious instruction belonged in the church and in the home.[82] Montgomery's response to the issue of sectarianism is in harmony with the position most Baptists have taken historically, and no evidence suggests she was insincere on this point. On the contrary, there is abundant evidence to suggest that, although Montgomery obviously shared the anti-Catholic bias of her Baptist denomination, she was willing and able to set aside sectarian concerns and work with all persons of goodwill to promote the common good as she understood it.

Ostensibly, the concerns of Montgomery's Roman Catholic critics were reasonable. Protestant Christianity was a dominant cultural and political force in Rochester at the turn of the century, although Roman Catholicism represented about 35 percent of the city's population.[83] In 1894 the state of New York passed its own version of the "Blaine Amendment," which was intended to prevent Roman Catholic parochial schools from receiving public funds. Anti-Catholic sentiment was resurgent nationally because of the Spanish-American War and locally because of the huge influx of Italian and other Roman Catholic immigrants into Rochester. But if her critics were sincere—and some suggested they were not[84]—they misunderstood Montgomery's attitude toward religious freedom. Where the missionary impulse of her Christian faith and the pluralistic demands of American citizenship produced tension, Montgomery defended the interests of pluralism because she believed that liberty of conscience was a necessary condition for the cultivation of authentic faith in God.

Apparently some antifeminists opposed Montgomery's candidacy, for Susan B. Anthony told the Local Council of Women about a "young girl" who claimed to have convinced her father, brother, and brother-in-law to vote against her. Anthony said that if "a slip of a girl could command three votes," then certainly the women's clubs of Rochester could get her elected. Anthony reminded the women that they "reigned in homes where there are fathers, husbands and brothers." She believed if the women used "their womanly influence" with the voters in their homes, they "had the power to enforce any reform," including Montgomery's election.[85]

Anthony's speech is an interesting example of how she modified her rhetoric to match her audience. When she spoke to the mixed public audience at the dedication of the YWCA building, she claimed that women had no political power because they lacked the vote. When she spoke to the all-female audience of the Local Council of Women in the context of their private meeting room, she emphasized the potential political application of a woman's moral influence.

Montgomery was elected by a substantial majority. Less than a week later, the clubwomen of Rochester welcomed the delegates of the New York State Federation of Women's Clubs to the city for their annual convention. The Rochester women's clubs distributed printed programs of the event to delegates and guests. The programs were distributed in envelopes, and the envelopes bore Susan B. Anthony's picture in the upper left-hand corner and Montgomery's in the lower right-hand corner.[86] It was a tribute to Montgomery's growing stature among the women of Rochester.

Montgomery welcomed the delegates to Rochester, and later, in a speech on "Political Study for Mothers and Teachers," said that women "must part with the past, and not consider that the editorial page has no interest for us."[87] That was a succinct statement of Montgomery's concept of womanhood: progressive and politically engaged, but not hampered by tradition.

Coeducation at the University of Rochester and the Death of Susan B. Anthony

The one nagging failure for Montgomery, as she entered the new century, was her inability to raise the $100,000 needed to open the University of Rochester to women. In January 1900 the fund stood at $33,000 and the Local Council of Women was divided over the best way to proceed.[88] On 12 June 1900, at the fiftieth annual meeting of the university board of trustees, the coeducation committee headed by Montgomery and Anthony informed the trustees that they had pledges and subscriptions for $40,000 and believed they could raise $50,000 but no more. The trustees decided to take what they could get and told the women $50,000 would be acceptable if they could raise it by the September board meeting. By September with the deadline looming, the fund was stalled at $42,000. The women worked through the summer, but the large contributions they expected did not materialize, and they met resistance from the alumni.[89]

On Friday, 7 September, Susan B. Anthony, who had just returned from a trip to Wyoming, was informed that the fund was short by $8,000, and the time would expire by the end of the trustee meeting the next day. On

Saturday morning, Anthony set out to complete the fund, which she was able to do at the very last minute by buttonholing some of her most reliable personal supporters. She met Montgomery at the trustee meeting late in the afternoon, and they reported to the trustees. The trustees were about to refuse one of the four $2,000 pledges, so Anthony guaranteed it with her life insurance policy. On Monday afternoon, she met with the secretary of the board of trustees to find out if all the pledges were legally acceptable to the university. Anthony wrote in her diary: "They let the girls in. He said there was no alternative." The university was coeducational, but the effort cost the aging Anthony dearly. She suffered an attack that was probably a stroke. It left her gravely ill for a week, and she required a doctor's care for more than a month.[90] That illness was the beginning of the long decline that led ultimately to her death.

Susan B. Anthony passed away on 13 March 1906. Ida Husted Harper, Anthony's biographer, noted that Montgomery was "now the most prominent woman of the city."[91] Montgomery, in a tribute to Anthony that was published in the local newspapers, said that Anthony "made all women feel that she had found the secret of keeping charm, interest and vitality to the end of a long life, in the unselfish abandonment of her whole being to the accomplishment of a great and unselfish purpose." The ideology of domesticity demanded that women abandon themselves unselfishly to home and family. Montgomery believed Anthony had demonstrated to the world an even higher womanhood by unselfishly abandoning herself in service to the women of the world. Montgomery wrote a resolution on behalf of the Rochester school board as a memorial to Anthony, which, among other things, lauded her "unselfish kindness and gracious womanliness."[92] On 23 March 1906 Montgomery led the effort of the women's clubs of Rochester to establish a memorial to Anthony. They decided to provide a building for the University of Rochester. The Susan B. Anthony Memorial Building would include "a gymnasium, rooms for social purposes, dormitories for out-of-town students, and also some personal memorial of Miss Anthony."[93]

Coeducation on equal terms at the University of Rochester lasted from 1900 to 1909, although the women faced various forms of discrimination. They were prohibited from using the gymnasium, joining college societies, or working on the school newspaper. The men did not want the women's pictures in the same section as theirs in the yearbook. Rush Rhees, who became president of the university only after the first women were admitted, did not favor coeducation. In a move that would have displeased Anthony, the champion of coeducation, he finally succeeded in moving the women to a so-called co-ordinate College of Women in 1909. The Men's and Women's Colleges remained separate until 1955. Rhees moved the College of Women into a separate building—the Susan B. Anthony Memorial Building.[94]

Seven

The Rochester Women's Educational and Industrial Union

Montgomery's Platform for Municipal Housekeeping

The Rochester Women's Educational and Industrial Union (WEIU) was Montgomery's stepping-stone to broad influence in the political and cultural life of Rochester. During the years of her presidency (1893–1911), the WEIU launched a remarkably broad range of municipal and educational reforms. While many prominent women were involved in the work of the WEIU, Montgomery was perhaps its most widely recognized spokeswoman and its guiding intellect. Under her leadership, the WEIU became the lead institution of the Rochester women's club movement and Montgomery became the most prominent woman in Rochester. Through the broad vision of political and cultural engagement that Montgomery and other leaders articulated, the WEIU became a powerful agent of Progressive reform in Rochester. Its members developed an expansive view of municipal housekeeping that justified their involvement in virtually any public enterprise.

Rochester's Models: Boston and Buffalo

The first WEIU was established in Boston by Harriet Clisby in 1877, a medical doctor born in London. The Boston WEIU had a particular focus on social ethics and practical benevolence, and it swiftly became one of the largest women's clubs in New England. The Boston WEIU set up an exchange where ladies could sell homemade crafts and foodstuffs for income. The union established downtown lunchrooms for women and a private tearoom for members. The Hygiene Committee investigated industrial labor conditions for women and children, sanitary conditions, the industrial smoke nuisance, and other sources of pollution. The WEIU created a job registry and encouraged female factory workers to seek domestic employment. The union established a Protective Committee to help working women with legal or financial complaints against their employers. Moreover the WEIU established training classes that taught job skills like dressmaking and trained young women to work in department stores.[1]

The second WEIU, and the one most important for the history of the Rochester WEIU, was established in Buffalo, New York, in February 1884. The Buffalo union, like Rochester's, was joined by the most prominent ladies in the city, as well as by many who were the wives of middle-class professionals or who were themselves working women of middle-class status. The Buffalo WEIU adopted the program of the Boston union almost without change and added to it several new activities. Like their Boston counterparts, the women of the Buffalo WEIU believed the interaction of wealthy women with poor and working-class women was morally beneficial to the poor and working-class women and so tried to create opportunities for such interaction to take place. One way that could happen was by employing the poor as domestics in upper-class homes. They also worked on a number of other reforms for women, such as hiring a police matron to work with female prisoners, placing female physicians in state institutions, and changing divorce law to make mothers equal guardians of children with fathers. Like the Boston and Rochester unions, the Buffalo WEIU sponsored public lectures and advocated a number of municipal reforms, including better management of truants, establishment of public parks, and abatement of industrial smoke.[2]

The Rochester WEIU's Agenda of Municipal Reform

The Rochester WEIU was modeled carefully after its predecessors, especially the Buffalo union. Its original committees were taken exactly from the Buffalo union's plan of organization. Early on, Montgomery declared that the WEIU existed for the purpose of "affording a higher and better life to the working women."[3] Nevertheless, despite the solidarity implied in the WEIU's name, the WEIU never succeeded at bridging class boundaries and engaging the participation and interest of working-class women. During

Montgomery's tenure as president, the WEIU remained a movement of middle-class and wealthy women whose altruism, compassion, and gentility did not erase their sense of cultural superiority.

Legal Protection for Working Women

The Rochester *Democrat and Chronicle* summarized the annual reports of the WEIU at its first annual meeting. The editors seemed especially impressed with the work of the Legal Protection Committee: "They Seek the Man-Eating Money Brokers and the Omnivorous Sewing Machine Agent in Their Native Jungle and Molify Their Rapacity." Women who worked as industrial or domestic laborers in the late nineteenth century were among the lowest-paid and least-protected workers in America. The wages, working conditions, and legal protection for working women became major issues for the women's rights movement.[4]

Women who were industrial workers often did piecework from their homes, especially if they had small children and no one to care for them. Children, too, provided extra hands for the work. These women were among the lowest-paid classes of industrial workers, and because the law offered such meager protection to the rights of working women, they were often the most abused by their employers and creditors. The Legal Protection Committee of the WEIU offered free legal services to these women as well as domestic workers and other working women. The committee helped them to collect debts and settle disputes with their employers. The Legal Protection Committee was one of the WEIU's most successful committees for many years, until work of the committee was transferred to the newly created United Charities and became autonomous as the Legal Aid Society in 1914.[5]

Domesticity and Culture for Poor and Working Women

The women of the Industrial and Employment Committee reported on the employment office they had established for women looking for employment as seamstresses, tailors, or domestic workers. They had also opened a cooking class at the Mechanics Institute. Committee chairperson Mrs. S. H. Linn shared her vision for their future work. The committee would sponsor classes in "sewing, housework and the care of little children" so that "those little girls too poor to attend the paid classes at the Mechanics Institute and who now drift about the streets learning vice, can come and learn the higher and moral side of life; for labor done well is always ennobling, and 'he liveth well who worketh well.'"[6] The Rochester ladies would train poor girls to do domestic work in respectable homes.

Young women were entering the workforce in large numbers in the late nineteenth century,[7] and maternalist reformers gave quite a lot of thought to the problem of young working women. Sheila Rothman found that when the YWCA engaged in job placement and training in the late nineteenth century, leaders tried to train young women in the domestic skills and direct them toward domestic employment. They believed that working in a good home, where a young woman was presumably protected by Victorian family values, was almost always preferable to working in the morally suspect environment of a factory or some other place where their virtue was presumed to be at risk. If domestic employment was not possible, office work was an acceptable second choice.[8] As more and more educated women entered the workforce, office jobs such as stenography, telephone operating, and typing became respectable occupations for women.[9] Laura S. Abrams found that the leaders of Hull House reached a quite different conclusion. They believed that domestic employment and factory work both threatened the virtue of young women, so they encouraged young women to marry.[10] Likewise, the ladies of the WEIU wanted to help young working women to learn to create what they considered a proper home atmosphere. The cooking class was a first step toward "educated motherhood." And to direct them to what they considered dignified employment in the homes of respectable families, they invited "persons who desire to employ worthy women for any department of household work" to contact them.[11]

In 1894 Mrs. Don Alonzo Watson gave a mansion she owned on Clinton Avenue to the WEIU as a headquarters,[12] and, like the Boston and Buffalo unions, the Rochester WEIU's Committee on Philanthropy opened a "Noon Rest" for young ladies who worked in the city. The operation also offered a few positions of paid employment for the women who cooked and served the food. The lunchroom served meals at cost and offered young women a respectable place to have a meal, socialize, and pursue self-improvement. Noon Rest subcommittees included a Social Committee to plan entertainment and a Library Committee to provide books, papers, and magazines.[13] In the first year, the committee reported great success, selling nearly eight thousand lunches, and more than one thousand suppers.[14] Nevertheless, the numbers soon dropped off. According to the committee report for 1896–1897, competition from other low-priced restaurants that opened as well as the choice of girls with bicycles to go home for lunch cut into their business. Despite their best efforts to attract customers with improved menus and advertisements, working women apparently preferred to eat elsewhere. The Noon Rest lost money and was forced to close in March 1896.[15]

The WEIU also tried to initiate young working girls into club life. The Guild of the WEIU was open "to any self-supporting girl." According to their rules of government, the young women of the Guild believed that "the only way to dignify labor is to infuse it with intelligence: and that to accomplish this we must both educate the worker and put science into the work, and that there is no sort of labor which cannot be thus elevated."[16]

The Guild instilled in its members the values of culture and self-improvement, and, at the same time, it allowed the ladies of the WEIU to exercise benevolence as they worked with young working-class women. During the summer of 1895, for example, Miss [Eleanor?] Lattimore of the WEIU took ten Guild girls for a week's lakeside vacation. Guild activities included a series of "Travel Talks" that were quite popular. These alternated weekly with so-called tea meetings, social events that included a light meal. There was also a gymnastics class, a literary class, a singing class, a German language class, and a library.[17]

There was an element of social control behind the attempts to initiate working-class women into middle-class values, as there was in many of the activities of the WEIU, and the working-class women often resisted. While they were apparently happy to have the clout of the ladies of the Committee on Legal Protection on their side, they were less willing to be told where to work or where to eat. The membership of the Guild in 1896 stood at thirty-six[18]—small in comparison to the WEIU—and it apparently did not last. It was not mentioned at all in the 1903 *Decennial Year Book*.

Culture and Self-Improvement for All of Rochester

Like many women's clubs, the WEIU valued opportunities for self-improvement, but the WEIU ladies did not want to improve themselves alone. The Civic Art Committee relished opportunities to offer enlightening and uplifting entertainment to the entire community—especially when they could somehow make the experience educational. For example, in 1898 the WEIU and the Mechanics Institute, a local technical school for industrial workers, cosponsored an exhibit called the "Eastman Photographs." Rochester was, of course, the home of the Eastman Kodak Company, so the exhibit served a number of purposes. The photographs were "the finest specimens of the photographic art," as well as a technical example of "the marvelous development of photography." To add to the beauty and charm of the exhibit, tea was served each afternoon, and an orchestra played most evenings.[19]

Many women's clubs focused on cultural opportunities in their programs because it was their purpose to offer their members opportunities for self-improvement. The WEIU never entirely gave up the social and self-improvement functions of the women's literary club.[20] What is more important is that the WEIU transformed the agenda of cultural self-improvement into a significant aspect of its public mission—its municipal housekeeping. For example, in 1898 the union combined culture with fund-raising when they exhibited a set of prints of modern copies of older masterpieces. On that occasion, as on several others, the Civic Art Committee charged admission and used the money to purchase prints to hang in the public schools.[21]

Patriotism and Political Training

Most nineteenth-century feminists of all sorts were enthusiastic patriots, and the connection is not difficult to understand. With progressives in general, feminists thought that the United States represented the leading edge of a wave of political democracy that would inevitably sweep the world. Furthermore, like Montgomery, many feminists believed that women in the United States, while still bound by law in anachronistic subordination to men, were the advance guard of women's global emancipation. It was, as Montgomery said, "merely a question of time."[22] Many domestic feminists in particular agreed with Montgomery that municipal housekeeping would "help women to gain full enfranchisement."[23]

During the Spanish-American War, the patriotism of the WEIU was especially visible. Perhaps to underscore their endorsement of individualistic-civic democratic institutions, they transformed their annual election of officers into a "Patriotic Day," which they hoped would afford their members and guests "a most social and enjoyable time." The newspapers reported that the WEIU ladies "showed their patriotism in a most interesting and emphatic manner." Large American flags and other emblems "festooned the walls," and the ladies displayed "Cuban curios." Perhaps to contrast what they regarded as the backwardness of Spain with the modernity and power of the American nation, they decorated one wall with several pieces of "old armor" and another with "cuts of all the United States battleships and their commanders." Each of the WEIU ladies wore "some national emblem, pinned to the corsage."[24]

The WEIU women were serious about citizenship. In 1898 the second Saturday of each month was devoted to a class in parliamentary procedure so that WEIU members could "become familiar with the usages governing public assemblies."[25] The journalist who reported on the class poked fun at the seriousness with which the all-female class formulated, presented, and debated mock resolutions. Perhaps he did not realize the significance of what he witnessed. The women were utilizing a familiar strategy of empowerment for women in the Cult of True Womanhood. The protective atmosphere of the all-female WEIU classroom gave them the freedom to master new knowledge and skills that they probably would never have attempted in a mixed-gender setting. Their gender-based segregation gave the class the legitimacy and protection of traditional womanliness, but the content was subversive of the limitations of the woman's sphere. The women were learning skills that were useful primarily beyond the domestic domain. In learning how to conduct themselves in the context of deliberative assemblies, the women looked forward to the day when they could exercise the full rights of citizens in civil society.

Educational Reform

When they took up educational reform work, the ladies of the WEIU became part of a broad movement of municipal housekeepers for whom educational reform was a central issue. William J. Reese found that before 1890 women's organizations were a marginal factor in the development of urban educational policy, but from 1890 to 1920, they influenced every significant development in educational reform.[26] It is not surprising that education reform became one of the largest and most successful programs of the WEIU. Rochester's schools were in crisis in the 1890s, and the women of the WEIU, steeped in the ideology of domestic feminism, believed it was their duty, as municipal housekeepers, to promote the public welfare by improving the schools. Helen Barrett Montgomery was particularly interested in education, and the

Educational Committee enjoyed strong and aggressive leadership. Of the fifty women on the committee, most were former teachers and mothers.[27]

Educational reform was about more than just education. It was also about the hierarchy of gender. The Rochester school system, like every other public school system in the late nineteenth century, was composed of a large, overwhelmingly female workforce that was controlled and directed by an exclusively male school board and an overwhelmingly male administrative staff. When the WEIU women inserted themselves into the questions of educational policy and administration, they challenged male authority. When they defended teachers against criticism, defended their authority in the classrooms, and chided apathetic parents, they asserted feminist solidarity. When they claimed that experience as mothers and former teachers made them competent to address questions of pedagogy, they transformed traditional women's roles into a source of public power and authority.

The women of the WEIU, like other domestic feminists who agitated for school reform in other cities, were advocates of the so-called "new education." Advocates of the new education emphasized the individualism of each student and discouraged corporal punishment and heavy dependence on rote learning and memorization. They criticized frequent testing and wanted promotions based on more than examinations alone. They wanted to integrate kindergartens and vacation schools into the public school system and expand the public school curriculum to include subjects such as manual training, domestic science, and nature study.[28]

The WEIU advocated all of these measures and more, but they encountered stiff resistance from the school board and from school superintendent Milton Noyes. The WEIU regarded the educational philosophy and methods of the Rochester schools as archaic. The superintendent and the board, which was at that time made up of representatives elected from each city ward, regarded the reforms proposed by the WEIU as faddish and socialistic.[29] Mrs. Susan H. Hooker, chairman of the WEIU Educational Committee, said that the committee found the challenge presented by the schools "appalling as well as inspiring."[30] The committee soon discovered the political limitations of the social status and moral authority they commanded. Although their influence was no doubt formidable, they could not force the school board to do anything it did not wish to do. When the reforms the committee recommended required the expenditure of significant funds or threatened to interrupt the stream of graft that riddled the school system, the women hit a brick wall of opposition. Sometimes the school board responded with vituperation and ridicule.

Despite the resistance and insults they suffered from the school board, the Educational Committee pressed for a remarkable array of reforms in the schools. They used several common Progressive Era strategies to achieve their goals: fact-finding investigations, muckraking reports, public lectures by "experts" promoting their cause, grassroots community organizing, and model programs. While the unreconstructed school board never totally acceded to the demands of the WEIU, the women were able to gather sufficient public support to achieve many of their goals. When the school board was reorganized under the Dow Law and Montgomery became a member of the board, their victory was complete.

Free Kindergartens

At the first public meeting of the Educational Committee, Boston kindergarten advocate Lucy Wheelock was one of two speakers who appeared to address the need for free kindergartens. At the end of the meeting, the Rochester women organized a kindergarten association on the spot. They set an initial subscription goal of one hundred dollars and made Rose Lattimore Alling treasurer of the fund.[31] With resolve and enthusiasm the women of Rochester joined the free kindergarten movement.

The free kindergarten movement in America was rooted in the Transcendentalist philosophy of early childhood education developed by Amos Bronson Alcott and Elizabeth Peabody at the Masonic Temple School in Boston in the 1830s. Alcott and Peabody proceeded from a behavioristic premise derived from faculty psychology. They believed the nature of the child was totally innocent at birth and depravity was learned. With the correct early childhood education, the so-called moral sense of the child could be perfected and depravity could be eliminated completely. From the very beginning of the Transcendentalist education movement, the ultimate goal was to move beyond individual learning to the "elevation of the moral life in society."[32]

To the social-ethical goal of Transcendentalist education, American kindergarten pioneers soon added the developmental educational psychology of German Transcendentalist and educational philosopher Friedrich Froebel, who also believed in the essential goodness of the child's nature. Froebel thought early education ought to match three basic stages of development: infancy, early childhood, and childhood. The middle stage, from age four to six, became the focus of Froebel's attention, and he created the *kinder-garten*, or "child's garden," as a new educational institution especially suited to the nature of early childhood.[33] Froebel intended the kindergarten to be a place of creative play, of self-directed activity and expression. Froebel said that the teacher helped the child to "produce outside of himself that which he conceives within himself." The aim was to help the child connect his or her natural presentiments with the exterior world—to externalize the interior life of the child.[34]

The fundamental ideas that Froebel wanted to reinforce in the child, which all his activities were designed to instill, were the unity and interde-pendence of society and the divine moral order of social relations. Froebel also believed that kindergartens and kindergarten training schools would help to emancipate women by bringing new dignity to their roles as mothers and edu-cators of children.[35] Froebel's kindergarten, thus, had a social principle that was quite compatible with the philosophy of the American Transcendentalist educators, and his philosophy was attractive to American advocates of domes-tic feminism.

In the 1860s and 1870s several of Froebel's students immigrated to America and attempted to establish kindergartens, but with few immedi-ately positive results. At this time, with the help of Elizabeth Peabody in New York and William T. Harris and Susan Blow in St. Louis, the first successful training programs for kindergartens in America were organized. In 1873 Harris, a Hegelian philosopher and superintendent of the St. Louis school system, opened the first public kindergarten in America under Blow's direction. Blow shared Harris' Hegelian views, and under their influence the Transcendentalism of Froebel was supplemented with an emphasis on disci-pline of the will and intellect.[36]

Kindergartens grew in popularity in America throughout the 1870s. More and more women were trained as kindergartners and adapted kindergarten methods and philosophy to the American cultural context. With greater popularity came increased criticism and opposition. Some critics regarded the kindergarten movement as the product of an esoteric European philoso-phy, too impractical and abstract to be useful to Americans. Others associated it with the woman's rights movement. They believed it was an attempt to entice women to abandon their proper sphere in the home and neglect their duty to provide moral education to their own children. Kindergartens, they believed, would subvert the family and destroy the social stability of state and society.[37]

Despite the critics, the kindergarten movement grew, and when it became combined with urban philanthropy, it was transformed into the free kindergarten movement. The direct stimulus to the free kindergarten movement was provided by the mounting crisis in America's expanding urban-industrial cities of the 1870s and 1880s. In the view of the founders of the free kindergartens, the institutions answered several pressing needs at once. The working poor were relieved of the responsibility for providing care for their children during working hours. The children were washed, clothed, fed, and taught middle-class moral values and habits. "Friendly visitors" from the kindergarten visited the homes of the children, who were mostly immigrants, to investigate conditions, provide benevolence, instruct parents in proper morals and child care, and invite them to participate in other educational programs associated with the kindergarten, such as cooking classes, language classes, or citizenship classes. Through the kindergarten, the movement leaders believed, they could "eliminate the problems of urban poverty, help the immigrant mother, save the child, and improve the nation."[38] The Woman's Christian Temperance Union, through its kindergarten department, developed a course for kindergartners in Froebelian literature and established kindergartens in at least twenty cities. Social settlements also frequently established free kindergartens as a part of their community outreach.[39]

The free kindergarten movement exemplified several aspects of domestic feminism. It relied upon leaders who believed in the ideals of educated motherhood and wanted to propagate domestic science among the immigrant mothers of the poor in the hope of enlisting them and their children in the task of municipal housekeeping. It combined benevolence and social control in an inextricable amalgamation of motives.

Implicit in the free kindergarten approach was a growing conviction that the causes of poverty were environmental. Truancy and delinquency were manifestations of "the stamp of the tenement."[40] In the view of the kindergarten supports, uneducated immigrant mothers, frequently absent because of work, were ill equipped to provide proper nutrition and hygiene, much less the high moral atmosphere needed to resist the pull of their surroundings. Kindergartens offered a way to save the child before he or she was ruined by the environment, and they promised to meliorate the family and the community as well. Between 1880 and 1890 more than one hundred free kindergarten associations were organized in American cities. In many locales, the free kindergarten work was funded by subscriptions in which a large number of women contributed small sums to the cause.[41]

The German population of Rochester stood at eleven thousand by 1880, and they helped to create substantial public sentiment in favor of kindergartens by 1883. Unfortunately there was no provision in the city charter to allow expenditures for kindergartens, so only private kindergartens operated before 1893. In that year, the New York State Legislature granted cities the right to fund kindergarten programs, and the school board opened kindergartens in nine pubic schools.[42] Nevertheless, the Women's Educational and Industrial Union was not satisfied.

Montgomery introduced the kindergarten discussion with comments that were characteristic of the assumptions and values of the free kindergarten movement, and of domestic feminism as a whole. She connected the middle-class home with moral virtue, and she linked poverty with immorality in the home. "There is a kindergarten on Phelps Avenue, and all the good little children in our neighborhood attend it," she said. "But they would grow up into very decent men and women probably, if they didn't have these advantages, because they are surrounded by the proper influences at home. We want to reach the children of the slums, who dwell in homes of vice and crime."[43]

Lucy Wheelock was a student of Elizabeth Peabody, a dedicated Froebelian who translated Froebel's autobiography into English, and a personal favorite of child psychologist and kindergarten theorist G. Stanley Hall. Wheelock lectured on behalf of the kindergarten movement wherever she could, never accepted fees for her lectures, and often paid her own expenses. She established a very successful training school for kindergarten instructors in Boston in 1888. She believed that moral character developed through proper early childhood education was a key to the success of a democratic society.[44] In her speech to the Rochester WEIU, Wheelock insisted that kindergarten programs incorporated "industry, temperance and religion" and gave attention to the child's physical, mental, and moral training.

The other speaker, Meta Brown of Buffalo, described how the kindergartens in her city were established "in those localities inhabited by the poorest class of citizens." In a comment that was probably particularly noteworthy to the ladies of Rochester, she observed that one kindergarten in particular served mostly Italian children. The "Italian colony" in Rochester was growing rapidly in the 1890s, and Italians were pilloried in public opinion. The press routinely stereotyped Italians as drunkards, thieves, and murderers. Stories sensationalized alleged Mafia violence, and headlines that touted "Italian with Knife" were commonplace.[45]

While the WEIU women dutifully funded and organized free kindergartens, their real goal was to have kindergartens integrated into the public school system. To that end, they asked the school board to establish a school to train kindergarten teachers. "There is a crying need for a normal college or training school for kindergartens," Mrs. Hooker reported. "Every school in the city is asking for a kindergarten, and is likely to get it. When we think of the large number of teachers that will be employed it behooves us to see that they are properly fitted for their work."[46] That goal became reality during Montgomery's tenure on the school board.

School Board Reform

In 1894 the Educational Committee recommended that the WEIU press the city for a night school on the eastern side of the Genesee River, and they recommended changing the city charter to provide for the appointment of a faculty member from the University of Rochester to sit on the Board of Education.[47] The committee was just beginning its work, and those modest proposals hardly reflected the strength of the committee's future work. Within a few years, the educational work of the WEIU would become the most significant agency of educational reform in the city of Rochester.[48]

Nevertheless, the proposal to place a University of Rochester professor on the board ignited a controversy that would eventually lead to an entire reorganization of the school board. After the WEIU recommendation, the Citizen's Educational Association, which was dominated by professors from the university, publicized its own recommendation for a reconstituted board of five members, with three elected at large and two appointed by the mayor. They further recommended that at least two members of the board should always be women. Rochester's mayor and Republican Party boss George

Aldridge then put forth his own recommendation. He agreed that the board was too large. He thought that five was a good number for the new board and that he should appoint them. The members of the Board of Education, who were elected from each city ward, rejected any suggestion that the board was too large and defended local representation as a cornerstone of American democracy against the city council's call for a smaller board.[49] By 1898 public sentiment was too powerful for the school board to resist. The board president appointed a committee of six to "consider what, if any, legislation is needed to improve the management of the schools." Dr. Frank F. Dow was the chairman of that committee. The report of his committee, after some emendation, became known as the Dow Law, under which Montgomery was elected in 1899 to the reconstituted board.[50]

Public School Reform

The most significant effort of the Educational Committee was reserved for the public schools. The ladies of the committee expressed a great deal of satisfaction with the schools, and, where there were problems, they believed the blame lay with the citizens of Rochester:

> Our citizens suppose they have made ample provision for commodious and well-ventilated school-rooms and for the employment of cultivated and thoroughly equipped teachers. They expect the superintendent to visit the schools frequently, to keep in touch with all progressive methods known to the best educators, and to lead in laying out such a course of study and training as shall develop the child into the ideal citizen. Having put it all under the supervision of a board of busy men, who, though chosen from among citizens peculiarly fitted for the work, could give but a small proportion of their time to it, they stand off and expect the machine to work perfectly.[51]

The ladies of the committee had no such expectation. If the men elected to the board and the superintendent were too busy to visit the schools regularly, the women were not. In the post-revolutionary period of American history, educating children for citizenship was considered one of the responsibilities of motherhood. The ladies of the committee were prepared to resume the responsibility, if "parents and those who should be most interested" faltered. The women of the committee wanted to make clear that they were not just busybodies intruding in matters that did not concern them. They approached the task in an organized, rational fashion, and they suggested that others could learn from their example. They appointed "public-spirited women" to visit schools in most of the districts in the city. These visitors were qualified for their office because most of them "have been teachers and are now mothers."[52]

The program of school visitation produced many beneficial effects, according to Hooker's report. Apathetic parents became interested in the schools, teachers felt appreciated and supported, school commissioners were engaged and informed. On the other hand, they discovered certain conditions that they found disconcerting. Administrators padded the payrolls with unnecessary teachers, and consequently teachers' salaries were abominably low. Teacher morale was low as well, and many teachers taught "'the art of passing'" rather than "the art of study."[53]

The Educational Committee also found a long list of defects in school buildings and equipment. In several schools, they found students in need of books and many children in need of suitable school clothes, and the committee provided them. They found overcrowding and inadequate janitorial service, which they deplored.[54] In the view of the Educational Committee, the schools were extensions of the home and ought to teach the moral values of the home. Education was a vehicle for the formation of middle-class values and upward social mobility.

The Educational Committee wanted to transform the Rochester public schools into models of progressive pedagogy, so they wrote to educational experts and studied the curricula of other urban school systems to try to discover the best plan for Rochester. They reported that the leaders with whom they communicated were all advocates of the "new education."[55] They criticized the use of a particular history text, which they found "dry and unprofitable."[56] The book may have been unprofitable for students, but the sale of textbooks was a major source of graft in the Rochester school system,[57] and the Educational Committee found that they had "a difficult problem to deal with."[58]

Manual Training and Domestic Science

The introduction of manual training and domestic science into the public school curriculum was one of the reforms the Rochester school board found most objectionable. From the reformers' perspective, manual training was a democratic initiative. It made education more practical for working-class students because it prepared them vocationally, as high school and college education did middle-class students. Also, it was seen as pedagogically progressive because it gave all students a means of creative expression, or as Montgomery put it, "the training of the whole child through brain and eye and hand."[59] The Rochester school board derided the idea as an extravagant and distracting novelty, a move toward socialism and an attack on parental responsibility.[60]

The WEIU worked for three long years to introduce manual training into the schools. In 1894 they received permission from the board to run a summer program in sewing at the No. 21 school. The WEIU regarded this as an entering wedge to open the way for a full manual training program. The sewing program was run at the WEIU's expense, and it was very successful. At the end of the summer, the WEIU held an exhibition of the students' work at Watson House and invited the school board, the superintendent, and the teachers to come. Hooker reported: "We regret that [the invitation] was not more generally accepted."[61]

The WEIU petitioned the board for permission to try the experiment in four schools during the regular school year at the WEIU's expense, and again the board gave permission. But Superintendent Noyes fretted that the introduction of sewing would interfere with the rest of the curriculum. Then the school board decided that sewing classes must be held after regular school hours. The WEIU regarded that as administrative sabotage.[62]

To marshal public support for manual training, the WEIU brought in lecturers from Philadelphia, Boston, and other cities where manual training was a part of the regular school curriculum. Following the lectures, Montgomery appeared before the school board once again to argue for manual training, and finally the board relented. They agreed to allow the program to proceed if the WEIU would pay the teacher. The board appropriated six cents per pupil for supplies.[63]

The following year, the WEIU introduced "sloyd" (*slöjd*), a type of manual training in woodworking, into the curriculum.[64] Domestic *slöjd* was a handcraft widely practiced in Swedish peasant households in the early nineteenth century. Families made practical items for themselves and to barter or sell. As industrialization progressed in Sweden, families began to abandon *slöjd* as a cultural tradition. Otto Salomon developed educational *slöjd* in Sweden in 1872 as a way to preserve traditional values. Deeply influenced by Froebel, Salomon designed educational *slöjd* to awaken and utilize the child's interest and curiosity in learning. Salomon's curriculum utilized useful household items and progressed gradually from the simple to the complex. Students worked from models and drawings, made their own drawings, and used simple tools to execute designs. Learning was hands-on, and instruction was individualized.[65]

Gustaf Larsson brought educational *slöjd* to the United States in 1888 and modified it for the American cultural and educational context. In America, Larsson made "sloyd" a part of the correlated curriculum of the child-centered "new education" that focused on the child's interest, self-expression, and multiple styles of learning. Larsson wanted sloyd to produce useful objects so that the child would realize immediately a practical benefit from education, but he also believed sloyd taught harmony and balance and the relation of beauty to form, proportion, utility, and ornamentation.[66]

The WEIU's introduction of sloyd indicated several things. First, in some respects the WEIU helped to position the Rochester schools on the leading edge of educational reform by the end of the nineteenth century. Second, under the influence of the WEIU, Froebelian ideas about early childhood education penetrated into the upper grades and affected the curriculum, making the educational process more interest-oriented and child-centered. Third, the WEIU pushed the Rochester school system to adopt a more practical approach to public education that made it more attractive and useful to new immigrants and other working-class families, whose children were crowding into the public school classrooms.

In 1897 the WEIU began to advocate the inclusion of domestic science in the public schools. They believed that by placing domestic science in the school curriculum in the lower grades, they could reach poor girls, who usually dropped out of school before high school, with the message of educated motherhood.[67] The WEIU continued to fund manual training and domestic science in the schools until the new school board, of which Montgomery was a member, integrated it completely into the curriculum in 1901.[68]

Vacation Schools

In 1899 the WEIU established two vacation schools for poor children "in the most crowded parts of the city."[69] Vacation schools, mostly organized by women's clubs, appeared in dozens of American cities around the turn of the century, and they were one of the most widely discussed educational reforms of the Progressive Era. Organizers underscored their "experimental" nature, and they integrated many features of the new education, such as manual training and nature study. Many of the vacation schools, like the ones in Rochester, eventually received municipal funding, and they reflected the grassroots struggle in the Progressive Era over issues such as the democratization of education and neighborhood control of schools, the right to exert social control over play and leisure, and the scope of the government's custodial control of children through the schools.[70]

The WEIU vacation schools ran for six weeks. A typical vacation school employed ten paid teachers and several unpaid volunteers, and it enrolled approximately 250 children daily with many more "sent sorrowing away."[71] Newspaper clippings in WEIU scrapbooks show that the curriculum included manual training for older boys, sewing, stories, music, games, singing, nature study, and weekly excursions. One year the entire curriculum was organized around nature study.[72]

In her report for the *Decennial Year Book*, Ita P. Farley, chairman of the Vacation School Committee, emphasized some of the progressive features of the vacation school curriculum, such as the emphasis on nature study and the "kindness and good fellowship" that made other forms of discipline unnecessary. She also believed that the manual training in the vacation schools would be "the starting point for increased efficiency and usefulness in the future lives of many of the children." She underscored the pride the children took in their work and declared that they were "in every way bettered" by the vacation school experience. In fact, she was convinced that the "experimental stage" of the vacation school was completed and that the work had proven its pedagogical and moral value by the interest the children showed and the quality of the work they produced.[73]

Not everyone was enthusiastic about the vacation schools. Apart from the resistance of the school board, newspaper clippings indicate that the WEIU faced criticism from some people in the communities where the vacation schools were held. Neighbors of the No. 18 school complained that the vacation school disturbed the peace of the community. In a petition, they claimed that "the children attending were of the rougher sort, and addicted to smoking cigarettes and use of swear words." They said recreational equipment was left outdoors at night so that "hoodlums" could get at it; consequently "the neighborhood is not reposeful either by day or by night." Due to the disturbance, they complained, "the numerous railroad employees and policemen" who lived in the community were "robbed of their few hours of sleep."[74]

It is possible that the real issue was social control—that some of the neighbors regarded the presence of the WEIU ladies and their vacation school as an unwelcome intrusion into the affairs of their community. The tone of the newspaper articles suggested that the neighbor's complaints were exaggerated. City officials appeared dismissive. A policeman who was sent to patrol the area around the school in response to the complaints found no unusual disturbance either during or after the school hours. According to the clippings, the WEIU women, who had picked that particular school because it was "the center of a densely crowded district," were "in a state of mind in which regret is mingled with indignation. Possibly the feeling of indignation predominates." Apparently they did not like having their altruism challenged by the working-class residents of the community. In any case, the criticisms were impotent. The vacation school remained open and the program grew.[75]

School Beautification

Art exhibits were a frequent part of the WEIU program, as were prize competitions aimed at city beautification. The majority of those efforts were designed in one way or another to benefit the schools. For example, in 1896 the WEIU's Civic Art Committee awarded two prizes of ten dollars each for the best answers to a set of ten questions that dealt with city beautification. The questions required contestants to describe and give examples of particular styles of architecture among the public buildings, churches, and houses in Rochester. They were to make suggestions for the best way to beautify the Genesee River, to evaluate the city parks, and to comment on the aesthetics of public memorials. Contestants had to be twenty years old or younger, and they were limited to twenty thousand words or less. The questions were designed to challenge the contestants to learn something that could be put to use for the public welfare. For example: "2.—(*a*) What proportion should the height of buildings bear to the width of streets? (*b*) What laws regulating this matter are in force in other cities?"[76]

The Civic Art Committee at first attempted to publicize their prize competition in the public schools, but the school board said that the circulars describing the competition were "'advertising matter'" and banned them from the schools. Myra S. Hall, chairman of the Civic Art Committee, regretted that "we failed to reach that part of the public for which our work was especially designed." In response, the committee changed its strategy. They decided to improve the educational atmosphere of the schools through interior decoration.[77] It was a clever strategy that employed domestic feminism as well as progressivism on several levels. It would have been difficult for the school board to object to the women engaging in such a womanly activity—especially when they offered their services at no cost to the school. Yet it was another opportunity to expand the municipal housekeeping responsibilities of the women—to highlight a public need and become indispensable in the process of meeting it. Through the press, the teachers, and the mothers' clubs, they were able to engage a great deal of publicity and interest.

The committee took an approach that was typical for the WEIU and for progressive reformers in general. They began with a model program—a single classroom—and used it to justify expansion throughout the school system. Their ultimate goal was to make interior decoration of the schools a neighborhood project and a community responsibility—an integral part of the planning, care, and maintenance for all schools.

The Civic Art Committee chose for its "object lesson" a room in the No. 10 school because the school was centrally located, and their aim was "to show what could be done to beautify a room at small expense." On the day the pictures were formally presented at a public ceremony, Superintendent Noyes remembered at the last minute a previous engagement and sent regrets that he could not attend.[78] Response from other quarters was enthusiastic, and within four years the committee was able place pictures in all of the "upper grade classrooms" of fourteen schools and in the library of Normal Training School for teachers. Additionally, several single pictures were placed in other schools. Inspired by the WEIU's work, teachers in several schools began independent projects to raise money for school art. Parents' associations and Mothers' clubs took over the work started by the WEIU in several other schools.[79]

The WEIU insisted that they would not hang pictures on "dirty or whitewashed backgrounds." They wanted walls painted with "restful tints" and windows hung with matching shades. Chairman Hall was happy to report that "the painting of walls is now included in all contracts for school buildings and the tint of the window shades had become the subject of intelligent study on the part of those in authority."[80]

In 1900, after Montgomery was elected to the school board, the Civic Art Committee had the opportunity to decorate an entire school building, the new No. 27 school building that had just been completed. The committee was allowed to pick the colors for the walls. At an expense of one thousand dollars, they placed a hundred and seventy pictures and forty-one casts throughout the building, which included reproductions of paintings, depictions of great architecture and sculpture, as well as less lofty depictions of animals and stories.[81]

The Educational Committee worked alongside the Civic Art Committee in school beautification. While the Civic Art Committee confined itself to interior decoration, the Educational Committee beautified school grounds with flower gardens. In this work, like so much else the WEIU did, the plan was to set an example and encourage community initiative. The WEIU chose four schools in the beginning and worked with the municipal Park Board to create the gardens. Other schools followed through the initiative of principals or Mothers' clubs. The WEIU supported the community initiative by offering annual prizes to the school that made the best improvements and by sponsoring an annual flower show in which public school students offered individual exhibits.[82]

The WEIU believed that such activities had significant moral as well as educational value. "Dull, discouraged children" were "quickened by industrial success" and engaged their schoolwork with "an awakened intellect surprising themselves and their teachers." But the influence spread beyond the schools to the all-important family life. The homes of some students had been "transformed from barren surroundings to beautiful gardens and vine-covered cottages," and the new beauty and vitality of the homes reflected the "character and good citizenship" that had taken root in the inhabitants.[83]

Teaching a Middle-Class Ethic of Money Saving

One of the reforms introduced by the Educational Committee was not aimed at the school board, the parents, the teachers, the curriculum, or the buildings, but at the pupils themselves. The Educational Committee began a "Penny Provident Station" at one of the schools in 1901; by 1903 over four hundred students were enrolled. The committee reported proudly that parents as well as students joined the savings bank. Depositors had learned the lessons of thrift so well that they had been able to use their savings to purchase items such as rent, coal, clothing, and Christmas gifts, while maintaining "goodly sums deposited in the savings bank." While penny by penny, the total deposits grew beyond four hundred dollars, the children developed "a sense of responsibility and self-respect," and many mothers were "helped out of a tight place" by their children's capital.[84]

Labor, Playgrounds, Mothers' Clubs, and More

By the turn of the century, the WEIU was one of the most influential organizations in Rochester. In addition to the activities already mentioned, the union sponsored dozens of public lectures on a remarkable range of cultural, political, and reform topics. Often the purpose of a lecture was to excite public support for the organization of a committee to study a particular problem. Members of the WEIU worked closely with other women's organizations and other progressive reformers to establish progressive reforms.

For example, the WEIU helped to establish a local chapter of the Consumers' League in 1900.[85] The National Consumers' League was organized in 1899 by Hull House veteran Florence Kelley, and its purpose was to organize grassroots consumer support for the passage and enforcement of protective labor legislation for working women. The main strategy of the National Consumers' League was to convince women, the main purchasers for American families, to boycott the products and services of employers that, in the league's view, treated women workers unfairly or maintained inhumane working conditions.[86] In December 1908 the Rochester Consumers' League tried to organize women's support for closing downtown stores at 6:00 p.m. on Saturday evenings. Mrs. W. L. Howard of the local Federation of Women's Clubs spoke to the WEIU at Montgomery's invitation. She advocated early closing to protect women who were store clerks from the ill effects of standing for long hours in the stores.[87]

The WEIU worked with a coalition of local progressive reformers and educators to establish the Children's Playground League in 1902,[88] four years ahead of the National Playground Association of America. The Playground League constructed and supervised a playground in a city park in one of Rochester's poorest and most crowded neighborhoods. After initial resistance from neighborhood residents, the work of the Playground League became so popular and successful that city authorities moved swiftly to expand the program. By 1908 the school board, of which Montgomery was a member, was given charge of the growing network of playgrounds because most playgrounds were connected with school property. The school board expanded the work into the social center movement (see chap. 9 below).

The WEIU also helped to facilitate the work of other organizations for municipal housekeeping. Although they did not create mothers' clubs, they were pleased when WEIU initiatives led to their formation. In addition to their own visits to the schools, the WEIU organized a "Mother's Congress" in 1898, whose purpose was to encourage mothers' interest in and cooperation with the public schools.[89] The National Congress of Mothers was organized in 1897 by Alice McLellan Birney, a kindergarten advocate and disciple of Froebel and G. Stanley Hall, and Phoebe Apperson Hirst, Birney's wealthy sponsor. The organization grew from two thousand members in 1897 to 1.5 million in 1930. The organization was renamed the National Congress of Mothers and Parent-Teacher Associations in 1908, and it became the National Congress of Parents and Teachers in 1924.[90] The National Congress was an important coalition of local organizations and the forerunner of modern parent-teacher associations, and it disseminated its philosophy of educated motherhood through group discussions, lectures, home visits, books, tracts, and a monthly periodical called the *National Congress of Mothers Magazine* (1908), later renamed the *Child Welfare Magazine* (1910). One significant aspect of the work of these municipal housekeepers was to press for wider community utilization of school facilities beyond school hours through such things as playgrounds, vacation schools, social centers, and civic clubs.[91]

The Mother's Congress of Rochester met at the WEIU headquarters on every fourth Saturday during the winter of 1898. Montgomery addressed the Mother's Congress at one of their 1898 meetings. Her message underscored the importance of educated motherhood for the future development of the child and of the community. She told the assembled mothers and teachers,

"The home influence is responsible for the first ideas and sentiments a child has concerning a world outside his little experience."[92] Montgomery and her colleagues wanted to make the home influence wholesome and intelligent, and they wanted to extend its influence through the school system to the entire community.

Because the WEIU believed that it was woman's duty to extend the influence of the home into the entire community, they led municipal coalitions to safeguard the health of children and improve nutrition. In partnership with Dr. George Goler, Rochester's public health officer, and the Rochester Public Health Association, the WEIU established a milk depot in the No. 26 school in 1900 and employed the first public school nurse in Rochester in 1907.[93] The WEIU also led the effort to provide school lunches for a penny.[94]

Often the WEIU's efforts transcended even the broad new scope of responsibility that they assigned to the school system. The earliest efforts to pass and enforce child labor legislation in Rochester were led by the WEIU,[95] and in 1911, they sponsored a sanitary survey by Rev. Caroline Bartlett Crane that excited much controversy in the city.

Caroline Bartlett Crane's visit to Rochester occurred while Montgomery was occupied with the Woman's Missionary Jubilee, and apparently Montgomery had little involvement in the event. Nevertheless, Crane's visit is symbolic of the new political power that women were able to leverage through the strategy of domestic feminism, as well as the potential of the women's new activism to involve them in unwanted controversy. Crane, a Unitarian minister, studied sociology at the University of Chicago and led her church in Kalamazoo, Michigan, to become a center of liberal Christianity and progressive reform. In 1901, while researching a lecture on meat handling, she discovered deplorable, unsanitary conditions at a local slaughterhouse.[96] That discovery eventually led her into a second career as a municipal sanitary inspector, a profession that she largely created for herself, and an endeavor in which she greatly depended upon her contacts in the women's club movement. In 1904 she founded the Women's Civic Improvement League in Kalamazoo, and she led that organization in a wide variety of municipal housekeeping reforms. In 1908 she began her national career, during which she executed sanitary surveys in more than sixty cities.

Crane's first appearance in Rochester as a lecturer on municipal sanitation was sponsored by the WEIU as early as 1903–1904.[97] Crane's 1911 survey in Rochester, although generally positive, stressed several problem areas. Her findings upset many people, although there was little news in what she reported. She found that Rochester's garbage handling and street cleaning were substandard. She criticized the city for having inadequate meat and milk inspections, and she found poor lighting and disregard for fire safety in several school buildings. She pointed out unsanitary conditions in boardinghouses and tenements and the near-slum conditions in certain areas of the city. The leadership and citizens of Rochester viewed their city as modern and progressive, and many people were stung by Crane's criticisms. The resentment that erupted over Crane's findings weakened the influence of the WEIU at the very time that some of its most creative leaders, including Montgomery, were curtailing their involvement.[98]

For Montgomery, the WEIU was a proving ground for her leadership skills and her ideas for political and social reform. Although her later career as a leader of the ecumenical woman's missionary movement overshadowed her career as a municipal housekeeper in Rochester, the second phase of her career would not have been possible without the early experience of leadership in Rochester. As Montgomery moved from her leadership of the WEIU to the leadership of the ecumenical woman's missionary movement, her basic reform agenda remained intact. Both institutions focused on social uplift for women and children, with education as the core strategy. The main distinction for Montgomery was that, as the leading intellectual of the ecumenical woman's missionary movement, it her responsibility was to make the theological underpinnings of her work explicit. In the nonsectarian context of the WEIU she found it more helpful to "bury" her creed, as she once said, for the sake of cooperation.[99] But whether her doctrine was implicit or explicit, in her mind she was always working for "the coming of the kingdom of which all good men dream."[100]

Eight

Helen Barrett Montgomery, Walter Rauschenbusch, and the Battle for Progressive Public Education

From time to time scholars have assumed that Helen Barrett Montgomery's social reform thought and activities were derived from the social gospel as expounded by Walter Rauschenbusch, who was Montgomery's contemporary in Rochester from 1897 until his death in 1918. That view is not supported by historical fact. Montgomery and Rauschenbusch were the same age. Both were Baptists and both were progressives committed to exploring the social implications of the gospel, so of course they agreed on a great many issues and were natural allies, but they came to their social, theological, and political views independently. For the most part, also, they worked on different issues through different organizational networks.

While it is clear that Montgomery knew Rauschenbusch and respected him, her views on progressive reform and feminism were developed independently. On at least one issue—educational reform—Montgomery and Rauschenbusch found themselves on opposite sides of a controversy. In 1908 Rauschenbusch led a citizen's rebellion against Montgomery's school board and the "new education" they had introduced. Montgomery was a central figure in the reformation of the Rochester school system, and nothing was more indicative of her values and the values of the municipal housekeepers of the WEIU than the new education. The fact that Rauschenbusch led the attack against the central feature of Montgomery's municipal reform work clearly indicates the divergence of their views. It illustrates an important distinction between the masculine orientation of Rauschenbusch's social gospel and the value-realization orientation of the German liberalism that he so admired, in contrast with the domestic feminist orientation of Montgomery's municipal housekeeping and the pragmatism of her educational philosophy. This chapter explains the main features of Montgomery's decade of work on the school board and why Montgomery's commitment to progressive education from the perspective of domestic feminism brought her into conflict with Rauschenbusch.

Walter Rauschenbusch in Rochester

The available evidence indicates there was a cordial relationship between Montgomery and Rauschenbusch,[1] but it is unclear to what extent Rauschenbusch actually influenced Montgomery's thought. No evidence has come to light that can establish a relationship between Montgomery and Rauschenbusch prior to 1897, yet Montgomery was actively involved in social reform through the Women's Educational and Industrial Union beginning in 1893. Rauschenbusch was born in Rochester in 1861, but spent the years from 1865 to 1868 with his mother and two sisters in Germany. Upon their return, Rauschenbusch attended Pfafflin's Private School in Rochester and then spent a year at the Rochester Free Academy, where he graduated in 1879.[2] Then Rauschenbusch returned to Germany, where he studied and traveled until 1883. When he returned to Rochester, he attended the University of Rochester, where he graduated in 1884, and he attended both the German and English departments of the Rochester Theological Seminary. In 1886 he completed his seminary education and accepted a call to the Second German Baptist Church in New York City's Hell's Kitchen.

Rauschenbusch gained a reputation for unorthodox theological views early in his career. In 1886, his Old Testament professor at Rochester prevented him from obtaining a missionary appointment to India, where his sister Emma served with John E. Clough. His parents were concerned that his liberalism might prevent his ordination, although it did not.[3] In New York City, Rauschenbusch's theological liberalism was augmented with socialist principles, which Rauschenbusch came to believe were implicit in the gospel when it was freed from the strictures and theological preoccupations of the Reformation and interpreted in light of the needs of urban industrial America. The socialist views of Henry George influenced him profoundly, and Rauschenbusch supported George's candidacy for mayor of New York City. In addition to political activities and his growing congregation, Rauschenbusch gave much of his time in New York to *For the Right*, a newspaper that he founded with Elizabeth Post, J. E. Raymond, and Leighton Williams in 1889 to provide an outlet for their Christian socialist thought. He and Williams also founded the Brotherhood of the Kingdom in 1892, a fellowship for select ministers and laymen interested in the social gospel, the central purpose of which was to promote the advancement of the kingdom of God on earth through Christian socialism.

In 1897 Rauschenbusch returned from more than a decade as pastor and taught in the German Department of Rochester Theological Seminary, where his father had taught before him. The impact of Rauschenbusch's liberal views upon the German department was profound, and many of the German students who emerged from his tutelage were forced to find places in English-speaking churches because they were too liberal for the German Baptist churches.[4] In 1902 he was promoted to a regular faculty position teaching church history, which he held until his death in 1918.

Today the name of Walter Rauschenbusch is probably the one name most closely associated with the social gospel, but Rauschenbusch was not yet famous when he returned to Rochester in 1897, and his first book was not published until 1907. Any influence on Montgomery had to come through personal acquaintance, his cooperation with the Good Government movement and his participation in municipal reform,[5] or because of his preaching or public lectures, such as those he gave to the "people's church" experiments at the Plymouth Church, the Brick Church, and the Labor Lyceum around the turn of the century.[6] In any case, Montgomery had become well acquainted with Rauschenbusch at least by 1904. Rauschenbusch chaired a YMCA committee to survey social conditions in Rochester, and the committee's report was released on 30 May 1904,[7] during Montgomery's tenure on the school board. Many of the YMCA committee's concerns were ultimately addressed by the school board in 1907 through the controversial social center movement, which opened neighborhood schools for community activities after school hours. Her husband, William A. Montgomery, joined the local chapter of the Brotherhood of the Kingdom founded by Rauschenbusch in 1904.[8] In fact, William Montgomery presided over a session of the chapter's annual conference two years later.[9]

An entry in Montgomery's diary on 19 November 1908 indicates that she heard Rauschenbusch speak at a "Socialist's meeting" and thought his speech was "great."[10] This event occurred in the midst of the controversy between Rauschenbusch's citizens' committee and the school board. Two brief handwritten notes from Montgomery to Rauschenbusch show her approbation of his thought. In the first, an undated note included in Rauschenbusch's correspondence from 1910, she was evidently responding to an address Rauschenbusch had given as a substitute speaker in the place of "Mr. Brandeis" (presumably Louis D. Brandeis), whose arrival "celestial powers had prevented." Montgomery was glad that "our Rochester people had the chance to listen to a greater prophet with a greater message." She wrote, "Every word you said had the sweet certitude of reason and justice." On a more personal note, she assured Rauschenbusch that she and her husband "often talk of you and often read you and often pray you [*sic*] though we so seldom see you."[11]

In the second note, dated 13 December 1910, Montgomery thanked Rauschenbusch for giving them a copy of his book, *Prayers of the Social Awakening* (1909). She recorded the gift in her diary on 11 December. In her note to Rauschenbusch, she wrote of her liking "the prayers of wrath and getting for the first time a glimpse as to the way people felt when those other prayers of wrath were written so long ago." Rauschenbusch's prayers allowed her to "feel fierce and religious at the same time." Nevertheless, she offered one critical suggestion. Always an advocate for missions, she hoped in the next edition Rauschenbusch would include a prayer for missionaries. "They need to see the big social side of their calling," she wrote, "and we need to enter into the spirit of the man on the thin warring edge of our far flung battle lines."[12]

Clearly Montgomery and Rauschenbusch had a friendly relationship, and she affirmed much of his theological perspective, but there is no reason to conclude from the evidence that her involvement in social reform was simply a reflection of his or anyone else's theology. Although it is evident that Rauschenbusch had some influence on her thought, at least by the mid-1900s, one must look elsewhere to explain her social activism in the 1890s. Indeed, the controversy surrounding the school board in 1908 is evidence that they had different ideas about how to implement progressive reforms on the practical level.

Montgomery and the WEIU: Advocates and Architects of the "New Education"

Under Montgomery's leadership the WEIU pressed for innovation and reform in the Rochester public schools. As a member of the school board from 1900 to 1910, Montgomery was in a position to promote the WEIU's agenda through official channels. As Marion Harris Fey noted, Montgomery's tenure on the school board was interlaced with her service to the WEIU, and it is sometimes difficult to differentiate between Montgomery's personal influence on the board and the influence of the WEIU.[13] Virtually all of the initiatives Montgomery supported as a member of the school board were either programs validated through pilot programs initiated and supported by the WEIU, or they were ideas advocated by the WEIU.

Montgomery's tenure on the school board was a time of unprecedented experimentation in Rochester's educational system. The curriculum in the public schools was revised to reflect the latest pedagogical thought, which assigned lesser value to rote memorization and greater value to self-expression, and to include manual and industrial training to meet the needs of the growing ranks of immigrant laborers. Superintendent Clarence F. Carroll, who was superintendent during most of Montgomery's tenure, from 1904 to 1911, emphasized the democratic impulse he felt was necessary in public education, so that it would "make no provision for an aristocracy of culture, but will make abstract culture subordinate to social efficiency." In his view, "abstract culture" was represented by the study of subjects such as Greek and Latin, which were rapidly disappearing from public schools and even universities, so that "the whole tendency is to give higher education a vocational organization using the word in the broadest sense of a preparation for definite life-work."[14] Democratic education was practical education.

Montgomery and the WEIU were perfectly in accord with democratic education thus conceived. Manual training in the schools, advocated and pioneered by the WEIU in 1896, eventually led to the creation of the Factory School in 1908, which its advocates claimed was the first of its kind in the nation.[15] It became so popular that within a month the plan had to be expanded to accommodate all the registrations.[16] But Montgomery and the WEIU pressed for more than the reorganization of the curriculum. They wanted the entire infrastructure of the educational system to benefit the city in every practical way possible.

In 1900 the WEIU opened the first playground in Rochester with the hope that "the educational authorities will take up the work."[17] Summer schools (or vacation schools, as they were called) were among the earliest educational pilot projects of the WEIU in 1894. The women established a vacation sewing school for girls—a part of their long battle for manual training in the schools. In 1907 the WEIU helped to convince the Common Council of the city to appropriate $5,000 to the school board for the supervision and support of a playground, a summer school, and something new—a social center that would serve the needs of adults as well as children after school hours (see chap. 9).[18]

The public funding of the playground was quite consistent with Montgomery's desire to make the infrastructure of the educational system yield practical benefits to the entire city. Montgomery told the WEIU that the money for the playground would actually reduce the burden on the taxpayer. According to Montgomery, statistics showed a substantial reduction in the number of juvenile arrests in the police precincts where the playgrounds run by the Playground League were, and the coroner reported a reduction in the number of juvenile drownings. She asserted that the city would ultimately benefit from savings on the cost of police protection, prisons, and charity work.[19] In the social center movement, Montgomery and her allies tried to use the resources of the educational system to provide practical benefits to the community and to extend social democracy.

Montgomery's impact on the nature and quality of public education in the schools was important because it endured. Thirty years after Montgomery's service on the board was finished, Herbert S. Weet found that "the basic philosophy of education that the new order had brought, remained."[20] After Montgomery's decade on the board, public education in Rochester was democratic and aimed at social efficiency, as Superintendent Carroll understood those terms. In other words, education in Rochester's public schools was focused on the needs of the individual student and practical in purpose.

The New Direction in Rochester's Public School System

The new school board, under the Dow Law, had unprecedented power over the administration of the school system. In earlier years, the mayor had veto power over all board actions, but the new law made the school board the final authority over the schools. The city's Common Council appropriated the funds for the school (based on the board's recommendation), and the board had sole responsibility for the expenditure of the funds. The city could audit the board's expenditures but could not control them.[21] Under these new conditions, the new school board set out in the first decade of the twentieth century on a journey of innovation and reform that was unprecedented in Rochester's history and made Rochester's school system exemplary.[22] As of 1 January 1902, due to a revision of the Dow Law, Rochester's school board members were paid an annual salary of $1,200. Montgomery would have received this salary for eight years, from 1902 to 1909. Apparently, it was the only salaried position she ever held after she was married.

The new school board came into office in January 1900 with what they believed was a mandate for change in the city's public school system. The most pressing issues for the new board were the elimination of corruption and cronyism, the renovation and construction of school buildings, the recruitment and training of competent teachers and administrators, and revision of the program of study. Three major factors exerted pressure on the Rochester school system at the beginning of the twentieth century. First, the many years of cronyism and corruption under the old school board had left Rochester with a substandard educational system, described by Blake McKelvey as "an abomination before 1900."[23] The situation had become so drastic that Wellesley College refused to recognize Rochester's high school diploma, and Cornell and Mt. Holyoke also held Rochester graduates in low esteem.[24]

Second, Rochester was growing rapidly, and immigration was a major source of growth. The school system, especially at the high school and evening school levels, was swiftly becoming overwhelmed with students (both children and adults) who presented new challenges. The number of high school students was 935 in 1900, but it grew to 2,353 by 1910. Yet the growing number of evening school students was even more problematic, increasing during the decade from 816 to 11,351 students. The explosive growth in evening school students is explained by the introduction in 1901 of music, domestic science, and vocational education attractive to adults; in 1902, of compulsory education for all factory workers sixteen years of age and under who had not completed grammar school; and in 1904, of classes for immigrants who needed to meet the requirements for naturalization.[25]

Third, urbanization and industrialization were changing the educational needs of all students, whether immigrants or native-born. The system of apprenticeship, which had long served those who were not interested in higher academic training, was disappearing, and many trades were made obsolete by industrial innovation. Those developments created a need in the public schools for manual and vocational education. Urban congestion and increasing reliance on technology rather than manual labor created the need for health education, physical education, and recreational programs.[26]

More and Better School Buildings

By far the simplest problem to address (although it was not inexpensive) was the need for more and better school facilities. During Montgomery's tenure on the board, Rochester erected five new grade schools and two new high schools, made additions to four buildings, remodeled numerous "sanitary closets," created assembly halls in ten schools, purchased land to enlarge school grounds and build new buildings, purchased all sorts of new equipment, constructed public playgrounds, redecorated buildings and beautified school property.[27]

Eliminating Corruption and Improving the Professional Staff

One of the first problems addressed by the new board was corruption in the system, and after a year of heated controversy, recalcitrant superintendent Milton Noyes was replaced after the board was able to demonstrate that he had misappropriated over $3,000 of school funds for his personal use.[28] The superintendent's office proved difficult to fill at first, with three different candidates (one of whom died before taking office) hired from 1900 to 1904. Still, the new superintendents shared the new board's philosophy and cooperated in its reforms; and when the office was vacant, a member of the board, Professor George M. Forbes of the University of Rochester, served as interim superintendent.[29]

Several teachers and principals were asked to resign for incompetence. Others were let go because the new board found school faculties bloated with patronage appointments. In an effort to reduce overcrowding and eliminate the need for "annexes," the board reduced kindergartens and first grades to half-day sessions. Montgomery voted against the reduction of kindergarten sessions, but she voted with the board on the reduction of first-grade sessions.[30] The number of annexes was reduced in the first year from twenty to two.

School board members were interested in more than eliminating political appointments from the ranks of the teachers. They set out to revise the professional standards for educators in Rochester's public schools. First they required all teachers and principals, both veteran and new, to master the revised curriculum, adapt new classroom methodologies, and implement new standards and goals (see below). All teachers and principals were required to attend ten half-day training "institutes" during the year. In these institutes, the subject supervisors (teachers who were considered experts in a particular subject and supervised its instruction throughout the school system) introduced, demonstrated, and trained teachers in the use of new techniques and subject matter. In addition, principals met as a group with subject supervisors and received detailed written instructions regarding material taught in the institutes, and subject supervisors visited classrooms to make sure teachers had mastered new material.[31]

New teachers coming into the Rochester system had to meet higher standards established by the new board in 1901. The teacher training school course was lengthened from one to two years, and the subjects of sociology, art, literature, and manual training were added to the curriculum. Half of the second year was given to practice teaching. In 1903 the board took official action to make two years of training the minimum requirement for teachers in the system. New teachers with fewer than two years of training were no longer considered qualified for service in Rochester, even if they held a valid teacher's license. For high school teachers, the requirement was graduation from an approved college.[32] In these requirements, the board came near to doing what Montgomery had promised she would not do—purge the less educated teachers from the ranks. Technically Montgomery kept her promise. The board did not remove competent veteran teachers who could adapt to the new measures. Nevertheless, the requirements for new teachers presented an impediment to the less affluent candidate who perhaps could not afford to meet Rochester's standards for teacher training, even if she or he held a valid license.

Program of Study

By far the most difficult and controversial changes brought to the Rochester school system by the new board involved revisions to the program of study. Several areas of the curriculum were revised and expanded, including manual and domestic training, music, the evening schools, and the kindergarten program. Some new items were added to the program of study, including vocational education, health education, and physical education. The new board decided to make kindergarten instruction universal in the city and opened a kindergarten in every primary school (a WEIU goal). Special classes were designed to address the needs of slow students, physically or mentally handicapped students, and students who did not speak English. The truant school was abolished, and truant students were sent to a special class in a regular school.[33] A special outdoor school was established for tubercular children.[34]

Of course, as more subjects were added to the course of study, the question of how to manage the limited amount of time for instruction became critical. While in the high schools it was possible to allow students to choose electives, in the elementary schools it was necessary to eliminate certain material from the course of study, which was controversial. In fact, the changes were so rapid and far-reaching that they were described as "revolutionary."[35]

Yet the board went even further and modified the entire educational approach. In 1900 the school board decided that passing the state's Regents examinations would no longer be a criterion for promotion and graduation for Rochester high school students.[36] (The Educational Committee of the WEIU had criticized the Regents examinations as a waste of time as far back as 1897.) In 1901 the board approved a completely revised curriculum on the recommendation of Superintendent Charles B. Gilbert. The new curriculum, a model of the progressive "new education," demanded more focus on the individual needs of the child, which resulted in what became known as the group method of instruction. Students in a grade were divided according to ability into three groups, and the teacher worked with each small group in turn, giving the teacher time with each student individually, while keeping the other groups busy with seat work or other activities.[37]

As difficult and disruptive to classroom discipline as this adjustment was, the board demanded even more of its teachers and administrators. The new curriculum required teachers to orient classroom instruction around students' interests by using "correlation" and student "self-expression."[38] It was no longer considered good pedagogy or good discipline to force a student to struggle over a subject for which he or she had little interest and aptitude.

Instead, it was up to the teacher to engage the student's interest in the subject by finding some correlation for it in another area where the student did show interest and aptitude.

Exploring the students' interest through self-expression was equally challenging to classroom discipline. According to the school board's mandate, "children of the first, second, third, and fourth grades will work in clay, paper, cardboard, wood, and materials used in weaving fabric and cane weaving. The children of the primary grades will be provided with wood cut into a variety of widths, which will enable them to construct toys and useful objects of an interesting nature. This work will involve the use of the measuring rule, try-square, saw, saw boxes, hammer and nails."[39] These materials were used by the children not only in manual training, but in an activity called "free construction"—that is, the children could make anything they wanted and the teachers were not to interfere. An elementary teacher might have one group involved in recitation, another in seatwork, and another in free construction. All of this creative freedom and individualization was supposed to help the student apply and externalize what he or she internalized by traditional recitations and drills. Even separate spelling lists were abandoned. Teachers were directed to draw daily spelling lessons from the words that emerged from the correlated lessons. Above all, it was supposed to be organized and purposeful. Under no circumstances were teachers supposed to give students work "to keep them busy."[40] A curriculum based on correlation and expression was the cutting edge of educational theory at the beginning of the twentieth century.[41]

The creative activities of the new educational methods yielded all sorts of artifacts that could be exhibited. Supervisors and administrators used the best examples to train and motivate teachers in the institutes and as empirical evidence to demonstrate the success of the new methods to the interested public. Exhibits became regular features for each grade and each school, and before long, a competitive spirit ensued.[42]

To those accustomed to the orderly and quiet classroom of the past, the classroom atmosphere created by the new wave of correlation and self-expression must have seemed noisy and chaotic. For teachers trained in the educational theories of an earlier era, all of these changes must have seemed overwhelming. Likewise, the teachers' problems and complaints must have made principals' jobs very difficult. Many parents and other citizens probably thought the school board had abandoned all reasonable standards of discipline and achievement.

Montgomery's Key Role in School Reforms

Montgomery came to the school board with definite ideas about how the reform of the system ought to proceed, and she became a major force in the progressive reforms that the board carried out. The school board proceedings from the ten years she served indicate that she was responsible for introducing the first revised course of study for the primary grades that the board adopted, although it was subsequently replaced.[43] Montgomery led the board to adopt the Prang drawing system (a WEIU goal); recommended numerous changes in textbooks; advocated more supervision, training, and better salaries for the overwhelmingly female professional staff of the schools; and was a consistent advocate for improved facilities and equipment. She convinced the board to appoint a special committee for school beautification (a WEIU goal), and she took a particular interest in the needs of special classes of students, such as truants and others with special needs. The proceedings also reveal that Montgomery was always prepared to defend her positions on matters of educational policy with facts drawn from the latest research, expert opinion, and a sharp wit.

One of the first lectures Montgomery gave in 1900 to the WEIU, just after her election to the board, was devoted to educational reform. The school board had just completed its budget process for the year and submitted its funding request to the city. She asked the ladies of the WEIU to "create public sentiment to the end that the amount shall not be cut down."[44]

She told the women that they were living in a period of "educational revolution." She directed the women to the Charles William Eliot's *Educational Reform*, William James' *Talks to Teachers on Psychology*, and Susan E. Blow's *Letters to a Mother on the Philosophy of Froebel* as evidence of the intellectual changes related to progressive education. According to Montgomery, "It is now universally recognized that education of the child is the sovereign right and duty of the state, and the most full and practical measure of education at that." The right and duty of the state in education superseded that of the community or the city, and the courts had repeatedly enforced the point that "no community can from short sightedness or lack of enterprise hamper the educational advantages" owed to the public. The basic requirements for educational facilities were heating, lighting, ventilation, and seating. But Montgomery thought these were "sadly lacking" in most school buildings in Rochester, and the buildings themselves were mostly outdated. Montgomery claimed there were twelve hundred children and fifty-three teachers crowded into twenty-four "annexes"—overflow facilities rented by the city. The city paid $6,000 yearly to rent the annexes, which were mostly "small rooms or hall bed rooms in dwelling houses, lighted by lamps, heated by stoves, with benches placed about the rooms, a teacher in the middle with her knees touching those of her pupils who are herded in like sheep." Rochester needed new school buildings, she said, and needed them immediately.[45] Montgomery's agenda as a member of the new school board was clear. She wanted the board to implement the newest ideas in progressive education and deliver the new education in new facilities that were bright, attractive, sanitary, spacious, and well equipped for the purpose.

Walter Rauschenbusch and the Popular Revolt against the "New Education"

While Montgomery worked hard to enlist support for the progressive reforms of the new school board, criticism from several quarters persisted. In addition to the old political interests and others who had lost jobs with the coming of the new school board, many parents and others interested in the schools thought the reforms introduced by the new board were too radical. Walter Rauschenbusch was among them.

Many teachers and parents, especially, responded to the new educational philosophy, so opposite to what they had always believed and been taught, with sharp criticism. The exhibits were especially disliked in some quarters, for they were thought to be dishonest and prideful displays. The criticism mounted as the school system prepared to enter items in an exhibit at a national educational convention, and it culminated in a public meeting at St. Paul's Parish House on 10 September 1908. In an open invitation to the public published in the *Democrat and Chronicle*, the ad hoc committee that organized the meeting asked parents to come and "give the results of the methods of teaching, school discipline and management as observed in their families." The organizers also hoped the meeting would shed light on "the alleged displacement of essentials by faddism, and the criticism that an unnecessary amount of time is devoted to the so-called 'show work' which should be devoted to reading, arithmetic, geography, etc."[46]

At the meeting a wave of frustration and anger burst forth against "an alleged lack of proper training in the fundamentals of education and the preponderance of so-called frills and fads in elementary grades." When one man attempted to speak in defense of the system, he was hissed and shouted down. Generally those in attendance thought the schools gave too much attention to "modeling in clay, sewing, music and drawing" and too little to "spelling, arithmetic, writing and geography." An anonymous letter from a teacher, in which the teacher claimed that "the time allowed for each subject [during the school day] was not a quarter of that needed," was read to the assembly. At the end of the meeting, a committee was appointed to arrange for another meeting.[47] Walter Rauschenbusch, as chairman of the committee, soon came to dominate the movement against the board of education.

Historian John R. Aiken believed that Rauschenbusch opposed the board's reforms because the American pragmatism and democratic egalitarianism they represented contradicted his own elitist and racist presuppositions about the proper goals and methods of education. Rauschenbusch believed, according to Aiken, that the purpose of education was to eliminate social evil by transmitting and perfecting the eternal moral values and ideals learned through classical German educational methods. In this way, individual and national character would progress. In Rauschenbusch's view, the board's commitment to individual self-expression and practical vocational education eroded respect for authority, promoted materialism, and undercut the achievements of German liberalism. Instead of preserving Teutonic values, the board surrendered them in an attempt to accommodate the Rochester public schools to the needs of immigrants, whom he believed were racially inferior. The reforms carried out by the Board of Education in the 1900s were not only ineffective, according to this view, but they were destructive to social ethics and an obstacle to the kingdom of God.[48] If Aiken's analysis was correct, Rauschenbusch's educational philosophy was consistent with Froebel's in many respects. Most importantly, Rauschenbusch believed that education's central purpose was the formation of individual and national moral character for the sake of eliminating evil from society.

In *Christianizing the Social Order,* Rauschenbusch attributed what he perceived as a decline in the quality of American education to the contaminating effects of capitalism:

> The business world sneers at anything in education that does not pan out immediate and material results. As its blaring bandwagon goes by the college walls, the students quiver to climb on board. They have lost interest in pure thought, which can never be converted into cash. The old love for the classics is gone, and the love of science for its own sake, which was to take its place, has failed to become general.[49]

Rauschenbusch's educational views were idealistic, but not necessarily elitist. In fact, he criticized the elitism of the German educational system. He believed public education had the potential to foster social equality, but only if it offered the same quality of education equally to all social classes. Although he conceded that every worker needed enough technical education to understand the contribution of his or her own task to the industrial process, he was suspicious of a system that limited the children of the working classes to vocational education only. He believed that they, like the children of the upper classes, needed broad intellectual stimulation and character formation. A stratified system of education "neither expresses nor creates democracy," he said.[50]

The Case against the "New Education"

Rauschenbusch entered the fray over public education for personal rather than theoretical reasons. He believed his own five children were not receiving an adequate education under the new school board's regime. Initially Rauschenbusch supported the new school board and the reforms they instituted, but his enthusiasm faded into "perplexity and dissatisfaction" at what he observed in his children.[51]

The citizen's committee, with Rauschenbusch as chairman, felt that clarity would enhance the value of the next meeting, so the committee published an appeal in the *Democrat and Chronicle* asking for public feedback on twelve items. The committee wanted "signed communications from parents, teachers, business men and all who have first hand knowledge of the educational conditions." They emphasized the need for "definite facts" rather than "vague denunciations." Specifically, they wanted to know if students got "sufficient drill" in subjects such as arithmetic, spelling, geography, and history. Had there been "any noticeable improvement in this direction within the last year"? Why could teachers find no time for drill, if that was the case? What subjects, if any, should be eliminated from the curriculum? What subjects deserved less attention? Were exhibitions and the time given to preparation for them useful? Was dramatization a useful technique, and if so, in what grades? Were institutes a valuable use of teachers' time? Was the group system a "wise arrangement"? Was vertical writing "desirable"? Was proper discipline being maintained? Should corporal punishment "be more freely used by the principals"? Did the teachers have confidence in the current system? Who was responsible for the "apparent discouragement of the teaching force"? Responses to these items were to be sent to Rauschenbusch and would be "treated with proper discretion."[52]

Apparently too few citizens disclosed their sentiments to satisfy the committee, for the *Democrat and Chronicle* printed another appeal for letters. The committee feared that some parents and teachers were withholding their views out of fear that their names would become public, and they wished to reassure the public of their discretion. They also wanted make clear that they welcomed positive comments: "If there is hearty approval of any of the methods under discussion, we want to know it and shall welcome every good word." The members of the committee wanted to assure the public that they did not view themselves as opponents of the board. In fact they believed "the Board of Education has served the people faithfully and earnestly to the best of its ability." Nevertheless they believed they had a public mandate.[53]

On 13 November Rauschenbusch and the committee were ready to report their findings at a public meeting at East High School. The report, printed verbatim in the *Democrat and Chronicle*, was much more conciliatory toward the board than many had perhaps expected.

Rauschenbusch reported that the committee had pored over "a large number of letters from teachers, parents and business men," visited ten schools and tested students, and interviewed "a large number" of persons. In the course of their investigation, they recognized the sincere and devoted work of the school board, so they "tried to do full justice to the . . . real progress made in the new educational system, but . . . we also set forth fully and emphatically the faults into which it seems to us to have fallen." The committee had met with the Board of Education for more than eighteen hours over five sessions, and they had been able to reach substantial agreement on many issues. So at the public meeting Rauschenbusch read an amended version of the report with the "controversial element" eliminated. "If we should publicly state the criticisms we made against the system with the arguments to support our criticism the board would justly feel compelled to make its defense against these criticisms and to state the arguments supporting its views. . . . Therefore we cut out our entire statement and argument, and confine ourselves to a concise restatement of the definite requests which we have addressed to the board."[54] Fortunately, a draft of Rauschenbusch's earlier version has survived to shed light on the "controversial elements" as he saw them.

While Rauschenbusch's comments in the draft were acerbic and sometimes sarcastic, the tone of the final public report was much more positive toward the board. Rauschenbusch and the committee did level some serious criticisms at the new system, but they did not ask for the abolition of a single feature of the new system except exhibitions. In every other case, they admitted the value of the school board's reforms and asked only that the board use moderation to remedy many unintended consequences the reforms had entailed. Nor did they even mention the movement of the board toward adult education, manual training, and vocational training—probably the school board's most important reforms in terms of opening the schools to Rochester's burgeoning immigrant population and accommodating their needs. This is perhaps an indication of the degree to which the school board was able to convince the committee of the general value of its reforms. Both in Rauschenbusch's draft of the report and its final published form, Rauschenbusch and the committee acknowledged the pedagogical value and appropriateness of nearly every curricular innovation introduced by the school board, even if they criticized particular new methods, ways in which they were implemented, or the degree to which they had displaced older ones.

Any differences Rauschenbusch and the committee had with the school board were "only differences of judgment," he told the audience at East High School. "We also found these differences largely disappearing as we discussed the questions involved." In fact, their views were so harmonious that the school board claimed it had already detected on its own many of the deficiencies noted by the committee in its report and planned to remedy them.

The committee's recommendations dealt with a very broad range of topics, from the value of a particular textbook to the ethical implications of the curriculum. The committee asked for more time to be devoted to drill work in spelling and geography, and they encouraged the board to investigate whether the formal grammar instruction was adequate. Rauschenbusch, in his draft, disparaged the instruction of mathematics in the grade schools as "kindergarten methods" and asked for more "mental arithmetic in the old-fashioned way."[55]

The committee recognized the "great advance" the new curriculum represented in the teaching of music and other artistic subjects, yet they believed that many grade school teachers, whose gifts did not lie in those areas, were needlessly pressured and made to feel incompetent when they could not lead artistic and musical activities. They asked the board to find a solution through team teaching.

Many of the committee's recommendations addressed the comparative value new teaching methods and particular activities in relation to traditional drill and recitation. Too much time was "frittered away," the committee thought, on preparations for holidays. While they did not want to extinguish the "festive spirit" entirely, they wanted holiday activities kept "strictly within limits so that the schools stick to their main business." Likewise, the committee believed that the curriculum had been overloaded with "expression work." They wanted the administrators and teachers to "keep perpetually in mind that the fundamentals of education must take precedence." In fact they believed some types of expression work ought to be discontinued and replaced with more valuable labor. For example, when the committee learned that grade school children were not required to do any homework at all they requested that a "moderate but increasing amount of home work be given" so that children would be prepared for homework when they reached high school. In his draft of the report, Rauschenbusch wrote that the children needed to "grapple independently with a set task and to chew their own food."[56]

Rauschenbusch and the committee also believed the group method of classroom organization, however well intended, wasted the teachers' time and energy. The committee recommended that teachers should consult with their principals, but that they should be free to organize their classes as they saw fit. In his draft, Rauschenbusch offered a sarcastic aside: "If under this arrangement some of the 'occupation' work goes overboard, we shall try to survive the loss, and if the 'occupation tables' went too, we should not mourn."[57]

The subject of the Regents examinations did not escape the committee's notice. They believed some sort of standardized testing was necessary because of its "moral effect upon the children" and so that the community could be assured that high standards were being maintained in all grades. What salubrious "moral effect" the committee had in mind can be inferred from Rauschenbusch's expression of regret, in his draft of the report, that students no longer "have to eat the bitter fruit of laziness and slovenliness by facing a defective percentage on their exam papers."[58] So eager were Rauschenbusch and the committee to see standardized testing reinstated that they proposed the appointment of a "committee of nine," composed of two members of the faculty of the University of Rochester, two faculty members from each high school, and three from the city at large, "to advise with the board in the preparation of such tests and to take under consideration any other matters relating to the welfare of the schools."[59] In effect, it was a recommendation to establish a shadow board to look over the shoulder of the elected school board. From the perspective of the school board, this was one of the most distasteful and controversial recommendations offered by Rauschenbusch and the committee.

The committee's most serious criticisms indicted the new system because of the negative moral implications of its unintended consequences. For example, they criticized the practice of "book making," in which teachers were required to collect sample books of student work and send them to the superintendent's office. Apparently, some teachers believed they were being evaluated on the quality of work in the sample books. In his draft report, Rauschenbusch wrote that the books were "perfected, elaborated, illustrated, until sometimes they were works of art. Some teachers 'fixed them over.'" Rauschenbusch felt that the sample books represented "a great leak of time and effort with pupils and teachers" and asserted that as many as fourteen sample books per student had been required of some teachers. Ironically, he believed, the sample books not only wasted time but "fostered that dull routine work which the new education condemns."[60] While the committee recommended a drastic reduction in the making of sample books, it is clear that Rauschenbusch would have preferred to see it ended completely.

Still, the sample books were merely symptomatic of what Rauschenbusch regarded as a deeper moral flaw in the new system. Rauschenbusch and the committee believed the school board, in allowing the schools to participate in local, regional, and national exhibitions, had "created in teachers and pupils a feeling that the chief end of education is to show off and get ready for an exhibition." Indeed, the school board had expended substantial resources to support exhibitions in which the Rochester course of study was put forth as an example for other school systems, and they had been lauded with praise and awards from educational experts.[61] Rauschenbusch and the committee believed that success had gotten the better of the board, and the preoccupation with creating successful exhibits had "produced exactly that machine-like work and dull routine against which the new education has protested nobly." Even worse, they had inadvertently fostered in the schools a spirit of deception and vanity. Some teachers, he claimed, had "'fixed over' the work of their pupils. Some had their gifted pupils do work for others and sign the names of others, thus misusing their time and health and undermining their sense of right. The papers of Italian children were taken to other schools and copied and the Italian names signed to them. . . . By these means Rochester has furnished far and away the finest exhibitions of public school work, but it has been at heavy cost."[62]

While Rauschenbusch could understand the pride that prompted those responsible to look the other way, he believed the public was justified in its moral outrage.[63] The public report of the committee recommended that the board should adopt a policy to refuse invitations to participate in exhibitions outside of Rochester and to limit them even in individual schools so that the "showy elements of school life" would be minimized and attention would be given to "solid education."[64]

Rauschenbusch was also highly critical of the quality of discipline in the Rochester schools. He was pleased that "the old reign of fear is gone. The children like to go to school, and seem free and happy in their contact with their teachers."[65] Nevertheless, he believed there was "a wide-spread laxity of discipline among American children: impertinence, disdain of authority, rowdyism in the higher schools." This defect he attributed to the too-frequent absence of fathers from the home. To make up for what was lacking in the home, Rauschenbusch thought the schools should "demand more prompt and unquestioning obedience, more respect for teachers and elders, and the prompt repression of noise and extravagance when they are selfish and unsocial." He believed the student population in the high schools needed culling. "If our High Schools dismissed 10% of the pupils as idle and incompetent, it would give the other 90% a chance to really profit by the special privileges of a High School course, and would create a new spirit in the student body."[66]

Rauschenbusch thought it would be difficult for the school system as it stood to fill the void of manly discipline in the lives of Rochester's students. In a section of his draft of the report entitled "The Mental Effects of the New Education," he asserted that the current system traded "precise knowledge" for "an atmosphere of mental freedom." He charged that

> the children of to-day are readily interested, but they want all things made interesting for them. They are not willing to rivet their attention on a piece of work and see it through. They do not learn to 'dig'. They turn out slovenly work and have no conscience about doing things just right. Even the older pupils are not able to take a text-book and wrestle a subject out for themselves. As soon as the stimulating influence of the teacher is withdrawn, their interest flags and they droop.[67]

The school board had set out in 1900 to make Rochester's high school diploma respected among colleges, but Rauschenbusch thought they had failed. "The colleges feel no mighty uplift of a new mental energy as the results of the new education. . . . Many professors feel that they can no longer expect the same level of work as in past generations of college men." Rauschenbusch saw this as evidence that the new education had eroded the intelligence and willpower of students in a way that threatened civilization. "The fundamental distinction between civilized man and the savage," Rauschenbusch argued, "is that the civilized brain can concentrate attention and keep it up, while the wandering interest of the savage picks things up with a grunt of delight and swiftly wearies of them."[68]

Rauschenbusch thought he knew the root of the defect. The "Kindergarten idea" was indulged for too long. In the upper grades, playfulness ought to give way to "the stern grip of work and duty as the child matures." Instead, childishness was indulged and study periods were too short. For Rauschenbusch the cause of the problem was clear. "Our schools have been feminized." While he agreed that "our politics need the purifying influence of woman," he believed that the schools needed "the energizing influence of men. However high the level of culture is rising among women, the really creative mental work thus far has been done by men, and men are still the great teachers of the race."[69]

Evidently, the committee agreed with these sentiments, for they asserted that "the teaching force would be improved" if more male teachers were hired and that growing boys needed "masculine influence for their proper discipline and development." They recommended that the board should hire more male teachers and not base decisions on "considerations of cheapness alone, but also the desirability of the masculine element in the teaching force" when choosing between male and female applicants.[70]

Implicitly and explicitly, Rauschenbusch and the committee accused the board of allowing the schools to waste valuable time on showiness and vanity, subornment of deception, and inculcating in children a playful immaturity that left them unprepared for responsible adulthood and robbed them of essential (and allegedly masculine) virtues such as focused concentration, endurance of adversity, and obedience to legitimate authority. Still, it was not so much what was being taught in the schools as it was the way in which it was taught. Anticipating Ann Douglas by almost seventy years, Rauschenbusch asserted that feminization was eroding American culture.

The School Board's Response

The school board found a way to agree with every recommendation of the committee, but in explaining their agreement they often sought to deflect the explicit or implied criticism. While the school board claimed that exhibit work had made a "great contribution to the knowledge of our principals and teachers by illustrating the progressive development of the course of study," they agreed that "the work had been overdone." In fact, they had already turned down four invitations to exhibitions and would "heartily assent" to the policy recommended by the committee.[71]

Like Rauschenbusch and the committee, the school board felt that "an increase in the number of men in the teaching force is desirable," but they thought it would be impossible to make much progress along that line in the lower grades because of the "existing conditions"—that is, the meager salaries those positions paid. They pledged to try to hire men in the upper grades and high schools, where the pay was better. Like the committee, the board wanted to increase teachers' salaries. They claimed they had done what they could to increase both the minimum and maximum salaries and to shorten substantially the time required to move from the minimum to the maximum scale. They could do no more without additional funding.[72]

Modern readers might assume that Montgomery took exception to the position of the committee regarding the need for male teachers, but she probably sincerely agreed that more men in the teaching force "would be desirable." While she was an advocate for the women teachers during her tenure and a lifelong advocate for expanding women's role in society, she was essentially complementarian in her gender views. She believed there were things for which men, like women, were especially suited. In fact, when Wellesley was searching for a new president in 1894 and again around 1910 or 1911, Montgomery expressed the preference for a male president. In 1894 she wrote that Wellesley needed someone "to start the golden stream flowing Wellesley ward. I don't know whether a woman can do that or not."[73] In 1910 or 1911, she wrote to fellow Wellesley alumna Louise McCoy North, "There is an academic hardness about the college that can only be broken up by a man big enough to *dominate* the college and create a new atmosphere."[74]

There were a few areas where the school board politely took issue with the committee's analysis. The problem of discipline was one of those areas. Forbes told the audience at East High School that the board was well aware of its responsibility to the public in regard to teaching and maintaining moral discipline in the schools. The committee's recommendation, he said, "refers indirectly to the training of the American home and the necessity of providing in the school training what is so generally urged upon Americans as lacking in their home training." Rauschenbusch had been anything but indirect in his draft, and the school board had seen the complete version of the report, with its criticisms and arguments intact. Forbes denied the suggestion that the school board's new system was subversive of moral discipline in the classroom. In fact, he viewed the climate of free expression that prevailed in the new system as a tremendous step forward. Forbes asserted to the audience:

> If I were asked to state what I regard as the greatest achievement of the new administration, I should name without a moment's hesitation the transformation of the moral attitude of teacher to pupil, and corresponding to this, the development of self-respect and self-control in the pupil

which creates, in its ideal form, perfect freedom and perfect order in the schoolroom. This transformation from repression to moral freedom is by no means complete, but it is so far advanced that there are now hundreds of schoolrooms in Rochester where it exists in approximately ideal form. The change in moral attitude involved in this conception of discipline receives its finest illustration in the rooms devoted to truants, so-called incorrigibles and defectives.[75]

This strong statement was perhaps a rather pointed reply to Rauschenbusch's comment about culling the ranks of the high schools.

Regarding the matter of standardized testing, the school board was convinced that no further testing was really needed because its current policy already provided for "substantially such tests as are requested." The board did not want to institute a testing regime that would require "long periods of strain and anxiety on the part of both pupils and teachers, and stamps the idea into the pupil's mind that the end and consummation of education is to pass examinations." Nevertheless, they agreed to the recommendation of the committee because "they have made it in a form entirely consistent with the above mentioned views." In fact, the school board declared it would "most heartily welcome the opportunity" to work with the committee of nine as long as everyone understood that "the final responsibility must rest upon us, a responsibility that we cannot in any case either avoid or transfer" because they were elected by the citizens of the city and "responsible to the entire community for discharging that duty."[76] The school board wanted everyone to know that they regarded themselves as the legitimate authority responsible for the schools and would not be usurped by a committee serving the narrow interests of a few.

Despite those areas of disagreement, the school board followed through with its pledges to the public. Forbes met with the principals and told them that he had dealt with the committee "in good faith" and that he wanted the changes promised by the board implemented immediately and in detail, and the board took other measures to assure compliance.[77]

The Aftermath of the Controversy

Rauschenbusch's committee had its way, but not the final word on the controversy. A year later, School Superintendent Carroll complained about the new "Committee of Nine" in his annual report. He believed their criticisms were biased and that the schools needed "a period of rest from irresponsible criticism."[78]

Montgomery also fired a few parting shots at the critics of the school board. In a draft of a letter to the editor of the *Post-Express,* she denied the charge made by Rauschenbusch and others that the school board rigidly controlled the teachers through the course of study. She claimed that the course of study was "only suggestive typical programs worked out for the assistance of teachers, who are left free to make out their own programs in consultation with the principal of the school." She believed that teachers were most effective in an atmosphere of structured freedom. She abhorred "the mechanical, cut-and-dried, uniform program, by which every teacher at the same moment was imparting the information which every other teacher of like grade was giving."[79]

Montgomery defended the group method of teaching as highly preferable to "mass teaching" which she regarded as justifiable only as a last resort. "The massing of little children may be easier for the teacher, but it is at the cost of the child's best interests," she declared.[80] With characteristic confidence, she laid out her case:

> The whole weight of present-day educational authority, and of experience in schools for many years past is on the side of the group method of teaching. It helps the teacher disentangle the individual child from the mass. Instead of grinding them all through at one pace, it adapts the instruction to the capacity of the child, putting him in his own, happy group of equals. The slow child is not embittered by always being compared with the brilliant, nor the clever child made lazy & uninterested by having too little to do.[81]

Montgomery and the school board were forced to moderate the pace of their reforms, but they maintained with certainty that theirs was the right course for the Rochester schools.

The End of Montgomery's School Board Career

Republican Party boss George Aldridge saw to it that Montgomery was not renominated for the school board in 1909. The Good Government forces that had brought her and the other reformers into office against his will had become too weak to be a political factor, and the controversies associated with Montgomery's tenure on the school board had weakened her public support.[82] Aldridge saw an opportunity to regain control of the school board and initially planned to replace Isaac Adler and James B. P. Duffy as well as Montgomery. Three Aldridge candidates would have given him control of the school board, but when his plans became apparent and met resistance, he decided to settle for removing Montgomery as a first step.[83] In a deft political move, Aldridge nominated another woman, school teacher Helen Gregory, in Montgomery's place, so that the voices of the women would be divided.

While many women remained loyal to Montgomery and petitioned for her renomination, it was clear they did not speak for all women.[84] Even Montgomery's good friend and longtime WEIU colleague Harriet Brown Dow, given the choice between supporting Gregory or having no woman on the school board, chose to support Gregory.[85] Montgomery wrote in her diary on 8 October 1909 that the women of the WEIU were "pretty mad,"[86] but the political mood had turned against them and their indignation could not produce the change of conditions they desired.

Clearly Montgomery relished her years of service on the school board. She was constantly on the move, from meeting to meeting, and from school to school. In January 1906 she recorded ten appointments related to the schools in her diary; on 20 December 1907 she visited seven schools, attended a three-hour board meeting, and gave a speech at the social center—all in one day.[87] Even when she traveled abroad, her beloved Rochester schools were never far from her mind. In 1902, while in Egypt, she sent accounts of her journey to the teachers and students of particular schools, which were published in the newspaper. In these letters, she suggested subjects for student readings and even sent some Egyptian sand for students to examine under a microscope.[88]

Montgomery's last meeting with the school board occurred on 31 December 1909. The board passed appreciative resolutions in her honor. They said that she had made "a very exceptional contribution to the arduous work of these years" and that her "wisdom and insight and broad experience" was "embodied" in the board's accomplishments. They claimed she had an "expert knowledge of the literature of childhood." Moreover, they lauded her contributions to the course of study in recommending supplementary readings and providing school libraries "the best literature which the world affords." The board took special care to recognize her concern for "the special welfare of teachers and children," her spirit of conviction, and her "inspiration, courage, good cheer, and saving humor."[89] Afterward, Montgomery reported in her diary that she felt "pretty sad at heart. End of ten years of service." The next day, she wrote, "HOUSE FULL OF ROSES from School Board and principals. Had forty young people here to supper."[90]

Nine

THE HACKETT HOUSE EPISODE
AND THE BIRTH OF SOCIAL CENTERS

Montgomery, like many progressives, approached social ethics with her religious presuppositions intact, and she saw no injustice in proscribing behavior that appeared to her to be destructive to public morality. At the same time, she believed that the social environment was a powerful factor in the development of personal character. Consequently she believed that a great deal of criminality and public immorality could be eradicated by improving the social conditions in which persons lived and developed, and that people, if properly educated and given the opportunity, would choose good over evil.

This chapter is an exploration of the connections that link Montgomery's involvement in two controversial episodes from Rochester's history. First, in the Hackett House episode, Montgomery led the women of Rochester to attempt to purge Rochester of its brothels. Their attack was two-pronged. The women tried to use the force of law to crack down on the brothels and put them out of business, and they advocated for "wholesome" recreational alternatives to the young men who patronized the brothels. Second, as a member of the school board, Montgomery participated in the social center movement, an attempt to use public school buildings as neighborhood centers where community residents could create for themselves the institutions of civil society and participate in a broader democratic public.

Although Montgomery, as a private citizen, failed to achieve the changes she desired in Rochester's social environment in the Hackett House episode, she persevered. As a member of the school board, through her support of the social center movement, she succeeded, at least temporarily. The social center movement, which became a controversial issue for the school board, drew support from many of the leading citizens of Rochester. It seemed to provide a practical way to meet a growing need for wholesome socialization, especially among the working class—a problem that had troubled Rochester's leaders for several years.

In 1903 Walter Rauschenbusch chaired a committee that conducted a year long survey of social conditions in Rochester on behalf of the YMCA. The committee discovered, among other things, that Rochester had plenty of prostitution and many cheap music halls and saloons, where the growing population of immigrant laborers spent their time and money, but few outlets of wholesome entertainment for the poorly paid and poorly educated working masses.[1] One of the key recommendations of the report was to provide wholesome recreational outlets.

The Hackett House Episode

In June 1904 Patrick N. Hackett, the proprietor of a local saloon known variously as "Hackett House" or "It," was arrested for running a "disorderly house"—a brothel. The establishment had long been the source of much trouble and was the subject of a widely publicized hearing that involved many young women who were arrested there. Nevertheless, on 4 March 1905 the State Excise Department issued the proprietor's wife a license to run the establishment on the same day that her husband's license was revoked, thereby allowing the establishment to remain open without the interruption of business.[2] The leading women of Rochester were outraged. Twenty-five leaders of women's organizations, including Montgomery, signed a call for a public meeting of women. They wrote: "In the name of our homes, in the name of the moral purity of our children, for the sake of a decent city where honest folk may rear their families uncontaminated and unafraid, let the women of this city assemble." They wanted every woman in Rochester to help in the struggle against "organized greed and impurity," and they asked the ministers of the churches to sound the call to the women at the midweek services.[3]

In an interview before the meeting, Montgomery told a reporter the women planned to try to get the new license revoked, take away the proprietor's bonding, and pressure the landlord who owned the property to evict the establishment. She said the women also wanted to know why judges did not use their discretion to imprison rather than fine "divekeepers" and "pool room managers." They wanted the mayor to station police officers in front of "notorious dives" and "take the names of all persons entering or leaving." The women felt this use of the "police power" was justifiable to "protect the morals of the young girls of the city." They had not decided if they should mention by name the establishments they thought merited such action, but the women's "investigations" had proved that many of the saloons in Rochester were "nothing more than houses of assignation."[4]

Six hundred women gathered in response to the call. Montgomery was elected chairman of the meeting, along with a secretary and nearly fifty vice presidents, including Susan B. Anthony. In Montgomery's address to the assembly, she presented a social justification of women's political action in municipal affairs, once again likening it to "housekeeping." She said:

> Not all of us realize how imperfect our organization in communities still is. We have learned fairly well how to live as individuals, but life in communities is still imperfectly understood. The good woman living in the country or small community may know very well how to regulate her life there, but the situation is changed in a city of more than 100,000 persons. There she cannot limit her housekeeping to her own home and still be considered a good housekeeper. In the country her duties may end with her own dooryard, but when houses adjoin hers on both sides on a street, when the conditions in these affect her and her children, it is the shallowest individualism to say that her whole duty has to do with her own family. Notwithstanding her best efforts, her boys and girls are endangered by the conditions in other homes and by the temptations that are set to ensnare them.[5]

Rose Lattimore Alling, who was the chairman of the Legal Protection Committee of the WEIU and a probation officer in the city, and whose husband was a leader of the Good Government movement and a prominent industrialist, wanted to goad the women to action. Because of the publicity over Hackett House, she said, "We have put our jeweled fingers over our hearts and gasped." The events that brought them together were commonplace, she said, but the women were so affected by it because they sat in their parlors on Sunday afternoons blissfully unaware of the conditions surrounding them. She told the audience that "the child is never the criminal." In most cases, wayward children were the victims of ineffective parents. The "fine theory that parents should be left to bring up their own children is dissipated" by the shocking ignorance or inability to cope with conditions she found in many homes. In her view, young people turned to places like Hackett House because they had no alternative, and well-intentioned reformers were "almost helpless," once a girl was caught in "the frightful undertow" of a place like Hackett House. She asked the women: "Shall I sit in my home . . . and do nothing to protect the children of these people?" Of course she would not. She was convinced that "some of our smug, complacent Christians" must abandon "their Sunday prejudices." She hoped some of her "good sisters" would not "fall off their seats" with shock, but she thought the playing of pool was "a good thing" when it could be done in a wholesome atmosphere. It was time to listen to "the cranks and heretics" and allow wholesome amusements on Sunday.[6]

Montgomery agreed with her friend. "Amusement of a wholesome kind must be provided just as much as churches," said Montgomery. "Every kind of innocent human amusement that appeals to boys and girls ought to be open. I am told there is only one bowling alley in this city that is not connected with a saloon. The $26,000 spent in convicting boys and girls might have been put to good use in work of this sort." Montgomery and the other leaders among the women had more in mind than "what President Roosevelt calls the 'big stick.'" They wanted to offer a carrot to the youth of Rochester who strayed into the saloons and pool halls. They wanted to provide alternative activities—even on Sunday.[7]

Montgomery was in no mood to hear complaints about the burden on the taxpayers. "We are the wives of the dear taxpayers," she told the women. They should use their influence to convince the city aldermen to fund alternative amusements or the women "ought to retire them from office if they don't." She wanted a variety of activities. She knew that "you can't catch all boys with a library" nor all girls with "a lecture on Browning." Some boys "just want to get out and holler," and they should have a place to do it "without going to the devil."[8]

The idea of expanding city services to include recreational opportunities was not new. Rauschenbusch had recommended it in his YMCA report nearly a year earlier. Rauschenbusch apparently accepted an assumption that was common among some Social Darwinists, that the development of society was reflected in the growth of each individual. He believed that boys were "young savages" who were "in their personal lives living through the primitive ages of humanity."[9] He believed more recreational outlets for boys would decrease juvenile delinquency and prevent adult male criminality. "Let the city scatter public playgrounds through its territory, provide out-door swimming places in Summer, a public swimming tank in Winter, better chances for skating, and let the religious and other organization [*sic*] provide trained leaders for gymnastic and other sports, and clubs for the evenings, and it would save dollars and save boys."[10]

Rauschenbusch was advocating "muscular Christianity," which viewed athletics as a means of restoring robust manhood to the allegedly feminized white middle-class male, and of building "moral character" among the working-class, immigrant, and black males.[11] He and his friend and ally, Paul Moore Strayer, pastor of Third Presbyterian Church, worked closely with the YMCA in Rochester,[12] and the YMCA was the foremost institution in the promotion of muscular Christianity in America.

Clifford Putney found that muscular Christianity was in large part a reaction against the influence of the Cult of True Womanhood in American Protestantism—a critique of the influence of women in the churches. How, then, is one to account for the fact that Montgomery and her domestic feminist sisters joined this push for muscular Christianity? What was different in the women's proposal was the type of amusements they recommended, such as pool halls, and the fact that they wanted them open on Sunday. If anything, the women's position was more radical, and their recommendations provoked heated criticism from conservative clergy.

If Montgomery ever felt threatened by masculinity, she never articulated it. On the contrary, she consistently maintained the Victorian view that men and women had complementary roles in home and society. She never advocated a smaller sphere of activity and influence for men, only a larger one for women. Apparently she was perfectly happy to support efforts to promote manliness—especially Christian manliness characterized by chivalry and moral virtue. In her view, Christian manliness would enhance Christian womanliness and protect social purity.

Nevertheless, as a domestic feminist, Montgomery offered her justification for organizing the women's response that addressed maternal values and concerns. She did not place all the responsibility for the current conditions on men, not even the elected officials. "We women are back of these evil conditions," she declared, "because we are living a sort of sweet, refined existence." She told her audience there were many "harem women" in the United States, who "might as well be carried through the world in a palanquin to-day for all we know about the real world."[13] She knew that many women feared "that in doing something in this way for others we would be immodest, grow strong-minded and altogether undesirable."[14] Nevertheless she encouraged her audience to "cut off the blinders" and discover the real conditions of the world, but to "keep as sweet and womanly as we can through it all."[15] This was True Womanhood turned on its head. These women still believed they were responsible for the moral state of society, but instead of congratulating themselves for keeping to the "woman's sphere," they blamed themselves for being out of touch with the real conditions of life outside their own comfortable homes. They indicted themselves, as women of privilege, for indulging in ignorance out of fear of the truth, yet at the same time they tried to reinvigorate their roles as moral guardians in the home and community.

The women passed resolutions condemning Hackett House and asking the governor to close the loophole in the excise law that permitted such abuse. They called upon judges to impose the strictest penalties available under the law upon those convicted of "keeping disorderly houses or gambling dens." They commended the mayor of the city in his struggle against vice, and they thanked the press covering the meeting. Most importantly, they established a committee to continue the work of the meeting.[16]

Montgomery, as chairperson of the meeting, was responsible for naming the permanent committee to continue the work of the meeting—the Committee of Fifteen. She announced the names a few days later, and most of them were prominent in the WEIU and the Ethical Club. One notable choice that did not often appear in lists of Rochester women active in public affairs was the name of Mrs. Walter Rauschenbusch.[17]

In comments to the press, Montgomery said the women meant only to "support honest public officials" and that "all evidence that may come to us" would be given over to them. The women intended to make a "systematic study of Rochester," to know what actual conditions prevailed and what the provisions of the law were so that they could "back up" their statements. Montgomery thought it might be possible to accomplish much by working quietly and without publicity with the landlords, some of them women who were perhaps unaware of how their property was being used. In any case, she wanted to work "in a sane way that shall commend itself to the good sense of the community" and "accomplish some practical results."[18]

Religious Backlash

Resistance to the women's efforts quickly developed from an unanticipated direction. On Sunday, 26 March, a volley of sermons congratulated the women for speaking out but opposed their suggestion of Sunday amusements. Rev. Horace A. Crane, pastor of Glenwood Methodist Church, even took aim at Montgomery personally, if indirectly, when he accused the public schools of fueling the "craze for amusement which characterizes this age." He thought that teaching children to dance in school gave them "the taste and knowledge for the public dance," which led to "the downfall of multitudes of young women." He blamed the "fad for dramatization, with the recommendation to see certain plays at the theater" for feeding the "theater habit" that eroded their moral virtue. While he understood the necessity of opening the parks on Sunday so that laborers, who had no other opportunity, could enjoy nature, he was against "the inducements of the toboggan slide, the merry-go-round and the vaudeville," which he thought drew crowds "chiefly reflecting to the benefit of the street railway company." Rev. J. M. Walters, pastor of Spencer Ripley Methodist Church, also took a swipe at Montgomery, telling his congregation that "the only way to save the boy from going to the devil is to get into him the words of the eighth verse of the first chapter of Acts. . . . What are billiards and pool, to save boys who never enter a church?"[19]

On the following Monday, the Rochester Ministerial Association, with sixty-five members in attendance, representing some of the leading Protestant churches in the city, met in the same YMCA hall the women had used. The Ministerial Association was an organization of evangelical churches created in response to an attempt to organize a Federation of Churches. When organizers of the federation, including Rauschenbusch, decided to omit the word "evangelical" from the charter to permit the membership of Unitarian and Jewish congregations, influential Methodist leaders refused to participate. The effort to organize a federation was abandoned, and the Ministerial Association was organized two years later along strictly evangelical lines.[20]

While the men of the Ministerial Association also condemned the Excise Department, they were unhappy with the women's call for Sunday amusements. Dr. S. Banks Nelson, pastor of St. Peter's Presbyterian Church, supposed that the women's advocacy of Sabbath "desecration" could only be explained by their near hysteria. "Since the days of the Pilgrim Fathers, the American Sabbath has been recognized as one of the foundation stones of the Republic," he said. He could not support the establishment of a "continental Sunday."[21]

Paul Moore Strayer tried to offer a defense of Sunday amusements based on muscular Christianity. Strayer was an ally of Rauschenbusch who participated with him in the YMCA survey and the People's Sunday Evenings.[22] He said Sunday amusements ought to be tried as long as those who wanted to enjoy them did not bother anyone else. He said the question was not "preservation of the sanctity of the Sabbath" but "preservation of the sanctity of man." Against cries of opposition, he said, "true manhood, Christian manhood, God's manhood, is of more importance to society in general, to the community, to the state and to the nation, than the Sabbath or the Westminster confession." He believed the churches were failing to reach the young people of the city, and merely condemning vice would do nothing to reverse the situation.[23]

Dr. C. E. Hamilton of the First Methodist Church told the ministers that the committee as appointed by Montgomery was stacked with "women who may be said to be possessed of liberal ideas" and complained that there were no representatives of his denomination, "the largest Protestant communion in the United States." Hamilton declared that he had "no sympathy with the modern effort to regenerate the world with skating rinks and bowling alleys." While the women had claimed that the $28,000 spent convicting boys and girls could have been better spent providing amusements, he thought the same money spent to entice twenty boys from a pool room to a bowling alley would, "if rightly used, put 200 boys into Sunday School and save their souls."[24]

Rev. George D. Miller, pastor of the First Presbyterian Church, thought the women were naïve about the innocence of the amusements they proposed. It was the "spirit of gambling" rather than the "instinct for the freedom of play" that made pool tables and other similar amusements attractive. Remove the gambling, and boys would lose interest. They would move on to even worse debauchery, "and you will have broken down your Sabbath in a futile attempt to reclaim the boy." Rev. A. J. Graham of Christ Episcopal Church thought the women were sincere but acted with "effervescence." The ministers voted unanimously, by a rising vote, to dissent from the call for Sunday amusements.[25]

Among several voices raised in defense of the women, the *Herald* fueled the controversy by suggesting on its editorial page that the ministers had misunderstood the sentiments of the women.[26] Banks replied that he had attended the meeting of the women and was not misled. In fact, he felt that "more than one-half of the ladies present did dissent, and some of them more warmly and emphatically than did the clergymen." Banks reiterated his view of the larger issue, that to allow Sunday amusements "would be untrue to our Christian calling and to the principles enunciated by the founders of the Republic, and that the un-American factors in our midst would ruin us to the undoing of genuine Americanism." Still he was not completely opposed to "reasonable liberty of the individual on the Sabbath" and would not oppose the opening of "swimming pools and baths in tenement neighborhoods on Sunday, say from 6 to 10 o'clock in the morning."[27] Apparently Banks thought cleanliness was next to godliness.

The women of the Committee of Fifteen were unwilling to engage in controversy with the ministers. They insisted the ministers had misunderstood them.[28] But rather than make a reply to the ministers, Montgomery said the committee would "have just as little publicity as possible" in the future. They would not announce their future meetings or disclose their plans in detail, but they did want to develop more opportunities for "innocent amusement" in the city. Also they wanted to "arrest conditions of vice" where they could. They would pass on whatever information they discovered that could be helpful to law enforcement. "We are not courting notoriety and shall not try to obtain it. In a womanly way we want to do all the good we can."[29]

Religion, Dancing, and the Custodial Mandate of the School Board

Unfortunately, Montgomery could not escape further controversy with certain ministers. This time it was the Methodist ministers in Rochester who wanted to limit the freedom of the school board to define its educational mandate and its custodial role. The board, on the other hand, moved to defend its right to define for itself what was and was not legitimate to teach in the schools. They also showed a clear determination to respect the rights of grassroots communities, in this case represented by Mothers' clubs, to make their own decisions about what was morally acceptable recreation and entertainment for their children. Finally, they resisted the effort of the ministers to limit the board's authority to permit noneducational use of school buildings for community purposes after hours. These issues—the expanding mandate of public education and community control of schools—were the sources of the controversy with the Methodist ministers years before the social centers were created, and the failure to resolve them to everyone's satisfaction eventually contributed to the death of the social center movement in Rochester.

A few weeks after the controversy with the Ministerial Association, on 21 April 1905, the members of the Rochester school board read into the minutes of their meeting a communication that they received from the Methodist Episcopal Preachers' Meeting of Rochester, New York, and vicinity. The Methodist ministers wrote to inform the school board that they were "a large constituency committed against the sanction of the dance" and to complain that dancing was taught in the seventh and eighth grades of the public schools under the guise of "rhythmic exercises." The ministers were convinced that "it is no part of the duty of the State to teach [dancing] at public expense" and that "dancing between the sexes should never be permitted in the public school buildings either in school hours or at any other time." They wanted the board to refuse permission to use the buildings for any purpose that would be offensive to a large constituency of citizens.[30]

The school board assigned to Montgomery the responsibility of crafting a response to the Methodist ministers. On 19 May 1905, she presented her response to the full board for approval. Montgomery began the letter with a polite and extended expression of appreciation for the Methodist ministers and their interest in the schools. The board shared the ministers' desire for academic and moral excellence among the children in the schools, even if they did not share their view of "rhythmic exercises." Montgomery wrote, "That we cannot fully agree with either your premises or conclusions is a matter of regret to us" because the board shared the ministers' "desire to promote the best and highest interests of the children of the public schools."[31]

Although it is not explicit in the ministers' initial communication, apparently they believed the Mothers' clubs of some schools were responsible for organizing dances after school hours. In the course of investigating the question of dancing in Rochester schools, the board sent letters to each principal in the school system. The board asked, "First, Have you dancing in your school? Second, Has any dancing entertainment ever been given by the Mothers' Clubs?"[32] The board received replies from all principals, and from the replies Montgomery concluded that "the accounts of frequent dancing in many schools, and of the part played in promoting it by Mothers' clubs had been somewhat exaggerated."

As far as dancing as a part of the course of study was concerned, Montgomery made a careful distinction between "rhythmic work," such as "gymnastic dancing," and "social dancing." The board agreed, according to Montgomery, that social dancing was not an appropriate subject for instruction. "Some of the steps and rhythms used in social dancing are employed in the gymnastic dancing or rhythm work," but the purpose of gymnastic dancing was "purely educational." It was designed "to select such movements, postures, and exercises as shall develop control over the body, poise, grace, flexibility and strength." In Montgomery's view, the educational value of the exercises was clear beyond doubt. "Our school principals, without dissenting voice, have testified to the physical betterment of the children from the use of these exercises, and not to that alone, but to the remarkable improvement in spirit, zest, good nature and eagerness in their school work noticeable after the introduction of the rhythmical exercises. The child is waked up, his blood put in more rapid circulation, his nervous tension relaxed, and his repressed animal spirits given a channel for harmless expression."[33]

In her customary fashion, Montgomery consulted a dozen experts in physical education. She reported that the experts were unanimous in their hearty endorsement of the physical and educational virtues of dance and rhythmic exercise. She declared, "The rhythmic exercises or steps already introduced are too valuable to discard from our system of physical culture."[34]

While the board would not allow the ministers to determine educational policy, they wanted to be sensitive to the scruples of parents. Those who could not in good conscience allow their children to take part in the exercises could have their children excused. Then, in a statement with a remarkably contemporary ring, Montgomery argued that after-school dances were legitimate as long as they reflected community standards. The school board "never felt it was its function to legislate on the matter," Montgomery wrote. They refused to allow school buildings to be used for private dances, but after a lecture or some other function, if parents, teachers, and students "wished to enjoy a little informal dancing," the board left it to "the good sense of the principal and patrons." According to Montgomery: "Where it was approved by the standards of the community, and done under the sanction of the principal and parents, we have not felt that we had the right or call to interfere." Montgomery's next sentence was a politely phrased but stinging rebuke to the ministers: "You will pardon us for saying that it seems to us that you are urging us to maintain a discipline over the social customs of the whole city, which it is found difficult or impossible to maintain in regard to the membership of your own churches." The board would remain vigilant against "the evils associated with indiscriminant and unregulated dancing," but they would not interfere with "the pleasant and informal neighborhood gatherings of the patrons and pupils of the public schools," which they regarded as "innocent recreation for all."[35]

Predictably, the Methodist ministers were deeply dissatisfied with the response they elicited from the school board. Their next letter, read into the school board minutes on 6 June 1905, was much more accusatory. They questioned the ethics of the board members in teaching dance under the guise of "rhythmic exercise" and said that it was unjust to foist a "fad" of "minor if any value" upon parents who were compelled by law to send their children to school. The ministers believed that the school board's expanding definition of its educational mandate was a threat to the authority of home and church. They were convinced that school dancing was the first step toward "a total disregard of home influence and religious training." They feared that, if parents who objected to dancing followed their consciences and prevented their children from participating, their children would be "ostracized from the companionship of their set." Once again they insisted that it was not the state's business to teach dancing in school, that school buildings should be used for educational and not social or recreational purposes, and that it was unjust that "parents or pupils shall be put to the humiliation of asking to be excused."[36]

Clearly, the Methodist ministers joined the growing conservative backlash against the broadening social agenda of Montgomery and the school board. The school board believed their mandate required a more comprehensive view of education that transcended traditional classroom instruction in the basics of reading, writing, and arithmetic. Furthermore, they saw in the educational system a means to address more than strictly educational needs. They tried to use the resources of the system to empower parents, teachers, and grassroots community organizations like the Mothers' clubs to meet the broader social needs in the neighborhoods. A growing number of conservative critics believed the school board was abusing its power, permitting unwarranted use of school buildings for noneducational purposes, pursuing educational fads, and taking advantage of the compulsory education law to force its social agenda on a defenseless public.

Social Centers: An Experiment in Participatory Democracy

The Committee of Fifteen passed out of public view, and the dancing controversy subsided, if only temporarily; but Montgomery and the other leading women of the city did not stop looking for ways to provide alternative amusements. In 1907 the Local Council of Women urged all the local women's clubs to endorse the public funding of playgrounds and the opening of school buildings for neighborhood meetings.[37] In conjunction with the Playground League, many of the city's most influential women's clubs lobbied the mayor to fund the social center idea and place it under the administration of the school board. Social centers would include "reading rooms, quiet game rooms, gymnasiums, and meeting places for discussions of affairs" for those beyond school age.[38] The school board appropriated five thousand dollars for the experiment. They began with one center at the No. 14 School, and they planned to expand the program if all went well.[39]

The board hired Edward J. Ward to direct the playgrounds and develop the first social center.[40] Ward was a graduate of Hamilton College and Auburn Theological Seminary. While pastor of a Presbyterian church in Silver Creek, New York, from 1905 to 1906, he used the church manse to create a community center. Next, he taught English at Hamilton College for a year, and then he went to Rochester to organize the social centers.[41] Under Ward's direction the first social center developed clubs for boys, girls, men, and women, and provided a forum for lectures and social gatherings for the entire community. The opening of the first social center generated great enthusiasm and was applauded in the press. George M. Forbes, president of the school board, gave an address at the opening of the center in which he said the social center idea was to address the "social instinct" in a "wholesome and uplifting way."[42]

The Rochester social centers were the culmination of decades of grassroots political and educational work aimed at creating a broader democratic public. Montgomery had participated in several of the earlier attempts, including the extension lectures offered by the University of Rochester, the educational program of the Women's Educational and Industrial Union (WEIU), and other women's clubs. In addition to those, Rochester had many other privately organized and funded public lecture programs, religious and secular, such as the Sunday evening programs offered by the YMCA, the People's Sunday Evenings, Algernon Crapsey's Brotherhood lectures at the Lyceum Theater, and the socialist-oriented program of the Labor Lyceum organized by the trade unions, just to name a few. There were also the Good Government clubs and the many other privately organized civic clubs in the city. What made the social centers different, according to historian Kevin Mattson, was the fact that they were publicly funded, and they offered opportunities for the development of an open and democratic citizen's forum. The programs, clubs, lectures, and debates of the social centers were, for the most part, organized and led by members of the community rather than professional experts. In the civic clubs, which soon became the most significant aspect of the social centers, the ruling principles were free speech, open deliberation, and democratic self-government.[43]

Much like the WEIU under Montgomery, or the ward-based Good Government clubs, the civic clubs of the social centers became training schools for participatory democracy. They offered a forum for discussion of a broad range of topics, from municipal to national issues, and they created a deliberative institutional base for confronting corruption in the municipal government.[44] Unlike the WEIU, however, the constituency of the men's civic clubs could vote. Consequently they eventually presented more of a threat to the political establishment.

Montgomery's support for the social centers represented an important benchmark in her trajectory away from the punitive measures and toward the effort to create a broader, more inclusive democracy in Rochester. The social centers reflected the optimism inherent in progressivism. They were an attempt to improve the social environment and give troublemakers a chance to choose the good. School board president Forbes wrote, "The gangs of boys and young men who have been such a nuisance in various quarters of the city are not inherently vicious, but are driven to loafing and mischief by the lack of any opportunity for wholesome activity. They eagerly welcome the opportunity of the social center." Likewise, Forbes believed the social center could help to eliminate social tensions and create social unity. He wrote that the centers were essential in "the broadening of narrow lives, the breaking down of prejudice and class distinction, the development of a community spirit, and best of all for the welfare for the city as a whole, the development of broad, civic intelligence and devotion."[45]

The social centers also represented a commitment on the part of the school board to community control over the schools. Basically the board authorized a budget and the use of a school building for a center and allowed community residents to organize their own programs with little or no outside interference. The only condition the board set down for expansion and continued funding was public participation. The board required communities to petition for a social center in their school, and social centers had to maintain a minimum attendance of twenty-five persons on the evenings when they were open or lose their funding. The social centers were increasingly popular, however. The board had all the requests for new centers that they could manage, and attendance figures at each center often ran into triple digits.[46]

The progressive obsession with efficiency created another justification for the social center movement.[47] With the pilot program less than a month old, Montgomery was ready to expand on the grounds of efficiency and community need. In response to a lecture in Rochester by muckraker and progressive reformer Jacob Riis,[48] who advocated opening school buildings to the general public for meetings, Montgomery told a reporter from the *Herald* that, both as an individual and as a school board member, she favored opening the school buildings to "reputable citizens to discuss matters of general interest." The reporter wanted to know if that included trade unions. Montgomery did not think it was necessary to make such distinctions. All citizens ought to be able to use the buildings, and that included trade unions. Riis claimed that the scarcity of meeting halls often forced people to meet in saloons, when the schools, built at public expense, stood empty. Montgomery agreed that there were too few "wholesome environments" where citizens could assemble to discuss issues. She did not think it would hurt the buildings to allow the citizens to use them when they were unoccupied by schoolchildren.[49]

The social center movement was an instant success, and in the fall of 1908 two additional centers were opened. Each social center had gymnasium equipment, table games, a library, shower facilities, and a staff of several persons to oversee the various clubs, recreational programs, and other activities.

Because of the civic clubs, the social centers quickly became more than alternative amusements. Ward, Clarence F. Carroll, superintendent of schools, and George M. Forbes, president of the school board, frequently claimed that Rochester's social center movement was unique. Ward emphasized the grassroots democratic nature of the Rochester social centers when he declared that there would be "no teachers and no teaching" at the social centers.[50] For him the social centers represented "brotherhood, the duty of every man to reveal himself as the brother of every other man and woman."[51]

Forbes thought that the social center was the answer to "the spirit of competition," which he believed was "robbing men and women of the highest happiness that they may know." Rather than competition, the social center was established "for the lodgment of the communal spirit" where the "ideals of brotherhood" could be developed. Without such ideals "the great democracy, of which a nation dreamed," was impossible.[52]

According to Carroll the uniqueness of the social center was in its renewal of the "natural" type of "fellowship tendencies." Churches, labor organizations, clubs, and fraternities were "inevitable and helpful and desirable," but they were also "artificial" in their fellowship tendencies. The social center would renew the natural type that was "higher and stronger" because it was "common, mutual and unselfish." It was characterized by the same spirit that marked "the neighborhood life in the New England rural community of former days," where everyone knew his neighbor and they were genuinely concerned with one another and "all shared much in common." The New England communities were "powerful units in a great democracy" and trained great leaders. He believed the social center had "no less power socially or politically.[53]

The social centers were so popular that the leaders of the movement were even able to convince the Ministers Association to support the opening of the centers on Sunday, as long as they were used "in a quiet way."[54] A fourth social center opened at No. 26 School, and in the four centers, fourteen men's civic clubs were organized into a League of Civic Clubs. Many other schools were opened to adult use even though they had no formal social center programs. But as the clubs grew, they attracted attention from those with a cause to promote as well as from those with interests to protect.[55]

Montgomery achieved her goal of opening the schools as a "whole-some environment" for the discussion of public affairs, but not everyone was pleased with the direction of the discussions. All sorts of speakers soon flocked to the social centers, whose topics ranged from the proper mastica-tion of food for good health to labor unions. Religious zealotry and political punditry attracted the most press coverage. Republican Party boss Aldridge, never an ally of reform, resented being criticized from platforms paid for by the city. A larger community debate over whether or not the schools ought to provide free textbooks to students dominated discussion in the Civic Men's Club of West High School social center for a while in 1908. Opinion gen-erally divided over religious lines, with Protestants mostly in favor of free textbooks and Catholics mostly opposed. The issue surfaced in the school board controversy with the citizens' committee, and a majority of the school board declared itself in favor of providing free textbooks if the money could be found. The Mother's clubs and the WEIU supported free textbooks and garnered over 65,000 signatures on a petition in support of the idea.[56] Father A. M. O'Neill, an outspoken critic of free textbooks,[57] also became a critic of the social centers. He complained that the taxpayers were supporting "Socialistic Centers."[58]

Controversy of another sort erupted when it was discovered that a club of Jewish girls at the social center of the No. 9 School had sponsored a mas-querade dance on a Sunday afternoon. The girls regularly used the center on Sunday afternoon because Saturday was their Sabbath, but dancing on Sunday offended the sensibilities of many within the Christian community. Once again, dancing was the presenting issue, and the school board was in the middle. It was the beginning of the end for the social centers, and the Common Council reduced the school board's appropriation in an attempt to kill them.[59]

Although the social centers endured for a few more years, they became known as hotbeds of socialist rhetoric. Ward, the director of the social cen-ters, caused a stir among local ministers when he said in print that the centers were replacing decadent churches in the community. The end was finally precipitated when University of Rochester professor K. P. Shedd, who was a socialist and also the director of the social center at No. 9 school, held a discussion of socialism at the social center in 1911. During the discussion, he made remarks that were interpreted as insulting to the American flag.

Another controversy over the social centers erupted, resulting in an end to their funding and of Shedd's professorship at the university.[60]

Neither Republican Party boss George Aldridge nor Rochester's mayor, Hiram H. Edgerton, who was an Aldridge man, were particularly fond of the social centers. Discussions at the civic club meetings turned too often to the subject of corruption in municipal government. After Aldridge arranged to have Montgomery removed from the school board and Ward left Rochester to organize social centers in Wisconsin under the auspices of the University of Wisconsin extension program, the remaining supporters of the social centers on the school board were unable to protect the program. Funding for the social centers was cut in 1911, and at the very moment when the movement was becoming popular nationwide, it withered in Rochester.

It is important to remember that the events recounted in this chapter occurred between 1904 and the end of Montgomery's school board tenure in 1910. Meanwhile, she was emerging as a leading intellectual of the ecumenical woman's missionary movement. Although she never articulated an explicit connection, events in Rochester clearly influenced her missiological thought and practice. As a mission theorist, Montgomery was concerned not only with the conversion of individuals, but with the Christianization of cultures. Of course, Christianization meant planting churches, evangelizing individuals, translating the Bible into the vernacular, and placing it in the hands of the people. But it also meant much more. Among other things, Christianization as Montgomery understood it required efforts to improve social conditions along Reform Darwinist lines. On the mission field, as in Rochester, she advocated the elimination of certain social customs and influences, worked for improved educational opportunities, and urged reforms that led to the democratization of society. And, as in Rochester, Montgomery hoped that positive initiatives begun on the mission field at the grassroots level would be adopted by governments and receive public support. If the social environment was a powerful factor in the development of personal character, then the institutionalization and government sponsorship of social reforms that reflected Christianization would improve the quality of individual lives and contribute to a social environment that was more conducive to evangelism.

Ten

"A Great Theme"

Domestic Feminism and the Gospel of the Women's Jubilee

When the coast-to-coast Golden Jubilee tour of the ecumenical woman's missionary movement, the largest mission celebration in the history of the United States, rolled into New York City for its grand climax in 1911, *The New York Times* took notice. "Big Missions Jubilee Opens Here To-Day"; "Pageant of Missions Opens Big Jubilee"; "6,000 Women at Luncheon"; "Missionary Jubilee Ends. More Than $869,350 Raised in Two Weeks Is Announced at Carnegie Hall." Some of the most notable women in the city, including Mrs. Russell Sage, Grace Dodge, Helen Gould, and Mrs. J. P. Morgan, attended the Jubilee events. The New York City celebration raised over $130,000.[1]

Why did American women respond so enthusiastically to the Woman's Missionary Jubilee of 1910–1911? What brought multitudes in seventy cities to the pageants, rallies, and luncheons? What motivated them to raise more than $1 million dollars for missionary causes? Why did they work, pray, and give with such energy and passion? At the risk of oversimplification, they did it because Helen Barrett Montgomery asked them to do it.

By 1910 Helen Barrett Montgomery was one of the key organizers and intellectual leaders of the ecumenical woman's missionary movement. The movement existed two generations before Montgomery emerged as one of its leaders, yet her influence in the early decades of the twentieth century was vital and unsurpassed. Dana L. Robert's work on women as mission theorists showed that Montgomery helped to define two mission theories that were profoundly important to that movement: "Woman's Work for Woman" and "World Friendship." Patricia R. Hill identified a connection between the ecumenical woman's missionary movement and the progressive movement.[2] The connection was not accidental. Montgomery brought her experience as a domestic feminist and municipal housekeeper to her work as missionary organizer and intellectual. Her effectiveness in the latter two roles was due in part to the fact that she did not have to invent a language to use in describing the work of the ecumenical woman's missionary movement. She used a language with which the women were already quite familiar: the language of domestic feminism and progressive reform.

Montgomery's Transition to the Missionary Movement

The year 1910 was full of transitions for Montgomery. Her career on the school board was ended, and her husband sold his interest in Venor & Montgomery. In her diary for 15 June, Montgomery wrote: "Will witnessed Mr. Halbeib's application for a wonderful new patent to start an auto without the necessity of cranking."[3] Not only did he witness the application, he also invested all his capital into the development of the invention. While ultimately successful, the venture was slow to turn a profit. In 1913 William Montgomery was forced to sell the family home and support his family with the proceeds. Helen Montgomery had to sell her grand piano, and the family moved into a duplex apartment, where they lived for three or four years. With her characteristic good humor, she referred to the experience as "camping out."[4]

Montgomery's work for the Women's Educational and Industrial Union (WEIU) continued to demand much time. In addition to her organizational responsibilities and her frequent lectures, she was directly involved in what would today be called social casework. On 17 December 1910 she recorded in her diary that she "spent morning at police court helping women arrested in Washington Hotel case." Again, on 19 December she interviewed women involved, and on 20 December she spoke with the detectives responsible for the case. Two days later, she wrote that she had investigated three possible places of employment that she had found for the women she was helping, and the following day, she took the women to their new jobs. She wrote: "The whole lot paroled. Police Chief congratulated us."[5]

Because of her growing involvement in the ecumenical woman's missionary movement, Montgomery withdrew from active leadership in the WEIU in 1911. She was reelected that year for another term as president but declined to serve.[6] From then on, the lion's share of her energy was dedicated to the ecumenical woman's missionary movement and to her own Baptist denomination.

While Montgomery grew in prominence in Rochester, she also expanded her activities beyond the city through her involvement with the ecumenical woman's missionary movement. In 1900 Montgomery traveled to New York City as a representative of the Woman's Baptist Foreign Missionary Society to attend the Ecumenical Missionary Conference, which was headquartered at Carnegie Hall. The ten-day conference was the largest religious event ever organized in America to that point. It attracted between 160,000 and 200,000 attendees, including 2,500 delegates from around the world, representing 162 mission boards (exclusive of the women's denominational societies). Six hundred missionaries attended, bringing with them a vast number of artifacts and photographs for the exhibit hall, which were examined by 50,000 interested visitors. Attendees chose from more than five hundred addresses that were given in the main hall as well as in dozens of churches and auditoriums in the area. *The New York Times* and the *New York Tribune* covered the meetings in detail, and honorary speakers included former U.S. President Benjamin Harrison, sitting U.S. President William McKinley, and the larger-than-life progressive and governor of New York, Theodore Roosevelt.[7]

Montgomery spoke twice during the conference. On Tuesday, 24 April, she addressed an audience at Central Presbyterian Church on "The Systematic Study of Missions: A Union Scheme for All Woman's Organizations." On the evening of Thursday, 26 April, she addressed the audience in Carnegie Hall on "The Outlook in Woman's Foreign Mission Work."

The meeting at Central Presbyterian Church was perhaps one of the most significant in the history of American mission theory, for it was the meeting at which the women's missionary boards announced their plan for united mission study—the plan that created the Central Committee on the United Study of Foreign Missions. Thomas A. Askew judged the Ecumenical Missionary Conference less than successful as a consultation on missions, despite its vastness and "vigorous exchange," because it produced so few "concrete results" that yielded "long-term effectiveness."[8] In his assessment of women's participation in the conference, Askew failed to note what was to become perhaps the most concrete and significant result of the Ecumenical Missionary Conference—the Central Committee. Through its annual mission study texts, the Central Committee helped to shape women's understanding of missions, history, culture, and international relations for thirty-eight years.[9]

Abbie B. Child introduced the seven-year united study plan to the women leaders at Central Presbyterian Church, but it was Montgomery who argued the need for such a course of action. She said that the women needed a "broader and more intellectual and more thoughtful grasp" of the subject of missions. She complained of the "smallness of treatment" in missionary meetings. "We have trusted to leaflets, and tracts, and items, and excerpts. We have done very little original work. We have made very few demands upon the brains of the women in our missionary circles," she told her audience. She believed that the lack of creative, intellectual effort accounted for their "smallness of vision in our missionary life."[10]

As she had done with the WEIU women in Rochester, Montgomery wanted to broaden the vision of missionary women with knowledge. When she led the WEIU, Montgomery challenged the women to move beyond culture study and self-improvement to municipal housekeeping, and to see the connections between the needs of their own families and communities and the municipal, national, and international political issues of her day. Likewise, she wanted missionary women to see that the study of Christian missions was much more than a religious exercise. Like the women of the woman's club movement, missionary women could make their movement inclusive of culture study and self-improvement as well as religion. She told her audience, "I believe that when we come to realize that in this cause of foreign missions are included statecraft, and civilization, and geography, and history, and biography, and philosophy, and poetry, and art, and the living history of the living kingdom of God, we shall find we have so much material for programmes that we will not be able to get on with meetings once a month, but we will have to have them once a week, to accommodate the women in our churches."[11]

Montgomery thought the women needed more information than "the customary mission literature . . . prepared for us by our Boards and given to us in homeopathic doses" could provide. Such literature did not allow women to dig deep, to stretch themselves intellectually. The women did not have to settle for "little leaflets" if they would only take some initiative. Montgomery adapted a strategy she had suggested to the women of the WEIU in 1896 for working with underprivileged children—a traveling library. City women might be able to go to the library and have all the books they needed set aside for them. Those with no easy access to a library could arrange for a traveling library of "fifty or a hundred volumes" to come to them.[12]

The plan adopted by the women called for them to study mission history from apostolic times through the end of the eighteenth century during the first year. Montgomery argued at the Ecumenical Conference that learning the history of missions was an essential first step. The women must "realize that Christianity in its growth has always been and must be missionary" and that "our missionary societies are built upon the foundations of 1,900 years."[13]

The Central Committee eventually translated the plan of study into a publication plan, and the books they published became some of the most successful mission study texts ever produced. Although Yale mission professor Harlan Page Beech subsequently advised the Central Committee against starting with a history book because he believed it would not sell, the women were undeterred.[14] The women's determination to begin with the study of history was validated when the first volume, *Via Christi,* by Louise Manning Hodgkins, sold fifty thousand copies. Montgomery wrote six books for the Central Committee and produced study notes for a number of others.

Montgomery's Defense of the Women's Mission Boards

In her second address, at the midweek celebration of women's role in missions, which Askew called the "most dramatic public rally" of the conference,[15] Montgomery addressed one of the perennial complaints against the women's missionary societies: their alleged redundancy. Some critics claimed that the denominational boards met the need for organization and that the women's boards were superfluous and wasteful of resources. On the program, Montgomery followed Lilavati Singh, professor of English literature at Lucknow College and protégé of Isabella Thoburn, whose remarks inspired the oft-quoted exclamation of Benjamin Harrison: "If I had given a million dollars to foreign missions, I should count it wisely invested if it led only to the conversion of that one woman."[16] Harrison apparently viewed Singh's testimony as an eloquent confirmation of the value of missions in general; Montgomery wanted him and others to recognize the particular contribution of organized women's work to missions.

The din of criticism struck Montgomery as "one of the surest signs of the abounding vitality of the women's foreign missionary Societies." Among the most troubling critics, in her view, were the intelligent, informed friends of missions who echoed perennial claims that it was time to merge the women's boards with the denominational boards. These critics argued that the women's work duplicated that of the denominational boards and that the "opulence" of women's boards was gained at the expense of the denominational boards. "They say we are robbing Peter to pay Paul, Paulina, perhaps I should say; that we are getting pennies when dollars are due, and are dividing denominational strength." Others, according to Montgomery, argued against a perceived feminism in the women's work. "'We have enough,' they tell us, 'of women's clubs, women's papers, women's charities; let us not have *woman* in religion. The gospel is one, the work is one, let us then unite in one great missionary reservoir all the streams of beneficence now turning the wheels of many societies.'"[17]

Montgomery believed that more *"woman* in religion" was precisely what was needed. The complaint against the women's boards was in part a reflection of the tremendous popularity of gender-based institutional separatism among American women in many religious and secular contexts, and gender-based institutional separatism was popular because so many women found it empowering. In the context of the mission movement, the reasons for women's support for separate mission boards were clear. Although a numerical minority in the churches,[18] men monopolized institutional power in the churches and denominational mission boards, and they persistently resisted sharing power with women. On the missionary field, many missionary wives literally worked themselves into an early grave trying to meet the needs of their families and the needs of native women and children at the same time. Nevertheless, the male leadership of the denominational mission boards was reluctant to appoint single women as missionaries and to provide adequate funds for the missionary enterprises that American women believed were most essential for women and children in mission lands. Without denominational support, and sometimes under heavy criticism and harassment, the women's mission boards grew and flourished, so that by 1900 there were more than forty in the United States with a combined membership of over 3 million women. Due to the support and influence of the women's boards, in 1890 more than 60 percent of American foreign missionaries were single women.[19] In the view of the women of the ecumenical woman's missionary movement, who believed they had a special calling from God to evangelize women and children around the world, the autonomy of their institutions in relation the male-dominated churches and denominational mission boards was a self-evident necessity.

According to Montgomery, women brought to the general work of missions "a thousand dollars for every one spent" by the women's boards. They fielded an "army of unpaid officers and helpers," who benefited the denominational boards as well as the women's boards as they brought the missions endeavor into "close contact with the local church." These women, Montgomery claimed, were the "advance agents of missionary prosperity." With careful attention to detail, they educated supporters and publicized mission efforts, utilizing a "network of meetings and conferences," and producing "a flood of missionary literature" that cost the denominational boards nothing. In her view, the women's societies were "the John the Baptists preparing the way for the denominational boards." Montgomery thought the complaints of the denominations against the women's boards were nonsense. "It is as unreasonable for the denominations to complain of the expense of the women's organizations as for a business house to grudge the salaries of its paid agents, or the expenses of its advertising department."[20]

Montgomery also believed the "different conditions of the lives of men and women" made it possible for women to work without wages. Montgomery's middle-class Victorian gender assumptions were apparent when she said, "Men are the bread-winners, ability must be paid for." Nevertheless, as a domestic feminist, Montgomery knew that women were more than homebodies. Women could bring "wide vision and high ability" at no cost to the general boards, and they would not settle for second-class status. The necessary passion and expertise could only be developed "by women's sharing the burden of missionary administration." According to Montgomery, women would not accept the drudgery without sharing in the responsibility for the missionary endeavor. She believed the women who worked through the women's boards had achieved so much "only because we have been given a definite work for which we are solely responsible" and had taken the responsibility to heart. If the responsibility were taken from them, their enthusiasm for the work would quickly dissipate.[21]

The women's missionary societies did not drain support from the denominational boards, Montgomery declared. To the contrary, she asserted that those churches in which women's societies were strongest were also the ones most generous in their support of the denominational boards, that those denominations in which the women's societies were strongest also had the largest per-capita gifts to missions, and that women supported the general boards as well as the women's societies. The accusation that women's societies were hurting the mission enterprise "impeaches the loyalty and good sense of two-thirds the membership of the Church." The women in the churches loved the gospel and made their gifts accordingly.[22]

Montgomery denied that the women's boards represented a feminist agenda in the missionary cause, but her response reflected her affirmation of what scholars today call "domestic feminism." To the charge that the women's boards proclaimed a "woman's gospel," she said, "we accept all the premises and deny all the conclusions. We want no woman's gospel, but we remember that the first commission on the resurrection morning was to Mary Magdalene; that the kingdom of heaven is likened not only to the shepherd seeking the lost sheep in the wilderness, but also to the woman sweeping the house for the lost coin."[23] It is interesting that Montgomery alluded to a parable about housekeeping to defend the role of the women's boards. Montgomery saw women's involvement in municipal reform as extended housekeeping, and her allusion to that parable suggested that she viewed the women's mission boards as something like municipal housekeeping on a global scale. While the leaders of the women's missionary societies did not proclaim an alleged woman's gospel, they certainly believed they had a particular mandate to be the servants and bearers of the gospel of Christ to women and children, a mandate that was complementary and equal to that of men. To that end, they contextualized mission education for women in the language and style of the women's club movement, domestic feminism, and progressive reform.

Montgomery cherished great hope for the future of the women's missionary societies. She believed they would help women to achieve an "enlarged conception of life" so that they could be more faithful disciples. For Montgomery, faithful discipleship meant less romanticism and more practical, joyful Christianity. She thought that "until all Christian women have learned that the cross of Christ is not to be sung about, nor wept over, nor smothered in flowers, but set up in our pleasures; that He never commanded us to cling to that cross, but to carry it, the work of the missionary circle will not be done nor its warfare accomplished."[24] Like the WEIU and other municipal housekeeping organizations that grew out of the culture study of the women's club movement, the purpose of the women's missionary societies was service, not sentiment.

Just as the WEIU and other municipal housekeeping organizations of the domestic feminist movement focused on the needs of women and children through the ideology of "educated motherhood," the ecumenical woman's missionary movement adopted missionary work "for women and by women" as its special calling. Montgomery told her audience in Carnegie Hall

> the final citadel of heathenism is in the home, and that fortress can be taken by women only. It seems such slow work, this gathering of children into kindergartens, this friendly contact with little groups of mothers, this teaching of needlework, this living one's own home-life through long, lonely years that seem to count for nothing. It is women's work, the patient hiding of the leaven in the lump until the whole is leavened. And there is no one agency which has such power to hasten the triumph of the kingdom of our Lord as this hidden work committed into the hands of women.[25]

Implicitly, the goal of the ecumenical woman's missionary movement was the Christianization of non-Christian civilizations. Montgomery's statement reflected the Victorian assumptions that home and family were the foundational institutions of any civilization, and that the home was the realm of woman's moral authority and influence. Apart from the evangelism that Montgomery assumed was common to all aspects of the missionary enterprise, the "slow work" of women's missions she described was not very different from the work she had been doing in Rochester through the WEIU for years. She believed the needs of women and children were roughly the same everywhere—education, socialization, and empowerment. The difference was in the degree of the needs and the context in which they were to be met.

There is no reason to disconnect Montgomery's domestic reform work in Rochester from her work for the ecumenical woman's missionary movement.[26] While it is debatable whether or not Montgomery and the ecumenical woman's missionary movement ought to challenge historians to reconsider the definition of the social gospel,[27] the connections between Montgomery's municipal reform work and her work for the ecumenical woman's missionary movement are apparent.

The Jubilee Celebration

Abbie B. Child, the first chairperson of the Central Committee, died unexpectedly in 1902. Montgomery's good friend Lucy Waterbury, with whom she had shared a podium at the Monroe Baptist Association many years before, was chosen to replace Child. Waterbury called upon Montgomery frequently to write and speak on the Central Committee's behalf. She and Peabody planned and organized the first summer school of missions, at which women were prepared to lead a study of the text for the coming year, in 1904. Montgomery was a prominent figure at these popular events. Lucy Waterbury remarried in 1906 and became Lucy Waterbury Peabody. The same year Montgomery's first book for the Central Committee, *Christus Redemptor: An Outline Study of the Island World of the Pacific,* was published. Two years later, Peabody was widowed again, and she reemerged more involved than ever before in the ecumenical woman's missionary movement. In 1909 she proposed to the Central Committee the idea of publishing literature for native women in their own languages, a suggestion that eventually led to the Interdenominational Committee on Christian Literature for Women and Children in Heathen Lands.[28]

The Central Committee chose Montgomery for the important task of writing a textbook for the movement that would commemorate fifty years of women's organized missionary work in America. Reading the manuscript of Montgomery's *Western Women in Eastern Lands* (1910) inspired Peabody. She believed the movement could claim much "actual achievement" in the emancipation of women around the world through education, health care, and the mitigation of oppressive cultural and religious practices. In the process, American women had devoted from their meager resources $41 million to the movement, in addition to much prayer and hard work.[29] Peabody suggested that Montgomery close the book with an appeal for a national celebration of the movement.[30] A "Year of Jubilee" would culminate with a grand event in New York City. Montgomery wrote a new concluding paragraph inviting the women of the movement to mark the anniversary with "a great thank offering" of money so that hospitals, schools, and orphanages could be built. Quoting the famous sentiment of the Haystack Prayer Meeting, she ended her appeal: "'We can do it, if we will'; 'We can do it, and we will.'"[31]

Western Women in Eastern Lands sold fifty thousand copies in six weeks, and total sales reached one hundred thousand.[32] According to Cattan, it was the bestselling missions study text ever printed.[33] From the germ of Peabody's idea came the Golden Jubilee tour—the largest and longest celebration of missions in American history. Peabody organized committees in Chicago and New York to make arrangements for the western and eastern celebrations, respectively. She recruited a group of speakers with Montgomery at the head that included missionaries on furlough, such as Dr. Mary Riggs Noble, a Presbyterian physician who served as a missionary in India; Kate Boggs Schaffer, a Lutheran missionary to India; and Jennie V. Hughes, a Methodist missionary to China. There were several other speakers as well, and the lineup changed over time due to the length of the tour, but Montgomery was a constant presence. Worried that her husband would feel neglected, Montgomery (in good Victorian fashion) asked his permission before agreeing to be away from home for so long. Faithful to the pledge he made before they were married, he gave her his blessing.[34]

The Jubilee tour traversed the continent, starting in Oakland, California, on 12 October 1910. The tour visited thirty-three major cities across the country, and there were satellite celebrations in many smaller cities as well, which brought the total number of cities involved to seventy.[35] Attendance at the meetings grew, along with the enthusiasm of the women, as the tour progressed. The organizers of the tour had set a fund-raising goal of $1 million, and in each city they gave the women an opportunity to contribute. The system they devised typified the spirit of the entire movement. Though the women gathered in what Montgomery called a "United Protestantism"[36] to hear the inspirational speakers and enjoy the other activities of the Jubilee, "at a preconcerted signal, these multitudes drawn from many Christian communities would separate into their distinctive denominations, where would be found at exactly the right moment their own Board officers waiting to instruct them in the work needing their aid."[37] In these meetings, they pledged or contributed to the love offering, and the money they collected made its way into the treasuries of the various boards. That was characteristic of the movement. Women cooperated not only as Christians but as women, and they addressed issues affecting women around the world; yet they did not sacrifice their denominational loyalties or identities.

The Jubilee schedule was unrelenting. For forty days after the initial celebration in Oakland, Montgomery and the other speakers persevered through a series of two-day celebrations in thirteen different cities, sometimes speaking nine times in a single day.[38] Often it was necessary to shuttle the speakers from place to place by automobile—still a rare luxury in those days—to make their appointments. Dr. Noble summed up the furious pace in a limerick:

> The Jubilee troupe superfine
> Was asked, "Do you speak and what time?"
> They replied, Ten, eleven,
> Three, four, five and seven,
> Six, eight and quarter to nine.[39]

After a break for the Christmas holiday, the tour resumed its frantic pace, with additional speakers to meet the demand of the larger crowds in the more populous eastern cities, where the local committees had had more time to prepare and publicize the events. In Pittsburgh, the Jubilee luncheons attracted forty-eight hundred in one day, while in Buffalo, the organizers had to remove the tables from the convention hall in order to accommodate the overflow crowd of twenty-four hundred who bought luncheon tickets. Presumably, the women rested their lunch plates on their laps.[40] Of course the tour could not bypass Washington, D.C., and New York City, the political and commercial capitals of the nation. In Washington, President Taft gave a reception at the White House for the Jubilee speakers, and Montgomery presented a leather-bound, autographed copy of *Western Women in Eastern Lands* to Mrs. Taft. Nannie Helen Burroughs, a leader of the black Baptist women's missionary movement and president of the National Training School for Women and Girls, presided over a meeting of two thousand African American women at the Metropolitan African Methodist Episcopal Church[41]—an indication that race-based segregation, while usually unspoken, probably characterized the entire tour.

In New York City, the immense celebrations required the facilities of the Metropolitan Opera House; the Astor, Waldorf-Astoria and Plaza hotels; and Carnegie Hall, in addition to several local churches. At the Met, the women produced a "pageant of missions," in which more than one thousand actors, assisted by a chorus from the Musical Art Society, directed by Frank Damrosch, and a sixty-six-piece orchestra from the Philharmonic Society and the New York Symphony, under the direction of David Mannes, illustrated the progress of missions in tableaux. The house was sold out. The hotels hosted the luncheons for more than six thousand women, and Carnegie Hall was the sight of an author's meeting and a closing mass rally.[42] Montgomery gave the final triumphant address of the Jubilee at to an overflow crowd at Carnegie Hall, almost eleven years after her first appearance there for the Ecumenical Conference, where the Central Committee was created.[43]

Looking back years later, Peabody wrote that the success of the Jubilee was due to "a spontaneous uprising of the womanhood of the United States against the entire conception of society as a selfish, sectional, material paganism." As the primary organizer of the Jubilee, Peabody knew better than anyone that the event had been the product of a great effort and the culmination of long years of cooperation and education—hardly spontaneous. But the "clamorous enthusiasm" of the women had surpassed expectations. It was certainly not a product of organizational efficiency. Peabody believed women were making a response to the evil of "militarism, oppression, [and] violence." The women offered more than protest; they proposed an "alternative good" that included "arrangements for the care of mothers, for the upbringing of children, for the kindly progress of the community under the influence of Christ."[44] In Peabody's assessment, the Jubilee transcended what is commonly understood by the term "foreign missions." It represented a gender-based, faith-based, prescriptive cultural criticism from the perspective of domestic feminism that did not exempt Western culture from its scrutiny.

If the men who ran the member boards of the Foreign Missions Conference of North America were slow to act on the cooperative spirit of the Ecumenical Conference,[45] the Jubilee is clear evidence that the women of the Conference of Woman's Boards were not. In little more than a decade their efforts at cooperative missions education gave the ecumenical woman's missionary movement a remarkable cohesiveness and effectiveness. Although the events of the next decade contributed to the drastic erosion of that cohesiveness and effectiveness[46] and led eventually to the collapse of the movement, it was a stunning accomplishment.

The Gospel of the Women's Jubilee

In 1900 Montgomery claimed that the ecumenical woman's missionary movement did not have a woman's gospel. Nevertheless, in 1910 Montgomery elaborated a domestic feminist apologetic for the engagement of women in Christian mission in *Western Women in Eastern Lands*. She argued that non-Christian religions were inherently debasing to women, and she attributed the relative emancipation of Western women directly to the influence of Christianity in Western culture. Furthermore she insisted that it was the responsibility of Western women to bring the emancipating power of Christianity to their non-Christian sisters around the world. While the liberation of individual women was important, the real target of Montgomery's strategy was the home, which she regarded as the most important institution of any civilization. If Western women could reach Eastern women with the gospel and Christianize the home, Montgomery believed the entire civilization would follow. Thus, in Montgomery's view women were the key agents in the civilizing mission of Christianity.

Many of the assumptions of domestic feminism were apparent in Montgomery's argument. Most obvious was the theoretically limitless expansion of woman's sphere based on the rationale of home protection. At the beginning of the Protestant missionary movement, the involvement of women in the enterprise was viewed as auxiliary to the work of men. By Montgomery's time, that was no longer true, and Montgomery's apologetic epitomized the missiology of "Woman's Work for Woman," which did not depend upon male missionaries and their work. At the same time, the rationale reflected the conservative nature of domestic feminism and its respect for True Womanhood. While missionary women and their indigenous helpers pursued autonomous careers in evangelism, education, medicine, Bible translation, and other fields, the ultimate goal was the transformation of the non-Christian home into a Christian home. In a Christian home, the purity and moral authority of women were supposed to manifest their deepest significance and greatest power.

Montgomery's Apologetic for the Ecumenical Woman's Missionary Movement

In the first chapter of *Western Women in Eastern Lands*, Montgomery outlined the history of the nineteenth-century women's missionary movement and related it to the broader context of women's changing status in the nine-

teenth century. In particular, she related the women's missionary movement
to the battles over women's education, the suffrage movement, and the abolition of slavery in America. Montgomery believed the women's missionary
movement was the culmination of the nineteenth century, which she called
"the Woman's Century." She wrote, "In it [the Woman's Century] forces
long at work crystallized so as to revolutionize many conceptions regarding
the proper sphere and activities of women. This readjustment of thought and
practice was not confined to one country, but was felt in varying degrees
throughout all nations." The women's missionary movement was in her view
"a special phase" of the global movement for the emancipation of women.[47]
Indeed, it was the catalyst that would ignite the movement worldwide.

In Montgomery's view, the motivating force behind the ecumenical
woman's missionary movement was Western women's sense of solidarity with
the suffering of their Eastern counterparts. She wrote, "The appeal to the
women of England and America was winged by the recital of the intoler-
able injustices and oppressions under which the women of the non-Christian
lands spent their lives; an appeal whose force fifty years has not dulled."[48]
Montgomery believed that Christian mission offered the only hope for permanent change in a positive direction for Eastern women because religion
was at the root of their oppression. She admitted there were "terrible wrongs
against women in our own land," but she maintained that there was an essential difference:

> The wrongs of Hindu, Chinese, and Moslem women are buttressed behind
> the sanctions of religion and are endorsed by the founders of their faith;
> while in our own land these wrongs flaunt themselves against the spirit and
> plain provisions of our religion. If women fully recognized the emancipa-
> tory nature of the pure religion of Jesus, the force of the religious mission-
> ary arguments would be tremendously strengthened.[49]

In 1894 Montgomery argued that the social and political subordination
of women in American culture was an anachronism in the global spread of
democracy that would eventually be resolved in favor of women's full freedom
and political participation.[50] In 1910 the terms were different, but the reasoning was much the same. Wrongs against women in Western culture were
serious, but they could potentially be resolved because they were contrary
to the "spirit and plain provisions" of Christianity. They were indications

that the Western world had not completely realized "the pure religion of Jesus." As a longtime municipal reformer, Montgomery was well aware that "in Christendom we have the white-slave trade, the red-light district, and other hateful and debasing traffics in womanhood." In her view the existence of such evils in Western lands was no reason to impede the missionary movement. Christianity's influence in the Western world was undeniable, and its influence on the status of women beneficial. According to Montgomery, "The Bible, as the authoritative source of Christianity, and the teachings of the greatest exponents of Christianity constantly honor women, and inculcate purity of life." The Christianization of culture was already far advanced in the Western world. "Strictly speaking, there is no Christian nation, but only nations in process of becoming Christian. But even so, the steady pressure of Bible ideals, exerted slowly and against tremendous difficulties, has already brought a revolution in the position of women."[51]

In contrast to the situation in the Western world, wrongs against women in non-Christian lands could not be resolved from within because they were essential to the religious culture. In the Eastern world, Montgomery wrote, woman "is nowhere accepted as man's equal, nowhere free, nowhere educated, nowhere is her right to her person recognized."[52] If Eastern women were to be freed from oppression and subordination, the missionary influence of Christianity was necessary. Montgomery wrote:

> Confucius and Mohammed, Code of Manu, and Buddhist scriptures alike agree in assigning woman to a position of inferiority and subordination, and in treating her as a "scandal and a slave, a drudge and a disgrace, a temptation and a terror, a blemish and a burden." . . . The evils that in Christian lands are recognized as sin, known to be contrary to all religious standards, and practiced only by those who do not accept these standards, are in non-Christian lands unashamed because embedded in the religious sanctions of the nation.[53]

If women in the non-Christian world could be made to see Christianity as a liberating force in their mundane experience, they would be more open to conversion, Christianity would gain a foothold in the home, and Christian mission would meet with greater success.

Montgomery believed she could demonstrate that "the reforms of Christendom which affect women are based squarely upon the principles of the Bible." In her reading of the Bible, Montgomery found a religious ethic that almost perfectly mirrored the Victorian ideals of domestic feminism. She found that the Bible assigned prominence to women, in contrast with the teachings of other religions, and that women as the Bible portrayed them were characterized by all the qualities of the ideal woman. They were "meek wives and loving mothers" as well as women of "high courage and noble daring." More importantly, she thought the Bible upheld sexual purity and morality in a way that was unique in world religious literature. "Where in all literature will one find such terrible, searching denunciation against impurity of life and thought, such faithful holding up of the consequences of evil?" In contrast to "the levity and impurity with which the facts of sex have been approached in life and literature," Montgomery believed "the white glory of the Book shines out."[54]

Not only did the Bible portray exemplary women and defend their purity and honor with an ideal sexual ethic. The Bible also *enunciated the principles which will finally lead to the complete emancipation of women.* Even the Old Testament, which Montgomery characterized as "partial and preparatory" in its relation to the New Testament, demanded "consideration for the rights of the weak and dependent, of women, children, the poor, the slave" that she found unique in antiquity. She believed that the prophets of Israel, in their insistence on ethical individualism, "laid the foundation for a democracy that should at last abolish the caste of sex." Jesus himself built upon that foundation in his teachings and example. "He took up the old teaching of the prophets, obscured by the prejudice of the centuries, brushed aside the dishonoring conventions which the rabbis had built up, and associated with women in the plane of a beautiful, free, human relationship."[55]

Of course, Montgomery recognized that Paul's limitations on the activities of women in 1 Corinthians were a problem for her argument. She regarded Paul's instructions to the Corinthian church as exceptions to the general rule of freedom and equality in the New Testament churches, which were imposed because of the special circumstances of the church in Corinth. But even Paul, Montgomery argued, laid down freedom and gender equality as the general rule for Christians everywhere. In the record of his missionary career in Acts and in his own epistles, Paul "lays down the Magna Charta of womanhood in a Christianity in which there is neither male nor female, bond nor free, but in which all are one in Christ Jesus. He sees clearly that the duty of subordination and service is laid on all alike in Christ's great democracy and only those who love most are most honored."[56]

During her entire career as a municipal reformer, Montgomery worked to make democracy broader and more inclusive, especially in regard to the participation of women. Yet she never gave up the Victorian conviction that men and women were by nature different and complementary. Although she believed men and women were equal, she did not believe they were the same. From this conviction, she reasoned theologically that the democracy of Jesus would manifest itself in a "new world" of fully developed humanity that was already in process, although it had not yet arrived. The new world was "not a man's world, hard, cruel, bitter toward the weak, nor a woman's world, weak, sentimental, tasteless, but a world of humanity in which for the first time the full orb of all the qualities that serve to mark the human shall have free course and be glorified."[57]

To the skeptic who wondered why the alleged democratic ideals of the Bible were so long delayed and so imperfectly realized, Montgomery appealed for time. She claimed that the Bible was only placed in the hands of "the people" during the last two or three centuries, and even so only a small part of the world's population had yet received it. Furthermore, Montgomery believed full equality for women was "the last word in democracy," and in most of the world "the first word is just getting itself uttered." Nevertheless, despite the opposition of vested interests and prejudice, Montgomery was convinced that "steady progress" was discernable in "Christian countries." She listed a number of progressive reforms as evidence: "laws are ameliorated, violence is curbed, child labor is limited, women do come to their rights in exact proportion as Christian ideals become dominant in a nation." Likewise, democracy accompanied the civilizing mission of Christianity in non-Christian lands.[58]

In Montgomery's view, the duty of Christian womanhood in America was clear. The "ethnic faiths" lacked the inner resources for the "emancipation of woman and child." Consequently it was up to the Christian women of America to intervene on their behalf. "The great Emancipator of the mother and child must be made known in every dark corner of the earth,"[59] Montgomery wrote, and in her reasoning she globalized the logic of municipal housekeeping. Municipal housekeepers rationalized their intervention in municipal affairs on the assumption, widely shared in Victorian culture, that women were best qualified to understand, care for, and defend the needs and interests of other women and children. Montgomery transformed the rationalization for municipal housekeeping into an apologetic for the ecumenical woman's missionary movement and their missiology of "Woman's Work for Woman." Frances Willard once said, "Woman will bless and brighten every place she enters, and will enter every place."[60] Montgomery and the women of her movement interpreted that mandate to include "every dark corner of the earth."[61]

"The New Woman of the Orient"

Montgomery offered her readers evidence that the ecumenical woman's missionary movement, as the lead institution in a worldwide democratic movement for the emancipation of women, was effective. In the non-Christian world, traditional degradation and oppression of women, legitimized by religion, was giving way to a new, emancipated womanhood, inspired and supported by the American Protestant missionary movement. Montgomery believed the changes were part of a "worldwide woman's movement," and that "this reaching out of women for fuller freedom and juster [sic] opportunities is confined to no race nor country." Whether in America, Europe, or the non-Christian world, the reforms had a single source: "They spring from the gradual penetration into common consciousness of certain principles which Christ enunciated and of which the New Testament is full. These principles are (1) the supreme worth of the individual, (2) his direct responsibility to God, (3) the obligation of unselfish service laid on all irrespective of sex, (4) human brotherhood, (5) divine fatherhood."[62]

These principles reflected the ideals of Christian chivalry in the Victorian Era, and in various combinations and versions they were commonly associated with many Christian reform movements in the Progressive Era, including the Social Gospel movement. But Montgomery gave the third principle a special relevance for the ecumenical woman's missionary movement when she made the obligation of service "irrespective of sex." In her view, these principles made the gospel "the most tremendous engine of democracy ever forged," and she expected it to "break into pieces all castes, privileges, and oppressions." Admittedly, the "corollary" issue of women's rights would not be solved completely while the "main problem of democracy" persisted, but Montgomery found it remarkable that the women's movement made progress nevertheless, even in those countries that were "the most backward and despotic, so far as women are concerned." The only explanation, in her view, was the movement of the spirit of Christ, who was "drawing the whole world unto His own perfect charity, justice, friendliness, democracy, to that redeemed humanity in which there shall be neither male nor female, bond nor free, but only free men and free women, whose lives, like His, are given them not to be ministered unto, but to minister."[63]

Montgomery went on to describe the main features and leading women of the movement in several non-Christian lands. In many ways, the movement Montgomery outlined was a reflection of the New Womanhood of America, which Montgomery represented. In various countries, the movement communicated through women's magazines, opened schools for girls, trained women as teachers, and formed women's and girls' clubs. In Siam (now Thailand), there was a woman's club affiliated with the Federation of Women's Clubs in America; in Japan, a National Women's Christian Temperance Union; in Egypt, a national organization of women's rights activists.[64] Women opened libraries and reading rooms, organized petition drives, and pressed for dress reform and legal redress against oppressive marriage customs. Women were trained as physicians and nurses, and they specialized in the treatment of women and children.[65]

Of course, the missionaries supported by the ecumenical woman's missionary movement were responsible for the initial leadership in many of these endeavors, but they generally took great pride in the accomplishments of indigenous women who became leaders. In Montgomery's view, however, two signs of progress stood above all others as indicators of success for the civilizing mission of the women's ecumenical movement because she believed they were evidence of more or less permanent cultural change. First, as an experienced municipal reformer, Montgomery knew that when some agency of the government adopted a reform it was usually because the reform was popular and regarded as practical or effective. Second, as a domestic feminist, Montgomery regarded Christianization of the home life as the ultimate goal. When desired reforms became a matter of course for indigenous families, Montgomery regarded them as profoundly successful.

Physical exercise for Chinese schoolgirls was a reform that Montgomery regarded as successful because it was adopted by the government. It is particularly interesting because Montgomery's description of the reform process was so similar to the process that took place in the United States when physical education was introduced in the first female colleges, such as Montgomery's own Wellesley College. According to Montgomery, "Formerly teachers in mission schools had to force girls to play, to exercise. They were sulky and mortified, it seemed so undignified and unwomanly to use the body freely. Now beautiful calesthenic exercises, dancing, gymnastics, are not only taught in the missions, but required in the government schools."[66]

When the Japanese emperor violated precedent and allowed his wife to ride by his side in an open carriage, Montgomery pointed with guarded optimism at an example of reform in government policy and home life. According to Montgomery, the emperor's liberality gave his wife "a new legal status" while it also did much to "elevate the position of women" through "courtesy and respect."[67]

In Japan, as in many other Eastern lands, Montgomery believed the reformation of family life testified to Christianity's growing social influence.[68] Montgomery believed that because of the influence of Christianity in general and the educational work of the ecumenical woman's missionary movement in particular, female children in many cultures were increasingly regarded as valuable and desirable, concubinage was in decline, and wives received new respect for their work in the home.

Montgomery believed the consequences of the "world movement" for women's rights remained in doubt, and the gospel was the key component in determining the outcome. She wrote, "What the women appropriate in the opening years of this new freedom will be wrought into the texture of national life for a century to come. When they ask for bread, shall we give them a stone? In their eagerness for fuller life and liberty and learning, shall we allow them to get only the garment of civilization and not its heart?"[69] Western civilization without the gospel was a hollow shell, in Montgomery's view, and it was in no way spiritually superior to Eastern civilizations.

In an earlier book for the Central Committee, in which she studied missionary activity in the Pacific Islands, Montgomery defended the missionary enterprise as a necessary feature of the Western contact with other cultures. Without the mitigation of Christianity, there was nothing to curtail "the white man's brutality, lust, and cruelty," and she believed the technological superiority made Western culture a curse to other peoples. She wrote:

The question is not missions or no intercourse, but intercourse without missions, or intercourse with missions added. To withdraw missionaries would not stop a single trader, nor a gallon of rum, nor one cruel exploitation; it would simply leave to run riot the forces of evil. The strongest reason why the conscience of Europe and America ought to continue and immensely strengthen its missionary forces in the island world is because we owe it to these people to make the largest, most costly, and statesmanlike reparation for the ills inflicted on them by unworthy representatives of our race, and by our still unchristianized governments. To take away the missionary would be to take away the one man who is in the islands, not for what he can get out of them, but for what he can give to them; the one man who gives the natives books in their own tongue, schools, hospitals, churches; who nurses their sick, teaches their children, resents their wrongs, protects them against imposition and fraud, teaches them new arts of practical life,—in short, who is their brother.[70]

Montgomery would not have American women abandon their Eastern sisters to a spiritually barren Westernization without the gospel. In her view, Jesus Christ was at the heart of Western civilization's distinctive regard for women. Any attempt to remove the influence of the ecumenical woman's missionary movement and liberate Eastern women with a secularized women's rights movement would be mistaken and potentially disastrous.

The tremendous success of the ecumenical woman's missionary movement raised issues that necessitated such a cautionary tone. Montgomery realized that great energy, enthusiasm, devotion, and sacrifice made the vast growth of the movement in the past fifty years possible. Still, Montgomery believed there was much more work to be done—difficult and costly work that required still more growth and still greater sacrifice. She asked, "What are 140 physicians among a half-billion women? What are 6000 schools to the 250 million children who ought to be in school? We congratulate ourselves on our great work. The glory is God's, the shame is ours. He has taken our scant gifts and multiplied them, but what are they? Let us never think we are meeting the need of the heathen world; we are only touching its edges."[71] Montgomery argued that it was not a question of money. American women had at their disposal more than adequate wealth for the task of Christianizing the world. Nor did they lack organization, spiritual resources, or opportunity. In Montgomery's view, the barriers to success were motivation and organizational effectiveness.[72]

There was another reason for Montgomery's concern for the future of the movement. Even as the leaders of the movement contemplated a Jubilee celebration, other voices called for the integration of the movement with the denominational boards. Just as in 1900, the very success of the movement motivated some to call for an end to its alleged competition with the denominational boards. Montgomery believed that the women's boards had "tapped a new vein of contributions that would not and could not be reached" by the male-dominated denominational boards.[73]

Montgomery believed women needed the sort of stimulating, meaningful, and challenging work they found through the women's boards just as much as men did. She objected sharply to the idea of separating women from the responsibility for spending money they had raised. She believed women were just as competent as men to make decisions regarding the appropriation of missionary funds and that to separate women from their responsibility would be harmful to their development as persons. "The opportunity of self-expression and the development that comes through responsibility are as necessary to women as to men," she wrote. Montgomery doubted that men were sufficiently "emancipated from the caste of sex" to accept women as peers if the women's boards were combined with the denominational boards. Despite the progress of women in American society, she believed that "we still have a long stretch of unexplored country to be traversed before the perfect democracy of Jesus is reached." Montgomery was not interested in tokenism, and that was all she believed women could expect from a merged board "in the present state of civilization."[74]

Nor would merger serve the best interests of the missionary cause, Montgomery warned. Instead it would tend to weaken the vital emotional connection that women felt to the special work of the ecumenical woman's missionary movement and ultimately weaken their devotion to the missionary enterprise. Montgomery believed that most of the women in the movement were motivated by their affinity for "that intimate, near appeal made by work for women and homes and little children."[75] For generations American women had been taught that those were their special concerns, and the missiology of "Woman's Work for Woman" was built on that conviction. Montgomery believed a merger would destroy the special focus of the

"Woman's Work for Woman" because it would destroy the boards that were the institutional base of its existence.

Instead of a merger, Montgomery advocated cooperative diversity. She believed that men were rightly and naturally attracted to certain features of the missionary enterprise and women to others, and she believed that if men and women pursued their respective interests, the missionary cause as a whole would be advanced and strengthened. "It is only natural and right that the work of establishing churches, training ministers, educating future leaders, should absorb the energies of men," she wrote. Women also had special tasks. Montgomery wrote, "It is a woman's task to see that the poor, downtrodden, backward women of the non-Christian world have a chance. Let us take care of the kindergartens, orphanages, asylums, and schools that appeal most to us; let us touch the home side of life, believing that in so doing we are aiding the whole great enterprise to which as men and women we are committed."[76] Montgomery believed the answer was not to merge the women's boards with the denominational boards, but to find a way to motivate men to support missions with the same sacrificial devotion as women.

Like women's clubs, women's colleges, and women's settlement houses, the women's missionary societies were manifestations of what women's historians have called the strategy of "separatism."[77] Montgomery's reluctance to relinquish separatism reflected in part her belief that separate institutions nurtured women's power and expedited women's progress. She feared that the loss of those institutions would mean the loss of autonomy and power. If, as Montgomery believed, the kingdom of God was "the perfect democracy of Jesus," America might be on the way, but clearly the nation had not yet arrived. For Montgomery, the women's boards represented Jesus' gospel of emancipation for women, the greatest achievement of the New Womanhood of America, and the best hope for the progress of the global women's movement, but they also represented an institutional defense against chauvinism.

Eleven

AFTER THE JUBILEE
Women's Colleges and "World Friendship"

In the wake of the 1910–1911 Jubilee, Montgomery helped guide the ecumenical woman's missionary movement through several important transitions, and she lived long enough to see the beginning of the movement's decline. Despite the changes she experienced, she never wavered from her basic commitment to progressivism and the ideology of domestic feminism.

New Priorities for the Movement

After the Jubilee tour, Montgomery returned home, as Peabody noted, "to her customary Sunday-school class," but she suffered another serious bout of ill health. During the Jubilee tour Dr. Mary Riggs Noble had diagnosed a liver disorder that required surgery. When she had fully recovered from the operation, she felt better than she had in years.[1]

Plan of Federation

Given the overwhelming success of the Jubilee, Lucy W. Peabody was convinced that the women's boards needed a more formal cooperative structure than the triennial meetings of the International Conference of Woman's Boards of Foreign Missions could provide. They needed an organization that would allow them to "keep in touch with each other and with womanhood as a whole." At the 1912 meeting of the conference she proposed a plan of federation. The women agreed to try the plan, but the first attempt, with regional divisions, proved unsatisfactory. The organization was not finalized until 1916, when a modified version of the original plan was adopted and the Federation of Woman's Boards of Foreign Missions was created.[2]

Day of Prayer

At the same 1912 meeting where Peabody proposed the federation, several other important ventures took shape. Apparently Montgomery had been advocating the adoption of a day of prayer since the 1890s, and at the 1912 meeting she and Peabody encouraged the conference to adopt a single day on which all of the women's boards could join in a World Day of Prayer. The idea was not an innovation; days of prayer had a long history in American culture, but this was the first time the women's boards agreed to unify their efforts. In 1919 the women's boards of foreign missions joined the women's boards of home missions, and the World Day of Prayer became a global institution.[3]

Committee on Christian Literature for Women and Children

As early as 1909 Lucy W. Peabody drew the attention of the movement to the need for "helpful literature, not only on Christian themes, but on hygiene, care of children, and the like," for women in the non-Christian world.[4] The International Conference of Woman's Boards of Foreign Missions launched a committee to study the issue, and in 1912 Clementina Butler read the committee's report. They found there was a substantial amount of Christian (and some non-Christian) literature produced for the East, but very little was aimed at women and children. Butler's report concluded that it was up to the women to "send in humbler ways the water of life into the very hearts and homes of women and children." The International Conference created the Interdenominational Committee on Christian Literature for Women and Children in Heathen Lands, later renamed the Committee on Christian Literature for Women and Children in Mission Fields.[5] The first publications were for women and children in China, but the work expanded globally. Dana L. Robert noted that the many magazines supported by the committee in various countries around the world encouraged the work of indigenous Christian artists and writers, who contributed to the magazines.[6] It also helped to spread the movement ideals for the "New Woman of the Orient," such as the basics of educated motherhood that Peabody mentioned in her original challenge in 1909. Because it received some substantial bequests—including one from Helen Barrett Montgomery, another from Lucy W. Peabody, and a third from Marguerite Doane, the daughter of hymn writer William Howard Doane—the Committee on Christian Literature for Women and Children in Mission Fields was able to operate autonomously long after the other institutions of the movement merged with the denominational boards or the National Council of Churches. It continued its independent existence well into the 1980s.[7]

World Tour

Peabody recruited Montgomery for a world tour of mission stations in 1913. Peabody hoped to combine a number of purposes into the tour. Once a missionary in India, she was eager to see her former mission field again and to share the experience with her good friend and their daughters, both of whom had finished college. At the same time, the Central Committee needed a textbook "based on first hand impressions," and Peabody wanted Montgomery to write it.[8] Furthermore, both Peabody and Montgomery were members of the Education Commission of Continuation Committee of the Edinburgh Conference. They had to travel to Holland for a meeting of the committee anyway, so why not take the opportunity to continue on with a tour of mission stations? Finally, as members of the Education Commission, the tour would give them an opportunity to assess the growing need for Christian colleges for women in Asia, which they were eager to fulfill.[9]

After the meeting in Holland, where they were invited to the palace of Appledoorn and received by Queen Wilhelmina, they traveled to Egypt, Ceylon (now Sri Lanka), India, Burma (now Myanmar), Singapore, Malaysia, Hong Kong, China, Manchuria, Korea, Japan (where for some reason Montgomery and Peabody parted company), Hawaii, and then to the west coast of the United States. The tour took nearly six months. Everywhere they went they found what they thought they would find and hoped to find—missionaries and their converts asking for women's colleges. The need provided validation of the decades of primary and secondary education for women and girls supported by the women's boards and a daunting new challenge, considering the vast resources that would be needed. No single denomination could possibly meet such a need, so the women's boards planned to work ecumenically. Almost everywhere Peabody and Montgomery found a need for new institutions or substantial support for existing ones.[10]

Union Christian Colleges for Women

As Dana L. Robert pointed out, higher education for women was fundamental to the development of the missiology of the ecumenical women's
missionary movement in that era—"Woman's Work for Woman"—and the
women of the movement regarded education as essential to the emancipation
of women everywhere.[11] It is not difficult to see why the leaders of the ecumenical women's missionary movement believed so strongly in education.
Women's colleges were essential in the development of domestic feminism
in the United States. In the language of Estelle Freedman, women's colleges and other gender-based institutions, such as women's clubs, were com-
ponents in the strategy of separatism.[12] Women built separate institutions
that functioned to their advantage in a number of ways. Women's colleges
in particular allowed women who were socialized in the ideology of True
Womanhood to gain advanced education, political leadership skills, and practical reform experience in a safe, morally appropriate environment. Women
emerged from women's colleges motivated to extend "womanly influence"
into unprecedented social and political arenas, and they were armed with a
strong apologetic for women's involvement in an expanding array of social
and political issues. They were able to compete more successfully with men
for what Kathryn Kish Sklar called "the distribution of social resources,"[13]
and they were prepared to cooperate with male allies as peers.

Women's colleges in America contributed powerfully to the development
of domestic feminism. Initially, supporters of women's colleges in America
argued that higher education would make women better wives and mothers.
A few visionaries, like Henry Fowle Durant, wanted to educate women for
social reform. In any case, women's higher education facilitated the modi-
fication of Victorian True Womanhood into the New Womanhood of the
Progressive Era. Montgomery and the leaders of the ecumenical women's
missionary movement hoped and believed that institutions of higher education on the mission field could have the same transforming effects on women
in other cultures around the world.

The movement lent its support to seven union colleges. In 1920 the
leadership of the movement formed the Joint Committee for Women's
Union Christian Colleges in Foreign Fields and embarked on a four-year
fund-raising drive. Peabody was chairman, and Montgomery was a member

of the committee.[14] Peabody, looking back years later, pointed with pride at the achievement of the women these institutions produced.[15]

While the leadership of the movement was enthusiastic, one wonders what the average woman's mission circle member thought of the plan to support college education for women in mission lands. After all, in 1910 only 3.8 percent of American women from eighteen to twenty-one years of age attended college. By 1920 the number had risen to 7.6 percent.[16] For most of the history of the women's missionary movement, the leadership made its appeals to the rank and file of American women partly on the basis of advantages they enjoyed as American women when compared to women around the world. The appeal to support higher education must have struck some women as a request to fund advantages for women in missionary lands that were superior to their own.

In any case, the initiative to fund women's colleges on the missionary field was not as successful in gathering grassroots support as other initiatives of the movement were. The Joint Committee was forced to turn to the Laura Spelman Rockefeller Memorial Fund and other institutional sources of support for about half of its fund-raising goal. In 1924 the name of the Joint Committee was changed to the Cooperating Committee for Women's Union Christian Colleges in Foreign Fields, and Montgomery became the chairman.[17] The World Day of Prayer offerings became the main source of funding after 1924.[18]

In 1920 Montgomery gave a speech at the National Conference of Church-Women in Washington, D.C. In that speech, which *Missions* called a "Thrilling Address," she reaffirmed her commitment to missions as an enterprise of civilizational conversion and of civilization as a means of God's mission in the world. She also restated her abiding commitment to the missiology of "Woman's Work for Woman," and she articulated her growing critique of American culture as inadequately Christianized, materialistic, and licentious. In 1920, of course, the push was on to support the Union Christian Colleges for Women. Montgomery's speech was optimistic and enthusiastic about the possibilities of the women's missionary movement, and it was slanted to build support among American women for the cause of women's higher education. Yet at the same time one can detect in Montgomery's tone a growing sense of frustration that American women were taking their advantages for granted and ignoring their duties and God's calling.

Montgomery challenged her audience to look upon "the mother-half of the race which holds the key to the future; that half of the race which from the dawn of time has been shut out from the kingdom of art, and shut out from the schools of philosophy, and shut in to ignorance, and superstition, and suffering, and degradation." Men had set things up, she said, so that the one half of the race with the greatest task—"the mothers of men!"—are forced to accomplish it "without tools, without training, without association—in solitude, and ignorance, and youth, and inexperience." Furthermore, in the whole of human history, Jesus Christ was the one great philosopher or religious teacher who ever saw the problem with that arrangement.[19]

Every civilization of the past or present that men tried to build on "a foundation of ignorant mothers and secluded wives" had failed, Montgomery claimed, and "every present civilization, except so far as the light of the Cross of the Son of God shines on it, has failed or is failing." Even America, where women enjoyed great political and social freedom, was imperiled by a lack of faith. According to Montgomery, "one of the menaces today is the enfranchised women whom Christ has not enfranchised, and their very education and their very culture and their very freedom, they are twisting to use them for things that will tear down the country that our forefathers built up."[20]

Turning to the global situation, Montgomery lamented that "the mothers of the world are illiterate." She believed that it was no exaggeration that "three-fourths of the women of the world are in the prison of illiteracy." Why? Because they lived in lands "where Christ is not named." The one exception was Japan, where in the previous half-century the government had instituted public education. But even there the government "took her seed from the hand of Christ, for it is only where Christ has gone that you ever get public education, that you ever conceive of democracy, that you ever think that common folks are good enough to educate." She took Japan's commitment as evidence that, even though it was not yet Christian, it was going to become Christian.[21]

In an effort to help her audience imagine what Christianity had meant to the world, she asked them to try to understand what it meant to live as a woman in a non-Christian land. "Take out your schools, take out your hospitals, take out your insane asylums, take out your schools for the feeble-minded, take out your blind schools," for all of those institutions she attributed to the influence of Christianity.[22]

Montgomery was especially irritated by the fact that some American women were attracted to Hindu spirituality:

> The whole civilization of India is built up on child marriage, child motherhood, perpetual widowhood, and seclusion of women. And there are American women born under the shadow of the Cross of Christ who are dabbling in Hinduism—such a lovely system, such a wonderful philosophy!
>
> And it is Hinduism that curses the women of India. It is Hinduism that says in its highest religious sanctions, as if I should pick up our Bible and find right in the center of it, "Read not this Holy Text to a woman; she is impure as hell." That is in the Bible of Hinduism that these suave individuals come over here to teach our women. Oh, the condition of the women without Christ![23]

Montgomery attributed the respect and honor with which women were regarded in American culture, and the relative public safety they enjoyed, to the influence of Christianity. For that reason, if for no other, she believed American women ought to believe in Christ. She thought it was an "unlovely thing" to see a man who did not believe in Jesus; but to find "a woman who walks the streets in safety, and goes into the elevators ahead of men, and goes into her Pullman at night and has the protection which Christ has thrown around her—to see her worldly, unlovely, selfish, parasitic, it is a spectacle that makes the demons laugh, it is so hideous."[24]

She told her audience that the privileges of education that so many women enjoyed in America were "a miracle" and a calling from God to "take up the burden for the women of the world." Then in comments that revealed clearly her belief in the cultural influence of women and how the progress of civilization depended upon God's blessing, she said, "You cannot raise this world until you have raised the mothers of this world. You cannot hold up America while America is being pulled down by these lower, lesser, un-Christian ideals about women."[25] Montgomery always thought America's Christianization was incomplete, but in 1920 the nation seemed to her to be losing ground spiritually.

Likewise, Montgomery believed that a culture's attitude toward its children was a barometer of its moral well-being. When Jesus told his disciples they must become like little children to enter the kingdom, "He spoke the

Magna Charta of childhood." In Montgomery's view, much of the agenda of municipal housekeeping and educated motherhood was implicit in Jesus' words. "The kindergarten was in those words. Our study of child nature was there. The playgrounds were there. The whole new attitude toward the child was there. Jesus is the emancipator of women and little children. Why, we can't help but tell the women of the world about him, can we?"[26]

Montgomery believed that the greatest contribution of the ecumenical woman's missionary movement was that "in those fifty years they laid the foundations of a new civilization" that valued and respected women as equals. "We started with little groups of thrown-away girls and slave girls and the lowest off-scourge of the population, but we demonstrated, as the Christian Scientists say. We demonstrated, until today we have changed the opinion of the world."[27]

Indeed, she thought that America's greatest contribution to world civilization as a nation was "that we sent out groups of school-teachers, men and women, who changed the opinion of the world about the educability of girls." In China and Egypt, where women were scorned, opinion was changed and the leaders wanted to educate women. Even in India, she said, "the leaders of thought" were convinced that they needed "an educated motherhood" to be strong nationally.

Montgomery proudly listed the colleges and medical schools supported by the movement. But her last word was one of warning and reproof. American women were no longer turning to the women's boards for missionary careers as they once did. Medical women in particular were in short supply. "Why is it that American medical women will volunteer by the score and hundred to go to Europe, and cannot hear the call of Christ for those neediest parts of all the world?" Montgomery believed American women needed a new commitment to Christian service and a new certainty in their faith: "We have got to challenge our colleges for that, and we have got to challenge our colleges to give us girls with the gospel and not an interrogation point, for Christ cannot use in his fight in the dark with the powers of evil, a woman who has lost her certainty and her gospel, and sometimes I think that while we are disputing about nice questions of the law and of interpretation and of scholarship and of standards, the world is burning up."[28]

From "Woman's Work for Woman" to "World Friendship"

In the aftermath of World War I, in which the nations of Christendom brutalized each other, the optimistic spirit and sense of cultural superiority that characterized both progressivism and the nineteenth-century Protestant missionary movement was shattered. The missiology of the ecumenical women's missionary movement, "Woman's Work for Woman," which assumed the superiority of Western civilization, required reformulation. In the United States, the ratification of the Nineteenth Amendment, which granted suffrage to women, tended to undercut another main feature of "Woman's Work for Woman," the strategy of separatism.[29]

The revised missiology of the movement was "World Friendship." The new term suggested a gender-neutral strategy of partnership. It retained many of the salient features of "Woman's Work for Woman" (and consequently of domestic feminism), such as women's rights and the special needs of women and children, and it supplemented them with new emphasis on social justice and world peace. Given the new strategy of partnership, the responsibility for direct evangelism was increasingly left to indigenous Christians and churches, and the women missionaries felt at liberty to cultivate cooperative relationships with government agencies, secular civic organizations, and men's Christian organizations.[30]

The first major document of the new missiology was Caroline Atwater Mason's *World Missions and World Peace.*[31] Mason's book constituted a strong rebuke of the violence of Western civilization, which Mason attributed to the incomplete conversion of Western civilization to the gospel of the Prince of Peace. Although it was the first book that the Central Committee ever published that lost money, it was also the first of several that dealt seriously with the issue of world peace.[32]

Montgomery's main contribution to the missiology of World Friendship was her 1929 study book, *From Jerusalem to Jerusalem.*[33] It was the last study book she wrote for the movement, and it contained her most mature reflection on the missionary movement in general and on the ecumenical women's missionary movement in particular. It was written in response to the International Missionary Conference in Jerusalem in 1928, and as an overview of the history of mission. Ostensibly Montgomery took the Pentecost event in Jerusalem as her starting point, but the book made it clear that she believed mission was much older than the Christian church.

Perhaps influenced by Southern Baptist missiologist William Owen Carver,[34] whose book *Missions and Modern Thought* she listed in her recommended readings,[35] Montgomery articulated a theory of *missio Dei* in which the mission of the Christian church is not rooted merely in biblical mandates such as the Great Commission (Matt 28:19-20), but in the very nature of God's interaction with humanity throughout history. Montgomery believed God had a plan for the salvation of the world before the foundation of the world, and that the plan was progressively revealed in history. The kingdom of God that Jesus announced and inaugurated was the plan in its "developing phases," and the missionary enterprise was synonymous with the growth of the kingdom of God.[36]

In Montgomery's view the plan of God was "(1) universal, (2) all-embracing, (3) redemptive, and (4) sacrificial." It was for everyone, everywhere, and it included all aspects of human life and culture. Christianity was the engine of authentic human progress, and the missionary was "the builder of Christianity, the pioneer of faith, the forerunner of progress."[37] Implicit in that statement was Montgomery's conviction that even Christianity was dependent upon a process of historical development. Dana L. Robert pointed out that in *From Jerusalem to Jerusalem,* Montgomery anticipated the missiological emphasis on Christianity's translatability as the key to its success.[38] But Montgomery did not believe that the success of any particular expression of Christian mission was inevitable. She believed human beings could make choices that thwarted the will of God and impeded the coming of the kingdom of God. For example, she blamed Boniface's allegiance to the papacy and his refusal to allow the translation of the Bible into the language of the people for what she regarded as "the gradual militarizing of the Church" in Germany. If Boniface had given the gospel to the German people in their own tongue, she believed Christianity would have developed differently in Germany and Luther's reforms might have been unnecessary.[39]

Patricia Hill claimed that *From Jerusalem to Jerusalem* represented a shift in Montgomery's thought from an "apocalyptic reading of history that had led her to see, in the successive opening of widely dispersed mission fields, the rapid approach of the Kingdom of God," to a postwar "cyclical view of history" in which "the church might fail in the historical moment, although the Gospel would ultimately triumph."[40] While it is true that Montgomery, like progressives in general, was much less optimistic in her appraisal of Western civilization after the First World War than she was before, there is no evidence that her prewar view of mission history was "apocalyptic" nor that her postwar view was "cyclical." Hill's use of the word *apocalyptic* in connection with the phrase *kingdom of God* suggested that Montgomery's view of the kingdom of God was an otherworldly reality. On the contrary, Montgomery understood the coming of the kingdom of God to be signified in worldly realities such as the emancipation of women, the expansion of literacy and health care, or the extension of democracy—and these she understood as the fruits of Christian conversion.

It is also a mistake to characterize her view of church history as "cyclical." Montgomery viewed church history as a complex process of development in which the gospel of Christ was the catalyst for the growth of the kingdom of God. Once the gospel took root and influenced the development of a particular culture, there were possibilities for progress and regression at the same time. The mission of the church was to Christianize all civilizations. Even the cultures of the so-called Christian nations needed redemption to some extent. Because people were free in relationship to God, there was always the possibility for failure in the missionary movement. In fact the entire last chapter of *Western Women in Eastern Lands,* written in 1910 at the apex of the influence of the ecumenical women's missionary movement, implied the possibility of failure. Montgomery called upon the women of the movement to move beyond complacency to renewed enthusiasm and to avoid mistakes and compromises that could cripple the movement. Montgomery believed that the mission movement was a historical development like all others. No other view can be found in any of Montgomery's writings.

Hill charged the prewar Montgomery with legitimizing Western imperialism, but to make her case she misquoted Montgomery. As evidence to show that Montgomery believed that "European and American imperialism was in partnership with the evangelical churches in the great enterprise of ushering in the Kingdom," Hill quoted from *The King's Highway:*

> And are not these empire-builders also builders of the King's Highway? Is it not profoundly true that all the great accomplishments of civilization by which anarchy is put down, property rendered safe, communications opened up, education made possible, are John the Baptists crying in the wilderness: "The Kingdom of Heaven is at hand"?[41]

That certainly does seem to implicate Montgomery in the evils of Western imperialism, but it is not what Montgomery wrote. Hill omitted a complete sentence after the first sentence of the quotation. The entire quotation should read:

> And are not these empire-builders also builders of the King's Highway? Did not the Roman soldiers who stretched firm roads like radii to the circumference of the Empire make paths on which the Gospel could travel swiftly? Is it not profoundly true that all the great accomplishments of civilization by which anarchy is put down, property rendered safe, communications opened up, education made possible, are John the Baptists crying in the wilderness: "The Kingdom of Heaven is at hand"?[42]

The inclusion of the sentence that Hill omitted shows that Montgomery believed that the King's Highway included civilization as an enterprise, not just Western civilization. Montgomery did not single out Western civilization as the only vehicle for the gospel message. She believed that the presence of the gospel message in a civilization was a catalyst for progress; but as her reference to Roman roads indicated, she defined "accomplishments of civilization" as anything that elevated human life and made it more humane, or that facilitated the progress of the gospel message.

The particular historical context of Montgomery's comments was the involvement of the British Empire in Egypt. Montgomery held no illusions about the reasons for Britain's intervention. She knew that England and France intervened in Egyptian affairs "primarily to protect the interests of their subjects who had made Egyptian investments." But she believed the British influence in particular had been salubrious. British economic reforms, land reclamation, legal and judicial reforms, and educational reforms constituted a "great work for civilization accomplished by the British."[43]

It is significant that Montgomery characterized that work as "work for civilization accomplished by the British." Montgomery was interested in underscoring how civilization in general was a highway for God. She believed that the progress of Christianity was incomplete in the West, and she never shrank from criticizing aspects of Western civilization that she found dehumanizing, especially when it reflected poorly on the mission of the church in non-Western cultures. Nevertheless, she believed that God could use Western civilization as a vehicle for the gospel message. For Montgomery the issue was not whether the churches were in partnership with imperial powers, but whether the churches were awake to the fact that God was at work through civilization, and that Christians of her era had opportunities for mission that were unprecedented in the history of the world.

Montgomery's explanation of the rapid spread of Christianity around the ancient world illustrated her understanding of how God used civilization as a vehicle for the gospel message. She believed the diaspora of the Jews provided early Christian evangelists with a ready audience in every part of the Roman Empire; the Greek language provided a convenient and nearly universal medium of communication; missionaries followed wherever the Roman Empire extended its roads and established its law to facilitate travel, trade, and communication; Christian preachers offered a spiritual message that appealed to people in a sensual, cynical, materialistic culture; the Christian message offered redemption, hope, peace, love, and liberation.[44]

It is true, as Hill recognized, that Montgomery was more thorough in her critique of Western civilization in 1929 than she had ever been before. No doubt the disillusionment that followed the First World War was a major motivating factor in the development of Montgomery's critique of the West. Even so, many of the elements of the critique were scattered throughout her earlier writings. Writing a historical overview of the missionary enterprise provided Montgomery with an opportunity to present her critique of the West in a more complete and systematic fashion, and to place it in the context of the Christian church's continuing struggle to maintain faithfulness to the gospel message in the face of temptations to compromise.

On two issues in particular, Montgomery found that the ancient church was guilty of compromise. First, the church compromised on the issue of pacifism. According to Montgomery, it was "the increase of wealth and numbers" that caused the church to abandon two centuries of peaceful nonresistance to violence and "drag the pure gospel of Jesus in the mire of war."[45] Second, the church reneged on its original commitment to the equality and freedom of women, and placed women in a position of subordination to a male-dominated hierarchy.

Montgomery reiterated her long-held position that the positive attitude of Jesus toward women made Christianity distinctive among the world religions. "Jesus alone of all the great religious teachers of the world made no sex bar in his religion. He had one law of faith and purity for men and women. He invited both sexes into the deepest mysteries of his faith without discrimination." She observed that women were the first witnesses to the resurrection and received the first commission from the risen Christ to proclaim the resurrection. They participated in the events of Pentecost and "in them was fulfilled the ancient prophecy of Joel that upon both men and women God would pour out his spirit and they should prophesy."[46]

Montgomery went on to build an argument from the New Testament that the early church included women in every aspect of the life and ministry of the church. The four daughters of Philip were prophets, Priscilla and Aquila instructed Apollos and had a church in their house, and perhaps Priscilla was the author of Hebrews. Phoebe was the minister of the church in Cenchrea, despite the efforts of later English translators to obscure the fact by translating the word as "servant" rather than "minister." Junia was noted among the apostles, and Tryphena and Tryphosa were probably preachers like Paul. Montgomery was certain that the evidence of the New Testament revealed in early Christianity "a democracy of the spirit in which men and women shared alike." Paul's injunctions against women in his epistles were "given in view of special circumstances," and in fact served as evidence of "the prevalence of speaking and teaching on the part of women."[47]

Unfortunately, according to Montgomery, the church was no more able to maintain its commitment to gender equality than it was to maintain its commitment to nonviolence. In the second and third centuries, "ecclesiastics gained control of the Church. As the hierarchy waxed great the position of women declined."[48] So deep was the betrayal of the "clear witness of the gospel" that some women began to believe that Christianity discriminated against women.[49]

Montgomery believed the ecumenical women's missionary movement was restoring the democracy of spirit in early Christianity that the compromise of centuries had obscured. She wrote:

> The hands of Jesus, their liberator, summon them [the women of the movement] out of their secluded lives to serve with him in the redemption of the world. Yet his organized Church is slow to avail itself of the talents of women, slow to set them free to express what God gave them to express. And while the Church hesitates and mumbles over formularies, business and society and politics are freely opening to women new doors of opportunity.[50]

The language of seclusion that Montgomery used to describe Christianity's limitation of women was almost identical to that which she once used to describe the attitude of middle-class Victorian culture in 1905, when she called women to activism in the cause of municipal housekeeping during the Hackett House episode. Twenty-four years later culture ran ahead of the Christian church in the liberation of women, in Montgomery's view, and Christianity paid a heavy price in the lost gifts and energy of women.

At the Jerusalem Conference in 1928, the nature of the relationship between the "older churches" of Christendom to the "younger churches" of the mission lands became a major topic of discussion. In response to this discussion, and in keeping with the partnership missiology of World Friendship, Montgomery reminded her readers again and again that Christianity came to the West from the East as she told how Europe was evangelized. She told heroic stories of many indigenous people who served the cause of Christ as missionaries or leaders of indigenous churches. It was nothing new for Montgomery to celebrate the work of indigenous missionaries. Her first study book for the movement, *Christus Redemptor,* was filled with such accounts. But in *From Jerusalem to Jerusalem,* Montgomery emphasized the autonomy of indigenous Christians and even their resistance to the negative aspects of Western civilization. For example, she told how Khama, an African prince of the Bechuanas, stood against the pagan influence of his own father and even endured exile in a way that was reminiscent of David and King Saul. When he became king by the will of the people, he established social and religious reforms in keeping with his Christian faith. His greatest reform, according to Montgomery, was Prohibition of imported liquor as well as native beer. King Khama called liquor a great evil and banished all white men involved with the liquor trade.[51]

The irony of this story, in which a black African king stood bravely against the paganism of his own culture and then lectured white Europeans on faithfulness to the word of God, obedience to the law, and the evils of the liquor trade, could not have been lost on Montgomery's audience. Here was a leader of one of the "younger churches" teaching the people of Christendom how to be Christian.

In her penultimate chapter, "The Unfinished Task," Montgomery made explicit what was implicit throughout the narrative. The unfinished task of missions was a global task. There were still, in 1929, many geographic areas of the world where no missionary had ever traveled, or where, in Montgomery's view, the missionary force was grossly inadequate. In Asia, Central and South America, Africa, and in the Arab world, there were hundreds of millions who had never heard the gospel.

Montgomery also worried that the mission movement had neglected its responsibility to evangelize Moslems and Jews. She viewed Islam as the major competitor to Christianity as the dominant world religion because of the loyalty and zeal of its adherents and the absence of racial prejudice among them. Nevertheless, she believed Islam was inferior to Christianity because "its code of ethics is limited and, in some respects evil; it tolerates, when it does not foster, slavery; it degrades womankind; it fails to reveal the fatherhood of God." Despite those defects, Islam posed a major challenge to the missionary enterprise. "If we continue to despair of the Moslem and to neglect him, the time may come when, gathering all his fanatical strength for one more onset, he may again disturb the peace and security of the world as he did in the seventh century of our era."[52]

Montgomery was just as dissatisfied with the Christian record toward the Jews, but for a different reason. "The treatment of the Jews by so-called Christian nations only serves to show how terribly far short his followers have come from sharing or manifesting the spirit of Jesus," she declared. Instead of persecution and oppression, the Jews needed the gospel message of redemption. "The Jew like the Gentile must be saved by Christ and by him only. He has brought life and immortality to light for both Jew and Gentile. The Jew has a right to the Gospel; it flowed out of his life, his story."[53] Perhaps Montgomery was reflecting on her own experience in Rochester and in the women's club movement when she commented on Christian apathy toward evangelism of the Jews: "We live beside them every day. They are our neighbors; they are our fellow citizens; yet we pass them by without a thought of responsibility in regard to their acceptance of Christ."[54] She believed the time had come for renewed effort toward the Jews—evangelism, distribution of the New Testament, ministries of care and compassion, and prayer. She thought Christians ought to pray for reconciliation with Jews and approach God in "penitence and confession of failure" so that their lives and witnesses might be winsome to the Jews.[55]

The "unfinished task" also included Christendom. Montgomery looked at the West from a non-Western perspective. "People in China and India and

Japan and Africa read of our lynchings, of our bootleggers, of our defaulting public officials, of our divorces." She was convinced that "the unchristliness of the West is the greatest obstacle to the Christianizing of the East." The World War was perhaps the clearest indictment of Christendom. "We cannot have war and Christ too. We must choose between abandoning the war system with its appeal to force, and giving up Christ and his appeal to goodness and self-sacrifice." She called war the "worship of Moloch" and called on the Christian church to find a peaceful alternative to settling international disputes.[56]

America in particular must give up the "unjust discrimination" of racial prejudice because it was a scandalous indictment against "Christian America" in the eyes of the world. Likewise, unjust business practice, such as child labor and oppressive wages must be abandoned.[57]

Montgomery also condemned Western imperialism as anti-Christian:

> Christ cannot live in a world that tolerates imperialism. The stronger nations must consider the weak. We cannot exploit weaker nations for our selfish advantage and hope to export our religion to those same nations. Christ must win his seat at the council table, must be accepted as the ruler of nations as well as individuals. What is unchristian in an individual cannot be allowable in a nation.[58]

The liquor trade was closely associated with imperialism in Montgomery's mind. It too had to be abandoned "if we want to keep Christ." She believed that Prohibition was tantamount in moral significance to the abolition of slavery in America. "We testified grandly for Christ as a nation when we abolished slavery; when we abolish an even more terrible slavery, the bondage to strong drink, we shall even more gloriously witness to him who came that we might have life and have it more abundantly."[59] Thus it was up to every Christian to be a conscientious and active citizen—to vote, to speak, to lobby for progressive reforms. Montgomery was concerned not only for the moral purity of America, but for the image and character of the missionary movement in which American Christianity played so dominant a part. Most importantly, she believed that civilization itself was a highway for God, and all of civilization was implicated in the missionary mandate of the gospel. "For whenever the spirit of Jesus triumphs in a law that protects the weak, or enlarges the life of a submerged tenth, that spirit is glorified among the nations." There were no Christian nations, only nations becoming Christian, and every victory in every culture, Eastern or Western, glorified God and brought the kingdom of God one step nearer to fulfillment.[60]

The idea that the gospel was a catalyst for cultural change was not a new one for Montgomery. In 1913 Montgomery published a centennial history of Baptist missions for the American Baptist Foreign Mission Society and the American Baptist Publication Society. In *Following the Sunrise,*[61] Montgomery articulated an interpretation of mission history that was consistent with her theology of culture in *From Jerusalem to Jerusalem.* In her view, the success of Baptist missions depended upon the power of the gospel as a catalyst for cultural change. Baptist readers would have recognized her theology as a theology of conversion, but in her view success depended upon the spiritual conversion of civilizations as well as individuals.

In two remarkable introductory paragraphs, Montgomery outlined what she considered providential preparations for the Baptist mission movement of the nineteenth century. Two seventeenth-century developments in particular she thought were key: the spirit of democracy and individualism that emerged through the English, American, and French revolutions and the globalization of consciousness that emerged from the age of colonization. In the eighteenth century, these two developments took on new spiritual significance when they were combined with the Methodist revivals in England and Jonathan Edwards' revival movement in America. Evangelical Protestants in both countries prayed with expectation for the global spread of the gospel and the consummation of the kingdom of God. In Montgomery's view, these historical developments converged by divine providence to prepare nineteenth-century evangelical Protestantism for a great missionary century.[62]

Montgomery's account of nineteenth-century Baptist missions was in many ways typical of her approach to mission history. In telling the story of pioneer missions, she often relied on a pattern that appeared in several of her books. She told how the missionaries took savage peoples and, with the power of the gospel, made of them "men and Christians."[63] The pattern illustrated her unwavering commitment to missions as individual spiritual conversion combined with cultural change. In Montgomery's view, that was the only really successful pattern for missions.

According to Montgomery's typical pattern, a primitive, marginalized, oppressed, and ignorant minority was transformed by the message of the gospel into a civilized, productive, prosperous, and intelligent people. In such cases, Montgomery usually depicted some providential preparation, such as an indigenous belief in one true God, which differentiated the people from the surrounding majority. After the first contact with missionaries and the gospel message, Montgomery portrayed a moment of breakthrough and mass evangelism. Once the people accepted the gospel message, they were ready for education and training in domesticity, industry, and other aspects of what Montgomery regarded as civilized existence. Finally, the people developed self-supporting churches and began their own missionary work to other groups.

Montgomery repeated variations of this basic pattern several times in *Following the Sunrise.* She used it to describe the conversion of the Karens and Muhsos of Burma, the Garos and many other tribes of Assam, and of outcastes in India. Montgomery employed an interesting variation, in which the breakthrough conversion occurred in the heart of the missionary, to describe the Baptist mission to the African Congo. Yet another version, in which Montgomery highlighted ecumenical cooperation, described Baptist missions to the peasants in the *barrios* of the Philippines.[64]

Montgomery called her chapter on the Philippines "Buttressing Democracy in the Philippines," and she called 1898 "The Wonder Year."[65] World events, she believed, moved providentially in the direction of world peace, the expansion of democracy, and broader opportunities for world mission. The United States' control of the Philippines was a prime example of both expanded democracy and broader mission opportunities, for "the protection of the American flag meant the right to free thought, free speech, and a free Bible in a free state."[66] Consequently Montgomery was a strong advocate of translating the Bible into the common languages of the Filipino people, of education and industrial training, medical missions, and direct evangelism. She supported comity agreements and ecumenical cooperation among evangelical churches, but she criticized the Baptists for an inadequate response to the need in the Philippines. When God opened a door of opportunity in the Philippines, she said, "The great Baptist denomination hardly stirred in its sleep."[67]

Twelve

A "MIDDLE-OF-THE-ROAD BAPTIST"
Creedalism and the Defense of Baptist Liberty, 1921–1922

Montgomery served one term as president of the Northern Baptist Convention (1921–1922), and it is one of the few periods of her life for which there is a record of unpublished correspondence reflecting her personal theological views. People sometimes assume that Montgomery was a theological liberal because of her social activism, her positions on suffrage and women in church leadership, and her association with Walter Rauschenbusch in Rochester. On the contrary, she was theologically conservative in many respects.[1] Her correspondence during her term as president of the Northern Baptist Convention provides ample evidence of this fact. Montgomery found herself caught in a power struggle between fundamentalists and modernists, and in the beginning she tended to favor the fundamentalists' call for a confessional statement. However, as the intolerance of fundamentalism became clear to her, she decided that fundamentalism had to be defeated and a creed avoided. Although she remained a self-described "Middle-of-the-Road Baptist" theologically, her commitment to liberty (which, in her view, was deeply rooted in the pages of the New Testament) took precedence.

In 1921, after Montgomery presented the Northern Baptist Convention with a gift from the "Jubilee" fund-raising campaign of the Woman's American Baptist Foreign Missionary Society, which totaled more than $450,000, the convention elected Montgomery president. It was the first time a woman ever served as the president of a major American denomination.

Although Montgomery was very active during her year as president, nothing she did was more significant than her opposition to the fundamentalist attempt to establish a confessional statement at the 1922 Northern Baptist Convention. It is indisputable that Montgomery opposed the statement at the June 1922 convention meeting, but that was not her intention as late as February 1922. Montgomery was at first an advocate of a confessional statement because she believed that it might help to unify the deeply divided Northern Baptist Convention and because she was not convinced that the convention's conservative critics were completely wrong. At first she tried to appease the fundamentalists, and it was their refusal to abandon militant tactics that finally convinced Montgomery to oppose them.

The Des Moines Statement

Montgomery was elected president of the Northern Baptist Convention in Des Moines, Iowa, in June 1921. In a preconvention meeting, Baptist fundamentalists affirmed a creedal statement that they felt ought to be the confession of faith for the entire Northern Baptist Convention. The statement said:

1. We believe that the Bible is God's word that it was written by men divinely inspired, and that it has supreme authority in all matters of faith and conduct.
2. We believe in God the Father, perfect in holiness, infinite in wisdom, measureless in power. We rejoice that he concerns himself mercifully in the affairs of men, that he hears and answers prayer, and that he saves from sin and death all who come to him through Jesus Christ.
3. We believe in Jesus Christ, God's only begotten son, miraculous in his birth, sinless in his life, making atonement for the sins of the world by his death. We believe in his bodily resurrection, his ascension into heaven, his perpetual intercession for his people and his personal visible return to the world according to his promise.
4. We believe in the Holy Spirit who came forth from God to convince the world of sin, of righteousness and of judgment, and to regenerate, sanctify and comfort those who believe in Jesus Christ.
5. We believe that all men by nature and by choice are sinners but that "God so loved the world that he gave his only begotten son

that whosoever believeth in him should not perish but have ever-lasting life"; we believe therefore that those who accept Christ as Savior and Lord will rejoice forever in God's presence and those who refuse to accept Christ as Savior and Lord will be forever separated from God.

6. We believe in the church—a living and spiritual body of which Christ is the head of which all regenerated people are members. We believe that a visible church is a company of believers in Jesus Christ, baptized on a credible confession of faith, and associated for worship, work, and fellowship. We believe that to these visible churches were committed, for perpetual observance, the ordinances of baptism and the Lord's Supper, and that God has laid upon these churches the task of persuading a lost world to accept Jesus Christ as Savior, and to enthrone him as Lord and Master. We believe that all human betterment and social improvement are the inevitable by-products of such a gospel.

7. We believe that every human being has direct relations with God, and is responsible to God alone in all matters of faith; that each church is independent and autonomous and must be free from interference by any ecclesiastical or political authority; that therefore Church and State must be kept separate as having different functions, each fulfilling its duties free from the dictation or patronage of the other.[2]

The Des Moines statement was essentially a restatement of the Philadelphia and New Hampshire confessions of faith, and its tone was relatively mild. It affirmed Baptist distinctives and it did not restrict orthodoxy to the so-called fundamentals, such as the verbal inspiration of the Scriptures, the substitution theory of the atonement, eternal conscious torment in hell, or premillennialism. Instead of rejecting the social implications of the gospel, the statement affirmed "human betterment and social improvement" as "inevitable."

Nearly three months after the convention, on 8 September 1921, Montgomery wrote to Rev. H. Lee McLenden of Cleveland, Ohio. In the letter, she described her theological views and her attitude toward the Des Moines statement. "I am one of the large number of Middle-of-the-Road Baptists," she wrote. "I believe fully in the great verities of our faith—the inspiration of the Scriptures, the deity of Christ, His atoning death, the reality of the resurrection, the Kingdom of God, and the binding nature of the command of Jesus to make disciples of all nations. The creedal statement which was adopted at Des Moines seems to me to represent the beliefs of the great majority of the Baptist denomination."[3]

Nevertheless, Montgomery opposed preconvention meetings on the ground that they were divisive. "Can we not, my brother, abandon this fighting spirit and the use of these party shibboleths? It seems to me that we are very much in the position of that church in Corinth to whom Paul wrote—it was weak because it was divided into parties, and Paul reminded them that it was Christ who was their Master."[4] Montgomery wanted unity, not because she did not care about doctrine, but because she believed that the command of Jesus to make disciples was the most important doctrine of the church. She wrote:

> We have a great task awaiting us. An agonized world calls on us to do our share in building the Kingdom. I do not believe we can afford to go aside for definitions, however necessary they may be. I have faith in God, to believe that He will clarify the situation as we obey Him. You remember once when the disciples asked Jesus to forbid some one because he followed not them, that He reproved them, and I believe that would be His attitude today. Can we not all, Conservatives and Progressives, love and trust one another, and speak the truth in love?[5]

Attempt at Reconciliation

In September 1921 Montgomery believed it was possible to work with the fundamentalists and maintain denominational unity. On 27 September she wrote to W. C. Bitting, secretary of the Northern Baptist Convention, that for the 1922 annual meeting she wanted "the strongest program we have ever had, and my thought is that if we can loosen it up somewhat, give an opportunity for the Evangelistic and Fundamentalist people to present their cause before the Convention, we might obviate the necessity of the pre-Convention meetings."[6]

Bittings replied with a stern warning against any attempt to mollify the fundamentalists. He thought that it would be unwise to open the convention meetings to discussions of a theological nature because the Northern Baptist

Convention was organized for fellowship and for missionary, philanthropic, and educational purposes. He warned Montgomery that the fundamentalists would take advantage of the ignorance of the vast majority of the Baptist constituency and gain control of the Northern Baptist Convention and its agencies. He believed that allowing a special-interest group a place in the convention program would threaten the convention's "very existence." He preferred preconvention meetings to theological debate in the convention sessions. "I believe the best thing to do is not to coddle a lion, nor to fondle a rattlesnake. Let them stay in their own cages."[7]

Bittings' letter did not convince Montgomery. She wrote to Professor R. M. Vaughan at the Newton Theological School, on 5 October 1921, that "some opportunity for an uncontroversial presentation of the important doctrines that are felt by many to be imperiled, would be very helpful." Montgomery still believed peace was possible and that an open discussion would unify everyone behind the missionary task. On the same day she wrote to Rev. William S. V. Robinson of Renssleaer, New York, "I believe that if we can once establish confidence in our institutions and our missionary agencies, it will do a great deal."[8]

Montgomery's interest in a creedal statement grew out of her concern to restore confidence in the work of the denomination and to protect its unity, not from a desire for conformity. She did not believe that a creed had the power to inspire devotion or ensure fidelity, but if a statement was to be adopted, she wanted one that was faithful to the Baptist tradition. On 18 November 1921 she wrote with some ambivalence to U. R. Batchelder of the First Baptist Church of East Milton, Massachusetts:

> In all the years I have been a member of a Baptist church, I have never known any candidate for membership to be asked whether he believed in the confession of faith. All have come in on their personal experience of the Lord Jesus, and I believe that the living spirit of God may be trusted to lead His church into all truth and keep us from error, if we keep close to Him. I am not one who believes that we can be kept true by a formal or creedal statement. I think all the history of the past has proved how impotent these statements are to either defend or protect the faith of the church. I have always been rather proud to belong to a church which had no authorized creedal statement, where every man was perfectly free to go out and make his own statement, if he wished. Do you not think that the time has come

for us to make some pronouncement, some Confession of Faith that will tell the ordinary person where we stand as Baptists?

I think the statement made at Des Moines was good, though perhaps not as inclusive as I would have wished. But something like that I certainly think we need. The New Hampshire and Philadelphia Confessions are both outgrown. They do not fully express the life that is in the Church today.[9]

Montgomery soon settled on the idea of a new confession of faith that would restate the Baptist faith for her own time. She was aware that many Baptist churches refused to adopt a statement of faith. Those churches usually stated that the New Testament, interpreted in the light of the best available scholarship, was their confession of faith. Montgomery doubted whether that position would serve the needs of the Northern Baptist Convention any longer. She thought it would be wise for the Northern Baptist Convention to appoint a committee that would study the issue for two years, and at the end of that time to bring to the convention a statement of faith that "the great majority of churches" would find acceptable. She knew that the Northern Baptist Convention had no power to compel a church to adopt a statement of faith, and she believed the convention should never use such a statement for "creedal purposes." She believed that "loyalty to Jesus Christ" was the only valid test of faith, rather than a "formal or fixed statement drawn up by any body of men."[10]

Regarding the content of a new statement of faith, on 5 December 1921 Montgomery wrote to Rev. J. Y. Aitchison of New York City that she "would almost be willing to adopt the Des Moines Confession, but I find that many feel it would be better to take time and make a fuller and better statement." The two items that she personally wanted most to be included in a new statement were "Missions and the Kingdom of God."[11]

While Montgomery was no fundamentalist, she agreed with the fundamentalists that doctrinal fidelity was important in Baptist institutions. In her 1 November 1921 reply to Rev. Charles H. Fountain of Plainfield, New Jersey, who wrote to complain about some of the teachers in Baptist colleges, she wrote:

I believe the agitation will make our boards of trustees more careful regarding the Christian character of the men whom they appoint to teach. While as Baptists we ought to give the greatest latitude to individual interpretation and the greatest freedom of thought, I do not think for a moment that we should permit the teaching of destructive critical theories to our boys and girls.[12]

Montgomery was equally concerned about ignorance in the pulpit. "I believe that an even more serious question than the occasional laxity of belief of certain teachers, is the admission into the ranks of our ministers of great numbers of poorly educated men." They were "bringing down the standards of our denominational life," and she believed that training schools for ministers who were not college graduates was a "life and death matter to us."[13]

Nevertheless, Montgomery could not avoid the conclusion that theological liberalism—or as she called it, "radicalism"—in the schools sponsored by the Northern Baptist Convention was a source of much of the controversy in the denomination. She personally deplored the idea of allowing teachers supported by denominational funds to undercut Christian orthodoxy in the classroom. On 12 December 1921, she wrote to Rev. Floyd H. Adams, secretary of the Executive Committee on Baptist Fundamentals, "I agree with you absolutely that we ought to get rid of any man who is teaching things that are subversive of the faith of our students, or any man whose personal attitude is known to be that of an unbeliever." She assured him she would use any personal influence at her command to "get rid of these teachers."[14] The next day, she wrote to Shailer Mathews, dean of the University of Chicago Divinity School, in whom she apparently had great personal confidence and trust:

> I wish you people in Chicago would get rid of some of the brethren that are continually getting your institution in hot water. . . . I have a sneaking idea that there is not really much difference between them and the Unitarians. . . . I do not know which is more to be dreaded, the hidebound reactionary or the gentle radical who is apparently bound to stand for every theory put forth by any crack-brained German theologian that shows that "the Bible ain't much, any way, and it does not mean what it says, and therefore we have got to get some theory that will let us out gently."[15]

She told Mathews that she believed the theological controversy could seriously harm the denomination, and she wished that the colleges and seminaries would see the difficulty and "quietly get rid of all their destructive radicals."[16]

Despite her personal desires, she wrote to Rev. C. H. Fountain on 27 December 1921, that "anything approaching a heresy trial" was too risky to be contemplated because such events had "wide-spread and unexpected results." She dreaded the possibilities. "The most evil of all evil passions, theological hatred, is stirred up, and sometimes an active persecution begins. I confess to you that I have not the wisdom to see how we can purge our body of heresy without doing more harm than good."

Instead of a purge, Montgomery continued to work for a new confession of faith. At the same time, she still wanted to include some major fundamentalist figures in the program of the 1922 meeting of the Northern Baptist Convention and allow them to proclaim their message to the delegates.

Always an optimist, Montgomery had high hopes for a new confession of faith. At the invitation of James M. Wood, president of Stephens College in Columbia, Missouri, Montgomery and a number of other Northern Baptists participated in a conference with several Southern Baptists, including E. Y. Mullins, president of the Southern Baptist Theological Seminary and of the Southern Baptist Convention. The Southern Baptist Convention was enduring its own fundamentalist controversy, and one of the recommendations of the Columbia Conference was to form a committee with both Northern and Southern Baptist representatives to draft a new joint confession of faith for both denominations. Montgomery believed it might be possible to include Canadian, English, and European Baptists as well.[17] In fact, Southern Baptists rejected the recommendation of the Columbia Conference, but they did approve a new confession of faith in 1925.

Defense of Women in Ministry

In the context of the growing controversy in the Northern Baptist Convention, Montgomery received a letter (no longer extant) from Mr. Ure Mitchell from Edwards, New York, who apparently challenged the propriety of a woman serving as president of the Northern Baptist Convention on the basis of his interpretation of the New Testament. Mitchell believed that women were banned from leadership roles in the church. On 18 November 1921 Montgomery answered Mitchell's letter with her defense of women's ministry, which she based on her own reading of the New Testament.

Montgomery challenged Mitchell's interpretation of Paul on the basis of her interpretation of "the highest authority—Our Saviour, Jesus Christ." She reasserted much of what she had already said in *Western Women in Eastern Lands*. She told Mitchell that Jesus "swept away the barriers imposed by men, in regard to sex. He made one law of purity for men and women. He allowed women to follow Him and minister to Him, though this must have subjected Him to misunderstandings."[18]

From Jesus' encounter with the Samaritan woman, Montgomery concluded that Jesus "flouted the ideas of his own time in regard to the proprieties for a Rabbi and a teacher," and that He revealed to her things that He had not, so far as we know, up to that time told to any of His disciples." Furthermore, she pointed out, a woman was the first witness to the resurrection.[19]

Montgomery believed that early Christianity gave women unprecedented liberty, which was often abused. In Corinth, for example, "the curse of the city was enshrined in its worship of Aphrodite." According to Montgomery, the only women who spoke to men or associated freely with men in public were cultic prostitutes, and when Christian women exercised their liberty they subjected the Corinthian church to "very grave suspicion of immoral conduct." The restrictions Paul placed on women in the Corinthian church were situational rather than universal, and the ruling principle was 1 Corinthians 14:40, "Let all things be done decently in order."[20]

Montgomery believed that if Paul had written to Baptist churches in Ohio in 1824, "He would have said, 'Let your women sit on their own side of the church', as at that time for women to sit with their own husbands, even at worship, would have shocked the congregation." She declared that the same rule still applied in churches in China, Korea, and Japan, but "by the spirit of the living Jesus working in the hearts of His believers," families would someday sit together as in America.[21] Montgomery turned next to the command for wives to be submissive to their husbands, found in the fifth chapter of Ephesians. Just before that command, she said, Paul gave the same command to all church members. Likewise, Peter commanded young Christians to submit to their elders and all to one another. So, Montgomery reasoned, if we quote Paul's command in Ephesians for wives to submit to their husbands, we must also quote the other injunctions. In her view, "All men and women, young and old, are to be in an humble, submissive frame of mind. I think this would be very good doctrine for some leaders."[22]

More importantly, Montgomery believed that Paul demonstrated his principles by his actions, and "in his actions he gave the widest liberty to women. He made use of them in every way in the propagating of the Christian Gospel." In his greetings in Romans and Philippians, Paul named women among the leaders in the church, and they contributed much to the advance of the gospel. Montgomery cited the example of Priscilla, and she raised the possibility that the epistle to the Hebrews was written by her. Montgomery believed Paul's ruling principle of equality for women and men was found in Galatians 3:28, "In Christ there is neither Jew nor Greek, there is neither bond nor free, there is neither male nor female; for ye are all one in Christ Jesus."[23]

Montgomery concluded with one of her strongest, most direct affirmations of the gospel as the source of women's emancipation: "I think it is the impact of the Gospel of Christ that has led to the emancipation of women from restricting and man-made laws. I believe that that living spirit is behind woman's suffrage and the education of women and the elevation of women to places of dignity and authority."[24] Interlocutors like Mitchell, who apparently wanted to use the specter of theological liberalism to taint the women's movement, did little to endear the fundamentalist cause to Montgomery. Eventually she abandoned hope for reconciliation and adopted a new strategy.

A New Strategy: "What We Want Is to Win"

In the months leading up to the 1922 meeting of the Northern Baptist Convention in Indianapolis, Indiana, Montgomery became increasingly frustrated by the unwillingness of the fundamentalist leadership to forego a preconvention meeting in return for the limited role in the program that she was offering to them. By March it was clear to her that she could not stop the fundamentalists from organizing a preconvention meeting. She wrote to Rev. Frederick E. Taylor, pastor of First Baptist Church, Indianapolis, on 13 March 1922, that the Executive Committee of the convention had "tried in every way we could to insure the cooperation of the Fundamentalists . . . but they declined to consider anything except the Executive Committee's turning over to them one entire session of the Convention, they to nominate the speakers and arrange the program. This of course was impossible."[25] Montgomery knew that the fundamentalists planned to push for the denomination to adopt the Des Moines statement, and she wanted to be ready with an organized response.

On 14 March 1922 Montgomery wrote to Rev. Cornelius Woelfkin, the liberal pastor of Park Avenue Baptist Church, where John D. Rockefeller Jr. was an active layman, and which subsequently reorganized as Riverside Church in New York City. She told him that she hoped the recommendation of the Columbia Conference might be adopted. In that case, the Northern Baptist Convention would have to appoint a committee, the members of which could be carefully selected by the Executive Committee of the convention, and the committee would have a year to work on its recommendation. But if the Columbia Conference recommendation was not accepted, they had to be ready with a strategy to oppose the Des Moines statement. She wanted Woelfkin to plan the strategy. "I wish you would put your clear brain at work on this thing," she wrote. What they needed, she thought, was a substitute confession of faith. If that failed, then they should be ready to offer amendments to the Des Moines statement, and they should have the amendments printed so that the delegates could read them before voting. She also recommended that the person offering the amendments ought to be "a man who is known to have conservative opinions" because she thought many delegates would vote "not intelligently but according to party." She did not think many delegates would support an amendment if "a *dangerous radical* (?) like yourself" offered it. Once again she encouraged Woelfkin to take charge of the strategy. "What we want is *to win,* and we do not care about personalities, so long as we can win."[26]

Still thinking strategically, Montgomery wrote to the convention's Corresponding Secretary, W. C. Bitting, on 17 March 1922. She wanted him to organize a card index for the registrars at the meeting. "I do not want to have any packing of the Convention, and I know, on very good authority, that there were some tiny churches that sent ten or twelve delegates last year, and these delegates all voted."[27]

Montgomery was shrewd enough to understand the importance of public opinion, so she continued to encourage the leaders of seminaries, divinity schools, and colleges to try to reign in faculty members whose public statements might inflame conservative passions. She wrote to Shailer Mathews on 25 April 1922, apparently in regard to some criticism she had heard of a book written by New Testament scholar Shirley Jackson Case, "I shall certainly read the book. . . . The sentences which were quoted certainly sound bad enough. I hope Dr. Case did not have the insolence to call Jesus an 'impressive individual.' But I will take your word for it that the book is a fine exegesis and shall hope not to find that sentence in it."[28]

Likewise, she tried to find ways to find ways to swing conservative opinion away from the fundamentalists. She wrote to Dr. Carlos M. Dinsmore on 17 April 1922, "I believe that one of the strategic things for us to do is to stress the fact that this Fundamentalist Movement is an INTERDENOMINATIONAL Movement, and as such is as objectionable to our conservative brethren as other interdenominational movements."[29]

The Indianapolis Meeting

Montgomery saw no hope for peace as she prepared for the Indianapolis meeting. "The skies look pretty stormy, and none of us know what the outcome is to be," she wrote to Bitting on 2 May 1922. "I confess that I look forward with a good deal of dread to the meeting in Indianapolis."

In her President's Address to the meeting, she confronted the issue head on. Only six months before, she had advocated for a new statement of faith for the denomination. The fundamentalists had proved inflexible in their demands, and Montgomery saw no way to save the denomination except to do battle and defeat them. She was determined to do everything she properly could to derail an official confession. She told the delegates that if they did authorize a committee to write a new confession of faith, they should see to it that the committee never reported back to the convention. They should provide the committee with adequate funds to publicize its statement to the churches and let the churches individually decide what to do with it. "For we Baptists to have an official confession of faith," she said, "would come perilously near to abandoning one of our fundamental principles."[30]

On Friday afternoon, 16 June 1922, the showdown over the confession finally occurred. The Southern Baptist Convention had rejected the recommendation of the Columbia Conference, so that part of Montgomery's strategy was a dead letter. When fundamentalist leader William Bell Riley moved for the adoption of a confession, Cornelius Woelfkin himself (contrary to what Montgomery had advised) offered a substitute motion, "that the Northern Baptist Convention affirm that the New Testament is our all-sufficient rule of faith and practice and that we have need of no other statement."[31] A long debate followed, which was interrupted by the passing by of a circus outside the auditorium. According to *The New York Times*, "For almost half an hour it was calliope versus Baptist creed." When one speaker was drowned out by the noise of the circus procession, Montgomery told him, "The elephants are passing by now, brother." He replied that he had met all sorts of difficulties in preaching, but he "never had to talk against a steam whistler before." Montgomery led the throng in hymn-singing until the procession passed by.[32] When the vote was finally taken, Woelfkin's substitute motion passed by a margin of 1,264 to 637.[33]

Montgomery's presidency of the Northern Baptist Convention is remembered, and rightly so, for her efforts to fend off the fundamentalist insurgency in 1922. But the evidence is clear that she acted in defense of the cherished Baptist principle of liberty, rather than in defense of liberal theology. In her view, the bedrock principle of liberty was clearly demonstrated by the gospel's power to emancipate women. Once she became convinced that fundamentalism posed a serious threat to her understanding of Baptist freedom in general, and to the freedom of women in particular, she used all of her influence to defeat fundamentalism in the Northern Baptist Convention.

Thirteen

CONCLUSION

On 5 October 1931, Helen Barrett Montgomery wrote to her friend Miss Clementina Butler, who was vice chairman of the Methodist Episcopal Church Women's Foreign Missionary Society and a fellow leader of the ecumenical woman's missionary movement. Montgomery was seventy years old and her health was declining rapidly. She wrote with the news that she was resigning as chairman of the Committee on Christian Literature for Women and Children in Mission Fields. With her resignation, Montgomery severed the last formal tie that bound her to the movement she had influenced so profoundly for thirty years. Only excerpts from the letter to Butler have survived, but even in the excerpts the enduring impact of domestic feminism on Montgomery's life and work are apparent. As she approached the end of her life, she was still convinced that the minds of men and women operated differently. While the men were "still studying the question" of providing Christian literature in mission lands, the women "saw a concrete need . . . and went at once to work." She thought it was best to "let others be the investigators" while the women "stick to our long accepted role of helpers." Nevertheless, she found it "a little amusing . . . that masculine sex pride makes the translators of the New Testament called [*sic*] Phoebe a servant of the Church and translates the same words used in regard to Timothy as minister of the Church." She encouraged the committee to continue the "fascinating line of Bible study opened up by mistranslation of words which are

made to mean different things when applied to women from their accepted meanings as usually employed."[1]

In 1931 many American women no longer found their "long accepted role of helpers" adequate. Educated women could choose rewarding secular careers rather than contend with the danger and discomfort of missionary service. Given their political enfranchisement and the new social freedoms that they enjoyed, the idea of a woman's sphere seemed increasingly implausible to American women. Nevertheless, Montgomery apparently refused to concede the loss of her moral world, even though, as a leader of the ecumenical woman's missionary movement, she had unwittingly participated in its deconstruction. The world was changing, in part because the ecumenical woman's missionary movement had been so successful at changing it, but Montgomery's moral vision maintained its fundamental connection to the Victorian values in which she was nurtured.

Montgomery is remembered today primarily among Baptists, and she is remembered among them because of her service in many capacities to the Northern Baptist Convention. Montgomery was active at almost every level of Baptist life, from her local church to the Baptist World Alliance, and several of her later publications were written for her denomination.[2] She served as president of the Woman's American Baptist Foreign Missionary Society from 1914 to 1924, with the exception of 1921–1922, when she served one term as president of the Northern Baptist Convention. Following her year of service as president of the Northern Baptist Convention, Montgomery attended the 1923 meeting of the Baptist World Alliance as a delegate from the United States and was one of only two women to address the meeting.[3]

Montgomery was widely honored in her own day. She received an honorary master's degree from Brown University in 1917; she received honorary doctorates from Franklin College and Denison University in 1922 and from Wellesley College in 1925. In 1929 she delivered the John M. English lectures on preaching at the Newton Theological Institution, Newton, Massachusetts. The lectures were published as *The Preaching Value of Missions*.[4] There is a stained glass window memorializing her in First Baptist Church, Washington, D.C. Helen Barrett Montgomery died on 19 October 1934, at the age of seventy-three.

Summary

Helen Barrett Montgomery's childhood experiences, religious training, and early education inclined her to believe in a process of progressive Christianization of culture. Her belief in the redemptive potential of progress was foundational for her work as a municipal reformer and as a mission advocate and educator. Montgomery was not converted to Christianity so much as she was nurtured into her faith. Her education taught her to believe that freedom and enlightenment were rooted in the gospel of Christ, and that all of the political and scientific progress in Western culture was a consequence of Christianization. While she believed and practiced personal evangelism, her fundamental concern was to create a social environment in which people, especially women, could experience liberation, enlightenment, and empowerment. Even in the context of municipal reform, where Montgomery consciously set her evangelical convictions aside for the sake of broader cooperation, she interpreted the work as a contribution to the kingdom of God.

Montgomery's initiation into feminist consciousness began with her education at Cathro Mason Curtis' Livingston Park Seminary, but it was established and confirmed at Wellesley. As an undergraduate, Montgomery came to view the emancipation and social uplift of woman as an integral part of Christian mission. As she attained emotional and intellectual autonomy from her father's powerful influence, the faculty at Wellesley became her most important mentors, and they helped Montgomery to redefine the meaning of womanly virtue in a way that mandated social activism on behalf of women and children.

Feminist scholars have tended to minimize the connections between the ecumenical woman's missionary movement and the liberal feminist position. While Montgomery was clearly more representative of the second-generation domestic feminist movement, her long friendship and partnership with Susan B. Anthony and her lifelong concern for the social and political emancipation of women seem to indicate that a sharp distinction would be unwise in her case. There is ample evidence in Montgomery's record to suggest that the difference between her variety of feminism and Anthony's was a matter of style and emphasis. Anthony was older, and she was from a more radical religious tradition. A veteran of many reform causes and suffrage battles, she was more combative, and she viewed suffrage as the political key to women's emancipation. Montgomery's generation benefited from the trailblazing work of Anthony's generation. Religiously and socially, Montgomery was more mainstream and conservative, and she tended to view suffrage as one goal among many in the cause of women's emancipation. In practice, however, those distinctions made little difference. Anthony and Montgomery supported one another's endeavors and worked as allies in the same causes.

The relationship between Anthony and Montgomery could be interpreted to suggest that the liberal feminists and domestic feminists needed and supported one another. While the aggressive tactics of the liberal feminists drew public criticism, many people found the relative conservatism of the domestic feminists reassuring. The liberal feminists pressed for social change from the margins, using the language of individualistic-civic nationalism, while the domestic feminists used the language of True Womanhood to press for social change from within. While the language of the liberal feminists touched the democratic spirit of progressivism, the rhetoric of domestic feminism resonated with its Victorian moral sensibilities.

The Women's Educational and Industrial Union (WEIU) was the key institution in Montgomery's career as a municipal reformer and an essential training ground for her later role as leader of the ecumenical woman's missionary movement. The initiatives of the WEIU were intended to help empower women economically, socially, and politically, while at the same time inculcating late Victorian middle-class values. While the WEIU was officially nonsectarian, for Montgomery its mission was implicitly Christianizing. Consequently, it was a simple matter for her to transfer the basic reform agenda of the WEIU to her work for the ecumenical woman's missionary movement. In both movements, education was the core strategy in the social uplift of women and children, but in the ecumenical woman's missionary movement, Montgomery was free to make the theological foundations of her reform agenda explicit.

Montgomery's decade on the school board in Rochester coincided with her emergence as a leader of the ecumenical woman's missionary movement, and her experiences on the school board influenced her work for missions. Montgomery worked for a decade to represent and empower women and mothers in the governance of the schools and to bring maternal values into the educational system in Rochester. She wanted to broaden the educational mandate of the state to include a broad range of social services and to expand democracy by funding community-controlled activities after hours in school buildings. While these are questions of political and social policy, they also had important theological implications for Montgomery as a mission theorist.

Montgomery was evangelical and orthodox, and she believed in individual conversion. But her understanding of conversion extended to cultures. As a progressive, she believed that the social environment shaped the character of individuals and that the social environment could be shaped and controlled. She also believed that the progress of civilization providentially prepared the way for the advance of the gospel. As a domestic feminist, she emphasized the emancipation of women and the penetration of maternal values into the public sphere as an indication of the progress of global democracy. Montgomery believed that Christian mission and human progress went hand in hand and that both were evidence that the kingdom of God was coming—a kingdom with ideals and values very much like those of domestic feminism. Though it would be unfair to overlook the deep spirituality that supported Montgomery's theology, its most striking feature and its most inspirational aspect for the women of the movement was found in its implications for mundane reality.

Ann Douglas indicted the Victorian Age that was so influential for Montgomery because it created a middle-class culture of sentiment rather than substance—of commercialization rather than real creativity.[5] In Douglas' view, male political culture excluded women from real power, and industrialization deprived them of productive economic roles. In response, middle-class women created a special status for themselves by exploiting the Victorian feminine ideal. Woman's religious and moral influence was supposed to compensate them for the lack of political power, and the time they once filled with productive economic activity was transformed into leisure and filled with consumerism.

It is clear that Helen Barrett Montgomery lived in the world that Douglas described, but she did not simply accept it uncritically. She showed no affinity for the idea that women were to confine themselves to poetry readings, shopping trips, and tea parties. She believed that women's virtue and moral influence needed to move from the parlor into the street, and that women's leisure ought to be invested in the cause of women's emancipation rather than wasted in conspicuous consumption.

Montgomery was a reformer, not a revolutionary. She wanted to expand the woman's sphere, not explode it. Nevertheless, Montgomery's case is evidence that Victorian culture was not as devoid of nobility as Douglas thought. At least there was enough moral fiber in Victorian womanhood to produce an insurgency if not an outright revolution.

No assessment of Montgomery would be complete that overlooked her persistent optimism. Montgomery believed that the kingdom of God was coming, and its coming had profound positive implications for individuals as well as for civilization. "The Bible is always forward-looking," she wrote. "Its golden age is never in the past. A great hope blows across its pages. A divine Adventure summons the souls of men to work together with God for the creation of a new earth in which righteousness, no longer pilgrim and stranger, is at home; and in which the Lamb for sinners slain is loved and worshipped by every heart."[6] Montgomery's vision of the kingdom was both spiritual and mundane, and with it, she inspired a generation of Protestant women to believe that they could change the world.

NOTES

Chapter 1

1   W. T. Whitley, *Third Baptist World Congress. Stockholm, July 21–27, 1923. Record of Proceedings.* Introduction by J. H. Shakespeare (London: Kingsgate Press, 1923), 99.

2   Whitley, 102 (italics in original).

3   Helen Barrett Montgomery, *Western Women in Eastern Lands* (New York: Macmillan, 1910), 205–6.

4   Montgomery, *Western Women*, 206.

5   Lucy W. Peabody, "Widening Horizons," in *Helen Barrett Montgomery: From Campus to World Citizenship* (New York: Fleming H. Revell, 1940), 120.

6   Montgomery, *Western Women*, 206–7.

7   Dana L. Robert, *American Women in Mission: A Social History of Their Thought and Practice* (Macon, Ga.: Mercer University Press, 1997), 263.

8   "New Opportunity for Baptist Women," *The Baptist*, 25 August 1923, 944.

9   Robert, 263.

10 Robert, 302–16; R. Pierce Beaver, *All Loves Excelling: American Protestant Women in World Mission* (Grand Rapids: Eerdmans, 1968); reprint, *American Protestant Women in World Mission: A History of the First Feminist Movement in North America* (Grand Rapids: Eerdmans, 1980), 179–200.

11 Nancy F. Cott, *The Grounding of Modern Feminism* (New Haven: Yale University Press, 1987), 3–7. See also Nancy A. Hardesty, *Women Called to Witness: Evangelical Feminism in the Nineteenth Century* (Nashville: Abingdon, 1984), 9.

12   Nancy F. Cott, "The Bonds of Womanhood: 'Woman's Sphere'," in *New England, 1780–1835* (New Haven: Yale University Press, 1977), 4–9; Barbara Welter, *Dimity Convictions: The American Woman in the Nineteenth Century* (Athens: Ohio University Press, 1976), 21.

13   Aileen S. Kraditor, ed., *Up from the Pedestal: Selected Writings in the History of American Feminism* (Chicago: Quadrangle Books, 1968), 13.

14   Cott, *Bonds of Womanhood*, 86–87.

15   Arthur S. Link and Richard L. McCormick, *Progressivism,* American History Series, ed. John Hope Franklin (Arlington Heights, Ill.: Harlan Davidson, 1983), 3.

16   James H. Moorhead, "Engineering the Millennium: Kingdom Building in American Protestantism, 1880–1920," *Princeton Seminary Bulletin*, Suppl., no. 3 (1994): 105.

17   Richard Hofstadter, "The Vogue of Spencer," in *Social Darwinism in American Thought* (Boston: Beacon Press, 1955), 31–50; Arthur A. Ekirch Jr., *Progressivism in America: A Study of the Era from Theodore Roosevelt to Woodrow Wilson* (New York: New Viewpoints, 1974), 20–24.

18   David B. Danbom, *The World of Hope: Progressives and the Struggle for an Ethical Public Life* (Philadelphia: Temple University Press, 1987), vii. See also Janet Forsythe Fishburn, *The Fatherhood of God and the Victorian Family: The Social Gospel in America* (Philadelphia: Fortress, 1981).

19   Jean B. Quandt, "Religion and Social Thought: The Secularization of Postmillennialism," *American Quarterly* 24, no. 4 (1973): 390–409.

20   Fishburn, *Fatherhood of God*, 32.

21   E.g., Wendy J. Deichmann Edwards and Carolyn DeSwarte Gifford, eds., *Gender and the Social Gospel* (Urbana: University of Illinois Press, 2003).

Chapter 2

1   Helen Barrett Montgomery, "Her Own Story," in *Helen Barrett Montgomery: From Campus to World Citizenship* (New York: Fleming H. Revell, 1940), 19–20.

2   Helen Barrett Montgomery, "In Memoriam: A. Judson Barrett" [1889], 5, American Baptist Historical Society Archives, Mercer University, Atlanta.

3   Montgomery, "In Memoriam," 6.

4   See Cott, *Bonds of Womanhood*; see also Barbara Welter, "The Cult of True Womanhood: 1800–1860," in *Dimity Convictions*, 21–41.

5   Letter to Miss Coolidge, 19 November 1915, TMs [photocopy], Baptist Missionary Training School Bible Conversations, 1915–1916, Ambrose Swasey Library, Colgate Rochester Crozer Divinity School, Rochester, N.Y.

6   Montgomery, "Her Own Story," 25–26.

7 Welter, 4.
8 Welter, 6–7.
9 *Democrat and Chronicle*, 11 October 1899, 10.
10 Montgomery, "Her Own Story," 22.
11 Montgomery, "Her Own Story," 52.
12 Montgomery, "Her Own Story," 73.
13 Montgomery, "Her Own Story," 22.
14 Diary, TMs, Montgomery Collection, American Baptist Historical Society Archives, Mercer University, Atlanta.
15 Conclusion in *Helen Barrett Montgomery*, 140.
16 Louise A. Cattan, *Lamps Are for Lighting: The Story of Helen Barrett Montgomery and Lucy Waterbury Peabody* (Grand Rapids: Eerdmans, 1972), 108.
17 Thomas A. Bailey and David M. Kennedy, *The American Pageant: A History of the Republic*, 6th ed. (Lexington, Mass.: D. C. Heath, 1979), 452–53.
18 Montgomery, "Her Own Story," 25.
19 "Rev. Dr. Barrett Is Dead," *Democrat and Chronicle*, 21 October 1889, 6.
20 Montgomery, "Her Own Story," 22.
21 Adelbert Cronise, "The Beginnings of Modern Spiritualism In and Near Rochester," in *The Rochester Historical Society Publication Fund Series*, vol. 5, ed. Edward R. Forman (Rochester, N.Y.: Historical Society, 1926), 13.
22 See Ann Braude, *Radical Spirits: Spiritualism and Women's Rights in Nineteenth-Century America* (Boston: Beacon Press, 1989).
23 Letter to Miss Coolidge, 19 November 1915.
24 Helen Barrett Montgomery, "If a Man Die, Shall He Live?" *The Baptist* 1, no. 1 (31 January 1920): 14, 16.
25 Montgomery, "Her Own Story," 28.
26 Lewis H. Batts, "Doctorate on the History of Lake Ave. Baptist Church (vol. 1)," 14–17. This document (four scrapbooks) is made from what are apparently draft pages and other material related to Batts' Ph.D. dissertation, which he wrote at the Hartford Seminary Foundation in 1935.
27 Montgomery, "Her Own Story," 29.
28 Montgomery, "Her Own Story," 30–31 (italics in original).
29 Sydney E. Ahlstrom, *A Religious History of the American People* (New Haven: Yale University Press, 1972), 745.
30 Montgomery, "Her Own Story," 23–31.
31 Cott, *Bonds of Womanhood*, 104–18.
32 Barbara Miller Solomon, *In the Company of Educated Women: A History of Women and Higher Education in America* (New Haven: Yale University Press, 1985), 16–17.

33 Robert, 92–114; Solomon, 20–21.

34 Solomon, 23.

35 Cott, *Bonds of Womanhood*, 122–25.

36 *The Story of Sixty Years, 1858–1918: Livingston Park Seminary, Rochester, N.Y.* [privately printed 1918], title page.

37 *Memorial Exercises of the Alumnae Association Held at Livingston Park Seminary, Rochester, New York, on Thursday, June Ninth, 1892* (Rochester, N.Y.: Post-Express Printing, 1892), 7.

38 *Memorial Exercises,* 16.

39 *Story of Sixty Years,* 20; Francis Wayland, *The Elements of Moral Science,* rev. ed (Boston: Gould & Lincoln, 1865); William Paley, *Natural Theology: or, Evidences of the Existence and Attributes of the Deity, Collected from the Appearances of Nature* (1802; repr. Houston: St. Thomas Press, 1972); Joseph Butler, *The Analogy of Religion, Natural and Revealed, to the Constitution and Course of Nature* (London: H. G. Bohn, 1860).

40 George M. Marsden, *The Soul of the American University: From Protestant Establishment to Established Nonbelief* (New York: Oxford University Press, 1994), 90–93; idem, *Fundamentalism and American Culture: The Shaping of Twentieth-Century Evangelicalism 1870–1925* (New York: Oxford University Press, 1980), 15–17; Ahlstrom, 353–56.

41 *Memorial Exercises,* 18–19; Harriet Brown Dow, "Influence of Women in the Life of Rochester," *Centennial History of Rochester, New York*, vol. 2, *Home Builders*, ed. Edward R. Foreman, Rochester Historical Society Publication Fund Series 11 (Rochester, N.Y.: Historical Society, 1932), 191.

42 Dow, 202.

43 Karen J. Blair, *The Clubwoman as Feminist: True Womanhood Redefined, 1868–1914* (New York: Holmes & Meier Publishers, 1980).

44 *Memorial Exercises,* 32.

45 *Memorial Exercises,* 35–36.

46 *Memorial Exercises,* 39–44.

47 *Story of Sixty Years,* 10–11.

48 Montgomery, "Her Own Story," 31.

Chapter 3

1 The arguments of Edward Clarke, for example, had frightening Social Darwinist implications for those already nervous about the declining reproductive rate among native-born whites. See Rosalind Rosenberg, *Beyond Separate Spheres: Intellectual Roots of Modern Feminism* (New Haven: Yale University Press, 1982), 7–12; Solomon, 56–57.

2   Rosenberg, 20–24; Solomon, 57.

3   Rosenberg, 42–51; Solomon, 58–61.

4   Patricia Ann Palmieri, *In Adamless Eden: The Community of Women Faculty at Wellesley* (New Haven: Yale University Press, 1995), 6–9.

5   Montgomery, "Her Own Story," 69.

6   Palmieri, 10, 11–13.

7   "The First Wellesley Announcement, December, 1874," (reprint, Wellesley Department of Education, 1934), 3-4.

8   "Wellesley College Calendar, 1879–80" (Wellesley College Archives), 78–79.

9   "Wellesley College Calendar," 21.

10 "Wellesley College Calendar," 79–80.

11 "Wellesley College Calendar," 80.

12 Martha H. Verbrugge, *Able-Bodied Womanhood: Personal Health and Social Change in Nineteenth-Century Boston* (New York: Oxford University Press, 1988), 145–46, 149.

13 Montgomery, "Her Own Story," 37 (italics in original).

14 Montgomery, "Her Own Story," 39–40.

15 Palmieri, 13.

16 Montgomery, "Her Own Story," 39.

17 Montgomery, "Her Own Story," 33.

18 Quoted in Palmieri, 34.

19 E.g., see Lori D. Ginzberg, *Women and the Work of Benevolence: Morality, Politics, and Class in the Nineteenth-Century United States* (New Haven: Yale University Press, 1990), 20–21; Cott, *Bonds of Womanhood*, 152–53; Braude, *Radical Spirits*, 117–27; Barbara Leslie Epstein, *The Politics of Domesticity: Women Evangelism, and Temperance in Nineteenth-Century America* (Middletown, Conn.: Wesleyan University Press, 1981), 89–90.

20 Palmieri, 28.

21 Montgomery, "Her Own Story," 67, 34.

22 Montgomery, "Her Own Story," 61 (italics in original).

23 Montgomery, "Her Own Story," 43.

24 Montgomery, "Her Own Story," 34.

25 Montgomery, "Her Own Story," 38 (italics in original).

26 Montgomery, "Her Own Story," 61–62.

27 Mrs. Curtis Lee Laws, "Her Baptist World," in *Helen Barrett Montgomery: From Campus to World Citizenship*, ed. P. W. W. (New York: Fleming H. Revell, 1940), 103–4.

28 Montgomery, "Her Own Story," 56.

29 Eliza Hall Kendrick, *History of Bible Teaching at Wellesley College, 1875–1950* (Wellesley, Mass.: n.p., 1950), 7.

30 Kendrick, 9.

31 Kendrick, 10.

32 Kendrick, 11.

33 Montgomery, "Her Own Story," 42, 57–58.

34 This was probably Katherine Coman, who taught political economy at Wellesley beginning in 1883. See Palmieri, 169.

35 Montgomery, "Her Own Story," 68.

36 Palmieri, 81, 176–77.

37 Montgomery, "Her Own Story," 42.

38 Montgomery, "Her Own Story," 42–43.

39 Montgomery, "Her Own Story," 47 (italics in original).

40 Palmieri, 186.

41 Palmieri, 187.

42 Montgomery, "Her Own Story," 33–34.

43 Montgomery, "Her Own Story," 56.

44 Palmieri, 26, 30; Montgomery, "Her Own Story," 49.

45 Palmieri, 27–28.

46 Helen Barrett Montgomery, "Alice Freeman Palmer," *Wellesley Magazine* 11, no. 4 (1 February 1903): 148.

47 Montgomery, "Her Own Story," 61, 64–68, 62–63, 69–70.

48 Montgomery, "Her Own Story," 36–37, 39, 49.

49 Montgomery, "Her Own Story," 45–46, 49, 51.

50 Montgomery, "Her Own Story," 55.

51 Montgomery, "Her Own Story," 65, 50, 52.

52 Montgomery, "Her Own Story," 63.

53 Palmieri, 10.

54 Montgomery, "Her Own Story," 32–33, 36, 53.

55 Quoted in Palmieri, 10.

56 Verbrugge, 146 (italics in original).

57 Montgomery, "Her Own Story," 43–44.

58 Montgomery, "Her Own Story," 47.

59 Quoted in Roberta Wein, "Women's Colleges and Domesticity, 1875–1918," *History of Education Quarterly* 14, no. 1 (1974): 41.

60 Florence Converse, *Wellesley College: A Chronicle of the Years 1875–1938* (Wellesley, Mass.: Hathaway House Bookshop, 1939), 22.

61 Palmieri, 10.

62 Montgomery, "Her Own Story," 47.

63 Montgomery, "Her Own Story," 60.

64 Montgomery, "Her Own Story," 48.

65 Palmieri, 207–8.

66 Montgomery, "Her Own Story," 40.

67 Montgomery, "Her Own Story," 50.

68 Montgomery, "Her Own Story," 64.

69 Montgomery, "Her Own Story," 57–58 (italics in original).

70 Tennie C. Claflin, "Constitutional Equality a Right of Woman," in *Up from the Pedestal: Selected Writings in the History of American Feminism*, ed. Aileen Kraditor (Chicago: Quadrangle Books, 1968), 132, 133.

71 Montgomery, "Her Own Story," 64.

72 Montgomery, "Her Own Story," 75.

73 Montgomery, "Her Own Story," 47.

74 Wein, 41.

75 Montgomery, "Her Own Story," 59.

76 Wein, 35, 39–40.

77 Palmieri, 145–54.

78 Quoted in Palmieri, 149–50.

79 Montgomery, "Alice Freeman Palmer," 148.

80 Montgomery, "Her Own Story," 57, 68.

81 These are a few of her endorsements of Prohibition: "Results of National Prohibition: The Convention President's Letter to National Baptist Churches," *The Baptist* 2, no. 48 (31 December 1921): 1526, 1541; "Some More Prohibition Facts," *The Baptist* 3, no. 13 (29 April 1922): 396; "Prohibition Again," *The Baptist* 3, no. 38 (21 October 1922): 1178; "Helping Prohibition, a Task for Missionary Women," *The Baptist* 4, no. 26 (28 July 1923): 815; "The Crisis in Prohibition," *The Baptist* 5, no. 33 (13 September 1924): 795–96; "Liquid Bread," *The Baptist* 9, no. 32 (11 August 1928): 990; "Prohibition, an Adventure in Freedom," *The Baptist* 9, no. 44 (3 November 1928): 1330

82 "Thanksgiving at Wellesley" [photocopy], Letters and Papers from the Family of Storrs Barrett, personal collection; see also Montgomery, "Her Own Story," 46.

83 Fishburn, *The Fatherhood of God,* 41–42.

84 "Thanksgiving at Wellesley."

85 Montgomery, "Her Own Story," 55.

86 Lynn D. Gordon, *Gender and Higher Education in the Progressive Era* (New Haven: Yale University Press, 1990), 4; see also Estelle Freedman, "Separatism as Strategy: Female Institution Building and American Feminism, 1870–1930," *Feminist Studies* 5, no. 3 (1979): 512–29; Kathryn Kish Sklar, "Hull House in the 1890s: A Community of Women Reformers," *Signs* 10, no. 4 (1985): 658–77.

87 Montgomery, "Her Own Story," 40–42.

88 Palmieri, 158.

89 Montgomery, "Her Own Story," 69.

90 Gordon, 190–91.

91 Solomon, 64.

92 Montgomery, "Her Own Story," 45.

Chapter 4

1   Solomon, 32.

2   Solomon, 36–37.

3   Eleanor Flexner, *Century of Struggle: The Woman's Rights Movement in the United States*, rev. ed. (Cambridge: Belknap Press, 1975), 118.

4   Flexner, 118–23.

5   Solomon, 124–35.

6   Solomon, 119.

7   Solomon, 122.

8   Solomon, 118.

9   Jane Addams, *Democracy and Social Ethics,* ed. with an Introduction by Anne Firor Scott (1907; repr., Cambridge, Mass.: Belknap Press, 1964), 85–86.

10 Blake McKelvey, "A Panoramic Review of Rochester's History," *Rochester History* 11, no. 2 (1949): 3; idem, "Rochester Fifty Years Ago," *Rochester History* 3, no. 3 (1941): 2; Joseph W. Barnes, "Rochester's City Halls," *Rochester History* 60, no. 2 (1978): 5.

11 Barnes, "Rochester's City Halls," 9.

12 McKelvey, "Rochester Fifty Years Ago," 2; idem, *Rochester: The Quest for Quality 1890–1925* (Cambridge, Mass.: Harvard University Press, 1956), 133; idem, "The Population of Rochester," *Rochester History* 12, no. 4 (1950): 13; Joseph Barnes, "The City's Golden Age," *Rochester History* 35, no. 2 (1973): 3–4; Robert F. McNamara, *The Diocese of Rochester in America 1868–1993,* with a Foreword by Fulton J. Sheen (Rochester, N.Y.: Roman Catholic Diocese of Rochester, 1998), 179.

13 "The Bausch and Lomb Story," http://www.bausch.com/en_US/corporate/corpcomm/general/story.aspx (accessed 26 October 2007); McKelvey, *Rochester,* 272. See also M. Herbert Eisenhart, *J. J. Bausch (1830–1926): American Pioneer* (New York: Newcomen Society, American Branch, 1948); Clarence A. Barber, "An Appreciation of Henry Lomb," *American Journal of Public Health* 5, no. 11 (1915): 1120–23.

14 Elizabeth Brayer, "George Eastman," *Rochester History* 52, no. 1 (1990): 4–5; McKelvey, *Rochester,* 256–63. Biographies of Eastman include Carl W.

Ackerman, *George Eastman,* with an introduction by Edwin R. A. Seligman (Boston: Houghton Mifflin, 1930); Elizabeth Brayer, *George Eastman: A Biography* (Rochester, N.Y.: University of Rochester Press, 2006).

15 McKelvey, *Rochester,* 241–75.

16 Blake McKelvey, "The Irish in Rochester: An Historical Perspective," *Rochester History* 19, no. 4 (1957): 6; see also Robert F. McNamara, "Ecumenism and the Rochester Center for Theological Studies," *Rochester History* 52, no. 4 (1990): 4–5.

17 McKelvey, "Irish in Rochester," 11.

18 Blake McKelvey, "The Germans of Rochester: Their Traditions and Contributions," *Rochester History* 20, no. 1 (1958): 1–2.

19 McKelvey, "The Germans of Rochester," 21.

20 McKelvey, *Rochester,* 153; idem, "Rochester's Ethnic Transformations," *Rochester History* 25, no. 3 (1963): 16.

21 McKelvey, *Rochester,* 153–56.

22 McKelvey, *Rochester,* 150.

23 McKelvey, "Panoramic Review," 6.

24 McKelvey, "Panoramic Review"; see also Cronise, 1–22; Whitney R. Cross, *The Burned-Over District: The Social and Intellectual History of Enthusiastic Religion in Western New York, 1800–1850* (Ithaca: Cornell University Press, 1950).

25 McKelvey, *Rochester,* 21–23.

26 Winthrop S. Hudson, "Montgomery, Helen Barrett," *Notable American Women 1607–1950,* ed. Edward T. James (Cambridge: Belknap Press, 1971), 566.

27 Montgomery, "Her Own Story," 71.

28 Montgomery, "Her Own Story," 72.

29 Montgomery, "Her Own Story," 72. I have never seen any mention of William Montgomery's first wife in a primary source other than Helen Barrett Montgomery's assertion that he was a widower. Even his obituaries do not mention her.

30 Wein, 39–40.

31 Montgomery, "Her Own Story," 45.

32 Fishburn, *The Fatherhood of God,* 28.

33 Robert H. Wiebe, *The Search for Order, 1887, 1920* (New York: Hill & Wang, 1967), 40.

34 Conda Delite Hitch Abbott, *Envoy of Grace. The Life of Helen Barrett Montgomery,* (Valley Forge, Pa.: American Baptist Historical Society, 1997), 4.

35 Albert W. Beaven, "William A. Montgomery: A Tribute," TMs [1930], p. 4, American Baptist Historical Society Archives, Mercer University, Atlanta.

36 Montgomery, "Her Own Story," 72.

37 "Daniel A. Woodbury," *Post Express,* 13 January 1913, 9.

38 Batts, 1–2.

39 "Two Fires Yesterday," *Herald,* 9 May 1893, 6; William F. Peck, *History of Rochester and Monroe County New York from the Earliest Times to the Beginning of 1907,* vol. 2 (New York: Pioneer Publishing, 1908), 1147–48.

40 "North East Co. Founder Dies At Home Here," *Times-Union,* 10 July 1930, 9.

41 Beaven, "William A. Montgomery," 2–3; Hudson, "Montgomery, Helen Barrett," 567.

42 "North East Co. Founder Dies."

43 "Year 1933," History of IBM Exhibit, IBM Archives. http://www-1.ibm.com/ibm/history/history/year_1933.html (accessed 4 April 2002).

44 Helen Barrett Montgomery, ["Tribute to W.A. Montgomery"], TMs [1930], 3, American Baptist Historical Society Archives, Mercer University, Atlanta.

45 Montgomery, ["Tribute"], 1.

46 Welter, 7.

47 Beaven, "William A. Montgomery," 1.

48 "Brotherhood of Kingdom," *Herald,* 8 March 1906, 9.

49 Fishburn, *The Fatherhood of God,* 111.

50 Beaven, "William A. Montgomery," 3.

51 Montgomery, "Her Own Story," 75.

52 Montgomery, ["Tribute"], 5.

53 Beaven, "William A. Montgomery," 5–6.

54 Montgomery, ["Tribute"], 3.

55 Beaven, "Helen of Rochester," 97.

56 Montgomery, ["Tribute"], 4.

57 Montgomery, "Her Own Story," 76.

58 Lucy W. Peabody, "Widening Horizons," in *Helen Barrett Montgomery: From Campus to World Citizenship* (New York: Fleming H. Revell, 1940), 122.

59 "Her Qualifications As A Candidate," *Democrat and Chronicle,* 11 October 1899, 10; Papers and Letters from the Family of Storrs Barrett, TMs photocopy, p. 7, personal collection.

60 Papers and Letters, 7.

61 Abbott, 5.

62 Montgomery, "Her Own Story," 77.

63 Papers and Letters, 93.

64 "A Womanly Speech," *Union and Advertiser,* 1 November 1899, 4.

65 Julie Fewster, "Helen Barrett Montgomery: A Disciple of Jesus Christ 1861–

1934," TMs [photocopy], 12, Montgomery Collection, American Baptist Historical Society Archives, Mercer University, Atlanta.

66 *Monroe Baptist Association Minutes* (1887), 5–6.

67 *Monroe Baptist Association Minutes* (1888), 12.

68 *Monroe Baptist Association Minutes* (1888), 3, 10, 13.

69 *Monroe Baptist Association Minutes* (1889), 19, 20, 21.

70 *Monroe Baptist Association Minutes* (1897), 28.

71 Wilhermina C. Livingstone, "A Presentation of the Life of Helen Barrett Montgomery," TMs 1955, 9, Montgomery Collection, American Baptist Historical Society Archives, Mercer University, Atlanta.

72 "Tributes to a Brother." *Democrat and Chronicle,* 28 October 1889, 6.

73 Beaven, "Helen of Rochester," 93.

74 Alice A. Chester, "Exhibits Outlining the History of the Lake Avenue Baptist Church, Rochester, New York 1871–1933," 3, Lake Avenue Baptist Church Archives, Rochester, N.Y.

75 Papers and Letters, 92.

76 Fewster, 17.

77 Fewster, 17.

78 Beaven, "Helen of Rochester," 92; Wilhermina C. Livingstone, "Helen Barrett Montgomery," pamphlet, American Baptist Historical Society Archives, Mercer University, Atlanta.

79 Blake McKelvey, "Woman's Rights in Rochester A Century of Progress," *Rochester History* 10, nos. 2–3 (1948): 16–17.

80 Papers and Letters, 8.

81 "Sage, Russell," *The Columbia Encyclopedia,* 6th ed. (New York: Columbia University Press, 2002). www.bartleby.com/65/ (accessed 6 April 2003); Marsden, 117.

82 "Sage, Russell"; "About Us," About the Foundation, Russell Sage Foundation. http://www.russellsage.org/about/about_us.htm (accessed 6 April 2003).

83 Jacqueline Van Voris, *Carrie Chapman Catt: A Public Life* (New York: Feminist Press, 1987), 38.

84 Solomon, 57.

85 Flexner, 213.

86 Flexner, 237.

87 Dumas Malone, ed., *Dictionary of American Biography,* vol. 9 (New York: Scribner's, 1946), s.v. "Huntington, Frederic Dan."

88 Elizabeth Cady Stanton, *Eighty Years and More: Reminiscences 1815–1897,* with an Introduction by Gail Parker (New York: Schocken Books, 1971), 451.

89 Van Voris, 38.

Chapter 5

1 Elizabeth Battelle Clark, "The Politics of God and the Woman's Vote: Religion in the American Suffrage Movement, 1848–1895" (Ph.D. diss., Princeton University, 1989), 14–15, 22; Mary Jo Buhle and Paul Buhle, eds., *The Concise History of Woman Suffrage: Selections from the Classic Work of Stanton, Anthony, Gage, and Harper* (Urbana: University of Illinois Press, 1978), 2, 8.

2 Clark, 45–46.

3 Buhle and Buhle, 2–13.

4 Clark, 152–53.

5 Clark, 57–58.

6 Clark, 29–30.

7 Buhle and Buhle, 16–17.

8 Clark, 229.

9 Quoted in Clark, 246.

10 Quoted in Clark, 271.

11 See Blair.

12 For a more complete discussion of the WEIU, see chapter 7.

13 While I have been able to discover a remarkably broad range of topics for Montgomery's lectures from a variety of sources, I am sure my collection is still incomplete.

14 Blair, 73–74.

15 "Interview with Mrs. Mary T. L. Gannett," Biographical/Autobiographical file, Montgomery Collection, American Baptist Historical Society Archives, Mercer University, Atlanta.

16 McKelvey, *Rochester*, 16.

17 Natalie F. Hawley, "Literature in Rochester, 1865–1905," *Rochester History* 10, no. 1 (1948): 7.

18 Blake McKelvey, "Rochester's Literary and Book Clubs," *Rochester History* 48, nos. 1–2 (1986): 8–9.

19 Hawley, 8.

20 McKelvey, "Rochester's Literary and Book Clubs," 10.

21 "Interview with Mrs. Mary T. L. Gannett."

22 William H. Pease, "The Gannetts of Rochester: Highlights in a Liberal Career, 1889–1923," *Rochester History* 17, no. 4 (1955): 13–14.

23 Blake McKelvey, "Susan B. Anthony," *Rochester History* 7, no. 2 (1945): 16.

24 Pease, 14.

25 "After the Big Banquet," *Herald*, 4 December 1896, 8; Blake McKelvey, "Rochester at the Turn of the Century," *Rochester History* 12, no. 1 (1950): 13.

26 Helen Barrett Montgomery, "Equal Suffrage," *Harper's Bazaar* 27, no. 18 (5 May 1894): 354.

27 Montgomery, "Equal Suffrage," 354.

28 Montgomery, "Equal Suffrage," 354–55.

29 Cf. Aileen Kraditor, ed., *Up from the Pedestal: Selected Writings in the History of American Feminism* (Chicago: Quadrangle Books, 1968), 220–22; Dana Greene, ed., *Suffrage and Religious Principle: Speeches and Writings of Olympia Brown* (Metuchen, N.J.: Scarecrow Press, 1983), 121–30.

30 Kraditor, *Ideas of the Woman Suffrage Movement*, 43–45.

31 Kraditor, *Ideas of the Woman Suffrage Movement*, 43–45.

32 Cf. Kraditor, *Up From the Pedestal*, 253–65; Greene, 112–30; Buhle and Buhle, 337, 347.

33 Cf. Kraditor, *Up From the Pedestal*, 175–78; Greene, 109–11.

34 Cf. Kraditor, *Up From the Pedestal*, 159–67; Greene, 105.

35 Kraditor, *Ideas of the Woman Suffrage Movement*, 68.

36 Montgomery, "Equal Suffrage," 354.

37 Kraditor, *Ideas of the Woman Suffrage Movement*, 67–71.

38 "After the Big Banquet," *Herald*, 18 December 1896, 11.

39 "Arrogant Spain and Devoted Cuba," *Democrat and Chronicle*, 17 December 1896, 5.

40 "Interesting Discussion," *Democrat and Chronicle*, 10 November 1899, 11.

41 "Some Thoughts for Women," *Democrat and Chronicle*, 9 April 1896, 11.

42 "Some Thoughts for Women," 11.

43 "The New Woman," *Union and Advertiser*, 9 April 1896, 9.

44 "The New Woman," 9.

45 "Some Thoughts," 11.

46 "Some Thoughts," 11.

47 "The Woman's Union," *Herald*, 27 April 1893, 6.

48 McKelvey, *Rochester*, 125.

49 "New Woman," 9.

50 "New Woman," 9.

51 "Some Thoughts," 11.

52 Sheila M. Rothman, *Woman's Proper Place: A History of Changing Ideals and Practices, 1870 to the Present* (New York: Basic Books, 1978), 98.

53 "Some Thoughts," 11.

54 "Some Thoughts," 11.

55 "Some Thoughts," 11.

56 *Year Book of the Woman's Educational and Industrial Union, Rochester, N.Y., 1896–1897* [1897], 13.

57 "How They Manage Things in Glasgow," *Democrat and Chronicle,* 3 December 1896, 12.

58 *Year Book,* 15.

59 Kraditor, *Ideas of the Woman Suffrage Movement,* 50, 102–5.

60 "Arrogant Spain," 5.

61 "Anent the Congress," *Democrat and Chronicle,* 5 December 1895, 14; "Mrs. Montgomery Talks on Politics," *Democrat and Chronicle,* 4 March 1897, 12.

62 "Anent the Congress."

63 "Venezuela," *Union and Advertiser,* 19 December 1895, 10.

64 "Anent the Congress;" cf. "Political Affairs," *Union and Advertiser,* 5 December 1895, 9.

65 E.g., Robyn Muncy, *Creating a Female Dominion in American Reform, 1890–1935* (New York: Oxford University Press, 1991); Patrick Wilkinson, "The Selfless and the Helpless: Maternalist Origins of the U.S. Welfare State," *Feminist Studies* 25, no. 3 (1999): 571–97.

66 "A Socialistic Propagandist," *Herald,* 23 January 1897, 4.

67 "A Question of Interest," *Herald,* 25 January 1897, 8.

68 "Municipal Reforms," *Union and Advertiser,* 9 January 1895, 8.

69 "How They Manage Things in Glasgow."

70 "The Liquor Traffic," *Union and Advertiser,* 27 February 1896, 10.

71 "The Liquor Traffic," 10.

72 "Venezuela," *Union and Advertiser,* 19 December 1895, 10.

73 "Cuba and Its Wars," *Union and Advertiser,* 12 March 1896, 8; cf. "Story of the Cubans," *Democrat and Chronicle* 12 March 1896, 8.

74 Richard L. Kagan, "Prescott's Paradigm: American Historical Scholarship and the Decline of Spain," *American Historical Review* 101, no. 2 (1996): 423–46.

75 Charles Gibson, ed., *The Black Legend: Anti-Spanish Attitudes in the Old World and the New,* with an Introduction by Charles Gibson (New York: Alfred A. Knopf, 1971), 13–27. See also Phillip Wayne Powell, *Tree of Hate: Propaganda and Prejudices Affecting United States Relations with the Hispanic World* (Vallecito, Calif.: Ross House Books, 1985).

76 Bartolomé de Las Casas, *The Devastation of the Indies: A Brief Account*, trans. Herma Briffault, with Introduction by Hans Magnus Enzenberger (New York: Seabury Press, 1974).

77 Kagan, 425–26.

78 Kagan, 428–31.

79 Helen Barrett Montgomery, "A Book that Rome Suppressed," *The Baptist* 1, no. 21 (19 June 1920): 735.

80 "Arrogant Spain," 5.

81 See Winthop S. Hudson, "Protestant Clergy Debate the Nation's Vocation, 1898–1899," *Church History* 42, no. 1 (1973): 110–18.

82 Ahlstrom, 879; cf. Julius W. Pratt, "Manifest Destiny and the American Century," *Current History* 29, no. 172 (1955): 331–36.

83 "Problems of the War with Spain," *Democrat and Chronicle,* 6 November 1898, 18.

84 Christopher A. Vaughan, "The 'Discovery' of the Philippines by the U.S. Press, 1898–1902," *Historian* 57, no. 2 (1995): 303–14.

85 Hofstadter, 170–96.

86 Quoted in Hudson, "Protestant Clergy," 117.

87 Hudson, "Protestant Clergy," 114.

88 "Problems of the War with Spain."

89 Jacob Gould Schurman, president of Cornell University, headed the first presidential commission appointed by President McKinley to assess the situation in the Philippines following the Spanish-American War and make policy recommendations to Congress.

90 "Talk on Report of Commission," *Democrat and Chronicle,* 3 December 1899, 18.

91 Quoted in Hudson, "Protestant Clergy," 116.

92 Quoted in Hudson, "Protestant Clergy," 118.

93 "Problems of the War with Spain."

94 In international relations, the concept that Montgomery was articulating is called "trusteeship," and it is rooted in the British concept of colonialism as articulated by Edmund Burke in 1793. See Charmian Edwards Toussaint, *The Trusteeship System of the United Nations* (New York: Frederick A. Praeger, 1956), 5–10; H. Duncan Hall, *Mandates, Dependencies and Trusteeship* (Washington, D.C.: Carnegie Endowment for International Peace, 1948), 97–100.

95 The American government sent soldiers and teachers to the Philippines. Both the Schurman and Taft Commissions underscored the necessity of public education as a means of inculcating democratic ideals among the Filipinos. In fact, before American teachers arrived in great numbers (847 in 1901–1902), American soldiers ran schools. See Jo Anne Parker Maniago, "The First Peace Corps: The Work of the American Teachers in the Philippines, 1900–1910" (Ph.D. diss., Boston University, 1971), 49, 114.

96 "Talk on Report of Commission."

97 See, e.g., Sidney M. Milkis and Jerome M. Mileur, eds., *Progressivism and the New Democracy* (Amherst: University of Massachusetts Press, 1999).

98 "An Australian Commonwealth," *Democrat and Chronicle,* 13 January 1901, 20.

99 "Co-Education and the Chinese Empire," *Democrat and Chronicle*, 5 March 1899, 16.

100 Robert F. McClellan, "Missionary Influence on American Attitudes toward China at the Turn of This Century," *Church History* 38, no. 4 (1969): 475–85.

101 "Problems of the War with Spain."

102 "On the Proposed Nicaragua Canal," *Democrat and Chronicle*, 4 December 1898, 18.

103 Kraditor, *Ideas of the Woman Suffrage Movement*, 85–86.

104 Cott, *Grounding of Modern Feminism*, 20.

105 Montgomery, "Equal Suffrage," 354.

106 Livingstone, "Presentation on the Life of Helen Barrett Montgomery," 10; P. W. W., *Helen Barrett Montgomery: From Campus to World Citizenship* (New York: Fleming H. Revell, 1940), 13–14.

107 Nancy A. Hewitt, *Women's Activism and Social Change: Rochester, New York, 1822–1872* (Ithaca: Cornell University Press, 1984).

108 Cott, *Bonds of Womanhood*, 126–59, 204; see also Ann Braude, "Women's History *is* American Religious History" in *Retelling U.S. Religious History*, ed. Thomas A. Tweed (Berkeley: University of California Press, 1997), 90–92.

109 Shirley S. Garrett, "Sisters All: Feminism and the American Women's Missionary Movement," in *Missionary Ideologies in the Imperialist Era: 1880–1920*, ed. Torben Christensen and William R. Hutchison (Cambridge, Mass.: Harvard Theological Review, 1982), 224.

110 Carolyn Alice Haynes, "Women and Protestantism in Nineteenth-Century America," in *Perspectives on American Religion and Culture*, ed. Peter W. Williams (Oxford: Blackwell, 1999), 300–318.

111 Blair, 1.

Chapter 6

* A version of this chapter was published previously as "Susan B. Anthony and Helen Barrett Montgomery: An Intergenerational Feminist Partnership," *Baptist History and Heritage* 40, n. 3 (2005): 80–90.

1 Biographies include the following: Ida Husted Harper, *The Life and Work of Susan B. Anthony*, 3 vols. (Indianapolis: Hollenbeck Press, 1898–1908); Rheta Childe Dorr, *Susan B. Anthony, the Woman Who Changed the Mind of a Nation* (New York: Frederick A. Stokes, 1928); Katharine Susan Anthony, *Susan B. Anthony: Her Personal History and Her Era* (Garden City, N.Y.: Doubleday, 1954); Alma Lutz, *Susan B. Anthony: Rebel, Crusader, Humanitarian* (Boston: Beacon Books, 1959); Kathleen Barry, *Susan B. Anthony: A Biography of a Singular Feminist* (New York: Ballantine Books, 1988). See also Elizabeth Cady

Stanton, Susan B. Anthony, Matilda Joslyn Gage, and Ida Husted Harper, eds., *History of Woman Suffrage,* 6 vols. (New York: Fowler & Wells, 1881–1922).

2   Barry, 69.

3   *Decennial Year Book* (Rochester, N.Y.: Women's Education and Industrial Union, 1903), 11.

4   McKelvey, *Rochester,* 11–12; idem, "Susan B. Anthony," 19–20. Curiously, McKelvey repeatedly referred to Dolley as "Dooley" in the 1945 article.

5   McKelvey, "Susan B. Anthony," *Rochester History* 7, no. 2 (1945): 19–20.

6   Blair, 73–81.

7   Blair, 91; Jeannette W. Huntington, "Women's Educational and Industrial Union, 1893–1943," TMs, Local History, Rochester Public Library, Rochester, N.Y.

8   McKelvey, *Rochester,* 11.

9   "The Woman's Union," *Herald,* 27 April 1893, 6.

10 Blair, 80.

11 Blair, 76, 87.

12 McKelvey, *Rochester,* 271, 105, 2, 116–17, 195, 203.

13 Blair, 93–96.

14 "Some Thoughts for Women," *Democrat and Chronicle,* 9 April 1896, 11.

15 "Mrs. Montgomery is President," *Herald,* 14 November 1896, 7; "Rochester Lady Honored," *Union and Advertiser,* 13 November 1896, 13; cf. Hudson, "Montgomery, Helen Barrett," 567.

16 Blair, 98.

17 "Resolutions Adopted by the Convention of Women's Clubs at Syracuse," "Mrs. Montgomery In Her Home City" file; "Playmate," by Rose Lattimore Alling, 1, "Tributes" file; Storrs B. Barrett to Mrs. Franklin W. Knope, 17 March 1937, 2, "Correspondence: Storrs B. Barrett" file, Montgomery Collection, American Baptist Historical Society Archives, Mercer University, Atlanta.

18 Alling, 1.

19 Mrs. Franklin A. Knope to Storrs B. Barrett, 8 February 1937; Barrett to Knope, 17 March 1937, 2, "Correspondence: Storrs B. Barrett" file, Montgomery Collection, American Baptist Historical Society Archives, Mercer University, Atlanta.

20 "After the Big Banquet," *Herald,* 4 December 1896, 8.

21 "In Susan's Honor," *Union and Advertiser,* 21 November 1896, 13.

22 Rothman, 74–75.

23 Rothman, 76–77.

24 "The New Building Was Dedicated," *Democrat and Chronicle,* 7 June 1898, 8.

25 "The New Building Was Dedicated," 8.

26 "Way Open to Women," *Democrat and Chronicle*, 15 June 1898, 13.

27 Jesse Leonard Rosenberger, *Rochester: The Making of a University,* Introduction by Rush Rhees (Rochester, N.Y.: University of Rochester, 1927), 235–37; McKelvey, *Rochester*, 235.

28 *Forty-Fifth Annual Catalogue of the University of Rochester, 1894–95* (Rochester, N.Y.: University of Rochester), 78–79.

29 *Forty-Fifth Annual Catalogue,* 79.

30 *Forty-Fifth Annual Catalogue,* 80.

31 "Lecture on Dante," *Union and Advertiser,* 20 March 1895, 10; "Life in Old Florence," *Union and Advertiser,* 27 March 1895, 8.

32 Pease, 14; Rosenberger, 236.

33 McKelvey, *Rochester*, 234–35.

34 "When a Woman Wills She Will," *Democrat and Chronicle,* 17 June 1898, 11.

35 "When a Woman Wills She Will," 11.

36 "When a Woman Wills She Will," 11; "And Now for a Big Mass Meeting," *Democrat and Chronicle,* 19 June 1898, 16.

37 "And Now for a Big Mass Meeting."

38 "And Now for a Big Mass Meeting."

39 Solomon, 58–61.

40 "And Now for a Big Mass Meeting."

41 "Their Confidence Increases Daily," *Democrat and Chronicle,* 23 June 1898, 11.

42 "Girls May Enter the Class of '02," *Democrat and Chronicle,* 13 July 1989, 10.

43 Rosenberger, 235.

44 McKelvey, *Rochester*, 235.

45 Harper, 3:1222.

46 McKelvey, *Rochester*, 73–79; Herbert S. Weet, "The Development of Public Education in Rochester, 1900–1910," *The History of Education in Rochester. Selected Articles on Rochester History.* The Rochester Historical Society Publications 17, edited and compiled by Dexter Perkins (Rochester, N.Y.: Historical Society, 1939), 183–84.

47 Russell D. Murphy, "The Mayoralty and the Democratic Creed: The Evolution of an Ideology and an Institution," *Urban Affairs Quarterly* 22, no. 1 (1986): 4; Frank Mann Stewart, *A Half Century of Municipal Reform: The History of the National Municipal League* (Berkeley and Los Angeles: University of California Press, 1950), 10; Link and McCormick, 10.

48 Stewart, 13.

49 Stewart, 13–22, 24.

50 McKelvey, *Rochester,* 76–79.

51   McKelvey, *Rochester*, 80–83; Weet, 185–86.

52   Dow, 192.

53   McKelvey, *Rochester*, 34; William J. Reese, *Power and the Promise of School Reform: Grassroots Movements during the Progressive Era* (Boston: Routledge & Kegan Paul, 1986), 272 n. 60.

54   *Year Book of the Woman's Educational and Industrial Union, Rochester, N.Y. 1896–97*, 14–15, WEIU Papers, Local History, Rochester Public Library.

55   Reese, 111.

56   McKelvey, *Rochester*, 194.

57   "The Women Will Name a Candidate," *Democrat and Chronicle*, 4 October 1899, 11; "Mrs. Montgomery Named," *Democrat and Chronicle*, 6 October 1899, 13.

58   "Meetings in Many Wards," *Democrat and Chronicle*, 28 October 1899, 13; "Meeting of Mothers," *Democrat and Chronicle*, 29 October 1899, 10; "A Womanly Speech," *Union and Advertiser*, 1 November 1899, 7.

59   "Openly Advocated from the Pulpit," *Democrat and Chronicle*, 30 October 1899, 4.

60   "Her Qualifications as a Candidate," *Democrat and Chronicle*, 11 October 1899, 10; "A Vacant Place on the Ticket," *Herald*, 14 October 1899, 4; "A Womanly Speech," 4, 7.

61   "Political Equality Club," *Union and Advertiser*, 20 October 1899, in *The Papers of Elizabeth Cady Stanton and Susan B. Anthony* [microform], ed. Patricia G. Holland and Ann D. Gordon (Wilmington, Del.: Scholarly Resources, 1991), roll 40.

62   "Their Case Well Put," *Democrat and Chronicle*, 1 November 1899, 9.

63   Montgomery, "Equal Suffrage," 354–55; "'Our Susan,'" *Herald*, 21 November 1896, 11; "In Susan's Honor," *Union and Advertiser*, 21 November 1896, 13.

64   "Platform of Women's Council," *Union and Advertiser*, 20 October 1899, in *Papers of Elizabeth Cady Stanton and Susan B. Anthony* [microform], roll 40; "Adopted a Platform," *Democrat and Chronicle*, 20 October 1899, in *Papers*, roll 40.

65   "Adopted a Platform," roll 40.

66   "Adopted a Platform," roll 40.

67   "Adopted a Platform," roll 40.

68   "Clean the City of the Book Ring," *Democrat and Chronicle*, 4 November 1899, 16.

69   "Mrs. Montgomery Speaks," *Union and Advertiser*, 28 October 1899, 9.

70   "Grand Ovation," *Union and Advertiser*, 2 November 1899, 10.

71   "Clean the City of the Book Ring."

72 "A Womanly Speech," 7.

73 "German-Americans Endorse Carnahan," *Democrat and Chronicle*, 5 November 1899, 18.

74 "A Womanly Speech," 7.

75 "Grand Ovation," 10.

76 "Grand Ovation," 10.

77 "Grand Ovation," 10.

78 "Mrs. Montgomery Speaks."

79 "A Womanly Speech," 7.

80 "Baptists in Convention," *Democrat and Chronicle*, 6 October 1899, 13.

81 "Clean the City of the Book Ring."

82 "Meetings in Many Wards," *Democrat and Chronicle*, 28 October 1899, 13.

83 McNamara, "Ecumenism," 4.

84 "An Appeal to Religious Prejudice," *Democrat and Chronicle,* 3 November 1899, 14.

85 "A Woman's Influence," *Democrat and Chronicle* 4 November 1899, 13.

86 Papers and Letters.

87 "Gracious Words of Welcome," *Democrat and Chronicle,* 8 November 1899, 11; "Interesting Discussion," *Democrat and Chronicle* 10 November 1899, 11.

88 "Woman's Council and Coeducation," *Democrat and Chronicle,* 13 January 1900, 12.

89 "Opens Its Doors to Young Women," *Democrat and Chronicle,* 9 September 1900, 17; Rosenberger, 235–37.

90 Harper, 3:1223–27.

91 Harper, 3:1427.

92 "School Board Resolution," *Herald,* 16 March 1906, 10.

93 Harper, 3:1467.

94 McKelvey, *Rochester,* 236.

Chapter 7

1 Blair, 73–83; Sarah Deutsch, *Women and the City: Gender, Space, and Power in Boston, 1870–1940* (New York: Oxford University Press, 2000), 144–53.

2 Blair, 85–90.

3 "For the Working Girls," *Democrat and Chronicle,* 21 November 1895, 8.

4 Glenda Riley, *Inventing the American Woman: A Perspective on Women's History 1865 to the Present* (Arlington Heights, Ill.: Harlan Davidson, 1986), 54–58; Steven J. Diner, *A Very Different Age: Americans of the Progressive Era* (New York: Hill & Wang, 1998), 55, 68–70.

5 McKelvey, *Rochester,* 140.

6   "For Woman's Good," *Herald*, 19 January 1894, 7.

7   Riley, 54–55.

8   Rothman, 74–78, 90–93.

9   Diner, 156–65.

10 Laura S. Abrams, "Guardians of Virtue: The Social Reformers and the 'Girl Problem,' 1890–1920," *Social Service Review* 74, no. 3 (2000): 445–46.

11 "Woman's Union Meeting," *Democrat and Chronicle*, 19 January 1894, 10.

12 McKelvey, *Rochester*, 125.

13 WEIU Scrapbook 1893–1896, 122, WEIU Papers, Local History, Central Library of Rochester and Monroe County, Rochester, N.Y.

14 "Criticised the Schools," *Democrat and Chronicle*, 11 May 1895, 10.

15 *Year Book of the Woman's Educational and Industrial Union, Rochester, N.Y. 1896–97*, 24–25, WEIU Papers, Local History, Rochester Public Library.

16 WEIU Scrapbook 1893–1896, 340.

17 *Year Book*, 22–24.

18 *Year Book*, 24.

19 WEIU Scrapbook 1893–1896, 119.

20 Cf. Blair, 99.

21 WEIU Scrapbook 1896–1901, 7–8, WEIU Papers, Local History, Central Library of Rochester and Monroe County, Rochester, New York; *Decennial Year Book* (Rochester, N.Y.: Women's Educational and Industrial Union, 1903), 31–32.

22 Montgomery, "Equal Suffrage," 354.

23 Quoted in Reese, 43.

24 WEIU Scrapbook 1893–1896, 164.

25 WEIU Scrapbook 1896–1901, 13.

26 Reese, 40.

27 *Year Book*, 26.

28 Reese, 50–51.

29 Reese, 58–59.

30 *Year Book*, 25.

31 "Waifs of the Slums," *Herald,* 8 December 1893, 6; *Year Book*, 25.

32 Michael Steven Shapiro, *Child's Garden: The Kindergarten Movement from Froebel to Dewey* (University Park: Pennsylvania State University Press, 1983), 1–14.

33 Shapiro, 19–23.

34 Evelyn Weber, *The Kindergarten: Its Encounter with Educational Thought in America* (New York: Teachers College Press, 1969), 6.

35 Shapiro, 22–25; Weber, 8–9.

36 Shapiro, 31–63; Weber, 24–33.

37 Shapiro, 65–79; Weber, 35–36.

38 Shapiro, 85.

39 Weber, 38–39.

40 Shapiro, 92.

41 Shapiro, 97; Weber, 39–40.

42 Blake McKelvey, "Rochester's Public Schools: A Testing Ground for Community Policies," *Rochester History* 31, no. 2 (1969): 6–7.

43 "Waifs of the Slums."

44 Catherine C. DuCharme, "Lucy Wheelock: Her Life and Work," *Childhood Education* 76, no. 3 (2000): 164–69; Elizabeth D. Ross, "Wheelock, Lucy," *Dictionary of American Biography Supplement Four, 1946–1950*, ed. John A. Garraty and Edward T. James (New York: Scribners, 1974), 874–75.

45 For more on the "Italian colony" of Rochester, see Blake McKelvey, "The Italians of Rochester: An Historical Review," *Rochester History* 22, no. 4 (1960).

46 "Criticised the Schools."

47 "For Woman's Good."

48 Reese, 35.

49 Reese, 103–5.

50 Weet, 185–86.

51 *Year Book,* 26.

52 *Year Book,* 26.

53 *Year Book,* 26.

54 "Criticised the Schools."

55 *Year Book,* 27.

56 "Criticised the Schools."

57 Reese, 48.

58 "Criticised the Schools."

59 *Year Book,* 13.

60 Reese, 59.

61 *Year Book,* 28.

62 "Criticised the Schools."

63 *Year Book,* 28.

64 *Decennial Year Book,* 12.

65 June E. Eyestone, "The Influence of Swedish Sloyd and Its Interpreters on American Art Education," *Studies in Art Education* 34, no. 1 (1992): 28–29.

66 Eyestone, 31–33; Frederick M. Logan, *Growth of Art in American Schools* (New York: Harper & Brothers, 1955), 102–3.

67 "Household Economics," *Herald,* 14 November 1897, 8.

68 Weet, 192–93.

69 *Decennial Year Book,* 13.

70 Reese, 150–51.

71 *Decennial Year Book,* 28.

72 WEIU Scrapbook 1896–1901, 37, 39.

73 *Decennial Year Book,* 28, 29.

74 WEIU Scrapbook 1896–1901, 48.

75 WEIU Scrapbook 1896–1901, 49.

76 WEIU Scrapbook 1893–1896, 134.

77 *Decennial Year Book,* 31–33.

78 "Appreciation of a Noble Gift," *Democrat and Chronicle,* 25 November 1897, 9.

79 *Decennial Year Book,* 32, 34.

80 *Decennial Year Book,* 32.

81 *Decennial Year Book,* 33–34.

82 *Decennial Year Book,* 24–25.

83 *Decennial Year Book,* 25.

84 *Decennial Year Book,* 26.

85 McKelvey, "Rochester at the Turn of the Century," 13; cf. idem, "Historic Origins of Rochester's Social Welfare Agencies," *Rochester History* 9, nos. 2–3 (1947): 31.

86 Link and McCormick, 81.

87 "Action Taken on Early Closing," *Democrat and Chronicle,* 12 December 1908, 18.

88 Blake McKelvey, "An Historical View of Rochester's Parks and Playgrounds," *Rochester History* 11, no. 1 (1949): 15–16.

89 *Decennial Year Book,* 26; Marion Harris Fey, "Educational Reform in the Era of the 'New Woman': Helen Barrett Montgomery, 1861–1934," 1989, TMs [photocopy], 21, personal collection.

90 Lawrence A. Cremin, *American Education: The Metropolitan Experience, 1876–1980* (New York: Harper & Row, 1988), 280–81.

91 Reese, 41, 181–82; Cremin, 281–82.

92 WEIU Scrapbook 1896–1901, 16–17.

93 McKelvey, "Historic Origins," 30–31; idem, "Samuel Parker Moulthrop: Devoted Educator and Good Citizen," *Rochester History* 19, no. 2 (1957): 12.

94 Dow, 196.

95 Dow, 196; McKelvey, "Historic Origins," 31.

96 Charles F. Starring, "Crane, Caroline Julia Bartlett," in *Notable American Women, 1607–1950* vol. 1, ed. Edward T. James, Janet Wilson James, and

Paul S. Boyer (Cambridge, Mass.: Belknap Press, 1971), 401–2; Linda J. Rynbrandt, "The 'Ladies of the Club' and Caroline Bartlett Crane: Affiliation and Alienation in Progressive Social Reform," *Gender and Society* 11, no. 2 (1997): 200–214.

97 Pease, 14.

98 Blake McKelvey, "Walter Rauschenbusch's Rochester," *Rochester History* 14, no. 4 (1952): 25; idem, *Rochester*, 111; idem, "Historic Origins," 33.

99 "Some Thoughts for Women," *Democrat and Chronicle,* 9 April 1896, 11.

100 *Year Book,* 11.

Chapter 8

1 Biographical studies of Rauschenbusch include Christopher H. Evans, *The Kingdom Is Always but Coming: A Life of Walter Rauschenbusch* (Grand Rapids: Eerdmans, 2004); Vernon Parker Bodein, *The Social Gospel of Walter Rauschenbusch and Its Relation to Religious Education* (New Haven: Yale University Press, 1944); Klaus Juergen Jaehn, *Rauschenbusch: The Formative Years* (Valley Forge, Pa.: Judson Press, 1976); Paul M. Minus, *Walter Rauschenbusch: American Reformer* (New York: Macmillan, 1988); Dores Robinson Sharpe, *Walter Rauschenbusch* (New York: Macmillan, 1942).

2 Sharpe, 40.

3 Jaehn, 11–13.

4 Sharpe, 142.

5 Minus, 121–27.

6 McKelvey, "Walter Rauschenbusch's Rochester," 4–7.

7 McKelvey, "Walter Rauschenbusch's Rochester," 12.

8 McKelvey, "Walter Rauschenbusch's Rochester," 13.

9 "Brotherhood of Kingdom," *Herald,* 8 March 1906, 9.

10 Montgomery Collection, American Baptist Historical Society Archives, Mercer University, Atlanta.

11 To Walter Rauschenbusch, Rauschenbusch Family Papers, Box 25, American Baptist-Samuel Colgate Library, American Baptist Historical Archives, Rochester, N.Y.

12 To Walter Rauschenbusch.

13 Fey, "Educational Reform," 25–27.

14 Quoted in John R. Aiken, "Walter Rauschenbusch and Education for Reform," *Church History* 36, no 4 (1967): 462.

15 "Rochester Board Is Breaking New Ground in Establishing Its Public Factory School," *Democrat and Chronicle,* 29 November 1908, 20.

16 Weet, 195.

17 "The Playground Experiment," *Herald,* 16 July 1900, 7.
18 McKelvey, 95, 125; "Will Discuss Playgrounds," *Herald,* 12 April 1907, 11.
19 "To Lift Burden from Taxpayers," *Democrat and Chronicle,* 3 March 1907, 17.
20 Weet, 221.
21 Weet, 188–89.
22 Weet, 191; McKelvey, *Rochester,* 93.
23 McKelvey, *Rochester,* 93.
24 Fey, 16.
25 Weet, 202–3, 225–26.
26 Weet, 191.
27 Weet, 191; Fey, Figure 1.
28 McKelvey, *Rochester,* 84; Weet, 189; *Proceedings, Board of Education, City of Rochester for the Year 1900* (Rochester, N.Y.), 125–52.
29 Weet, 189–90.
30 *Proceedings . . . 1900,* 63.
31 Weet, 214.
32 Weet, 216.
33 Helen Barrett Montgomery, "The Last Ten Years of the Rochester Schools," *The Common Good* 5, no. 1 (1911): 10.
34 "Outdoor School for Children with Taint of Tuberculosis Likely to Be Established," *Democrat and Chronicle,* 28 September 1909, 16.
35 Weet, 206.
36 *Proceedings . . . 1900,* 147.
37 *Proceedings . . . 1901,* 86–101.
38 Weet, 210–12; *Proceedings . . . 1901,* 86–87.
39 *Proceedings . . . 1901,* 100.
40 *Proceedings . . . 1901, 87,* 91.
41 Weet, 212–13.
42 Weet, 214–15.
43 *Proceedings . . . 1900,* 102–3.
44 "Public Schools and Their Needs," *Democrat and Chronicle,* 4 February 1900, 18.
45 "Public Schools and Their Needs," 18.
46 "Meeting of Patrons of Schools," *Democrat and Chronicle,* 9 September 1908, 11.
47 "Parents State Objections to Public School Methods," *Democrat and Chronicle,* 11 September 1908, 15.
48 Aiken, 456–69. It is important to note that Aiken developed his analysis of Rauschenbusch's educational theory primarily from a commencement address

given by Rauschenbusch in 1902. Aiken devoted less than two pages of his essay to the controversy in Rochester. Rauschenbusch's actual criticisms of the Rochester schools during the controversy reflected an emphasis that was different from the themes highlighted in Aiken's analysis of Rauschenbusch's educational theory. While Aiken mentioned Rauschenbusch's attitude toward women teachers, it was far from the core issue in his analysis. Yet it was a key feature in the actual conflict with the Rochester school board.

49 Walter Rauschenbusch, *Christianizing the Social Order* (New York: Macmillan, 1912), 316.

50 Rauschenbusch, *Christianizing*, 143, 452–53.

51 Quoted in Sharpe, 150.

52 "Grievance Committee Seeks Definite Information as to Methods in Public Schools," *Democrat and Chronicle,* 25 September 1908, 13.

53 "Want More Letters on School Methods," *Democrat and Chronicle,* 2 October 1908, 15.

54 "Formal Request Submitted to Board of Education for Changes in School Methods," *Democrat and Chronicle,* 14 November 1908, 14–15.

55 Walter Rauschenbusch, "Draft of the Report of the Committee on Public Schools," TMs with handwritten notes [1908], 24, Rauschenbusch Family Papers, Box 49, American Baptist Historical Society Archives, Mercer University, Atlanta.

56 Rauschenbusch, "Draft of the Report," 33.

57 Rauschenbusch, "Draft of the Report," 16

58 Rauschenbusch, "Draft of the Report," 33.

59 "Formal Request," 14.

60 Rauschbusch, "Draft of the Report," 12.

61 *Proceedings . . . 1905,* 18–19.

62 Rauschenbusch, "Draft of the Report," 10.

63 Rauschenbusch, "Draft of the Report," 11.

64 "Formal Request," 14.

65 Cf. Rauschenbusch, *Christianizing,* 144–45, where Rauschenbusch included the abatement of corporal punishment among the liberating and democratizing consequences of the influence of Christianity on the American educational system. Although he lauded several particular reforms, such as extension programs, the push for universal literacy, and progressive taxation, he mentioned none of the main features of the "new education," such as manual training, the focus on student interest, and individual self-expression, which he apparently deplored.

66 Rauschenbusch, "Draft of the Report," 9.

67 Rauschenbusch, "Draft of the Report," 30.

68 Rauschenbusch, "Draft of the Report," 31–32.

69 Rauschenbusch, "Draft of the Report," 32.

70 "Formal Request," 14.

71 "Formal Request," 14–15.

72 "Formal Request," 15

73 Helen Barrett Montgomery, letter to "My dears," 17 May 1894, Ms [photocopy], personal collection.

74 Helen Barrett Montgomery to Louise McCoy North, undated postcard, "North, Lousie McCoy" file, Margaret Clapp Library, Wellesley College, Wellesley, Mass. (italics in original).

75 "Formal Request," 14–15.

76 "Formal Request," 15; "School System Changes Ordered," *Democrat and Chronicle,* 18 November 1908, 14; "Principals Discuss Changes in Methods," *Democrat and Chronicle,* 25 November 1908, 12; "Board Takes Secret Vote," *Democrat and Chronicle,* 26 November 1908, 8.

77 "School System Changes Ordered," 14; "Principals Discuss Changes in Methods," 12.

78 Clarence F. Carroll, "Superintendent's Report" [1909], *The Fifty-Fifth Report of the Board of Education of the City of Rochester, New York, for the Years 1908, 1909, 1910* (Rochester: Board of Education), 39.

79 Helen Barrett Montgomery to the Editor of the Post-Express, 14 January 1909, Ms, Autograph Letter File, Local History, Rochester Public Library, Rochester, New York, 1.

80 Montgomery to the Editor, 7.

81 Montgomery to the Editor, 8.

82 McKelvey, *Rochester,* 103–4.

83 "That School Board Nomination," *Herald,* 1 November 1909, 6; McKelvey, *Rochester,* 104.

84 "Renomination Asked for Mrs. Montgomery," *Evening Times* 24 September 1909, 8; "Federation Not Officially Represented," *Union and Advertiser,* 7 October 1909, 9; "For Woman on School Board," *Democrat and Chronicle,* 24 September 1909, 16; "Delegations of Women Ask That Mrs. Montgomery Be Returned to School Board," *Democrat and Chronicle,* 7 October 1909, 13; "Statement of Federation," *Democrat and Chronicle,* 13 October 1909, 15; "Civic Clubs Have Not Endorsed Miss Gregory," *Herald,* 1 November 1909, 8.

85 "A Woman on the School Board," *Herald,* 1 November 1909, 6.

86 "H.B.M.'s Diary," TMs, Biographical/Autobiographical File, Montgomery

Collection, American Baptist Historical Society Archives, Mercer University, Atlanta.

87 "H.B.M.'s Diary."

88 "From Mrs. Montgomery," *Democrat and Chronicle,* 16 February 1902, 18; "Mrs. Montgomery's Letter," *Democrat and Chronicle,* 23 February 1902, 20.

89 *Proceedings . . . 1909,* 59–60.

90 Montgomery Collection, American Baptist Historical Society Archives, Mercer University, Atlanta.

Chapter 9

1 McKelvey, *Rochester,* 95, 133.

2 McKelvey, *Rochester,* 135; "Women Call Mass Meeting to Fight Against Vice," *Herald,* 22 March 1905, 6.

3 "Women Call Mass Meeting;" "To Protest Against Vice," *Democrat and Chronicle,* 22 March 1905, 13.

4 "There Will Be Plain Speaking," *Herald,* 23 March 1905, 6.

5 "Make Appeal to Governor," *Democrat and Chronicle,* 24 March 1905, 13; cf. "Excise Law Criticised by Women of Rochester, Who Appeal to the Governor," *Herald,* 24 March 1905, 6.

6 "Make Appeal to Governor."

7 "Excise Law Criticised."

8 "Excise Law Criticised."

9 Walter Rauschenbusch, "Y.M.C.A. Report 1904," Rauschenbusch Family Papers, Box 49, 16, American Baptist Historical Society Archives, Mercer University, Atlanta.

10 Rauschenbusch, "Y.M.C.A. Report 1904," 17.

11 See Clifford Putney, *Muscular Christianity: Manhood and Sports in Protestant America, 1880–1920* (Cambridge, Mass.: Harvard University Press, 2001).

12 McKelvey, *Rochester,* 132–38.

13 "Excise Law Criticised."

14 "Make Appeal to Governor."

15 "Excise Law Criticised."

16 "Excise Law Criticised."

17 "Mrs. Montgomery Names Committee of Fifteen," *Herald,* 27 March 1905, 6.

18 "Mrs. Montgomery Names Committee of Fifteen," 6.

19 "Pastors Speak of Dangers Besetting Youth," *Democrat and Chronicle,* 27 March 1905, 9. The verse referred to is Acts 1:8: "But you will receive power when the Holy Spirit comes on you; and you will be my witnesses in Jerusalem, and in all Judea and Samaria, and to the ends of the earth" (NIV).

20   McKelvey, *Rochester,* 129.

21   "Ministers Do Not Agree With Women In Relation to Sunday Recreation," 28 March 1905, 7; cf. "Sunday Amusements Opposed," *Democrat and Chronicle,* 28 March 1905, 13.

22   McKelvey, *Rochester,* 132–38.

23   "Ministers Do Not Agree."

24   "Ministers Do Not Agree."

25   "Ministers Do Not Agree."

26   "The Women and the Clergy," *Herald,* 30 March 1905, 4.

27   "Ministers Not Misled by Inaccurate Press Reports," *Herald,* 30 March 1905, 7.

28   "May Not Reply to Pastors," *Democrat and Chronicle,* 29 March 1905, 10.

29   "Women's Committee at Work," *Democrat and Chronicle,* 1 April 1905, 15.

30   *Proceedings . . . 1905,* 51–52.

31   *Proceedings . . . 1905,* 64.

32   *Proceedings . . . 1905,* 64.

33   *Proceedings . . . 1905,* 65.

34   *Proceedings . . . 1905,* 65–66.

35   *Proceedings . . . 1905,* 66.

36   *Proceedings . . . 1905,* 68–69.

37   "May Ask Use of School Houses," *Herald,* 13 January 1907, 8.

38   "Wants Schools for Social Use," *Herald,* 17 February 1907, 8.

39   "Will Discuss Playgrounds," *Herald,* 12 April 1907, 11; "Experimental Work Outlined," *Herald,* 13 April 1897, 6; "New Movement Is Inaugurated," *Herald,* 2 November 1907, 12.

40   "Playground Supervisor," *Herald,* 19 June 1907, 9.

41   "Ward, Edward Joshua," *Who Was Who in America,* vol. 2 (Chicago: A.N. Marquis, 1950), 556.

42   "The Social Center," *Herald,* 1 November 1907, 6; "New Movement Inaugurated."

43   Kevin Mattson, *Creating a Democratic Public: The Struggle for Urban Participatory Democracy during the Progressive Era* (University Park: The Pennsylvania State University Press, 1998), 52–57.

44   Mattson, 55–56.

45   *Proceedings . . . 1908,* 51.

46   Mattson, 53–56.

47   Mattson, 48–49.

48   Jacob A. Riis, *The Making of an American* (New York: Macmillan, 1916); James B. Lane, *Jacob A. Riis and the American City* (Port Washington, N.Y.: National

University Publications/Kennikat Press, 1974). Riis' other works include *How the Other Half Lives: Studies Among the Tenements of New York* (New York: Scribners, 1890); *The Battle with the Slum* (New York: Macmillan, 1902); *The Children of the Poor* (New York: Scribners, 1902); *Theodore Roosevelt, the Citizen* (New York: Outlook, 1904).

49 "Permits to Use Schools," *Herald,* 28 November 1907, 7.

50 "Social Center's Highest Purpose," *Democrat and Chronicle,* 6 November 1908, 13.

51 "No. 9 Has Social Center At Last," *Democrat and Chronicle,* 8 November 1908, 20.

52 "Social Center's Highest Purpose."

53 "Good Start for Social Center," *Democrat and Chronicle,* 7 November 1908, 14.

54 "Social Centers Are Now Open on Sunday," *Democrat and Chronicle,* 9 November 1908, 12.

55 McKelvey, *Rochester,* 102.

56 "Debate on Text Books Arrested," *Democrat and Chronicle,* 22 December 1908, 15.

57 "Discussion Has Little Utility," *Democrat and Chronicle,* 29 December 1908, 10.

58 McKelvey, *Rochester,* 103.

59 McKelvey, *Rochester,* 103.

60 McKelvey, *Rochester,* 106, 240.

Chapter 10

1 "Big Mission Jubilee Opens Here To-Day," *The New York Times,* 27 March 1911, 20:3; "Pageant of Missions Opens Big Jubilee," *The New York Times,* 28 March 1911, 8:3; "6,000 Women at Luncheon," *The New York Times,* 30 March 1911, 11:1; "Missionary Jubilee Ends," *The New York Times,* 31 March 1911, 4:3.

2 Robert, 130ff., 272ff.; Patricia R. Hill, *The World Their Household: The American Woman's Foreign Mission Movement and Cultural Transformation, 1870–1920* (Ann Arbor: The University of Michigan Press, 1985).

3 "H.B.M.'s Diary."

4 Fewster, 5; American Baptist Historical Society Archives, Mercer University, Atlanta.

5 "H.B.M.'s Diary."

6 Katherine Talbot Hodge, "History of the Woman's Educational and Industrial Union, 1893–1943," TMs, 21, 48, Local History, Central Library of Rochester and Monroe County, Rochester, N.Y.

7   Thomas A. Askew, "The New York 1900 Ecumenical Missionary Conference: A Centennial Reflection," *International Bulletin of Missionary Research* 24, no. 4 (2000): 146–54.

8   Askew, 149.

9   See Federation of Woman's Boards of Foreign Missions of North America, "Historical Sketch 1900–1921," Sixteenth Interdenominational Conference, January 14 & 15, 1921 (New York: 1921), 55–60; Cattan, 36–47; Robert, 260–69, 274–77.

10   Ecumenical Conference on Foreign Missions, *Ecumenical Missionary Conference, New York, 1900,* vol. 1 (New York: American Tract Society, [1900]), 145.

11   Ecumenical Conference, 1:145.

12   Ecumenical Conference, 1:145.

13   Ecumenical Conference, 1:146.

14   Robert, 262.

15   Askew, 148.

16   Cf. Askew, 148; Robert, 280; Ruth Tucker, *Guardians of the Great Commission: The Story of Women in Modern Missions* (Grand Rapids: Zondervan, Academie Books, 1988), 143; Cattan, 37; Peabody, 118; Montgomery, *Western Women in Eastern Lands*, 227.

17   Ecumenical Conference, 1:215–16.

18   Ann Braude, "Women's History *Is* American Religious History," in *Retelling U.S. Religious History,* ed. Thomas A. Tweed (Berkeley: University of California Press, 1997), 93.

19   Robert, 129–30.

20   Ecumenical Conference, 1:216.

21   Ecumenical Conference, 1:216.

22   Ecumenical Conference, 1:216–17.

23   Ecumenical Conference, 1:217.

24   Ecumenical Conference, 1:217.

25   Ecumenical Conference, 1:217.

26   In a broader context, Janet F. Fishburn connected the social gospel to its missionary origins in her unpublished paper, "The Social Gospel as Missionary Ideology: Historiography of the Social Gospel and the Missionary Movement." TMs [photocopy] (1998), American Baptist Historical Society Archives, Mercer University, Atlanta, Georgia; cf. Wendy J. Deichmann Edwards, "Forging an Ideology for American Missions: Josiah Strong and Manifest Destiny," unpublished TMs [electronic copy] (1998), personal collection.

27   See Kendal P. Mobley, "The Ecumenical Woman's Missionary Movement: Helen Barrett Montgomery and *The Baptist*, 1920–1930," in *Gender and*

the Social Gospel, ed. Wendy J. Deichmann Edwards and Carolyn DeSwarte Gifford (Urbana: University of Illinois Press, 2003), 167–81.

28 For more on these events, see Cattan, 36–47.

29 Peabody, 120–21.

30 Cattan, 54.

31 Montgomery, *Western Women in Eastern Lands*, 278. Cattan wrote the best account of the Jubilee that is generally available, in chapter 4, "The Golden Jubilee Celebration," 48–61.

32 Peabody, 124.

33 Cattan, 66.

34 Cattan, 54–60.

35 Rachel Lowrie, *The Story of the Jubilee: An Account of the Celebration of the Fiftieth Anniversary of the Beginning in the United States of Woman's Organized Work for Foreign Missions/ 1860–1910* (West Medford, Mass.: Central Committee on the United Study of Missions, 1911), 5; Cattan, 55.

36 Montgomery, *Western Women in Eastern Lands,* 278.

37 Lowrie, 8–9.

38 Cattan, 55.

39 Peabody, 124.

40 Cattan, 56–57.

41 Lowrie, 32.

42 "Big Mission Jubilee Opens Here Today," *The New York Times,* 27 March 1911, 20.

43 Cattan, 60; Peabody, 124.

44 Peabody, 123.

45 Askew, 151–52.

46 On the decline of the ecumenical woman's missionary movement between the two world wars, see Robert, 302–16.

47 Montgomery, *Western Women in Eastern Lands,* 3–4.

48 Montgomery, *Western Women in Eastern Lands,* 45.

49 Montgomery, *Western Women in Eastern Lands*, 45.

50 "Equal Suffrage," *Harper's Bazaar* 27, no. 18 (5 May 1894): 354.

51 Montgomery, *Western Women in Eastern Lands,* 68–69.

52 Montgomery, *Western Women in Eastern Lands,* 66.

53 Montgomery, *Western Women in Eastern Lands,* 68.

54 Montgomery, *Western Women in Eastern Lands,* 69, 70.

55 Montgomery, *Western Women in Eastern Lands,* 71–72 (italics in original).

56 Montgomery, *Western Women in Eastern Lands,* 73.

57 Montgomery, *Western Women in Eastern Lands,* 73–74.

58 Montgomery, *Western Women in Eastern Lands,* 74.

59 Montgomery, *Western Women in Eastern Lands,* 75.

60 Quoted in Rothman, 67.

61 Montgomery, *Western Women in Eastern Lands,* 75.

62 Montgomery, *Western Women in Eastern Lands,* 206.

63 Montgomery, *Western Women in Eastern Lands,* 206–7.

64 Montgomery, *Western Women in Eastern Lands,* 219, 222–23.

65 Montgomery, *Western Women in Eastern Lands,* 207–16.

66 Montgomery, *Western Women in Eastern Lands,* 217.

67 Montgomery, *Western Women in Eastern Lands,* 222.

68 Montgomery, *Western Women in Eastern Lands,* 221.

69 Montgomery, *Western Women in Eastern Lands,* 223.

70 Montgomery, *Christus Redemptor,* 10–11.

71 Montgomery, *Western Women in Eastern Lands,* 245.

72 Montgomery, *Western Women in Eastern Lands,* 245–62.

73 Montgomery, *Western Women in Eastern Lands,* 266.

74 Montgomery, *Western Women in Eastern Lands,* 268, 269.

75 Montgomery, *Western Women in Eastern Lands,* 270.

76 Montgomery, *Western Women in Eastern Lands,* 271, 273.

77 Freedman; see also, Sklar, "Hull House in the 1890."

Chapter 11

1 Peabody, 125; Cattan, 66.

2 Peabody, 126; Cattan, 63.

3 Cattan, 64–65.

4 Beaver, 163.

5 Beaver, 165.

6 Robert, 271.

7 Beaver, 312.

8 Helen Barrett Montgomery, *The King's Highway: A Study of Present Conditions on the Foreign Field* (West Medford, Mass.: Central Committee on the United Study of Foreign Missions, 1915).

9 Peabody, 126–28; Cattan, 65–67; Robert, 269–71.

10 Peabody, 128–33; Cattan, 67–76.

11 Robert, 270.

12 Freedman; see also Sklar, "Hull House in the 1890s."

13 Sklar, "Hull House in the 1890s," 659.

14 Cattan, 93.

15 Peabody, 133.

16 Solomon, 64.

17 Cattan, 93–101.

18 Beaver, 170.

19 Helen Barrett Montgomery, "A Look at the Mother-Half of the Race," *Missions* 11, no. 5 (1920): 260.

20 Montgomery, "A Look at the Mother-Half of the Race," 260.

21 Montgomery, "A Look at the Mother-Half of the Race," 260.

22 Montgomery, "A Look at the Mother-Half of the Race," 260.

23 Montgomery, "A Look at the Mother-Half of the Race," 260–61.

24 Montgomery, "A Look at the Mother-Half of the Race," 261.

25 Montgomery, "A Look at the Mother-Half of the Race," 260.

26 Montgomery, "A Look at the Mother-Half of the Race," 260.

27 Montgomery, "A Look at the Mother-Half of the Race," 260.

28 Montgomery, "A Look at the Mother-Half of the Race," 262.

29 Robert, 272–73.

30 Robert, 273.

31 Caroline Atwater Mason, *World Missions and World Peace: A Study of Christ's Conquest* (West Medford, Mass.: Central Committee on the United Study of Foreign Missions, 1916).

32 Robert, 276–77.

33 Helen Barrett Montgomery, *From Jerusalem to Jerusalem: "Fly Abroad, Thou Mighty Gospel"* (Cambridge, Mass.: The Central Committee on the United Study of Foreign Missions, 1929).

34 William Owen Carver, *Missions in the Plan of the Ages: Bible Studies in Missions* (New York: Revell, 1909); idem, *Missions and Modern Thought* (New York: Macmillan, 1910).

35 Montgomery, *From Jerusalem to Jerusalem*, 231.

36 Montgomery, *From Jerusalem to Jerusalem*, 13–15.

37 Montgomery, *From Jerusalem to Jerusalem*, 14, 9.

38 Robert, 282 n. 61.

39 Montgomery, *From Jerusalem to Jerusalem*, 103.

40 Hill, 181, 182.

41 Hill, 181.

42 Montgomery, *King's Highway*, 17.

43 Montgomery, *King's Highway*, 17.

44 Montgomery, *King's Highway*, 32–43.

45 Montgomery, *From Jerusalem to Jerusalem*, 38.

46 Montgomery, *From Jerusalem to Jerusalem*, 39, 40.

47 Montgomery, *From Jerusalem to Jerusalem*, 40–41.

48 Montgomery, *From Jerusalem to Jerusalem*, 41.

49 Montgomery, *From Jerusalem to Jerusalem*, 42. This was perhaps an acknowledgment of the critiques made against Christianity by Elizabeth Cady Stanton.

50 Montgomery, *From Jerusalem to Jerusalem*, 42.

51 Montgomery, *From Jerusalem to Jerusalem*, 130–35.

52 Montgomery, *From Jerusalem to Jerusalem*, 169.

53 Montgomery, *From Jerusalem to Jerusalem*, 183, 185.

54 Montgomery, *From Jerusalem to Jerusalem*, 186.

55 Montgomery, *From Jerusalem to Jerusalem*, 188–89.

56 Montgomery, *From Jerusalem to Jerusalem*, 190, 191.

57 Montgomery, *From Jerusalem to Jerusalem*, 191.

58 Montgomery, *From Jerusalem to Jerusalem*, 192.

59 Montgomery, *From Jerusalem to Jerusalem*, 192.

60 Montgomery, *From Jerusalem to Jerusalem*, 193.

61 Helen Barrett Montgomery, *Following the Sunrise: A Century of Baptist Missions, 1813–1913* (Philadelphia: American Baptist Publication Society, 1913).

62 Montgomery, *Following the Sunrise*, 3.

63 Montgomery, *Following the Sunrise*, 53.

64 Montgomery, *Following the Sunrise*, 38ff, 55ff, 76ff, 84-86, 108ff, 226ff, 253ff.

65 Montgomery, *Following the Sunrise*, 247.

66 Montgomery, *Following the Sunrise*, 254.

67 Montgomery, *Following the Sunrise*, 260.

Chapter 12

* A version of this chapter was published previously as "Helen Barrett Montgomery: A 'Middle-of-the-Road Baptist' Bible Translator," *Baptist History and Heritage* 42, no. 2 (2007): 55–68.

1 The wife of denominational leader and editor Curtis Lee Laws wrote a warm tribute to Montgomery after her death. See Laws. Curtis Lee Laws coined the term *fundamentalist* and was an early leader of the movement in the Northern Baptist Convention.

2 "Fundamentals Conference at Des Moines," *The Baptist* 2, no. 22 (2 July 1921): 684.

3 Helen Barrett Montgomery, Papers and Letters from the Family of Storrs B. Barrett, TMs [photocopy], Personal Collection, 53–54. Some explanation of this source is merited. Toward the end of my dissertation research, I obtained photocopies of some material discovered by Sharon Dowd, which was in the possession of the Storrs Barrett family. Apparently Storrs Barrett gathered material

for a biography of Helen Barrett Montgomery that was never completed. Many of the typewritten items were related to her work as president of the Northern Baptist Convention. I have arranged them chronologically. I do not know what ultimately became of the originals, although it was my understanding then that the American Baptist Historical Society was attempting to obtain them.

4   Papers and Letters, 54.

5   Papers and Letters, 54.

6   Papers and Letters, 57.

7   Papers and Letters, 58.

8   Papers and Letters, 59.

9   Papers and Letters, 61–62.

10 Papers and Letters, 65.

11 Papers and Letters, 66.

12 Papers and Letters, 60.

13 Papers and Letters, 60.

14 Papers and Letters, 71.

15 Papers and Letters, 72.

16 Papers and Letters, 72.

17 Helen Barrett Montgomery, "The Columbia Conference," *The Baptist* 3, no. 3 (18 February 1922): 79.

18 Papers and Letters, 62.

19 Papers and Letters, 62–63.

20 Papers and Letters, 62–63. Compare this explanation with Montgomery's later position, as revealed in her Centennial Translation of 1 Corinthians 14:33-40. See Sharyn Dowd, "The Ministry of Women in Montgomery's *Centenary New Testament*: The Evidence of the Autographs." *American Baptist Quarterly* 20, no. 3 (2001): 320–28.

21 Papers and Letters, 62–63.

22 Papers and Letters, 62–63.

23 Papers and Letters, 63–64. C.f. Gal 3:28 in the *Centenary Translation*.

24 Papers and Letters, 64.

25 Papers and Letters, 74.

26 Papers and Letters, 78–79 (italics in original).

27 Papers and Letters, 79.

28 Papers and Letters, 81.

29 Papers and Letters, 81.

30 Helen Barrett Montgomery, "The Tasks That Confront Us," *The Baptist* 3, no. 20 (17 June 1922): 625.

31 Arthur W. Cleaves, "The Northern Baptist Convention," *The Baptist* 3, no. 21 (24 June 1922): 676.

32 Papers and Letters, 91.

33 Cleaves, 676.

Chapter 13

1   CCLWC RG 90 4/66, Day Mission Collection, Yale University Divinity School Library, New Haven, Connecticut. Thanks to Dana L. Robert for sharing this document with me.

2   Montgomery, *Following the Sunrise*; idem, trans., *Centenary Translation of the New Testament* (Philadelphia: American Baptist Publication Society, 1924). Sharyn Dowd has done the best research on Montgomery's translation. See "Helen Barrett Montgomery's *Centenary Translation* of the New Testament: Characteristics and Influences," *Perspectives in Religious Studies* 19, no. 2 (1992): 133–50; Dowd, "Ministry of Women."

3   F. Townley Lord, in his history of the Baptist World Alliance, claimed that she was elected recording secretary of the Women's Meeting in Stockholm, but that is not confirmed by the published proceedings of the Congress. According to that record, Miss S. T. Weber of London was elected to that office. There is no indication in the published proceedings that Montgomery was elected to an office. See F. Townley Lord, *Baptist World Fellowship: A Short History of the Baptist World Alliance* (Nashville: Broadman Press, 1955), 49; cf. Whitley, 145.

4   *The Preaching Value of Missions* (Philadelphia: Judson Press, 1931).

5   Ann Douglas, *The Feminization of American Culture* (New York: Knopf, 1977).

6   *Bible and Missions*, 93.

BIBLIOGRAPHY

Archives

Ambrose Swasey Library, Colgate Rochester Crozer Divinity School, Rochester, N.Y.

American Baptist Historical Society Archives, Mercer University, Atlanta.

Day Mission Collection, Yale University Divinity School Library, New Haven, Conn.

Lake Avenue Baptist Church, Rochester, N.Y.

Local History, Central Library of Rochester and Monroe County, Rochester, N.Y.

Margaret Clapp Library, Wellesley College, Wellesley, Mass.

Rush Rhees Library, University of Rochester, Rochester, N.Y.

Newspapers

The New York Times
(Rochester, N.Y.) *Democrat and Chronicle*
(Rochester, N.Y.) *Evening Times*
(Rochester, N.Y.) *Herald*
(Rochester, N.Y.) *Post Express*
(Rochester, N.Y.) *Times-Union*
(Rochester, N.Y.) *Union and Advertiser*

Unpublished Works

Alling, Rose Lattimore. "Playmate." "Tributes" file. TMs. Montgomery Collection. American Baptist Historical Society Archives, Mercer University, Atlanta.

Barrett, Storrs B., to Mrs. Franklin W. Knope, 17 March 1937. TMs. "Correspondence: Storrs B. Barrett" file. Montgomery Collection. American Baptist Historical Society Archives, Mercer University, Atlanta.

Batts, Lewis H. "Doctorate on the History of Lake Ave. Baptist Church." 4 vols. Lake Avenue Baptist Church, Rochester, N.Y. This document (four scrapbooks) is made from what are apparently draft pages and other material related to Batts' Ph.D. dissertation, which he wrote at the Hartford Seminary Foundation in 1935.

Beaven, Albert W. "William A. Montgomery: A Tribute." TMs. [1930]. American Baptist Historical Society Archives, Mercer University, Atlanta.

Chester, Alice A. "Exhibits Outlining the History of the Lake Avenue Baptist Church, Rochester, New York, 1871–1933." TMs. Lake Avenue Baptist Church Archives, Rochester, N.Y.

Clark, Elizabeth Battelle. "The Politics of God and the Woman's Vote: Religion in the American Suffrage Movement, 1848–1895." Ph.D. diss., Princeton University, 1989.

Edwards, Wendy J. Deichmann. "Forging an Ideology for American Missions: Josiah Strong and Manifest Destiny." TMs [electronic copy]. 1998. Personal collection.

Fewster, Julie. "Helen Barrett Montgomery: A Disciple of Jesus Christ 1861–1934." TMs [photocopy]. 1981. Montgomery Collection. American Baptist Historical Society Archives, Mercer University, Atlanta.

Fey, Marion Harris. "Educational Reform in the Era of the 'New Woman': Helen Barrett Montgomery, 1861–1934." TMs [photocopy]. 1989. Personal collection.

Fishburn, Janet F. "The Social Gospel as Missionary Ideology." TMs [photocopy]. 1998. American Baptist Historical Society Archives, Mercer University, Atlanta.

Hodge, Katherine Talbot. "History of the Woman's Educational and Industrial Union, 1893–1943." TMs. Local History, Central Library of Rochester and Monroe County, Rochester, N.Y.

Huntington, Jeannette W. "Women's Educational and Industrial Union, 1893–1943." TMs. Local History, Central Library of Rochester and Monroe County, Rochester, N.Y.

"Interview with Mrs. Mary T. L. Gannett." TMs. "Biographical/ Autobiographical" file. Montgomery Collection. American Baptist Historical Society Archives, Mercer University, Atlanta.

Knope, Mrs. Franklin A., to Storrs B. Barrett, 8 February 1937. TMs. "Correspondence: Storrs B. Barrett" file. American Baptist Historical Society Archives, Mercer University, Atlanta.

Livingstone, Wilhermina C. "A Presentation on the Life of Helen Barrett Montgomery." TMs. 1955. Montgomery Collection. American Baptist Historical Society Archives, Mercer University, Atlanta.

Maniago, Jo Anne Parker. "The First Peace Corps: The Work of the American Teachers in the Philippines, 1900–1910." Ph.D. diss., Boston University, 1971.

Montgomery, Helen Barrett. "H.B.M.'s Diary." TMs. Montgomery Collection. American Baptist Historical Society Archives, Mercer University, Atlanta.

———. To the Editor of the Post-Express, 14 January 1909. Ms. Autograph Letter file. Local History, Central Library of Rochester and Monroe County, Rochester, N.Y.

———. To Louise McCoy North. Undated postcard. "North, Lousie McCoy" file. Margaret Clapp Library, Wellesley College, Wellesley, Mass.

———. To Miss Coolidge, 19 November 1915. TMs [photocopy]. Baptist Missionary Training School Bible Conversations, 1915–16. Ambrose Swasey Library, Colgate Rochester Crozer Divinity School, Rochester, N.Y.

———. To "My dear Professor Rauschenbusch." Ms. [1910]. Rauschenbusch Family Papers. Box 25. American Baptist Historical Society Archives, Mercer University, Atlanta.

———. To "My dears," 17 May 1894. Ms [photocopy]. Personal collection.

———. ["Tribute to W.A. Montgomery"]. TMs. [1930]. Montgomery Collection. American Baptist Historical Society Archives, Mercer University, Atlanta.

————. To Walter Rauschenbusch, 10 and 13 December 1910. Ms. Rauschenbusch Family Papers. Box 25. American Baptist Historical Society Archives, Mercer University, Atlanta.

Papers and Letters from the Family of Storrs Barrett. TMs [photocopy]. Personal collection.

Rauschenbusch, Walter. "Draft of the Report of the Committee on Public Schools." TMs with handwritten notes. [1908]. Rauschenbusch Family Papers. Box 49. American Baptist Historical Society Archives, Mercer University, Atlanta.

————. "Y.M.C.A. Report 1904." TMs. Rauschenbusch Family Papers. Box 49. American Baptist Historical Society Archives, Mercer University, Atlanta.

"Resolutions Adopted by the Convention of Women's Clubs at Syracuse." TMs. "Mrs. Montgomery In Her Home City" file. Montgomery Collection. American Baptist Historical Society Archives, Mercer University, Atlanta.

Skilton, John Hamilton. "The Translation of the New Testament into English 1881–1950: Studies in Language and Style." Ph.D. diss., University of Pennsylvania, 1961.

WEIU Scrapbook 1893–1896. WEIU Papers, Local History, Central Library of Rochester and Monroe County, Rochester, N.Y.

WEIU Scrapbook 1896–1901. WEIU Papers, Local History, Central Library of Rochester and Monroe County, Rochester, N.Y.

Published Works

Abbott, Conda Delite Hitch. *Envoy of Grace: The Life of Helen Barrett Montgomery.* Valley Forge, Pa.: American Baptist Historical Society, 1997.

Abrams, Laura S. "Guardians of Virtue: The Social Reformers and the 'Girl Problem,' 1890–1920." *Social Service Review* 74, no. 3 (2000): 436–52.

Ackerman, Carl W. *George Eastman.* With an introduction by Edwin R. A. Seligman. Boston: Houghton Mifflin, 1930.

Addams, Jane. *Democracy and Social Ethics.* Edited with an Introduction by Anne Firor Scott. 1907; reprint Cambridge, Mass.: Belknap Press, 1964.

Ahlstrom, Sydney E. *A Religious History of the American People.* New Haven: Yale University Press, 1972.

Aiken, John R. "Walter Rauschenbusch and Education for Reform." *Church History* 36, no. 4 (1967): 456–69.

Allen, C. Leonard, and Richard T. Hughes. *Illusions of Innocence: Protestant Primitivism in America, 1630–1875.* Chicago: University of Chicago Press, 1988.

Anthony, Katharine Susan. *Susan B. Anthony: Her Personal History and Her Era.* Garden City, N.Y.: Doubleday, 1954.

Askew, Thomas A. "The New York 1900 Ecumenical Missionary Conference: A Centennial Reflection." *International Bulletin of Missionary Research* 24, no. 4 (2000): 146–54.

Bailey, Thomas A., and David M. Kennedy. *The American Pageant: A History of the Republic.* 6th ed. Lexington, Mass.: D. C. Heath, 1979.

Barber, Clarence A. "An Appreciation of Henry Lomb." *American Journal of Public Health* 5, no. 11 (1915): 1120–23.

Barnes, Joseph W. "The City's Golden Age." *Rochester History* 35, no. 2 (1973).

———. "Rochester's City Halls." *Rochester History* 60, no. 2 (1978).

Barry, Kathleen. *Susan B. Anthony: A Biography of a Singular Feminist.* New York: Ballantine Books, 1988.

"The Bausch and Lomb Story." http://www.bausch.com/en_US/corporate/corpcomm/general/story.aspx. Accessed 26 October 2007.

Beaven, Albert W. "Helen of Rochester." In *Helen Barrett Montgomery: From Campus to World Citizenship,* 85–97. New York: Fleming H. Revell, 1940.

Beaver, R. Pierce. *All Loves Excelling: American Protestant Women in World Mission.* Grand Rapids: Eerdmans, 1968; reprint *American Protestant Women in World Mission: A History of the First Feminist Movement in North America.* Grand Rapids: Eerdmans, 1980.

Blair, Karen J. *The Clubwoman as Feminist: True Womanhood Redefined, 1868–1914.* New York: Holmes & Meier, 1980.

Blevins, Carolyn DeArmond. "Women in Baptist History." *Review and Expositor* 83, no. 1 (1986): 51–61.

Bodein, Vernon Parker. *The Social Gospel of Walter Rauschenbusch and Its Relation to Religious Education.* New Haven: Yale University Press, 1944.

Bowden, Henry Warner. "Perplexity over a Protean Principle: A Response."

In *The American Quest for the Primitive Church,* edited by Richard T. Hughes, 171–78. Urbana: University of Illinois Press, 1988.

Brackney, William H. *The Baptists.* New York: Greenwood Press, 1988.

———. "Helen Barrett Montgomery 1861–1934, Lucy W. Peabody 1861–1949: Jesus Christ, the Great Emancipator of Women." In *Mission Legacies,* edited by Gerald H. Anderson et al., 62–70. Maryknoll, N.Y.: Orbis, 1994.

Braude, Ann. *Radical Spirits: Spiritualism and Women's Rights in Nineteenth-Century America.* Boston: Beacon Press, 1989.

———. "Women's History *Is* American Religious History." In *Retelling U.S. Religious History,* edited by Thomas A. Tweed, 87–107. Berkeley: University of California Press, 1997.

Brayer, Elizabeth. "George Eastman." *Rochester History* 52, no. 1 (1990).

———. *George Eastman: A Biography.* Rochester, N.Y.: University of Rochester Press, 2006.

Breisach, Ernst. *Historiography: Ancient, Medieval, and Modern.* Chicago: University of Chicago Press, 1983.

Browne, Benjamin P. *Tales of Baptist Daring.* Philadelphia: Judson Press, 1961.

Buhle, Mary Jo, and Paul Buhle, eds. *The Concise History of Woman Suffrage: Selections from the Classic Work of Stanton, Anthony, Gage, and Harper.* Urbana: University of Illinois Press, 1978.

Bullard, Roger A. "Feminine and Feminist Touches in the Centenary New Testament." *The Bible Translator* 38, no. 1 (1987): 118–22.

Bunyan, John. *Grace Abounding to the Chief of Sinners.* Edited by Roger Sharrock. Oxford: Clarendon, 1962.

Bushnell, Horace. *Christian Nurture.* New Haven: Yale University Press, 1916.

Butler, J. Donald. *Four Philosophies and Their Practice in Education and Religion.* 3rd ed. New York: Harper & Row, 1968.

Butler, Joseph. *The Analogy of Religion, Natural and Revealed, to the Constitution and Course of Nature.* Preface by Samuel Halifax. London: H. G. Bohn, 1860.

Carroll, Clarence F. "Superintendent's Report" [1907]. *The Fifty-Fourth Report of the Board of Education of the City of Rochester, New York, for the Years 1905, 1906, 1907.* Rochester, N.Y.: Board of Education.

———. "Superintendent's Report" [1909]. *The Fifty-Fifth Report of the Board of Education of the City of Rochester, New York, for the Years 1908, 1909, 1910.* Rochester, N.Y.: Board of Education.

Carroll, J. M. *The Trail of Blood.* Lexington, Ky.: Ashland Avenue Baptist Church, 1931.

Carver, William Owen. *Missions and Modern Thought.* New York: Macmillan, 1910.

———. *Missions in the Plan of the Ages: Bible Studies in Missions.* New York: Revell, 1909.

Cattan, Louise A. *Lamps Are for Lighting: The Story of Helen Barrett Montgomery and Lucy Waterbury Peabody.* Grand Rapids: Eerdmans, 1972.

Citations by President William Herbert Perry Faunce for Honorary Degrees Granted by Brown University MDCCCC–MCCCCCXIV. Boston: D. B. Updike, Merrymount Press, n.d.

Claflin, Tennie C. "Constitutional Equality a Right of Woman." In *Up from the Pedestal: Selected Writings in the History of American Feminism*, edited by Aileen Kraditor, 131–35. Chicago: Quadrangle Books, 1968.

Converse, Florence. *Wellesley College: A Chronicle of the Years 1875–1938.* Wellesley, Mass.: Hathaway House Bookshop, 1939.

Cott, Nancy F. *The Bonds of Womanhood: "Woman's Sphere" in New England, 1780–1835.* New Haven: Yale University Press, 1977.

———. *The Grounding of Modern Feminism.* New Haven: Yale University Press, 1987.

Cremin, Lawrence A. *American Education: The Metropolitan Experience, 1876–1980.* New York: Harper & Row, 1988.

Cronise, Adelbert. "The Beginnings of Modern Spiritualism In and Near Rochester." In *The Rochester Historical Society Publication Fund Series.* Vol. 5, edited by Edward R. Forman, 1–22. Rochester, N.Y.: Historical Society, 1926.

Cross, Whitney R. *The Burned-Over District: The Social and Intellectual History of Enthusiastic Religion in Western New York, 1800–1850.* Ithaca: Cornell University Press, 1950.

Danbom, David B. *The World of Hope: Progressives and the Struggle for an Ethical Public Life.* Philadelphia: Temple University Press, 1987.

Decennial Year Book. Rochester, N.Y.: Women's Education and Industrial Union, 1903.

Deutsch, Sarah. *Women and the City: Gender, Space, and Power in Boston, 1870–1940.* New York: Oxford University Press, 2000.

Dewey, John. *Democracy and Education.* New York: Macmillan, 1916.

Dilthey, Wilhelm. *Pattern and Meaning in History, Thoughts on Meaning and Society.* Edited with introduction by H. P. Rickman. New York: Harper & Brothers, 1961.

Diner, Steven J. *A Very Different Age: Americans of the Progressive Era.* New York: Hill & Wang, 1998.

Dorr, Rheta Childe. *Susan B. Anthony, the Woman Who Changed the Mind of a Nation.* New York: Frederick A. Stokes, 1928.

Douglas, Ann. *The Feminization of American Culture.* New York: Knopf, 1977.

Dow, Harriet Brown. "Influence of Women in the Life of Rochester." *Centennial History of Rochester, New York.* Vol. 2, *Home Builders,* edited by Edward R. Foreman, 189–207. Rochester Historical Society Publication Fund Series 11. Rochester, N.Y.: Historical Society, 1932.

Dowd, Sharyn. "Helen Barrett Montgomery's *Centenary Translation* of the New Testament: Characteristics and Influences." *Perspectives in Religious Studies* 19, no. 2 (1992): 133–50.

———. "The Ministry of Women in Montgomery's *Centenary New Testament:* The Evidence of the Autographs." *American Baptist Quarterly* 20, no. 3 (2001): 320–28.

DuCharme, Catherine C. "Lucy Wheelock: Her Life and Work." *Childhood Education* 76, no. 3 (2000): 164–69.

Durkheim, Emile. *The Rules of Sociological Method.* 8th ed. Trans. Sarah A. Solovay and John H. Mueller. Edited by George E. G. Catlin. Glencoe, Ill.: Free Press, 1938.

Ecumenical Conference on Foreign Missions, Ecumenical Missionary Conference, New York, 1900. 2 vols. New York: American Tract Society, [1900].

Edwards, Wendy J. Deichmann, and Carolyn DeSwarte Gifford, eds. *Gender and the Social Gospel.* Urbana: University of Illinois Press, 2003.

Eisenach, Eldon J. *The Lost Promise of Progressivism.* Lawrence: University Press of Kansas, 1994.

Eisenhart, M. Herbert. *J. J. Bausch (1830–1926): American Pioneer.* New York: Newcomen Society, American Branch, 1948.

Ekirch, Arthur A., Jr. *Progressivism in America: A Study of the Era from Theodore Roosevelt to Woodrow Wilson.* New York: New Viewpoints, 1974.

Epstein, Barbara Leslie. *The Politics of Domesticity: Women Evangelism, and Temperance in Nineteenth-Century America.* Middletown, Conn.: Wesleyan University Press, 1981.

Evans, Christopher H. "Gender and the Kingdom of God: The Family Values of Walter Rauschenbusch." In *The Social Gospel Today,* 53–66. Louisville, Ky: Westminster John Knox, 2001.

————. *The Kingdom Is Always but Coming: A Life of Walter Rauschenbusch.* Grand Rapids: Eerdmans, 2004.

Eyestone, June E. "The Influence of Swedish Sloyd and Its Interpreters on American Art Education." *Studies in Art Education* 34, no. 1 (1992): 28–37.

Federation of Woman's Boards of Foreign Missions of North America. "Historical Sketch 1900–1921." Sixteenth Interdenominational Conference, January 14 and 15, 1921. New York: 1921.

"The First Wellesley Announcement, December, 1874." Reprint Wellesley Department of Education, 1934.

Fishburn, Janet Forsythe. *The Fatherhood of God and the Victorian Family: The Social Gospel in America.* Philadelphia: Fortress, 1981.

Flexner, Eleanor. *Century of Struggle: The Woman's Rights Movement in the United States.* Cambridge: Harvard University Press, 1975.

Forty-Fifth Annual Catalogue of the University of Rochester 1894–95. Rochester, N.Y.: University of Rochester.

Frank, Meryl, and Blake McKelvey. "Some Former Rochesterians of National Distinction." *Rochester History* 21, no. 3 (1959).

Freedman, Estelle. "Separatism as Strategy: Female Institution Building and American Feminism, 1870–1930." *Feminist Studies* 5, no. 3 (1979): 512–29.

Garrett, Shirley S. "Sisters All. Feminism and the American Women's Missionary Movement." In *Missionary Ideologies in the Imperialist Era: 1880–1920,* edited Torben Christensen and William R. Hutchison, 221–30. Cambridge, Mass.: Harvard Theological Review, 1982.

Geertz, Clifford. *The Interpretation of Cultures.* New York: Basic Books, 1973.

Gibson, Charles, ed. *The Black Legend: Anti-Spanish Attitudes in the Old World and the New.* Introduction by Charles Gibson. New York: Knopf, 1971.

Ginzberg, Lori D. *Women and the Work of Benevolence: Morality, Politics, and Class in the Nineteenth-Century United States.* New Haven: Yale University Press, 1990.

Gordon, Lynn D. *Gender and Higher Education in the Progressive Era.* New Haven: Yale University Press, 1990.

Green, Jesse, ed. *Cushing at Zuñi: The Correspondence and Journals of Frank Hamilton Cushing, 1879–1884.* Albuquerque: University of New Mexico Press, 1990.

Greene, Dana, ed. *Suffrage and Religious Principle: Speeches and Writings of Olympia Brown.* Metuchen, N.J.: Scarecrow Press, 1983.

Greenfeld, Liah. *Nationalism: Five Roads to Modernity.* Cambridge, Mass.: Harvard University Press, 1992.

Hall, H. Duncan. *Mandates, Dependencies and Trusteeship.* Washington, D.C.: Carnegie Endowment for International Peace, 1948.

Handy, Robert T. "Biblical Primitivism in the American Baptist Tradition." In *The American Quest for the Primitive Church,* edited by Richard T. Hughes, 143–52. Urbana: University of Illinois Press, 1988.

Hardesty, Nancy A. *Women Called to Witness: Evangelical Feminism in the Nineteenth Century.* Nashville: Abingdon, 1984.

Harper, Ida Husted. *The Life and Work of Susan B. Anthony.* 3 vols. Indianapolis: Hollenbeck Press, 1898–1908.

Hawley, Natalie F. "Literature in Rochester, 1865–1905." *Rochester History* 10, no. 1 (1948).

Haynes, Carolyn Alice. "Women and Protestantism in Nineteenth-Century America." In *Perspectives on American Religion and Culture,* edited by Peter W. Williams, 300–318. Oxford: Blackwell, 1999.

Hewett, Furman T. "Mining the Baptist Tradition for Christian Ethics: Some Gems." *Perspectives in Religious Studies* 25, no. 1 (1998): 63–78.

Hewitt, Nancy A. *Women's Activism and Social Change: Rochester, New York, 1822–1872.* Ithaca: Cornell University Press, 1984.

Hill, Patricia R. *The World Their Household: the American Woman's Foreign Mission Movement and Cultural Transformation, 1870–1920.* Women and Culture Series. Ann Arbor: University of Michigan Press, 1985.

Hoadley, Frank T., and Benjamin P. Browne. *Baptists Who Dared.* Valley Forge, Pa.: Judson Press, 1980.

Hofstadter, Richard. *Social Darwinism in American Thought.* Rev. ed. Boston: Beacon Press, 1955.

Housley, Kathleen. "'The Letter Kills but the Spirit Gives Life': Julia Smith's Translation of the Bible." *The New England Quarterly* 61 (1988): 555–68.

Hudson, Winthrop S. "Montgomery, Helen Barrett." In *Notable American Women 1607–1950.* Vol. 2, edited by Edward T. James, 566–68. Cambridge: Belknap Press, 1971.

———. "Protestant Clergy Debate the Nation's Vocation, 1898–1899." *Church History* 42, no. 1 (1973): 110–18.

Hughes, Richard T., ed. *The American Quest for the Primitive Church.* Urbana: University of Illinois Press, 1988.

———. *The Primitive Church in the Modern World.* Urbana: University of Illinois Press, 1995.

Jaehn, Klaus Juergen. *Rauschenbusch: The Formative Years.* Valley Forge, Pa.: Judson Press, 1976.

James, William. *Talks to Teachers on Psychology: And to Students on Some of Life's Ideals.* New York: Henry Holt, 1915.

Jessup, Phillip C. *Elihu Root.* Vol. 1, *1845–1909.* New York: Dodd, Mead, 1938.

Kagan, Richard L. "Prescott's Paradigm: American Historical Scholarship and the Decline of Spain." *American Historical Review* 101, no. 2 (1996): 423–46.

Kendrick, Eliza Hall. *History of Bible Teaching at Wellesley College, 1875–1950.* Wellesley, Mass.: n.p. 1950.

Kraditor, Aileen S. *The Ideas of the Woman Suffrage Movement, 1890–1920.* New York: W. W. Norton, 1981.

———, ed. *Up from the Pedestal: Selected Writings in the History of American Feminism.* Chicago: Quadrangle Books, 1968.

Lane, James B. *Jacob A. Riis and the American City.* Port Washington, N.Y.: National University Publications/Kennikat Press, 1974.

Las Casas, Bartolomé de. *The Devastation of the Indies: A Brief Account.* Translated by Herma Briffault. Introduction by Hans Magnus Enzenberger. New York: Seabury Press, 1974.

Laws, Mrs. Curtis Lee. "Her Baptist World." In *Helen Barrett Mongtomery: From Campus to World Citizenship*, 98–113. New York: Revell, 1940.

Link, Arthur S., and Richard L. McCormick. *Progressivism*. American History Series. Edited by John Hope Franklin. Arlington Heights, Ill.: Harlan Davidson, 1983.

Livingstone, Wilhermina C. "Helen Barrett Montgomery." Pamphlet. American Baptist Historical Society Archives, Mercer University, Atlanta.

Logan, Frederick M. *Growth of Art in American Schools*. New York: Harper & Row, 1955.

Lord, F. Townley. *Baptist World Fellowship: A Short History of the Baptist World Alliance*.

Lowrie, Rachel. *The Story of the Jubilee: An Account of the Celebration of the Fiftieth Anniversary of the Beginning in the United States of Woman's Organized Work for Foreign Missions 1860–1910*. West Medford, Mass.: Central Committee on the United Study of Missions, 1911.

Lutz, Alma. *Susan B. Anthony: Rebel, Crusader, Humanitarian*. Boston: Beacon Books, 1959.

Malone, Dumas, ed. *Dictionary of American Biography*. Vol. 9. New York: Charles Scribner's Sons, 1946. S.v. "Huntington, Frederic Dan."

Marsden, George M. *Fundamentalism and American Culture: The Shaping of Twentieth-Century Evangelicalism, 1870–1925*. New York: Oxford University Press, 1980.

———. *The Soul of the American University: From Protestant Establishment to Established Nonbelief*. New York: Oxford University Press, 1994.

Mason, Caroline Atwater. *World Missions and World Peace: A Study of Christ's Conquest*. West Medford, Mass.: Central Committee on the United Study of Foreign Missions, 1916.

Mattson, Kevin. *Creating a Democratic Public: The Struggle for Urban Participatory Democracy during the Progressive Era*. University Park: The Pennsylvania State University Press, 1998.

McClellan, Robert F. "Missionary Influence on American Attitudes toward China at the Turn of This Century." *Church History* 38, no. 4 (1969): 475–85.

McKelvey, Blake. "The Germans of Rochester: Their Traditions and Contributions." *Rochester History* 20, no. 1 (1958).

———. "Historic Origins of Rochester's Social Welfare Agencies." *Rochester History* 9, nos. 2–3 (1947).

———. "An Historical View of Rochester's Parks and Playgrounds." *Rochester History* 11, no. 1 (1949).

———. "The Irish in Rochester: An Historical Perspective." *Rochester History* 19, no. 4 (1957).

———. "The Italians of Rochester: An Historical Review." *Rochester History* 22, no. 4 (1960).

———. "A Panoramic Review of Rochester's History." *Rochester History* 11, no. 2 (1949).

———. "The Population of Rochester." *Rochester History* 12, no. 4 (1950).

———. "Rochester at the Turn of the Century." *Rochester History* 12, no. 1 (1950).

———. "Rochester Fifty Years Ago." *Rochester History* 3, no. 3 (1941).

———. *Rochester: The Quest for Quality, 1890–1925.* Cambridge, Mass.: Harvard University Press, 1956.

———. "Rochester's Ethnic Transformations." *Rochester History* 25, no. 3 (1963).

———. "Rochester's Literary and Book Clubs." *Rochester History* 48, nos. 1–2 (1986).

———. "Rochester's Public Schools: A Testing Ground for Community Policies." *Rochester History* 31, no. 2 (1969).

———. "Samuel Parker Moulthrop: Devoted Educator and Good Citizen." *Rochester History* 19, no. 2 (1957).

———. "Susan B. Anthony." *Rochester History* 7, no. 2 (1945).

———. "Walter Rauschenbusch's Rochester." *Rochester History* 14, no. 4 (1952).

———. "Woman's Rights in Rochester, A Century of Progress." *Rochester History* 10, nos. 2–3 (1948).

McNamara, Robert F. *The Diocese of Rochester in America, 1868–1993.* With a Foreword by Fulton J. Sheen. Rochester, N.Y.: Roman Catholic Diocese of Rochester, 1998.

———. "Ecumenism and the Rochester Center for Theological Studies." *Rochester History* 52, no. 4 (1990).

Memorial Exercises of the Alumnae Association Held at Livingston Park

316 / Helen Barrett Montgomery

Seminary, Rochester, New York, on Thursday, June Ninth, 1892. Rochester, N.Y.: Post-Express Printing, 1892.

Milkis, Sidney M., and Jerome M. Mileur, eds. *Progressivism and the New Democracy.* Amherst: University of Massachusetts Press, 1999.

Minus, Paul M. *Walter Rauschenbusch: American Reformer.* New York: Macmillan, 1988.

Mobley, Kendal P. "The Ecumenical Woman's Missionary Movement: Helen Barrett Montgomery and *The Baptist*, 1920–1930." In *Gender and the Social Gospel*, edited by Wendy J. Deichmann Edwards and Carolyn DeSwarte Gifford, 167–81. Urbana: University of Illinois Press, 2003.

———. "Helen Barrett Montgomery: A 'Middle-of-the-Road Baptist' Bible Translator." *Baptist History and Heritage* 42, no. 2 (2007): 55–68.

———. "Susan B. Anthony and Helen Barrett Montgomery: An Inter-generational Feminist Partnership." *Baptist History and Heritage* 40, no. 3 (2005): 80–90.

Moehlman, Conrad H. "Mrs. Montgomery's Translation of the Gospels." *Watchman-Examiner* (26 June 1924), 809.

Monroe Baptist Association Minutes. American Baptist Historical Society Archives, Mercer University, Atlanta.

Montgomery, Helen Barrett. "Alice Freeman Palmer." *Wellesley Magazine* 11, no. 4 (1 February 1903): 146–49.

———. *The Bible and Missions.* West Medford, Mass.: Central Committee on the United Study of Foreign Missions, 1920.

———. "A Book That Rome Suppressed." *The Baptist* 1, no. 21 (19 June 1920), 735.

———. *Christus Redemptor: An Outline Study of the Island World of the Pacific.* Rev. ed. New York: Macmillan, 1909.

———. "The Columbia Conference." *The Baptist* 3, no. 3 (18 February 1922): 79.

———. "Equal Suffrage." *Harper's Bazaar* 27, no. 18 (5 May 1894): 354–55.

———. *Following the Sunrise: A Century of Baptist Missions, 1813–1913.* Philadelphia: American Baptist Publication Society, 1913.

———. *From Jerusalem to Jerusalem: "Fly Abroad, Thou Mighty Gospel."* Cambridge, Mass.: The Central Committee on the United Study of Foreign Missions, 1929.

———. "If a Man Die, Shall He Live?" *The Baptist* 1, no. 1 (31 January 1920): 14, 16.

———. "In Memoriam: A. Judson Barrett." Rochester, N.Y. Privately Printed. [1889].

———. "Her Own Story." In *Helen Barrett Montgomery: From Campus to World Citizenship*, 17–82. New York: Revell, 1940.

———. *The King's Highway: A Study of Present Conditions on the Foreign Field*. West Medford, Mass.: Central Committee on the United Study of Foreign Missions, 1915.

———. "The Last Ten Years of the Rochester Schools." *The Common Good* 5, no. 1 (October 1911): 5–11.

———. "A Look at the Mother-Half of the Race." *Missions* 11, no. 5 (1920).

———. "New Opportunity for Baptist Women." *Baptist* 4, no. 30 (25 August 1923): 944–45.

———. *Prayer and Missions*. West Medford, Mass.: Central Committee on the United Study of Foreign Missions, 1924.

———. *The Preaching Value of Missions*. Philadelphia: Judson Press, 1931.

———. "The Tasks That Confront Us." *Baptist* 3, no. 20 (17 June 1922): 625.

———. "Two Recent Books I Have Found Helpful." *Baptist* 5, no. 16 (17 May 1924): 378-79.

———. *Western Women in Eastern Lands: An Outline Study of Fifty Years of Women's Work in Foreign Missions*. New York: Macmillan, 1910.

———, trans. *Centenary Translation of the New Testament*. Philadelphia: American Baptist Publication Society, 1924.

"Montgomery, Helen Barrett." *Who Was Who in America*. Vol. 1. Chicago: A. N. Marquis, 1943.

Moorhead, James H. "Engineering the Millennium: Kingdom Building in American Protestantism, 1880–1920." *Princeton Seminary Bulletin*, Suppl., no. 3 (1994): 104–28.

Muncy, Robyn. *Creating a Female Dominion in American Reform, 1890–1935*. New York: Oxford University Press, 1991.

Murphy, Russell D. "The Mayoralty and the Democratic Creed: The Evolution of an Ideology and an Institution." *Urban Affairs Quarterly* 22, no. 1 (1986): 3–23.

Omanson, Roger L. "Bible Translation: Baptist Contributions to Understanding God's Word." *Baptist History and Heritage* 31, no. 1 (1996): 12–22.

Paley, William. *Natural Theology: or, Evidences of the Existence and Attributes of the Deity, Collected from the Appearances of Nature*, 1802; reprint, Houston: St. Thomas Press, 1972.

Palmieri, Patricia Ann. *In Adamless Eden: The Community of Women Faculty at Wellesley.* New Haven: Yale University Press, 1995.

Parkman, Francis. *Some of the Reasons Against Woman Suffrage.* Boston: Massachusetts Man Suffrage Association, [1894].

Peabody, Lucy W. "Widening Horizons." In *Helen Barrett Montgomery: From Campus to World Citizenship,* 114–35. New York: Fleming H. Revell, 1940.

Pease, William H. "The Gannetts of Rochester: Highlights in a Liberal Career 1889–1923." *Rochester History* 17, no. 4 (1955).

Peck, William F. *History of Rochester and Monroe County New York from the Earliest Times to the Beginning of 1907.* Vol. 2. New York: Pioneer Publishing, 1908.

Powell, Phillip Wayne. *Tree of Hate: Propaganda and Prejudices Affecting United States Relations with the Hispanic World.* Vallecito, Calif.: Ross House Books, 1985.

Pratt, Julius W. "Manifest Destiny and the American Century." *Current History* 29, no. 172 (1955): 331–36.

Proceedings, Board of Education, City of Rochester. Rochester, N.Y., 1900–1910.

Putney, Clifford. *Muscular Christianity: Manhood and Sports in Protestant America, 1880–1920.* Cambridge, Mass.: Harvard University Press, 2001.

P. W. W. "About this Book." In *Helen Barrett Montgomery: From Campus to World Citizenship,* 9–14. New York: Fleming H. Revell, 1940.

Quandt, Jean B. "Religion and Social Thought: The Secularization of Postmillennialism." *American Quarterly* 24, no. 4 (1973): 390–409.

Rauschenbusch, Walter. *Christianizing the Social Order.* New York: Macmillan, 1912.

Reese, William J. *Power and the Promise of School Reform: Grassroots Movements during the Progressive Era.* Boston: Routledge & Kegan Paul, 1986.

Reuther, Rosemary Radford, and Rosemary Skinner Keller. *Woman and Religion in America.* Vol. 3, *1900–1968.* San Francisco: Harper & Row, 1986.

Reynolds, David S. "The Feminization Controversy: Sexual Stereotypes and the Paradoxes of Piety in Nineteenth-Century America." *New England Quarterly* 53, no. 1 (1980): 96–106.

Riley, Glenda. *Inventing the American Woman: A Perspective on Women's History 1865 to the Present.* Arlington Heights, Ill.: Harlan Davidson, 1986.

Riis, Jacob A. *The Battle with the Slum.* New York: Macmillan, 1902.

———. *The Children of the Poor.* New York: Charles Scribner's Sons, 1902.

———. *How the Other Half Lives: Studies among the Tenements of New York.* New York: Charles Scribner's Sons, 1890.

———. *The Making of an American.* New York: Macmillan, 1916.

———. *Theodore Roosevelt, the Citizen.* New York: Outlook, 1904.

Robert, Dana L. *American Women in Mission: A Social History of Their Thought and Practice.* Macon, Ga.: Mercer University Press, 1997.

Robertson, A. T. Review of *Centenary Translation of the New Testament. Acts–Revelation,* by Helen Barrett Montgomery. *Review and Expositor* 22, no. 2 (1925): 245–46.

———. Review of *Centenary Translation of the New Testament. The Gospels,* by Helen Barrett Montgomery. *Review and Expositor* 21, no. 3 (1924): 342.

Robertson, Darrel M. "The Feminization of American Religion: An Examination of Recent Interpretations of Women and Religion in Victorian America." *Christian Scholar's Review* 8, no. 3 (1978): 238–46.

Rochester Theological Seminary. *General Catalog 1850–1920.* Rochester: E. R. Andrews, 1920.

Rosenberg, Rosalind. *Beyond Separate Spheres: Intellectual Roots of Modern Feminism.* New Haven: Yale University Press, 1982.

Rosenberger, Jesse Leonard. *Rochester: The Making of a University.* Introduction by Rush Rhees. Rochester, N.Y.: University of Rochester, 1927.

Ross, Elizabeth D. "Wheelock, Lucy." In *Dictionary of American Biography Supplement Four 1946–1950,* edited by John A. Garraty and Edward T. James, 874–75. New York: Charles Scribner's Sons, 1974.

Rothman, Sheila M. *Woman's Proper Place: A History of Changing Ideas and Practices, 1870 to the Present.* New York: Basic Books, 1978.

Rynbrandt, Linda J. "The 'Ladies of the Club' and Caroline Bartlett Crane: Affiliation and Alienation in Progressive Social Reform." *Gender and Society* 11, no. 2 (1997): 200–214.

"Sage, Russell." "About Us." About the Foundation, Russell Sage Foundation, www.russellsage.org/about/about_us.htm. Accessed 6 April 2003.

———. *The Columbia Encyclopedia.* 6th ed. New York: Columbia University Press, 2002, www.bartleby.com/65/. Accessed 6 April 2003.

Shapiro, Michael Steven. *Child's Garden: The Kindergarten Movement from Froebel to Dewey.* University Park: Pennsylvania State University Press, 1983.

Sharpe, Dores Robinson. *Walter Rauschenbusch.* New York: Macmillan, 1942.

Sklar, Kathryn Kish. *Catharine Beecher: A Study in American Domesticity.* New Haven: Yale University Press, 1973.

———. "Hull House in the 1890s: A Community of Women Reformers." *Signs: Journal of Women in Culture and Society* 10, no. 4 (1985): 658–77.

Smith, Harold S. "J. R. Graves." In *Baptist Theologians,* edited by Timothy George and David S. Dockery, 223–48. Nashville: Broadman Press, 1990.

Smith, Timothy L. *Revivalism and Social Reform: American Protestantism on the Eve of the Civil War.* Baltimore: The Johns Hopkins University Press, 1980.

Solomon, Barbara Miller. *In the Company of Educated Women: A History of Women and Higher Education in America.* New Haven: Yale University Press, 1985.

Stanton, Elizabeth Cady. *Eighty Years and More: Reminiscences, 1815–1897.* Introduction by Gail Parker. New York: Schocken Books, 1971.

Stanton, Elizabeth Cady, and Susan B. Anthony. *The Papers of Elizabeth Cady Stanton and Susan B. Anthony* [microform]. Edited by Patricia G. Holland and Ann D. Gordon. Wilmington, Del.: Scholarly Resources, 1991.

Stanton, Elizabeth Cady, Susan B. Anthony, Matilda Joslyn Gage, and Ida

Husted Harper, eds. *History of Woman Suffrage.* 6 vols. New York: Fowler & Wells, 1881–1922.

Starring, Charles F. "Crane, Caroline Julia Bartlett." In *Notable American Women 1607–1950.* Vol. 1, edited by Edward T. James, Janet Wilson James, and Paul T. Boyer, 401–2. Cambridge, Mass.: Belknap Press, 1971.

Stern, Madeleine B. "The First Feminist Bible: The 'Alderney' Edition, 1876." *Quarterly Journal of the Library of Congress* 34, no. 1 (1977): 23–31.

Stewart, Frank Mann. *A Half Century of Municipal Reform: The History of the National Municipal League.* Berkeley and Los Angeles: University of California Press, 1950.

The Story of Sixty Years, 1858–1918: Livingston Park Seminary, Rochester, N.Y. Rochester, Privately printed, [1918].

Tocqueville, Alexis de. *Democracy in America.* Vol. 1. With an Introduction by John Stuart Mill. New York: Schocken Books, 1961.

———. *The Old Regime and the French Revolution.* Translated by Stuart Gilbert. Garden City, N.Y.: Doubleday, 1955.

Toussaint, Charmian Edwards. *The Trusteeship System of the United Nations.* New York: Frederick A. Praeger, 1956.

Tucker, Ruth. "Female Mission Strategists: A Historical and Contemporary Perspective." *Missiology* 15, no. 1 (1987): 73–89.

———. *Guardians of the Great Commission: The Story of Women in Modern Missions.* Grand Rapids: Zondervan, Academie Books, 1988.

Van Voris, Jacqueline. *Carrie Chapman Catt: A Public Life.* New York: Feminist Press, 1987.

Vaughan, Christopher A. "The 'Discovery' of the Philippines by the U.S. Press, 1898–1902." *Historian* 57, no. 2 (1995): 303–14.

Vedder, Henry C. "Mrs. Montgomery's New Testament." *The Baptist* 6, no. 10 (11 April 1925): 312.

Verbrugge, Martha H. *Able-Bodied Womanhood: Personal Health and Social Change in Nineteenth-Century Boston.* New York: Oxford University Press, 1988.

"Ward, Edward Joshua," *Who Was Who in America.* Vol. 2. Chicago: A. N. Marquis, 1950.

Wayland, Francis. *The Elements of Moral Science.* Revised. Boston: Gould and Lincoln, 1865.

Weber, Evelyn. *The Kindergarten: Its Encounter with Educational Thought in America*. New York: Teachers College Press, 1969.

Weber, Max. *Economy and Society: An Outline of Interpretive Sociology*. Edited by Guenther Roth and Claus Wittich. Berkeley: University of California Press, 1978.

Weet, Herbert S. "The Development of Public Education in Rochester 1900–1910." In *The History of Education in Rochester. Selected Articles on Rochester History*. The Rochester Historical Society Publications 17. Edited by Blake McKelvey. Compiled by Dexter Perkins. 183–232. Rochester, N.Y.: Historical Society, 1939.

Wein, Roberta. "Women's Colleges and Domesticity, 1875, 1918." *History of Education Quarterly* 14, no. 1 (1974): 31–47.

"Wellesley College Calendar, 1879–1880." Wellesley College Archives.

Welter, Barbara. *Dimity Convictions: The American Woman in the Nineteenth Century*. Athens: Ohio University Press, 1976.

Whitley, W. T. *Third Baptist World Congress: Stockholm, July 21–27, 1923, Record of Proceedings*. Introduction by J. H. Shakespeare. London: Kingsgate, 1923.

Whitsitt, William Heth. *A Question in Baptist History*. Louisville, Ky.: Charles T. Dearing, 1896.

Wiebe, Robert H. *The Search for Order, 1887–1920*. New York: Hill & Wang, 1967.

Wilkinson, Patrick. "The Selfless and the Helpless: Maternalist Origins of the U.S. Welfare State." *Feminist Studies* 25, no. 3 (1999): 571–97.

"Year 1933." History of IBM Exhibit, IBM Archives. www-1.ibm.com/ibm/history/history/year_1933.html. Accessed 4 April 2002.

Year Book of the Woman's Educational and Industrial Union, Rochester, N.Y., 1896–1897 [1897]. WEIU Paper, Local History. Rochester Public Library.

Index of Personal Names

Abbott, Lyman, 29–31, 34, 95
Abrams, Laura S., 132
Adams, Floyd H., 251
Addams, Jane, 49
Adler, Isaac, 52, 180
Ahlstrom, Sydney, 92
Aitchison, J. Y., 250
Aiken, John R., 168, 289n48
Alcott, Amos Bronson, 137
Aldridge, George, 123, 142, 179–80, 199–200
Alling, Joseph T., 112, 114–15,
Alling, Rose Lattimore (Mrs. Joseph T.), 77, 107, 112, 137, 185
Anthony, Daniel, 102
Anthony, Mary S., 67, 78, 107
Anthony, Susan B., 8, 81, 97; career summary, 102–3; and coeducation at the University of Rochester, 110–11, 125–27; death of, 126; and Hackett House, 185; and liberal feminism, 74; memorial, 126–27; and Montgomery, 9–10, 101–27, 261; and the WEIU, 103–5; and YWCA, 107–10

Apollos (of the NT), 238
Aquilla (of the NT), 238
Askew, Thomas A., 203–5

Batchelder, U. R., 249
Barbour, Clarence A., 63, 64, 66, 115, 116
Barrett, Amos Judson, 2, 14–16, 58
Barrett, Anne Louise, 15, 37, 40
Barrett, Emily B. Barrows (Mrs. Amos Judson), 12, 14–15, 40, 79
Barrett, Storrs Barrows, 15, 64, 299n3
Bausch, Edward, 105
Bausch, Matilda G. Morell (Mrs. Edward), 105
Bausch, John Jacob, 50, 52, 105
Beaven, Albert W., 58, 63, 65–66
Beaven, S. W., 65
Beech, Harlan Page, 205
Birney, Alice McLellan, 151
Bitting, W. C., 248, 255–56
Blackwell, Elizabeth, 48
Blackwell, Henry, 74, 103
Blair, Karen, 76, 99, 106
Bloomer, Amelia, 103

Blow, Susan E., 138
Boniface, 234
Bradwell, Myra, 48
Brandeis, Louis D., 158
Brooks, Phillips, 29
Brown, Antoinette, 103
Brown, Meta, 141
Burroughs, Nannie Helen, 212
Butler, Clementina, 226, 259

Carroll, Clarence F., 159, 160, 178, 198
Carver, William Owen, 234, 298
Case, Shirley Jackson, 255
Catt, Carrie Chapman, 68
Chapman, Mariana W., 107
Chester, Alice A., 63, 66
Child, Abbie B., 204, 210
Claflin, Tennie C., 39
Clark, Elizabeth Battelle, 71, 75
Clarke, Edward, 26, 68, 268n1
Cleveland, Grover, 90
Clisby, Harriet, 129
Clough, Emma Rauschenbusch (Mrs. John E.), 156
Clough, John E., 156
Coman, Katherine, 45, 270
Confucius, 216
Cott, Nancy F., 5, 98
Crane, Caroline Bartlett, 152
Crane, Horace A., 189
Crapsey, Algernon, 196
Croly, Herbert, 9
Croly, Jane Cunningham, 76, 105
Cunningham, James E., 51
Curran, Michael, 51
Curtis, Cathro Mason, 19–23, 261

Damrosch, Frank, 213
Danforth, Henry G., 105
Danforth, Edwine Blake (Mrs. Henry G.), 77, 105
Dewey, George, 94

Dewey, John, 9
Dinsmore, Carlos M., 256
Doane, Marguerite, 227
Doane, William Howard, 227
Dodge, Grace, 210
Dolley, Sarah Adamson, 21, 104, 281n4
Douglas, Ann, 176, 263–64
Douglass, Frederick, 102
Dow, Frank F., 116, 142
Dow, Harriet Brown (Mrs. Frank F.), 104, 180
Duffy, James B. P., 180
Duffy, Walter B., 51
Durant, Henry Fowle, 26–29, 33, 36, 37–38, 228

Edgerton, Hiram H., 200
Edwards, Jonathan, 242
Eastman, George, 50, 272n14
Eliot, Charles William, 33
Elgin, William, 62
Ellwanger, George, 53
Ely, Richard, 9

Farley, Ita P., 146
Fey, Marion Harris, 159
Finney, Charles, 52
Fishburn, Janet Forsythe, 10, 58, 295n26
Forbes, George M., 162, 177–78, 195–98
Fountain, Charles H., 250, 252
Fox, John D., 16
Fray, Ellen Sully, 78
Freedman, Estelle, 228
Freeman, Alice; see Palmer, Alice Freeman
Froebel, Friedrich, 137–38, 145, 151

Gannett, Mary T. L. (Mrs. William C.), 77, 78, 83, 104
Gannett, William C., 78, 83

Garfield, James A., 44
Garrett, Shirley S., 99
Garrison, William Lloyd, 102
George, Henry, 156
Gilbert, Charles B., 164
Gladden, Washington, 95
Goler, George, 152
Gordon, Lynn D., 45
Gould, Jay, 67
Gould, Helen, 201
Graham, A. J., 191
Grant, Ulysses S., 15
Greanleaf, Jean Brooks, 67, 105
Gregory, Helen, 180

Hackett, Patrick N., 184
Hall, G. Stanley, 140, 151
Hall, Myra S., 148, 149
Hamilton, C. E., 190
Hancock, Winfield S., 44
Harper, Ida Husted, 126
Harper, William Rainey, 112
Harris, William T., 138
Harrison, Benjamin, 203, 205
Hau, Jacob, 51
Haynes, Carolyn, 99
Hewett, Nancy L., 98
Hill, Patricia R., 202, 234–37
Hirst, Phobe Apperson, 151
Hodgkins, Louise Manning, 205
Hofstadter, Richard, 93
Hooker, Susan H., 136, 141, 144
Howard, Ada, 28, 36
Howard, Clinton, 65
Howard, Mrs. W. L., 150
Howe, Julia Ward, 74
Hughes, Jennie V., 211
Huntington, Frederic Dan, 67–68

Jacobi, Mary Putnam, 67–69
James, William, 166
Jordan, David Starr, 94

Judson, Abby Ann, 16
Judson, Adoniram, 16
Junia (of the NT), 238

Kagan, Richard L., 91
Kelley, Florence, 150
Kimball, Mrs. William S., 105
Kraditor, Aileen, 5, 80–81, 87

Landsberg, Max, 83, 105
Landsberg, Miriam (Mrs. Max), 77, 83, 105
Larsson, Gustaf, 145
Las Casas, Bartolomé de, 91
Lattimore, Samuel A., 111
Laws, Curtis Lee, 299n1
Laws, Mrs. Curtis Lee, 299n1
Lea, Henry Charles, 92
Lincoln, Abraham, 16, 103
Livingstone, Wilhermina C. 63, 66
Lomb, Henry, 50
Luther, Martin, 234
Lyon, Mary, 20

Mannes, David, 213
Mason, Caroline Atwater, 62, 233
Mathews, Shailer, 251, 255
Mattson, Kevin, 196
McClellan, Robert, 96
McKelvey, Blake, 78, 161
McKinley, William, Jr., 93, 203, 279n89
McLenden, H. Lee, 247
McQuiad, Bernard J., 51
Meade, C. E., 56
Miller, George D., 190
Mitchell, Ure, 252–54
Moehlman, Conrad H., 66
Montgomery, Abel S., 56
Montgomery, Edith, 61
Montgomery, Helen Barrett; and Susan B. Anthony, 9–10, 101–27, 185, 261; birth and family, 12–16; church

membership, 17–18; as clubwoman, 77–79; death, 260; early education, 19–21 education at Wellesley, 25–46; election to Rochester school board, 2, 8, 114–25; honors and memorials, 260; marriage, 57–60; president of WEIU, 76, 83, 103–4; and Alice Freeman Palmer, 32, 33–35, 41; Lucy Waterbury Peabody, 3, 62, 210–13, 227–29; as New Testament translator, 2, 8, 35, 238, 259, 300n20; as president of Northern Baptist Convention, 2, 245–57, 260, 300n3; and Walter Rauschenbusch, 9–10, 155–81, 245

Montgomery, William A., 47, 49, 54–61, 64, 157, 202, 273n29

Morgan, Frances Louisa Tracy (Mrs. J. P.), 201

Motley, John Lathrop, 92

Mott, Lucretia, 103

Mullins, E. Y., 252

Nelson, S. Banks, 190

Noble, Mary Riggs, 211–12, 225

North, Louise McCoy, 177

Noyes, Milton, 136, 144, 148, 162

O'Connor, Joseph, 51

O'Grady, James, 51

O'Neill, A. M., 199

Palmer, Alice Freeman, 29, 30, 32, 33–35, 37, 40–41, 54

Palmieri, Ann, 34, 41

Paul (the apostle), 217, 238, 248, 252–54

Pattison, T. Harwood, 63

Peabody, Elizabeth, 137–38, 140

Peabody, Lucy Waterbury, 3, 62, 210–11, 213, 225–29

Peter (the apostle), 253

Philip (of the NT), 238

Phoebe (of the NT), 238, 259

Post, Elizabeth, 157

Prescott, William H., 91–92

Priscilla (of the NT), 238, 254

Putney, Clifford, 187

Quandt, Jean B., 9

Rauschenbusch, Walter, 52, 95, 184, 186–87, 189, 190, 288n1; and Helen Barrett Montgomery, 9–10, 155–81, 245, 289n48, 290n65; and William A. Montgomery, 57

Rauschenbusch, Mrs. Walter, 188

Raymond, J. E., 157

Reese, William J., 135

Rhees, Rush, 126–27

Ricker, W. G., 56

Riis, Jacob, 197, 293n48

Riley, William Bell, 256

Robert, Dana L., 201, 226, 228, 234

Robinson, William S. V., 249

Rockefeller, John D., Jr., 255

Roosevelt, Theodore, 93, 186, 203

Rose, Ernestine, 103

Rosenberg, Rosalind, 26

Rothman, Sheila, 85, 108, 132

Sage, Margaret Olivia Slocum (Mrs. Russell), 67, 69, 201

Sage, Russell, 67

Salomon, Otto, 145

Schaffer, Kate Boggs, 211

Scudder, Vida, 41

Selden, George B., 50

Severance, Caroline, 76

Shaw, Anna Howard, 48, 107, 118

Shedd, K. P., 199–200

Sibley, Margaret Durbin Harper (Mrs. Hiram W.), 105

Singh, Lilavati, 205

Sklar, Kathryn Kish, 228

Small, Albion, 9

Smith, Hannah Whitall, 75
Spencer, Herbert, 7
Stanton, Elizabeth Cady, 8, 69, 74, 102–3, 299n49
Stanton, Henry, 102
Stebbins, Henry H., 117–18
Stone, Lucy, 74, 103
Strayer, Paul Moore, 66, 187, 190
Strong, Augustus H., 16

Taft, Helen Louise Herron (Mrs. William Howard), 212
Taft, William Howard, 212
Taylor, Frederick E., 254
Thoburn, Isabella, 205
Thomas, M. Carey, 40
Townsend, Mrs. George W., 104
Tryphena (of the NT), 238
Tryphosa (of the NT), 238

Van Dyke, Henry, 94
Vaughan, Christopher A., 93
Vaughan, R. M., 249

Vella, Salvatore M., 52
Venor, Edmund, 56

Walker, Mary, 39
Wallin, Madeleine, 49
Walters, J. M., 189
Ward, Edward J., 195, 198, 199–200
Warner, George E., 115–16
Waterbury, Lucy; *see* Peabody, Lucy Waterbury
Watson, Matilda M. (Mrs. Don Alonzo), 132
Weet, Herbert S., 160
Wein, Roberta, 40
Welter, Barbara, 5, 13–14, 57
Wheelock, Lucy, 137, 140
Whiting, Sarah Frances, 29, 33–34
Wiebe, Robert, 56
Willard, Frances, 8, 75, 81, 219
Williams, Leighton, 157
Woelfkin, Cornelius, 255, 256–57
Wood, James M., 252
Woodbury, D. A., 56

INDEX OF SUBJECTS

American Anti-Slavery Society, 102
American Association of University Women, 78, 107; *see also* College Women's Club
American Baptist Foreign Mission Society, 242, 260
American Baptist Publication Society, 242
American Book Company, 123
American Equal Rights Association, 103
American Woman Suffrage Association, 74, 103
Anglo Saxon myth, 93

Baptists, 2, 8, 32, 70; and anti-Catholicism, 92, 124; and communion, 30–31; and creedalism, 245–57; and sectarianism, 124; and the University of Rochester; 53, 112; in Rochester, NY, 53; license to preach vs. ordination, 63–64; Montgomery's mission history of, 242–43; Montgomery's views of, 30–32, 247–51, 256; *see also names of specific organizations*
Baptist Missionary Training School, 62
Baptist World Alliance, Third World Congress of (Stockholm, Sweden, 1923), 1, 260

Bible, 12, 20, 42, 246, 264; and democracy, 218, 243; New Testament, 2; 8,
16, 35, 217, 219, 238, 240, 245, 250,
252, 255, 256, 259; Old Testament,
156, 217; and theological liberalism,
251; and women, 216–17, 259; study
of, at Wellesley College, 28, 30, 32–33;
translation of, 200, 214, 234, 243, 259
Black Hand, 52, 141
Black Legend, 91–92
Blaine Amendment, 124
Board of Education, Rochester, NY, 136,
150, 158, 168, 170; and curriculum
reform, 159–60, 179; and dancing,
191–95, 199; and the Dow Law, 116,
160–61; and free kindergartens, 137,
140; and free textbooks, 199; and
the Good Government movement,
116; and manual training, 143–45;
Montgomery's campaign and election to, 116–25; Montgomery's
membership on, 2, 8, 78, 114, 126,
155–57, 179–181, 183–84, 202, 262;
and the "new education," 159; and
playgrounds, 151, 160; and Walter
Rauschenbusch, 167, 169–78; reform
of, 141–42, 161–67; and school beautification, 147–49, 166; and social
centers, 160, 183–84, 195–200; and
vacation schools, 146, 160; and the
WEIU, 136–37
Brotherhood of the Kingdom, 57, 157
Brown University, 260

Canajoharie Academy, 102
Central Committee on the United Study
of Foreign Missions, 4, 210, 213, 221,
227, 233; significance of, 203–5
Children's Playground League, 151, 160,
195
Christendom, 216, 233, 239–41
Christian Endeavor Society, 59

Christianity, 29, 58, 69; evangelical,
11, 27; liberal, 152, Montgomery's
views of, 3–4, 8–9, 205, 209,
214–18, 221, 230–31, 234–41, 253,
261, 299n49; muscular, 187, 190;
Walter Rauschenbusch's views of,
187, 290n65; see also Protestantism;
Roman Catholicism
Christus Redemptor, 210, 239
citizen's committee, 167, 169–78
Citizen's Educational Association, 116,
141
citizenship, 19, 44, 96, 142, 149; and
domesticity, 41; educating women
for, 86, 97, 135; duties of, 45; of
immigrants in Rochester, NY, 52,
139; and the missionary impulse,
124; and the Political Equality Club,
78; and Republican motherhood, 84;
and True Womanhood, 55
Civic Art Committee; see under
Women's Educational and Industrial
Union (WEIU) Code of Manu, 216
coeducation, 26; see also under
Rochester, University of; Women's
Educational and Industrial Union
(WEIU)
Colgate-Rochester Divinity School, 57
College Woman's Club; see College
Women's Club
College Women's Club, 77–78, 107
Columbia Conference, 252, 255, 256
Committee of Fifteen, 188–91, 195
Committee of Nine, 173, 178–79
Committee on Christian Literature for
Women and Children in Mission
Fields, 226–27, 259
Conference of Woman's Boards; see
International Conference of Woman's
Boards on Foreign Missions.
Cooperating Committee for Women's

Union Christian Colleges in Foreign Fields, 228–32

Darwinism, 7; *see also* evolution; Reform Darwinism, social Darwinism
Daughters of Temperance; *see* temperance; Sons and Daughters of
democracy, 94–98, 142, 160, 169, 242–43, 279n95; and the Bible, 216–18, 238; and Christianity, 3, 9, 31, 215–20, 230, 235, 263; and the ecumenical women's missionary movement, 215–20, 223–24, 238; and feminism, 72–75, 79–81, 87, 98, 134, 263; and social centers, 195–200; Wellesley College community as, 37
Denison University, 260
Des Moines statement, 246–48, 254–55
domestic feminism, 73, 113, 134, 228, 262; defined, 75–76; and the ecumenical woman's missionary movement, 209; and the General Federation of Women's Clubs, 106; and the Jubilee tour, 201–2, 213; and the Ignorance Club of Rochester, NY, 21; and Montgomery, 8, 10, 11, 71, 76–77, 79, 97–100, 119, 140, 156, 187, 207–8, 214, 217, 220, 225, 259, 261–63; and the WEIU, 103–5, 135–40, 148, 152; and "Woman's Work for Woman," 233; and the YWCA, 108–10; *see also* evangelical feminism; feminism; liberal feminism
domesticity, 12–13, 76, 126, 243; defined, 5–6; and education, 20; and literature, 47–48; and Montgomery, 41, 49, 54, 59–60, 70, 100, 109, 119–21, 123; and teaching, 47–48; and the WEIU, 131–33; at Wellesley College, 25–26, 40
domestic science, 136, 139, 143, 145, 161
Dow Law, 116–17, 137, 142, 160–61

Ecumenical Missionary Conference (1900), 203–4
ecumenical woman's missionary movement, 2, 62, 259–60; defined, 3–4; and the Jubilee tour, 201, 210; and liberal feminism, 222, 261; missiology of, 214–15, 228, 233; Montgomery as leader and intellectual of, 8, 10, 31, 101, 153, 200–202, 203, 209–10, 225, 219, 228, 232–33, 235, 238, 260, 262; and the "New Woman of the Orient," 220–22; relationship to denominational mission boards, 207, 223
Edinburgh Conference, Education Commission of the Continuation Committee of, 227
Educational Committee; *see under* Women's Educational and Industrial Union (WEIU)
educational reform; and gender, 136; Montgomery's disagreement with Walter Rauschenbusch over, 155–56; Montgomery's role in, 166; and municipal housekeeping, 135; and sloyd, 145; and vacation schools, 146–47; and the WEIU, 129, 135–50
educated motherhood; *see* motherhood
Electromatic Typewriter Company, 57
evangelical feminism, 8, 73, 98; defined, 74–75; *see also* domestic feminism; feminism; liberal feminism
evangelicals 76; and conservatism, 98; and conversion, 12; and feminism, 75; and postmillennialism, 9
evolution, 23; Darwinian 7; and postmillennialism, 9; *see also* social Darwinism
Executive Committee on Baptist Fundamentals, 251

Factory School, 159

Federation of Woman's Boards of
  Foreign Missions, 226
feminism, 71–73; and Christianity, 99;
  after the Civil War, 73–76, 82, 103;
  and Cathro Mason Curtis, 21; definition of, 5; and democracy, 86–87;
  and education, 20, 26; hostility to
  male power, 29; and Montgomery,
  1–4, 6, 8, 39–40, 98, 101, 108, 155,
  261; and patriotism, 134; separatist
  strategy of, 44; at Wellesley College,
  29, 39–41, 44–45; and the WEIU,
  136; and the Woman's Ethical Club
  of Rochester, 78; and women's missionary boards, 208; see also domestic
  feminism, evangelical feminism;
  liberal feminism
Following the Sunrise, 242–43
Fortnightly Ignorance Club, 21, 23, 77,
  104, 116
Franklin College, 260
free kindergarten movement, 85, 138–
  41; and Transcendentalism, 137–38
From Jerusalem to Jerusalem, 233–34,
  239, 242
fundamentalism, 1, 245–50, 252, 254,
  256–57

General Federation of Women's Clubs,
  106
General Motors, Rochester Products
  Division, 57
Good Government movement, 114–17,
  157, 179, 185, 196
Guild; see under Women's Educational
  and Industrial Union (WEIU)

Hackett House, 183–88, 239
Harper's Bazaar, 67, 79
Hinduism, 215, 231
home, ideology of, 1–2, 5–6, 8, 11, 44,
  55–56, 74, 79, 126; and Montgomery,

61, 71, 80–81, 121, 123, 152, 184–86,
  214–16, 220, 223–24; at Wellesley,
  27–28; and "Woman's Work for
  Woman," 209, 214–16, 220, 223–24
Hull House, 85, 132, 150

IBM, 57
Ignorance Club; see Fortnightly
  Ignorance Club
imperialism, 92–93, 95, 235–36, 241
Industrial and Employment Committee;
  see under Women's Educational and
  Industrial Union (WEIU)
Interdenominational Committee on
  Christian Literature for Women and
  Children in Heathen Lands, 210,
  226–27, 259
International Conference of Woman's
  Boards of Foreign Missions, 213,
  225–26
International Missionary Conference
  (Jerusalem 1928), 233
Islam, 240

Joint Committee for Women's Union
  Christian Colleges in Foreign Fields;
  see Cooperating Committee for
  Women's Union Christian Colleges
  in Foreign Fields

Keuka College, 57
kingdom of God, 7, 58, 157, 168; Montgomery's views of, 4, 9, 32, 204, 224,
  234–35, 242, 248, 250, 261, 263–64
King's Highway, 235–236,

Lake Avenue Baptist Church, 16, 17, 54,
  56, 57, 115, 116; and Montgomery, 2,
  62, 64–66, 69
Laura Spelman Rockefeller Memorial
  Fund, 229
Legal Aid Society, 131

Legal Protection Committee; *see under* Women's Educational and Industrial Union (WEIU)

League of Civic Clubs (Rochester, NY), 198

liberal feminism, 8, 75, 261–62; defined, 73–74; *see also* feminism

Livingston Park Seminary, 19–24, 261

Local Council of Women, Rochester, NY, 116–18, 124–25, 195

Lucknow College, 205

Lyell Avenue Mission, 18

Mafia; *see* Black Hand

Maine Law, 103; *see also* Prohibition

manual training, 146, 163, 165, 171, 290n65; and sloyd, 144–45; and the WEIU, 136, 143–45, 146, 159, 160

Methodist Episcopal Preachers' Meeting (Rochester, NY), 191–95

missions, 203–6; and Montgomery, 34, 62, 101, 158, 205–10, 222, 229, 239, 242; women's impact on, 206–8, women's study of, 204–5; *see also* Woman's Missionary Jubilee

Monroe Baptist Association, 62, 64–65, 123, 210; Women's Home Mission Union of, 62–63; Women's Foreign Missionary Society of, 62–63

motherhood, 40, 44, 55, 75, 142; educated, 84–86, 132, 139, 145, 151, 209, 226, 232; Montgomery's views of, 2, 61, 70, 84–86, 100, 119, 121–22, 231

mothers' clubs, 148–51, 192–93, 195

Mother's Congress, 151

Mount Holyoke Female Seminary, 20, 27, 28

municipal housekeeping, 106, 152; and free kindergartens, 139; and Montgomery, 97, 100, 156, 204, 208, 218–19, 232, 239; and the WEIU, 76–77, 104, 129, 134, 148, 151, 156, 209

Municipal League of Philadelphia, 115, 117

muscular Christianity, 187, 190

National American Woman Suffrage Association, 74, 103

National Conference of Church-Women, 229

National Conference on Good Government; *see* Good Government movement

National Congress of Mothers, 151

National Congress of Mothers and Parent-Teacher Associations; *see* National Congress of Mothers

National Congress of Parents and Teachers; *see* National Congress of Mothers

National Consumers' League, 150

National Council of Churches, 227

nationalism, 16, 44, 55, 72–73, 96, 262

National Municipal League, 115

National Playground Association of America, 151

National Training School for Women and Girls, 212

National Woman Suffrage Association, 74, 78, 103

new education, 136, 143, 145–46, 155, 159, 164–67, Walter Rauschenbusch's opposition to, 167–75, 290n65

New England Woman's Club, 76

New Hampshire Confession of Faith, 247, 250

New Testament; *see* Bible; New Testament

Newton Theological School, 249

"New Woman," 34, 41, 220, 224; Montgomery as, 8, 47–49, 70; of the Progressive Era, 6, 79, 82–84, 228; of the Orient, 2, 219–21, 226

New York State Federation of Women's
Clubs, 82, 105–7, 125
New York State Suffrage Association,
107
Noon Rest; *see under* Women's
Educational and Industrial Union
(WEIU)
Normal Training School, 148, 163
North East Electric Company, 56–57
Northern Baptist Convention;
Montgomery as president of, 2,
245–57, 260, 300n3
Nunda Institute, 14–15

Old Testament; *see* Bible; Old
Testament

pacifism, 237
patriotism, 12, 13, 23, 79, 86, 134
Penny Provident Station, 150
Pentecost, 233, 238
People's Sunday Evenings (people's
church), 157, 190, 196
Pfafflin's Private School, 156
Philadelphia Confession of Faith, 250
Philanthropy Committee; *see under*
Women's Educational and Industrial
Union (WEIU)
Political Equality Club, 78, 104, 107, 118
postmillennialism, 9
Prang drawing system, 166
Preaching Value of Missions
premillennialism, 247
Prescott's Paradigm, 91–92
progress of civilization; as divinely
directed, 7, conservative views of, 7;
Montgomery's views of, 79, 94, 96,
97, 218, 220, 231, 234–36, 261, 263;
progressive views of, 7; and True
Womanhood, 23; *see also* Progressive
Era; progressivism
Progressive Era, 6–8, 84–85, 88, 105,

114, 137, 146, 219, 228; *see also* progressivism; progress of civilization
progressivism, 10, 56, 67, 115–16, 208,
290n65; defined, 6–8; and democratic
education, 110, and efficiency, 197;
and maternalist political influence,
88; and Montgomery, 11, 47, 49, 70,
84–88, 89, 105, 114, 125, 155–56,
166–67, 183, 219, 228, 234–35,
248, 263; and the WEIU, 129, 134,
137, 142–53; at Wellesley College,
27, 34, 39, 42–46; and the women's
missionary movement, 202; *see also*
Progressive Era; progress of civilization
Prohibition, 103; Montgomery and, 42,
89, 239, 241, 271n81
Protestantism, 5, 9, 17, 19, 55, 99, 124;
and anti-Catholicism, 91, 124; evangelical, 74, 99, 242; and missions,
214; and progressivism, 114, 233;
and the Spanish–American War, 92;
varieties of, in Rochester, NY; 52–53;
and women, 80, 187, 211, 219, 264
public schools; and dancing controversy, 189–95, 199; as extension of the home and object of
women's reform, 40, 120, 151; and
Montgomery, 123–24, 159–67; and
Walter Rauschenbusch, 167–76; and
the Regents examinations, 164, 173;
and social centers, 151, 157, 160, 180,
183–84, 192, 195–200; teachers
and principals of, in Rochester, NY,
66; and the WEIU, 134, 142–49

Reform Darwinism, 7, 200
Rochester Collegiate Institute, 16, 19
Rochester Common Council, 115, 142,
160, 199
Rochester Consumers' League, 150
Rochester Federation of Women's
Clubs, 150

Rochester Free Academy, 52–53, 156
Rochester Mechanics Institute, 57, 131, 134
Rochester Ministerial Association 189–91, 192
Rochester Public Health Association, 152
Rochester Theological Seminary, 16, 17, 18, 63; German Department of, 156, 157; *see also* Colgate-Rochester Divinity School
Rochester, University of, 23, 105, 114, 141, 162; the Susan B. Anthony Memorial Building, 126–27; and Judson Barrett, 15; and coeducation, 78, 110–13, 125–126; and the Citizens Educational Association, 116; the College of Women, 127; and the Committee of Nine, 173; and Helen Montgomery, 111–12, 125–26, 196; and William Montgomery, 57; and Walter Rauschenbusch, 156; and social centers, 196, 199
Roman Catholicism, 5; and anti-Catholicism, 51; and Montgomery, 92, 123–24; in Rochester, NY, 51, 53

salvation, plan of, 33, 234
school beautification; *see* Board of Education; school beautification
Schurman Commission, 94, 279n89, 279n95
sloyd; *see* manual training; and sloyd
social centers; *see* public schools; and social centers
Social Affairs Committee; *see under* Women's Educational and Industrial Union (WEIU)
Social Darwinism, 7, 93, 187, 268n1
social gospel, 9–10, 83, 155–57, 210, 219, 295n26
socialism; and Montgomery, 88; and Walter Rauschenbusch, 156–57, 158;

in Rochester, 196; and social centers, 199; and the WEIU, 136, 144
Sons of Temperance; *see* temperance; Sons and Daughters of
Sorosis, 76, 106
Southern Baptist Convention, 234, 252, 256
Southern Baptist Theological Seminary, 252
Spain; Montgomery's views of, 92–95; and the WEIU, 135
Spanish-American War, 92, 279n89; and ant-Catholicism, 124; Montgomery's views of, 87, 92, 96, 123; and the WEIU, 134
State Excise Department (New York), 184, 190
Stephens College, 252
suffrage, 53, 72–73, 86, 97, 105, 109, 233; and Susan B. Anthony, 101, 102–3, 261–62; and domestic feminists, 76; and educated motherhood, 85; and evangelical feminists, 74; Frederic Dan Huntington's views on, 68–69; and liberal feminists, 73–74; and Montgomery, 69–70, 79–81, 84, 88, 97–100, 102, 108, 118, 215, 245, 254, 262; movement for, in New York state, 66–69, 107; and the Political Equality Club, 78; at Wellesley College, 44–45; and the Woman's Ethical Club, 78; *see also names of specific organizations*
Symmetrical Womanhood, 40–41

temperance, 68, 76, 107–8; and Susan B. Anthony, 102–3; and domestic feminism, 99; and Montgomery, 42, and the "New Woman," 79; in Rochester, NY, 52–53; Sons and Daughters of, 102–3; at Wellesley College, 34, 42 theological liberalism, 29, 76, 105, 152, 190, 255; and Montgomery, 245, 251, 254, 257; and Rauschenbush, 156–57

Transcendentalism, 76; and free kindergartens, 137–38

True Womanhood, 8, 13, 15, 55; defined, 5–6; and domestic feminism, 76, 214; and educated motherhood, 84; at Livingston Park Female Seminary, 19–20, 23; and Montgomery, 8, 11, 41, 86, 119, 121, 188, 262; and Muscular Christianity, 187, and the WEIU, 135, at Wellesley College, 26–27, 29, 41; and women's higher education, 26, 228

United Charities, 131
United States Children's Bureau, 88

vacation schools, 136, 146,151, 160
Venor & Montgomery, 56, 202
Victorian Era, 5, 7, 11, 19, 55, 219

Watson House; see under Women's Educational and Industrial Union (WEIU)
Wednesday Morning Club, 77
Wellesley College, 24, 47, 53, 54, 61, 71, 161, 221; Bible study at, 28, 30, 32–33; and domesticity, 25–26, 40; and feminism, 29, 39–41, 44–45; and missions, 34, 43–44; and Montgomery, 24–46, 177, 260, 261, 270n34; and Mount Holyoke Female Seminary, 27–28; and progressive reform, 42–44; and religion, 29–32; and suffrage, 44–45; and Symmetrical Womanhood, 40–41; and True Womanhood, 26–27, 29, 41; and women's health, 26–28, 37–39, 41
Wellesley Preparatory School, 53, 60

Wellesley Magazine, 41
Western Union Telegraph Company, 67, 89
Western Women in Eastern Lands, 2, 210–11, 212, 214, 235, 253
Woman's Alliance, 104
Woman's American Baptist Foreign Missionary Society, 260
Woman's Baptist Foreign Missionary Society, 203
Woman's Christian Temperance Union, 53, 75, 79, 139
Woman's Ethical Club, 77–78, 84, 104, 116, 188
Woman's Missionary Jubilee, 2–3, 4, 67, 152, 201, 211–13, 223, 225, 296n31; and Montgomery, 60, 210–11, 214, 225; and segregation, 212
Woman's National Loyal League, 103
Woman's Political Club; see Political Equality Club
Woman's Rights Convention, 102, 103
woman's sphere, 20, 98, 260; defined, 5–6; and higher education, 26; and suffrage, 68, 108; and Montgomery, 69, 79, 86–87, 97, 108, 122–23, 188; and municipal housekeeping, 81, 86–87, 122–23, 188, 214, 264; and the "New Woman," 47–48, 79, 135
Woman's State Temperance Society, 103
Woman Suffrage Party of Monroe County; see Political Equality Club
Woman's Union Missionary Society, 4
"Woman's Work for Woman," 2, 228, 233; defined, 4–5; and Montgomery, 202, 214, 219, 223–24, 229
Women's Civic Improvement League, 152
Women's Educational and Industrial Union (WEIU); of Boston, Massachusetts, 104–5, 129–30, 132; of Buffalo, NY, 104–5, 129–30,

132; of Rochester, NY, 76–77, 83, 105, 109–110, 116; Civic Art Committee, 133–34, 147–49; and coeducation at the University of Rochester, 111, 118; and cultural self-improvement, 133–34; and domestic feminism, 103–6, 135–40, 148, 152; Educational Committee, 135–50; founding of, 103–5; and free kindergartens, 137–41; and the Good Government movement, 116; Guild, 133; Industrial and Employment Committee, 105, 131–33; Legal Protection Committee, 105, 131, 133, 185; and Montgomery, 8, 76–77, 82, 85–88, 98–99, 104, 106, 116–18, 129, 156, 196, 202, 262; and municipal housekeeping, 76, 85–86; Noon Rest, 132–33; patriotism and political training, 77, 82, 87–88, 134–35; Philanthropy Committee, 105, 132;

Social Affairs Committee, 105; vacation schools, 136, 146–47, 151, 160; Watson House, 111, 118, 144

Women's Foreign Missionary Society of the Methodist Episcopal Church, 259

Woodbury Engine Company, 56

World Day of Prayer, 226, 229

"World Friendship," 5, 202, 225, 233, 239

World's Missionary Committee of Christian Women, 4

World War I, 4, 5, 233, 235, 237, 241, 296n46

World War II, 5, 296n46

Young Men's Christian Association (YMCA), 53, 114, 189, 196; and Walter Rauschenbusch, 157, 184, 186–87, 190

Young Women's Christian Association (YWCA), 108–10, 124, 132